*British Naval Policy
in the Gladstone–Disraeli Era,
1866–1880*

JOHN F. BEELER

*British Naval Policy
in the Gladstone–Disraeli Era,
1866–1880*

STANFORD UNIVERSITY PRESS
STANFORD, CALIFORNIA
1997

Stanford University Press
Stanford, California

© 1997 by the Board of Trustees of the
Leland Stanford Junior University

Printed in the United States of America

CIP data are at the end of the book

Last date below indicates year of this printing:
05 04 03 02 01 00 99 98 97

In Memoriam
John H. Beeler, 1916–1985

Preface

A paper on Victorian naval architecture and technological change, written fifteen years ago, provided the genesis for this study. It was subsequently expanded into a master's thesis, and served as the point of departure for my doctoral dissertation. Over the past decade, however, my research has been increasingly directed toward the broader topic of British naval policy as a whole, in particular the men who formulated it and the politicoeconomic circumstances that guided, constrained, and otherwise influenced them, rather than the narrow realm of rivets and bolts, armor plate and guns, and engines and boilers.

Beyond generalities, the period and subject matter are fascinating. If human actions are inextricably tied to perceptions of the past, mid-Victorian politicians and naval administrators, like all who experienced the processes of industrialization and economic transformation—"modernization," as it was once fashionable to call it—suffered a disproportionate share of confusion. The comfortable foundations upon which their world views and assumptions were erected were swept away with disconcerting swiftness by the mechanization of naval warfare. The transformation went far beyond the realm of technology too, profoundly influencing naval tactics and strategy, government finance, political discourse, and public opinion. Moreover, for policy makers accustomed to the relative stability of preindustrial times, the phenomenon of continual—and rapid—technological change was itself revolutionary. Experience, in other words, seemed to lose much of its relevance, and until a new foundation of wisdom based on their own experience could be accumulated, they were forced to feel their way tentatively, often blindly, as if enshrouded in one of London's notorious fogs. This book is therefore as much a case study in human response to the process of modernization as it is an investigation of mid-Victorian British naval policy.

Rapid technological change has, of course, long since lost its novelty. I hope, however, that the value of this book transcends mere antiquarianism. Mid-Victorian British politicians, naval administrators, newspaper editors and, ultimately, the public at large, confronted an international situation in some respects analogous to that which Americans face in the waning years of the twentieth century. Like the British following France's disastrous defeat in 1870–71, we have seen the threat from our greatest military rival crumble; like them too, for the last several years we have been reaping the harvest of this "peace dividend." Yet the end of the cold war has not diminished the United States' role as *the* world power, just as the disappearance of overt challenges from abroad did not alter mid-Victorian Britain's status as the sole power with global reach. To such states peace brings with it a new set of challenges and responsibilities, in the realms of both international relations and domestic politics. Moreover, while the "peace dividend" permitted the down-scaling of military and naval establishments, Britain—like the United States in the 1990s—had to maintain forces for myriad peacetime duties, to say nothing of providing a deterrent to foreign aggression. In sum, the British had to discover the bottom-line requirements for national security in peacetime, while still maintaining a navy capable of upholding the nation's interests abroad. The bottom line was imperative for politicians seeking to win the support of a mass electorate, yet the technological revolution exerted a countervailing pressure on naval expenditure. Gladstone, Disraeli, and their contemporaries had to balance the mutually conflicting tasks of attracting voters through economizing while ensuring national and imperial security at a time when foreign threats were muted—yet when the march of technology, and the consequent imperative of maintaining, at minimum, technological parity served to push defense spending upwards. One could substitute the names of contemporary American leaders and the assertion would be as relevant to today's situation.

Of course, we must use extreme caution when drawing parallels between past and present. Analogies between the two are never complete; each historical era is unique and must be studied on its own terms, rather than those of today. Not only does history not repeat itself, it does not offer "lessons." Those we draw ourselves, based on our inescapably subjective understanding of the past. Yet if history per se offers us no "lessons," it does offer an inexhaustible stock of examples, and from those examples we may still gain a broader understanding of the past and, through it, not only the range of options facing us today, but their possible consequences as well.

Acknowledgments

As an aspiring historian I naively thought that acknowledgments were a polite formality, part of scholarly etiquette. I am still a novice in many respects, but writing this book has made me aware that, if nothing else, acknowledgments, no matter how formulaic they appear on the printed page, are heartfelt thanks rather than mere trappings of scholarship. Indeed, words are inadequate to express my feelings of gratitude and appreciation to the many people—friends, scholars, and colleagues—who have freely offered their support, wisdom, assistance, and advice during this volume's lengthy gestation.

Three scholars have played especially vital roles in helping bring my research to fruition. Professor Ron Cassell of the University of North Carolina at Greensboro fostered my interest in Victorian Britain in general and the Victorian navy in particular. This volume is the culmination of study that began in his class fifteen years ago. Professor Cassell subsequently directed my masters thesis, which benefited immeasurably from his knowledge and advice. At the University of Illinois, Professor Walter Arnstein played a similarly vital role in my professional development as my advisor, dissertation director, and mentor; I must acknowledge the encouragement and invariably valuable comments, suggestions, and criticisms he provided. Without the benefit of his expertise—offered both graciously and liberally—this study would be far weaker than it is, and words can convey neither my sense of appreciation nor indebtedness to him. Thanks are also due especially to Dr. Andrew Lambert of the War Studies Department at King's College, University of London, whose understanding of nineteenth-century British naval history far surpasses mine, and who has generously shared his comprehensive knowledge of the subject matter and the sources with me for almost a decade.

Many other individuals, institutions, and organizations have made vital contributions to my research. A University of Illinois Program in Arms Control, Disarmament, and International Security dissertation fellowship—funded by the MacArthur Foundation—enabled me to carry out several months of archival research in Great Britain during 1989–90. A Yale University International Security Program postdoctoral fellowship—funded by the John M. Olin Foundation—permitted me the luxury of a year in which to extensively revise and expand my dissertation. My thanks to both programs and to their respective directors, Professor Jeremiah Sullivan and Professor Paul Kennedy, and to the MacArthur and Olin Foundations for the funding that made writing this book possible.

Further acknowledgment must be made of the assistance provided by the staffs of the numerous archives and libraries in which I worked, especially the British Public Record Office (Kew), the National Maritime Museum, the British Library, the Bodleian Library (Oxford University), the archives of W. H. Smith, the Ministry of Defence Library, the Royal Commonwealth Library, the Liverpool Record Office, Liverpool Libraries and Information Services, the Northamptonshire Record Office, University of Illinois Library, and the Sterling, Beineke, and Mudd Libraries at Yale University. The librarians and archivists I have encountered have been unfailingly helpful and courteous, but Guy Robins, David Topliss, and Clive Powell of the National Maritime Museum rate special mention for their efforts on my behalf.

I must also acknowledge the kindness of the Controller of Her Britannic Majesty's Stationery Office for permission to quote from Crown copyright material, the Trustees of the National Maritime Museum for permission to quote from the papers of Sir Alexander Milne, Sir Geoffrey Phipps Hornby, and Sir William Houston Stewart in the museum's manuscripts collection, the present Earl of Derby for permission to quote from the papers of the 14th and 15th Earls of Derby, the present Viscount Hambleden for permission to quote from the papers of W. H. Smith, the National Trust for permission to quote from the Hughenden (Disraeli) papers, the Syndics of Cambridge University Library for permission to quote from the papers of Hugh C. E. Childers formerly held by the Royal Commonwealth Society, and G. E. Ward Hunt for permission to quote from the papers of George Ward Hunt.

Acknowledgments

Professors David McKenzie and Anne Pottinger Saab of the University of North Carolina at Greensboro aided me at an early stage by reading and commenting on my master's thesis. Professors John Lynn, John McKay, and Geoffrey Parker of the University of Illinois rendered similarly valuable service as members of my dissertation committee. Professor Parker—now at Ohio State University—also read the subsequent manuscript, provided numerous useful suggestions, and assisted me in finding a publisher. Sir Michael Howard, Dr. Keith Neilson of the Royal Military College of Canada, and Professor Emeritus Robert Johnson of the University of Alabama graciously read my manuscript and I am indebted to all of them for their helpful comments and suggestions. Thanks are furthermore due Professor Emeritus Bryan Ranft of the University of London, Professor Geoffrey Till of the Royal Naval College, Professor Jon Sumida of the University of Maryland, and Dr. Nicholas A. M. Rodger, all of whom furnished valuable assistance while conducting research.

I must also thank Dr. Norris Pope and Peter Kahn, Director and Associate Editor, respectively, at Stanford University Press, the former for his faith in this project, the latter for his valuable and unfailingly good-natured assistance in turning the manuscript into a book.

Numerous others have provided valuable advice and support. A few warrant special thanks, foremost among them H. W. Jones and his family, formerly of Neasden, London, who took a keen interest in both my research and well-being while living in London and who have become my adopted family. Dr. William Wilbur Sutton has likewise been a tireless source of encouragement. William Nash and Paul Wirth have furnished valuable creative and editorial assistance. All of them—friends, colleagues, scholars, and institutions—and many others as well, have helped to make this book far better than it would otherwise have been, and have contributed equally to my understanding of the collaborative nature of such endeavors. For any defects that remain I am solely responsible.

My thanks, finally, to all of those who have put up with me during the prolonged processes of researching, writing, revising, and editing, especially my family and the history faculties of Eastern Illinois University and the University of Alabama. And no words can adequately express my thanks and love to Amy.

J. F. B.

Contents

	TABLES	xvii
	A NOTE ON QUOTATIONS	xix
1.	Introduction: The Industrial Revolution and the Navy	1
2.	Strategic Parameters	6
3.	Administration, Politics, and Economics	38
4.	Derby, Disraeli, and a Mutinous Admiralty, 1866–1868	69
5.	Hugh Childers at the Admiralty, 1868–1870	83
6.	Of *Captains* and Lords	102
7.	Collapse and Recovery, 1870–1874	125
8.	Politics, Finance, and the Navy, 1874–1880	150
9.	Admiralty Administration: Childers, Goschen, and the Historians	171

10.	Rivals	191
11.	Strategic Planning and Imperial Defense	210
12.	Conclusion	237
13.	Epilogue: The End of an Era	260
	NOTES	281
	BIBLIOGRAPHY	325
	INDEX	345

8 pages of illustrations follow page 20

Tables

1. Ships on Overseas Stations, 1821–1900   28–29
2. Ships in Commission on Overseas Stations, 1821–1900   30–31
3. Army, Debt Redemption, Civil Service, Navy, and Total Expenditure, 1865–66 to 1880–81   54–55
4. Debt Redemption, Civil Service, Army, and Navy Expenditures as a Percentages of Total Expenditure, 1865–66 to 1880–81   56
5. Naval Estimates and Expenditures, 1865–66 to 1880–81   57
6. Naval Spending as a Percentage of the Total Budget, 1815–1913   58
7. Navy Estimates and Expenditure, 1865–66 to 1880–81   63–65
8. Shipbuilding Programs versus Tonnage Completed, 1865–80   86
9. Naval Spending, 1860–90   192

10.	Naval Spending, 1860–90: Percentage of British Outlays	193
11.	Battlefleets, 1860–90	198
12.	British and French Ironclads Laid Down, Ordered, Converted, or Purchased, 1858–90	206–7
13.	British Ironclads Laid Down and Completed, 1866–80	247

A Note on Quotations

Many of the quotations in this book are drawn from the letterbooks of William Gladstone, the Earl of Derby, Sir Alexander Milne, and others. In such books the writers or their secretaries commonly resorted to abbreviations: "w<u>h</u>" for "which," "H of C" for "House of Commons," "Admty" for "Admiralty," and so on. Most such abbreviations have been spelled out in full in the text, and the entire word enclosed in brackets, rather than leaving the reader to puzzle over word identities or, equally frustrating, decipher such awkward constructions as "Sec[retar]y," and "Com[mission]n[e]rs."

*British Naval Policy
in the Gladstone–Disraeli Era,
1866–1880*

CHAPTER I

Introduction:
The Industrial Revolution and the Navy

[T]he English navy undertakes to defend a line of coast and a set of dependencies far surpassing those of any continental power. And the extent of our operations is a singular difficulty just now. It requires us to keep a large stock of ships and arms. But on the other hand, there are most important reasons why we should not keep much. The naval art and the military art are both in a state of transition; the last discovery of to-day is out of date, and superseded by an antagonistic discovery to-morrow. Any large accumulation of vessels or guns is sure to contain much that will be useless, unfitting, antediluvian, when it comes to be tried.

—Walter Bagehot, *The English Constitution*, 1867.

During the three decades after 1850 the British navy entered the machine age. Prior to midcentury the battlefleet on which British maritime supremacy rested stood largely unchanged from the days of Nelson and even earlier. Thanks to new systems of internal bracing the ships themselves were larger than the vessels that had won command of the sea over the course of the eighteenth century and upheld it in the long struggle against Revolutionary France and Napoleon. But the essentials of the wooden ship of the line remained intact during the forty years that followed Trafalgar: an agglomeration of wood, canvas, iron, rope, and tar. It was an eloquent testimony to the ancient shipwright's craft and visually one of the most impressive achievements of the preindustrial era.

By the late 1840s, however, the winds of change were beginning to stir. Steam power had, by that point, been incorporated into many of the navy's smaller ships, especially since the appearance of the screw propeller in the late 1830s had provided an alternative to paddle wheels. The latter were objectionable in men-of-war on a number of counts, most notably their susceptibility to disablement by gunfire and the amount of space they consumed, space that had hitherto been occupied by guns. But as of 1847 the battlefleet itself—meaning specifically the largest units of the fleet, the ships of the line—remained wholly dependent on the wind.[1]

This comfortable state of affairs ended abruptly in May 1847, when the French navy laid down the *Napoleon*, the world's first steam ship of the line. Steam, it was quickly and alarmingly proclaimed in Britain, had "bridged" the Channel. A French steam fleet, it was believed, could easily evade British squadrons, and, as Lord John Russell warned his cabinet in 1847, "a French invasion with 40,000 troops might prove possible in the first week after war had been declared."[2] The Admiralty remained doubtful as to whether steam battleships would ultimately prove successful at sea and preferred to await the results of tests with converted seventy-fours and steam frigates, but events beyond its control were pushing the navy to act quickly on the question of constructing steam battleships.[3] By September 1848 the Whig First Lord, Lord Auckland, had become convinced that "the whole theory of shipbuilding will be diverted from the old notion of sailing ships to the manner in which the screw [propeller] auxiliary may be best combined with good sailing qualities."[4] Within a year all work on sailing ships of the line had been halted; henceforth building for the battlefleet would be confined to steamships.[5]

The construction of a steam battlefleet was but the opening chapter of a technological revolution. During the following three decades, iron supplanted wood and steel supplanted iron for the construction of ships' hulls. Armor was incorporated and modern, breech-loading, rifled ordnance firing explosive or armor-piercing shells replaced smoothbore muzzle-loading cannon. Gun turrets replaced broadside guns, and locomotive torpedoes, hydraulic machinery, and electricity made their appearance on warships, to cite only the most obvious transformations. In addition to the physical makeover of the battlefleet, the technological revolution had far-reaching ramifications in such spheres as naval architecture and tactics. In 1850 the battlefleets of the world looked much the same as they had in the days of Nelson. By 1890 the essentials of the predreadnought battleship design—heavy guns mounted in turrets on the centerline of a wholly steam-powered, steel-hulled, armored warship of about 14,000 tons displacement—had been realized, and capital ship design, after thirty-plus years of violent upheaval, finally reached a point of relative stability. It is those thirty years of rapid and far-reaching change—especially the late 1860s, 1870s, and early 1880s—with which this study is concerned.

Introduction 3

Almost forty years ago Dr. Oscar Parkes coined the resonant phrase "the Dark Ages of the Victorian navy" to describe the decade following 1873.[6] Parkes was referring to the fortunes of the navy during the years dominated by the great political rivalry between William Gladstone and Benjamin Disraeli, but the characterization "Dark Ages" is applicable in other senses as well. The early steam navy has been the subject of a spate of recent works and the Fisher-era service has long been a topic of scholarly research.[7] But in relative terms, the gap between the two periods, which witnessed the greatest technological change in the design and construction of ships of war since the broadside sailing ship supplanted the galley at the dawn of the modern era, has received less attention. To a considerable extent it remains a "Dark Age."

The period does receive coverage in numerous general works.[8] Moreover, a number of specific studies deal with parts of it: James P. Baxter's *The Introduction of the Ironclad Warship*, Stanley Sandler's *The Emergence of the Modern Capital Ship*, C. J. Bartlett's "The Mid-Victorian Reappraisal of Naval Policy," and, most recently, C. I. Hamilton's *Anglo-French Naval Rivalry, 1840–1870* all deal with the early ironclad era. Arthur Marder's *Anatomy of British Sea Power* covers the years from 1880 on.[9] Yet there remain several avenues for further investigation. No in-depth study addresses the decade between 1870 and 1880. In addition, earlier works have displayed an understandable tendency to focus principally on technology.[10] Finally, the mid-Victorian navy has routinely been viewed historically in the long shadow cast by the influence of Alfred Thayer Mahan. For Parkes, the Mahanian "Renaissance" rescued the navy from the "Dark Ages," and this assumption continues to inform most assessments of the period. Most modern scholars have accepted the post-Mahanian, "two-power standard" navy of the 1890s and 1900s as the norm by which to judge prior naval policy.[11] Indeed, there has been a widespread inclination to analyze pre-Mahanian British naval policy in a post-Mahanian framework, a tendency that, aside from its anachronism, distorts the interpretation of events prior to the Naval Defence Act (1889).

This study attempts, therefore, to assess the course of British naval policy from the mid-1860s through the mid-1880s in the context in which contemporaries viewed it, rather than through lenses supplied by Mahan. Moreover, rather than focusing primarily on the technological side of the story—admittedly its most visible element—the following pages will survey a much broader picture: the parameters that shaped British response to the technological revolution, including the domestic political scene, government fiscal policy, the administration (and administrators) of the navy, and, certainly not least of all, British perceptions of foreign governments and navies.

The era was complex, and not simply in light of technological change. In the domestic sphere the Second Parliamentary Reform Act (1867) fundamentally altered the nature of politics; henceforth the ruling class had to couch its policies with a view to appealing to an electorate that numbered more than a million and a half and contained for the first time a substantial working-class element. As a result, the organization of political parties subsequently underwent substantial alteration, and politicians, parties, and policy makers manifested an increasing awareness of the importance of public opinion and of the power of the press, both in framing their platforms and policies to garner public support and in responding to perceived shifts of opinion outside Westminster Palace. These factors and others, not least among them politicians' desire to appeal to the enlarged electorate through economizing, inexorably influenced the course of naval policy, whether indirectly or directly.

Overseas, there were further novel factors with which to contend. The Anglo-French naval rivalry of the early ironclad era had ended by the late 1860s with the British triumphant, an outcome that had major ramifications on the subsequent course of British naval policy in the realms of technology, deployment, and strategic planning. Moreover, following France's defeat by Germany in 1870–71, the British reaped what current usage would call a "peace dividend," as the Third Republic devoted most of its armaments expenditure to rebuilding the army, following the disastrous showing against its continental rival. The diminution of the perceived threat from France was an additional factor that shaped British naval policy in the decade and a half that followed.

The navy's administration also influenced the nature and direction of policy. Hugh Childers, the First Lord of the Admiralty from late 1868 to early 1871, undertook a comprehensive reform program that introduced mandatory retirement for flag officers, established a rational construction and repair policy, and restructured naval administration from the constitution of the Board of Admiralty to the manner of handling routine business. Childers' efforts garnered contemporary notoriety following the greatest naval tragedy of the era,

Introduction

the capsizing of H.M.S. *Captain* in September 1870, but their significance goes well beyond events immediately surrounding their implementation, and no attempt to comprehend the course of naval policy after 1869 can claim comprehensiveness without considering the causes and consequences of his work.

In short, the technological revolution that took place in warship design after 1850 did not occur in a vacuum. The aim of this book is to supply a context for this revolution. Technology was (and is) an important element in naval warfare, policy, and strategy, but technology should be viewed in its contemporary setting, for it is, ultimately, nothing more than a means to human ends—the product of human thought and effort. It cannot be fully understood without reference to the political, economic, administrative, international, and even ideological context within which it evolves.

CHAPTER 2

Strategic Parameters

The Force

The mid-Victorian navy was an amalgam of two forces designed for two largely incompatible, if not wholly unrelated, roles. One was suited for national defense and intervention in European affairs, the other was a peacetime police force that operated almost exclusively in extra-European waters. The former consisted after 1861 of ironclads first and foremost, the pride of the navy and, to Britons and many Europeans, the most visible and potent symbols of the country's power. The latter consisted of a multiplicity of types from tiny gunboats to corvettes almost 300 feet in length, most of which would have been of little use in the event of a European war, but which were quite useful in performing the duties for which they were designed: the tasks of a marine constabulary.

It has been argued that this divergence in ship types is explained by the largely prevailing Liberal ideology of the time; more likely, however, it was simply the contemporary response to a set of inherited assumptions, coupled with the growing divergence between the two parts of the fleet in terms of design and technical sophistication, itself the product of technological change.[1] For the battlefleet it was necessary to keep abreast of the latest advances in ordnance, armor, motive power, and design, in order to prevent a rival from attaining technological superiority. But for the peacetime ships of the "non-fighting" navy, that were ordinarily employed against countries without a powerful navy, or with, at best, a handful of modern vessels, the necessity for monster guns and armor plate vanished.

On distant stations, where coal depots were few or nonexistent, masts and sails retained their value even after the battlefleet was wholly steam-powered. And with the scarcity of dry docks overseas, wooden hulls with copper sheathing were actually preferable to iron, which rapidly became so covered with marine growth, especially in tropical waters, as to seriously impede the passage of the hull through the sea. Finally, and not surprisingly, the peacetime duties, valuable though they were in the eyes of most British politicians, were not so valuable as to justify squandering large amounts of money to provide overseas stations with state-of-the-art, cutting-edge designs or technology. To have done so would have been willfully extravagant. So while the ships of the battlefleet were changing dramatically, both inside and out during the 1860s and 1870s, the smaller vessels of the peacetime navy continued to look much as they had for a century and more.

There was near-universal agreement among political elites that it was necessary to maintain overseas squadrons to perform police duties and uphold British interests. The one prominent political grouping that dissented from this view was generally allied with the Liberal cause. Some of the Radical followers of Richard Cobden protested against the employment of the navy as a police force, even going so far as objecting to using it to disrupt the African slave trade.[2] During the 1840s, for instance, M.P. W. H. Hutt "denounced the blockade of the West African coast as based on 'erroneous principles' and 'mistaken humanity.'"[3] Three decades later M.P. Peter Rylands sounded a similar note regarding the whole scope of the peacetime duties of the navy: "[H]e entirely protested against the doctrine that the taxpayers of this country should be burdened to keep up a Navy 'not for ourselves alone, but for the benefit of the world at large.'"[4] Cobdenite Radicals aside, however, Britain's rulers through the mid-Victorian era, with one prominent exception, did not question the grounds upon which the overseas squadrons were maintained. Debate was restricted to questions of size and cost of the squadrons: their abolition simply did not enter calculations in the world of mainstream British politics. Even Cobden himself upheld the necessity of having a peacetime force scattered around the world.[5]

Under these circumstances the division of the fleet into "fighting" and "nonfighting" elements followed quite naturally: it was dictated by pragmatism, almost by necessity. It was wasteful to use larger ships than necessary to undertake the generally trivial duties of the "peacetime navy." Employing ironclads to chase down slave vessels or pirates, for instance, would be an expensive instance of overkill; besides, large, lumbering, and unwieldy armored vessels were next-to-useless for intercepting handy blockade runners or small pirate vessels. Ironclads, it is true, could intimidate recalcitrant foreign populations and authorities when pressing for redress of affronts to British honor or property, but on most stations smaller vessels were generally sufficient for this purpose, and were undeniably cheaper to build and maintain.

International Relations

The phrase "gunboat diplomacy" has come to symbolize both the nature of British foreign policy in the Victorian era and, to a large extent, the force used to implement that policy, but the exploits of the gunboat navy have tended to obscure the true foundation of British naval power and a large measure of its foreign policy influence in the nineteenth century.[6] With regard to Britain's relations with Europe, the battlefleet was far and away the more important element. Many Victorian statesmen may have disagreed with Palmerston's bellicose willingness to use the navy as a tool of foreign policy, but few quarreled with his underlying premise that there were no better keepers of the peace than the battlefleet, and even Gladstone—in many respects the antithesis of Palmerston in the foreign policy realm—was prepared to use the battlefleet to uphold British interests.

The general aims of British diplomacy in the early and middle decades of Victoria's reign were limited, due to the convergence of several factors. Most prominent among them were Britain's overwhelming economic, commercial, and industrial superiority over its rivals; geographic isolation of both the Home Islands and most of the empire; and the enduring legacy of the long struggle with revolutionary and imperial France, both in terms of the power structure on the continent and the situation with regard to the sea, the empire, and certainly not least of all, the navy itself.[7] Until the final quarter of the century Britain's industrial lead stood unchallenged. As of 1860, the United Kingdom's share of world manufacturing output was 19.9 percent: that of its next closest rival—France—was 7.9 percent. This share increased over the following two decades, reaching 22.9 percent in 1880, over two and a half times Germany's output, and 50 percent above that of the United States. As of 1860, Britain was responsible for two-fifths of the world's commerce in manufactured goods.[8]

Moreover, Britain's industrial, commercial, and economic advantages left it to a great extent a satiated power in the sphere of international relations. It boasted no irredentist agenda and it had no pressing need or inclination to enlarge the empire, although piecemeal expansion did continue throughout the early and mid-Victorian eras, especially in India and through the acquisition of strategic bases such as Singapore (1819) and Hong Kong (1842). In its position of industrial and commercial hegemony it made little sense to upset the status quo. After 1815, therefore, Britain had few deep-rooted quarrels with the nations of Europe and most of them had few quarrels with Britain.

In addition, given its geographic insularity from the Continent, and with its overwhelming naval predominance, countries that might quarrel with Britain would do so at a considerable disadvantage. In this respect the legacy of the French Revolutionary and Napoleonic wars, as embodied in the Vienna settlement of 1814–15, also worked distinctly to Britain's advantage, both in terms of the power structure within Europe and in the wider world. The final victory in the prolonged struggle against France left Britain without serious challengers to its maritime and naval hegemony or its near-monopoly of overseas colonies. As long as naval superiority was upheld there could be no substantive challenge to imperial predominance prior to the era of colonial nationalism.

There was another side of the coin. If Britain did not have to concern itself unduly with outside threats—the occasional invasion scare excepted—its power to intervene in Europe was similarly circumscribed, a situation that had substantial bearing on British foreign policy of the mid-Victorian era. Some writers have viewed the Schleswig-Holstein crisis of 1864, followed in October 1865 by the death of Palmerston, as a turning point in the formulation of British foreign policy. It would be more accurate, however, to suggest that Schleswig-Holstein and subsequent events illustrated the limitations of a foreign policy that relied largely on seapower for coercion and enforcement as least as much as they did on the shifting attitudes of the men who shaped that policy.[9]

The Crimean War marked the last noteworthy forceful British intervention in European affairs for twenty years; Britain stood on the sidelines during the Schleswig-Holstein crisis, the Austro-Prussian War, and the Franco-German War. One commentator has viewed this shift away from interventionism as part of a "mid-Victorian reappraisal of naval policy," which was manifested in a more cautious foreign policy following the death of Palmerston.[10] The circumstances of these crises, however, go a considerable way toward explaining the apparent isolationist turn in the mid-1860s.

Palmerston's government certainly did not disdain involving itself in an attempt to call off Austria and Prussia over Schleswig-Holstein. Rather, Palmerston and Earl Russell found that for all their bellicose words, Britain could do nothing to influence the course of events on the Continent. Indeed, having proclaimed British intent to uphold the territorial sanctity of the two duchies, Palmerston was publicly embarrassed, first because Bismarck paid no attention to his threatening words, and second because Britain, bereft of allies, was forced to stand aside meekly as Austria and Prussia did as they pleased.[11] Moreover, of the great European crises over the next decade and a half—the Austro-Prussian (1866) and Franco-German (1870–71) wars, Russian renunciation of Black Sea demilitarization (1870–71), the "War in Sight" Scare (1875), and the Eastern Crisis (1875–78)—only the last involved a region in which naval power could be utilized with any degree of effectiveness. The Austro-Prussian and Franco-German wars were both almost wholly military struggles. Sea power played no role in the outcome of either contest, and Britain's actions were limited to attempting to mediate between the combatants and concentrating the battlefleet in the Channel in 1870–71, owing to long-standing mistrust of Louis Napoleon.

When Russia announced in November 1870 its intent to disregard the Black Sea neutrality clauses of the Treaty of Paris (1856), Britain confronted the same strategic dilemma that had bedeviled Crimean War planning: Russia was the largest state in the world, but was exasperatingly difficult to attack by sea. No show of naval force was likely to influence the czar's counsels unless aimed at a strategically crucial point or accompanied by a major land campaign. On the purely practical level, both courses were out of the question in late 1870. The former would have involved a massive commitment of naval resources, and more important, would have drawn the battlefleet away from the Channel, a strategic impossibility given the still-raging Franco-German war. The second was equally impossible: Britain did not have available troops, France's and Germany's armies were otherwise occupied, and Austria-Hungary was still confronting the domestic political implications of the *Ausgleich* and was as usual disinclined to intervene in external matters that did not directly threaten its security.

Economic considerations also entered the foreign policy equation. Ardent free traders—Richard Cobden and John Bright especially—believed "that universal free trade would usher in an era of universal peace," and argued that the adoption of the doctrine should be accompanied by government retrenchment, especially in the spheres of national and imperial defense.[12] Most contemporaries were more skeptical of the pacific dividends of the doctrine, but if extreme claims by exponents were widely discounted, there still remained compelling arguments to resort to trade rather than war.[13] Moreover, whether or not the actions were consciously or solely based on free trade principles, British overtures to France and Germany on arms reduction in 1869–70 and the submission of the *Alabama* claims to outside arbitration and the subsequent obedience to the verdict—in the face of considerable domestic hostility and denunciation—suggest that "harmonization of mankind's general desires and ideals" was not absent from the thoughts of William Gladstone.

Of the political elites of the mid-Victorian era, Gladstone was the closest in ideology and temperament to Cobden and Bright. He was neither a doctrinaire free trader nor a pacifist—as Bright was—but the guiding principles of his foreign policy were unquestionably sympathetic to those of the "Manchester men."[14] These guiding principles were evident during the two most prominent foreign policy incidents of his first administration: British response to the Russian decision to remilitarize the Black Sea and the settlement of the *Alabama* claims. In the former instance, Gladstone himself never approved the neutralization of the Black Sea and therefore had no quarrel with Russian aims. But he had serious objections to unilateral action.[15] More significantly, in terms of realpolitik, British objections to Russia's action were sufficiently pointed that, at Bismarck's urging, the czar was persuaded to submit the matter to the London Conference (1871), at which the European Concert formally ratified the remilitarization of the Black Sea.

More substantive, and far less popular, was the Liberal ministry's course of action with regard to the *Alabama* claims. The *Alabama* was the most successful of several Confederate commerce raiders during the American Civil War. It and another Confederate commerce raider, C.S.S. *Florida*, were built in Liverpool, but British complicity went further, owing to Foreign Secretary Russell's failure to stop the Confederacy from taking delivery of the vessels. Moreover, the *Alabama* was supplied from England and manned primarily by

Englishmen. The United States therefore sought restitution from Britain for the losses it had incurred as a consequence of the vessel's depredations. As long as Russell remained in power—either as foreign secretary or, after Palmerston's death, prime minister—the British government refused to acknowledge any responsibility in the matter, but the fall of Russell's government in June 1866 removed the chief impediment to resolution of the claims. The succeeding Derby government began negotiations with the United States, talks that were carried through by Gladstone and the Liberals, first by signing the Treaty of Washington in May 1871, followed by submission of the American claims to Geneva. The United States was awarded £3,000,000 ($15,000,000) by the arbitrators. Gladstone's ministry, in turn, acceded to the verdict.

Some writers have regarded the method by which the *Alabama* claims were settled as an historic precedent for the cause of peaceful arbitration and for Gladstone's commitment to the policy.[16] On a less idealistic level the defenselessness of Canada made it highly desirable for Britain to reach an amicable agreement with the United States.[17] The unresolved dispute and the threat of American belligerence also hamstrung the British government in its dealings with Europe. Lord Clarendon, Liberal foreign secretary until his death in June 1870, stated in May 1869, "There is not the slightest doubt that if we were engaged in a continental quarrel we should immediately find ourselves at war with the United States." Clarendon's successor, Lord Granville, likewise "endorsed the resort to arbitration in the *Alabama* dispute on the grounds of the dangerous situation in Europe."[18] Yet the resolution of the *Alabama* claims by arbitration, and the government's uncomplaining acceptance of the substantial damages awarded to the United States struck many contemporaries as most un-Palmerstonian, not to say humiliating, behavior.[19]

That it did owed in considerable part to the efforts of Disraeli, who indeed made it one of his campaign issues. "Since the Liberals had left the patriot mantle of Palmerston lying on the ground, he would pick it up and use it, thus emphasizing the differences between the 'national' policy and the 'weak' and 'appeasing' stance of Gladstone, which could only lead to England's humiliation." Equally to the point, Disraeli was quick to sense "that political capital could be made out of a programme of imperial pride and diplomatic boldness." Hence, such pronouncements as those made in his famous Crystal Palace speech of 1872, which touted renewed pride in empire and national greatness, were "the first hints that the 1870s would see a far greater division between politicians over external affairs than in the 1860s."[20]

More substantive indicators were soon forthcoming. In response to French fears of a preemptive German military strike in the spring of 1875, Britain joined Russia in "express[ing] concern in Berlin at the rumours." The following November, in a much more famous coup, Disraeli purchased the Suez Canal shares belonging to the indigent khedive of Egypt, thus forestalling possible exclusive French ownership and control of the commercially and strategically vital waterway, and in 1876 he succeeded in winning parliamentary approval of the additional title of Empress of India for the Queen (she was thus proclaimed in January 1877). But not until the Eastern Crisis of 1875–78, which began as a revolt among the Ottoman Empire's Balkan subjects, did Disraeli find suitable circumstances for the exercise of his assertive foreign policy.

That Britain would play a major role in the crisis was not apparent from the outset. Alone among the great powers, it refused to agree to the solution adopted by Germany, Austria-Hungary and Russia in the Berlin memorandum of 13 May 1876, which would have applied coercive power to Turkey to reform the administration of its Christian provinces. Disraeli argued that to sign the memorandum would be "asking us to sanction them putting a knife to the throat of Turkey, whether we like it or not."[21] He succeeded in carrying his point, but his success placed the cabinet no closer to formulating a coherent policy. Indeed, Disraeli was faced with serious rifts among his colleagues over the direction of British policy, most notably between himself and the foreign secretary, Lord Derby, who was more cautious, more pacifistic, and more pro-Russian than the prime minister.[22] Notwithstanding the rejection of the Berlin Memorandum, so hesitant and indecisive was British policy that it was more the longevity of the crisis and its deepening as Serbia declared war on Turkey in June 1876 that eventually created the circumstances in which the government could evolve a coherent policy and, more difficult still, agree on its application. Even so, the ministry had to weather severe adverse public opinion aroused by Gladstone's famous pamphlet on Turkish massacres in Bulgaria, *Bulgarian Horrors and the Question of the East*. Only after Russia declared war on the Ottoman Empire (24 April 1877) and, more ominously, seemed poised to occupy Constantinople (late 1877) could the ministry articulate the "interests in the Near East for which ... [Britain, in Disraeli's opinion] ought ultimately to fight," but even then only at the cost of the resignations of Lords Carnarvon and Derby in early 1878.[23]

With the replacement of Derby by Lord Salisbury and a greater degree of cabinet solidarity, the government's policy quickly became interventionist. The Russian advance on Constantinople in December 1877–January 1878 prompted contingency plans for the use of the Mediterranean squadron. When Russian negotiators and the Porte signed the Treaty of San Stephano (March 1878), which called for the creation of a large Bulgarian state (presumably to be a Russian client) and reserved the question of Russian access to the Straits of Constantinople for future bilateral negotiations, the squadron was ordered to steam to Constantinople, ostensibly to protect British lives and property, but in reality to intimidate Russia.

The denouement was more lengthy than tense. Austria-Hungary, equally concerned at Russia's Balkan ambitions, sided with Britain, the more so since the creation of a large Bulgarian state contravened an earlier Austro-Russian agreement (the Reichstadt accord, 1877). Likewise, Bismarck, anxious to prevent a falling-out between Russia and Austria-Hungary—which might, in turn, provide France with an ally for its *revanchist* agenda—applied pressure on the czar to submit the Treaty of San Stephano to the powers for redrafting. Faced with potential war against both Britain and Austria-Hungary, without the support of Germany, and informed by his minister of war Dimitri Miliutin that the Russian army, still in the throes of post-Crimean reorganization, was unprepared for a major conflict, Alexander II relented, opening the way for the Congress of Berlin (June 1878), at which the great powers revised the Treaty of San Stephano.

From his viewpoint, Disraeli could count several accomplishments resulting from the government's handling of the Eastern Crisis. The closure of the Straits of Constantinople to warships—especially Russian warships—in peacetime, a longstanding principle that appeared threatened by the Russo-Turkish settlement, was reaffirmed by the Congress of Berlin. Likewise, the Congress reduced the size of the Bulgarian state created by San Stephano, in the process denying it access to the Aegean. Britain itself was permitted to occupy Cyprus, a point from which to counter the Russian threat to the eastern Mediterranean. And on a less tangible but nonetheless noteworthy level, Disraeli's "forward" policy stirred the popular imagination, in the process adding the word "jingo" to the lexicon.

Public approbation for foreign policy coups is often fleeting, however, and within two years of Disraeli's triumphant return from the Congress of Berlin the Conservatives were out of office, the victims of economic depression and a "forward" imperial policy gone awry, as the government managed to become entangled in embarrassing wars in South Africa and Afghanistan. Gladstone also contributed to his archrival's defeat. During 1879 and 1880 the former prime minister embarked on his historic Midlothian campaigns: popular appeals to the mass electorate, the chief of which was to discredit "Beaconsfieldism," Gladstone's term for what he believed to be the morally indefensible, economically irresponsible, and politically insupportable foreign and imperial policy of an ethically bankrupt government.[24] In the process, Gladstone tacitly reassumed the leadership of the Liberal party, from which he had retired in 1875, and following the party's victory in the general election of 1880, he became prime minister a second time, over the objections of the queen.

Gladstone's vision of proper British foreign and imperial policies differed substantially from that of Disraeli; he strived for the preservation of peace and a less aggressive imperial policy. He desired a return to cooperation with the Concert, rather than unilateral British action.[25] Yet in the sphere of foreign policy the practical difference between Gladstone and Disraeli was "barely noticeable."[26] Despite the cooperation of the Concert in forcing the Ottoman Empire to make concessions to Montenegro and Greece in 1881, Gladstone and the Liberals found themselves a year later inexorably sucked into Egyptian affairs. In this instance Gladstone was unable to arrange joint action by the Concert or even between Britain and France. Thus, in the wake of antiforeign rioting in June 1882 that threatened British commercial interests and, more ominously, the Suez Canal, the British Mediterranean squadron was ordered to bombard Alexandria, an action followed by amphibious operations, the long-term occupation of Egypt, and, ultimately, involvement in the Sudan as well.

The Afghan border crisis of 1884–85 also demonstrated the practical similarity between the foreign policies of Disraeli and Gladstone. In an attempt to stabilize its central Asian frontier, Russia's forces advanced toward Afghanistan during the 1860s and 1870s. The advance culminated in 1878 with the establishment of a military mission in Kabul, challenging British influence on the northwestern frontier of India. The immediate consequence was the Second Afghan War (1878–79), which concluded with the reestablishment of British predominance in the region. But continued Russian pressure in central Asia appeared to threaten both Persia and India and when on 30 March 1885 Russian and Afghan troops clashed at Penjdeh, "Gladstone recognized that a stand had to be made, [although] it must have saddened him enormously that after all his criticism of Disraeli's anti-Russian bias, his own Government should have come again to the brink of war with Russia."[27] Saddened or not, the reaction was forceful. Contingency plans were made for naval operations against Batum, on the eastern shore of the Black Sea, and the cabinet "even ordered the seizure of a Korean port (Port Hamilton) as a precautionary measure." Events were subsequently confused by domestic politics in Britain, as Gladstone resigned in June 1885 in the wake of the Gordon disaster in the Sudan; it was left to Lord Salisbury, at the head of the Conservatives, to reach an accord with Russia over their respective spheres of influence in central Asia, an accord completed just in time for the next Balkan crisis, over Bulgaria.

Such was the framework of European relations within which British naval policy functioned during the Gladstone-Disraeli era. Of course, such a short synopsis of the more noteworthy determinants and turns of British foreign policy can do justice neither to the complexities of the events nor to the motives of the participants; yet the general course of events must be borne in mind. The state of Britain's relations with the rest of Europe during the Great Rivalry naturally had a direct bearing on the deployment and utilization of naval power.

Strategic Considerations

The British response to crises in Europe, both prior to and during the mid-Victorian era, was conditioned not only by the attitudes of those in power, but also by the extent to which British force could be brought to bear as that "essential prop to British diplomacy." Hence, regardless of Gladstone's revulsion at the bloodshed of the Franco-German war, and notwithstanding his earnest attempts to mediate between the combatants, Britain lacked any effective means of compelling either one, especially Germany, of "the need to accord due weight to London's opinion." (One also wonders how the British government would have manifested its displeasure in 1870 had either France or Germany violated Belgian neutrality.) The same had been true in 1866, of course. Such was not the case, however, with the Russian menace to Constantinople in 1877–78 or Arabi Pasha's revolt four years later. Not only was support of the Ottoman Empire a hallmark of British foreign policy during the era, Britain could effectively influence events in the region through the application of naval force.[28]

The entire Mediterranean was a crucial link in the most direct route to the east, India in particular. Even prior to the completion of the Suez Canal (1869), in fact for the whole of the nineteenth century, the Mediterranean was a crucial theater for British strategic dispositions. It was largely coincidental that after 1815 the chief threats to British security arose in the eastern half of these waters, as the Ottoman Empire seemed to edge toward collapse or partition. But to compound headaches for British strategic planners, potential dangers were not restricted to the eastern half. France's best naval base, Toulon, threatened security to lines of communication at the western end, a threat magnified with the French conquest of Algeria beginning in 1830. "Indeed," notes Gerald Graham, "Britain was prepared in a pinch to fight both France and Russia to keep her Mediterranean corridor intact."[29]

Geographic factors further influenced the strength and disposition of British naval forces within the Mediterranean. The sea corridor was vulnerable to attack owing to three strategic "chokepoints": the Straits of Gibraltar, the central Mediterranean narrows between Cape Bon and the tip of Sicily, and the Dardanelles. The second of these essentially divided the Mediterranean into two halves, and determined the strategic importance of the British base at Malta (taken following Napoleon's Egyptian campaign of 1798) which, owing to its central location, afforded access to both halves. But despite the British presence at Malta, which remained the principal base of the Mediterranean squadron throughout the nineteenth century, there was a perennial danger that a rival might achieve local superiority in one half.

Between Malta and Gibraltar, supplemented at different intervals by Port Mahon in the Balearics and Leghorn on the west coast of Italy, the western Mediterranean could be secured. In the eastern half the situation was quite different, there being no strategically useful port beyond Malta, which was too far from the Straits of Constantinople and the Suez Canal to be of use as a supply base for a steam fleet operating at the eastern end. Hence, it is possible to appreciate the strategic impetus for the Disraeli ministry's acquisition of Cyprus in 1878. But Cyprus, despite its geographic proximity, lacked the harbor so necessary to buttress and secure British naval presence in the eastern Mediterranean (the same was true of Gibraltar at the other end, incidentally). Here the Liberals' reluctant involvement in Egypt paid unexpected dividends, for, once dredged, Alexandria possessed the excellent harbor that Cyprus lacked and quickly became the base of British naval power in the eastern Mediterranean, from which to counter threats to the Straits or Suez.[30]

The other nexus of British strategic concentration was, of course, the home islands where, at any given time during the mid-Victorian era, save in moments of crisis in the Mediterranean, the majority of the ironclad fleet was to be found. This strategic disposition close to home may have reflected the less aggressive British posture apparent to C. J. Bartlett and others. It is equally clear, however, that the ongoing technological revolution that began with the introduction of steam caused a significant shift in the strategic deployment of the British battlefleet for the ensuing four decades and more, a posture seemingly oriented more toward the defensive than the offensive.

The overriding reason for the shift was steam power itself. In 1847, spurred by the French decision to construct steam battleships, the Duke of Wellington envisioned a "bolt from the blue": a quick descent on the English coast by a French fleet which, thanks to its engines, could defy wind and tide and, more significantly, evade a blockading British fleet with an ease that had not existed in the days of sail. The most perceptible manifestation of this dramatic alteration of strategic circumstances was a succession of "invasion scares" from the mid-1840s through the early 1860s.[31] Nearly as obvious to subsequent historians was the evident abandonment of the traditional "blue water" strategy of national security that anchored defense of the Home Islands on naval blockade of enemy coasts. By 1859 a royal commission on national security had concluded that "the efficient blockade of an enemy's ports had become well nigh impossible."[32] In the face of such opinion a new approach to national defense was imperative.

As it evolved, the new approach revealed several facets. The royal commission itself stressed the need for coastal defenses and recommended an expenditure of £10,000,000 on fortifications. Palmerston, in turn, implemented the recommendation over the strident protests of his chancellor of the exchequer, Gladstone. The most visible consequence was a series of elaborate fortifications around the chief dockyards of the country, soon dubbed "Palmerston's follies." A further manifestation was Queen Victoria's 1859 letter to Lords Lieutenant, authorizing the formation and drilling of volunteer militia, which would provide a force for home defense in the event of a French invasion. On the basis of these two initiatives it indeed appears that the mid-Victorian era witnessed a distinct shift away from the traditional emphasis on naval power for national defense toward security arrangements based in considerable part on land forces: a tilt away from the "blue water" school to the "brick and mortar" school.

In addition, naval deployment, even the nature of the battlefleet, apparently reflected the altered circumstances of the period. As First Lord George J. Goschen informed the House of Commons in 1873, it was the Liberal government's policy to keep the newest and most powerful ironclads "at home prepared for any emergency and that older ships should be sent into their absent [i.e., overseas] squadrons."[33] Further, home defenses were bolstered by the practice, begun in 1868, of employing part of the ironclad fleet as coast guard vessels, stationed individually at major commercial ports. In peacetime these ships were manned by skeleton crews, but in the event of a crisis the complements would be quickly filled by calling out the naval reserve (also established in 1859), comprising men who had served ten years or more active service, who were paid a retainer to remain available in wartime, and who were drilled yearly on reserve squadron cruises.

Thus, as of 1868, five British ironclads patrolled the Mediterranean, but the Channel fleet numbered ten, bolstered by an additional three at coast guard stations and another at Portsmouth.[34] Six years later, at the close of Gladstone's first administration, the Mediterranean and Channel forces were evenly balanced, each with four ironclads, but the armored coast guard force had swelled to ten ships. Such dispositions became the norm in the mid-Victorian era, save for the period immediately surrounding the Eastern Crisis in 1877–78. While British capital ship deployment had traditionally been markedly Eurocentric, for the three decades after 1850 it would be more accurate to label it Anglocentric, the strategic centrality of the Mediterranean notwithstanding.

This defensive posture also appears to have been manifested in design policy between 1866 and 1885 by the construction of a number of ironclads intended expressly for coastal defense, a trend that was especially popular in the 1860s and early 1870s. The shift from "blue water" to "coastal defense" had several factors propelling it. Most compelling, at least from a purely naval standpoint, ships built specifically for operations in coastal waters fulfilled a real want of the service, that being of armorclads of shallow draft.[35] The great draft of large seagoing ironclads—typically 21–28 feet—rendered them incapable of operating safely in shallow coastal waters. The notion of coastal defense also found favor on political and ideological grounds, especially among those who, like Cobden, Bright, and Gladstone, regarded the proper role of the navy as defensive, and who furthermore saw in the coastal defense ironclad an (inexpensive) alternative to both seagoing ironclads (with their offensive capabilities) and Palmerston's follies.[36] Last, small armored ships were substantially cheaper than their seagoing counterparts, a fact lost on neither economy-minded M.P.s nor Admiralty administrators agitating for more ships. Thomas Brassey argued in 1871 that by suspending construction on the large ironclad *Devastation* and reallocating the sums voted for it, the Admiralty could "provide, by the end of three years, without any addition to the present Vote for shipbuilding, 36 vessels of a type admirably adapted for coast defence."[37] As a result of this conjunction of rationales, during the mid-1860s the navy built or acquired seven coastal defense turret ships and armored gunboats for home defense and, later in the decade, commenced work on a further six of the former type: three for home defense, two for India, and one for Australia. Moreover, a brief but acute alarm at the Admiralty that followed the outbreak of the Franco-German War led to the authorization and construction of four additional coastal defense turret ships.

Yet commentators, especially those who maintain that the "brick and mortar" school achieved ascendance over the traditionally dominant "blue water" school during the second half of the nineteenth century, have made too much of this apparent retreat from the time-honored aggressive, offensive naval strategy of the close blockade.[38] The conclusion is understandable, especially in light of the 1859 commission which concluded that with the advent of steam "we can no longer rely upon being able to prevent the landing of a hostile force in the country."[39] But arguing that "the nation could not be considered secure against invasion if it had to depend for its defense on the fleet alone" is not synonymous with arguing that the "blue water" strategy for national defense was wholly, or even largely, supplanted by the "brick and mortar" school.[40]

As an initial corrective to the prevailing view, it must be stressed

H.M.S. *Hotspur* (authorized 1868, launched 1870, completed 1871). As its name implies, *Hotspur* was designed with the concept of ramming foremost. Like other such vessels—*Rupert, Hero,* and *Conqueror*—it also sported low freeboard and so little coal bunkerage that it was effectively limited to coastal operations: harbor defense and, as far as Admiralty planners were concerned, coastal assault against enemy ports and shipping. This latter role was carefully concealed from the public to prevent outcry from parliamentary Radicals, such as John Bright. (All photos are courtesy of the National Maritime Museum, London.)

H.M.S. *Rupert* (authorized 1870, launched 1872, completed 1874). Another of the "coastal defense" rams, the disposition of *Rupert*'s main armament—two 10-inch guns in a single turret forward of the vessel's superstructure—rendered fire astern impossible. Such a design could be entertained only for the specific roles envisioned for it: ramming and coastal assault.

H.M.S. *Invincible* (authorized 1867, launched 1869, completed 1870). One of a class of four vessels designed to counter the small (3,000-ton) French *Alma*-class ironclads, designed for service on foreign stations. The four 5,700-ton *Invincibles*, plus the similar *Swiftsure* and *Triumph*, were not only decisively superior to their direct counterparts, but also most of the first-class French ironclads built prior to 1870, with iron, rather than wooden, hulls, extensive internal compartmentalization, and thicker armor.

H.M.S. *Captain* (authorized 1866, launched 1869, completed 1870). Designed by Captain Cowper Coles and built in a private shipyeard, *Captain* was foisted upon the Admiralty by the weight of public pressure with singularly tragic results. Its design attempted to combine the incompatible qualities of low freeboard and full sailing rig. Within nine months of completion *Captain* capsized in a squall in the Bay of Biscay, with the loss of all but 18 of its 492 crew members.

Top left: Hugh C. E. Childers (1825–97), Liberal politician and statesman. Childers served as Civil Lord of the Admiralty during the latter years of the 1859–66 Liberal government and as First Lord from late 1868 to early 1871. In the latter capacity he implemented a far-reaching program of naval reform.

Top right: Admiral Sir Alexander Milne (1806–96), naval officer and administrator. Milne entered the navy in 1817, and after extensive sea service, came to the Admiralty in 1847. He was unquestionably the greatest naval administrator of the Victorian era and the first to give systematic consideration to British deployment in the machine age.

Bottom: H.M.S. *Devastation* (authorized 1869, launched 1871, completed 1873). *Devastation* was the first of the "breastwork monitors," the first seagoing (as opposed to coastal) mastless ironclad, and in layout and armament disposition the prototype of the modern battleship. This shot also serves to emphasize how much it shared in terms of freeboard and profile with "coastal defense" monitors such as *Rupert* and *Hotspur*. Because of the state of steam technology, however, breastwork monitors were confined to European waters.

H.M.S. *Bellerophon* (authorized 1863, launched 1865, completed 1866). An improvement on the first-generation ironclads, *Bellerophon*'s shorter, fuller hull gave it increased maneuverability; its more powerful engines compensated for a loss of fineness. It was the first British capital ship to sport a full double bottom; its main battery was concentrated amidships, also a novelty.

H.M.S. *Sultan* (authorized 1868, launched 1870, completed 1871). Illustrative of the dichotomy that dominated ironclad building in the late 1860s and 1870s, the weight of *Sultan*'s sailing rig meant that its guns were smaller and its armor thinner than on breastwork monitors. Contemporary steam technology did not permit the abandonment of sails on vessels that might serve beyond European waters.

H.M.S. *Shannon* (authorized 1873, launched 1875, completed 1877). By the time *Shannon* was completed, fast, steam-powered vessels were needed to hunt enemy commerce raiders. *Shannon*'s masts and sails were hindrances to such a role, but the paucity of coaling stations abroad dictated their retention.

H.M.S. *Nelson* (authorized 1874, launched 1876, completed 1881). An armored cruiser, *Nelson* carried enough coal to steam forty days at seven knots. Due to the transitional nature of contemporary steam technology, such ships were not speedy enough to fulfill the cruiser role.

H.M.S. *Warrior* (authorized 1859, launched 1860, completed 1861). The first armored, iron-hulled, seagoing vessel, *Warrior* was decisively superior in speed, seaworthiness, and protection to France's *Gloire*, in response to which it was built. Nevertheless, it was obsolescent by 1870, a victim of rapid technological change.

H.M.S. *Inflexible* (authorized 1873, launched 1876, completed 1881). Designed in response to the Italian ironclads *Duilio* and *Dandolo*, the *Inflexible* epitomized the transitional character of capital-ship design in the 1870s. Beneath its brig-rig it boasted four 16.25-inch rifled muzzle-loaders in two turrets, mounted amidst an armored citadel of wrought iron two feet thick. *Inflexible* was also the first British warship with electric power. The torpedo launcher—another technological novelty—is visible at the bow.

H.M.S. *Alexandra* (authorized 1872, launched 1875, completed 1877). The leisurely construction pace indicates how insignificant the Admiralty thought foreign battlefleets and construction programs were in this decade. *Alexandra* was the last first-class ironclad with a full rig.

H.M.S. *Temeraire* (authorized 1873, launched 1876, completed 1877). *Temeraire* was the most unusual of the hybrid British capital ship designs of the 1870s. Originally conceived as a second-class, box-battery ironclad of the *Invincible* type, its design was subsequently much enlarged and the box-battery supplemented by two heavy guns mounted in armored *barbettes* on the upper deck.

H.M.S. *Ajax* (authorized 1876, launched 1880, completed 1883). The *Ajax* design was probably the worst of the compromised British capital ship designs between 1860 and 1890: cramming the ordnance and armor of a first-class ironclad on the hull and displacement of a "coastal defense" ship. The product of strategic and economic considerations, the results were termed "second-class" but were of doubtful utility: slow, clumsy, and lacking the fighting qualities of larger warships, either British or foreign.

H.M.S. *Collingwood* (authorized 1880, launched 1882, completed 1887). A return to the basic configuration of *Devastation*, with a significant departure: the center-line-mounted guns were in *barbettes*, whose lightness enabled them to be mounted ten feet further above the waterline than *Devastation*'s guns.

that even a commission composed largely of military engineers did not recommend total reliance on land defenses.[41] More crucially, much of the impetus for the Anglocentric battlefleet concentration followed necessarily, not from a defensive *mentalité* shared by politicians and naval administrators (whether professional or civilian), but from the limitations imposed by technological transition. The growing reliance on steam as the primary source of motive power tied the fleet to its coal depots far more thoroughly and tightly than had been the case in the days of sail. A sailing ship's radius of action and endurance were circumscribed only by the need for food and water for the crew. Not so the steamship, which required frequent refueling. In addition, the switch from wooden to iron construction, necessitated in large ships by the increasing burden of steam machinery, tied the fleet to the dry dock. Iron fouled much more rapidly than did wood sheathed in copper (copper could not be used over an iron hull owing to chemical reaction between the two metals), and a foul hull drastically reduced speed and operational range while similarly increasing coal consumption. The main units of the battlefleet, almost all of them iron-hulled, required frequent dry docking to clean their bottoms. The only dry docks big enough to accommodate them were at Portsmouth and Devonport. The steam—and subsequently, the ironclad—battlefleet was stationed close to home because it could not stray from its logistical support. Battlefleet deployment, in short, was dictated by technological limitations, regardless of the strategic mindset of the formulators of policy.

In addition, the largely deterrent role played by the battlefleet in the 1860s and 1870s can easily obscure both its centrality to British national security and its equally pivotal role as a tool for foreign policy, a role that was at times unmistakably offensive. The most visible instances of offensive operations took place, of course, in 1878 and 1882; that Hornby's squadron did not fire a shot while stationed off Constantinople cannot undercut the threat posed to Russia by its presence there. Beyond these incidents, there are a handful of others worth noting, despite the general peace in European and international relations. In 1873, factional strife in Spain between Republicans and Carlists resulted in the seizure of much of the Spanish fleet—including four ironclads—by radical *Intransigentes*. They were in turn proclaimed pirates by the Spanish government (20 July), prompting British and German naval authorities to act. Two of the rebel ironclads were seized on 1 August and subsequently turned over to

Spanish authorities. Following the blockade of Cartagena the *Intransigentes* surrendered, the whole business having lasted less than a fortnight.[42]

In 1880 warships from the British Mediterranean squadron participated in an international demonstration in the Adriatic, the object of which was to pressure Turkey into ceding Dulcigno to Montenegro. A similar action took place in 1886, when British, German, Austro-Hungarian, Russian, and Italian warships briefly blockaded Greece, out of fear of its designs on the Ottoman Empire.[43] Finally, in the tense period following the Penjdeh incident (1885) a special squadron of ironclads was assembled for possible service in the Baltic.

But it is more appropriate to judge the effectiveness of deterrent forces by how little, rather than how much they are actually used, and by this standard the mid-Victorian battlefleet was unmistakably successful, despite the seemingly insignificant number of ironclads at sea at any given point and regardless of their Anglocentric deployment. In 1860 the Channel fleet had numbered eighteen vessels, no less than ten of them steam battleships. Five years later the force in the Channel had shrunk to eight ships, but five of them were ironclads, and in terms of fighting power, the fleet of 1865 was unquestionably the stronger force. By January 1871 there were twenty-five ironclads in commission, the preponderance of them in European or home waters, and another twelve available in reserve. Five years later the reserve force numbered twenty. Many of these ships, to be sure, were old and, by the latest standards, insufficiently armed and armored. All, however, could have played a part in the defense of Britain had a foreign threat materialized. It never did.

In short, the British navy remained the first and the most important line of defense throughout the mid-Victorian era, despite allegations that it was supplanted by land defenses. Much of the seemingly defensive deployment was a consequence of technological factors rather than of the triumph of a noninterventionist policy. Given the blockades of Spain in 1873, the Adriatic in 1880, and Greece in 1886, the intervention at Constantinople in 1878, the bombardment of Alexandria in 1882, and the contingency plans and preparations for operations against Russia in 1885, it is clear that mid-Victorian battlefleet strategy was by no means as defensive in posture as some writers have maintained. Even the "coastal defense" ironclads were envisioned as dual-purpose vessels, designed to operate against enemy harbors and fortifications as well as defending British shores. In originally pressing for construction of several such ships in 1866, Controller Spencer Robinson described the design as "being intended either for coastal defenses, or the attack of shipping in an enemy harbour...."[44] The offensive capabilities were downplayed and even concealed from the public, presumably to avoid an outcry from the left wing of the Liberal party.

Two final observations regarding the battlefleet: the increasingly Anglocentric, if not defensive, concentration of British capital ships during the mid-Victorian era has come in for its share of criticism as an abandonment of the "blue water" strategy on which Britain's naval preeminence was constructed, and, hence, a violation of one of Mahan's cardinal tenets of seapower. Yet this trend continued after the mid-Victorian era; indeed, it accelerated. With the rise of German seapower in the early twentieth century the concentration became so Anglocentric that not only was local naval superiority abandoned in both the Americas and the Far East, but the Mediterranean, in many respects the strategic nexus throughout the nineteenth century, was turned over to former archrival France. Yet the concentration that took place after 1889 and accelerated after 1900 has been accepted without question as the simple consequence of strategic necessity.

In this respect, however, the continuity is clear; the same technological and international circumstances that impelled increasing concentration in home waters in the 1890s and 1900s were at work in the 1870s, albeit less obviously. In fact, the advent of steam made the concentration strategically logical as well as technologically necessary. No longer did the British face the possibility of a surprise descent by a large French force from the West Indies, *à la* Villeneuve in the summer of 1805. The limitations of steam technology, coupled with British imperial predominance and the spreading network of submarine telegraph cables all but precluded such an occurrence. British statesmen and naval officers knew where the serious threats could come from with a degree of assurance that did not exist in the days of sail. To have frittered away (to use Hugh Childers' expression) the strength of the navy through wider deployment—assuming it to have been technologically feasible—would have needlessly weakened the battlefleet in the few places where its presence was crucial.

Last, arguing that the "brick and mortar" excesses of the mid-to-late nineteenth century represent an anomaly in British security policy and strategy is to overlook a continual hedging of national security bets. The era of Nelson, the heyday of British seapower, the era in which the boast "I do not say they cannot come; I only say they cannot come by sea" rang loud, was also the era of the coastal defense Martello Towers, as unnecessary as their direct descendants, Palmerston's follies, but nonetheless eloquent testimony to ever-present British fears that a French invasion *might* somehow evade the blockading forces of the Royal Navy. Clarke notes that the remains of Palmerston's follies can still be seen, "close to the antitank ditches and air-landing obstacles devised against another threat of invasion."[45] In short, the "brick and mortar" school has existed for as long as the "blue water" school, side by side with it, Mahan notwithstanding. At some points its sway was greater than at others, and the mid-Victorian period was undoubtedly one such point, but at no time did the "brick and mortar" school achieve such ascendance as to cause Britain to abandon the traditional reliance on the navy as the bulwark of national security.

Overseas Deployment

Beyond Europe, few situations called for the overwhelming force of a capital ship, much less a squadron or a fleet. After 1870 two coastal defense monitors were stationed in India and one in Australia. Not one of the three fired its guns in anger during its lengthy career.[46] The role of deterrent was once again amply fulfilled. Elsewhere the standard practice was to maintain a token ironclad force on stations where Britain might face rival ships of similar power or, alternatively, where the French stationed armored ships. This situation meant, in practical terms, that ironclads were stationed on the North American and West Indies command to counter the United States' armored fleet; on the Pacific station, where by the 1870s both Chile and Peru possessed small but potent ironclads, and on the China station, where the French, Russian, and eventually the Japanese posed potential armored threats.

The standard armored force in North American waters was two or three vessels, one of them a stationary harbor-defense ship at Bermuda. Similar practice was followed on the China station, where an obsolescent ironclad was permanently stationed at Hong Kong and another armored ship was designated to cruise the entire command and serve as a suitably impressive flagship for the squadron commander. In the Pacific a solitary ironclad was deemed sufficient from 1866 to 1877. Indeed, when pinched for vessels in the latter year, the

Admiralty substituted the large unarmored frigate *Shah* for a cruising ironclad. Following the precepts of Murphy's Law, this juncture, naturally, witnessed the lone noteworthy action involving British forces against an ironclad. On 29 May 1877 the *Shah* and the smaller unarmored warship *Amethyst* exchanged rounds with the Peruvian coastal defense ironclad *Huascar*, manned by mutineers. The action was indecisive, the *Huascar* surrendered to Peruvian authorities the following day, and none of the participants suffered serious damage. But the Admiralty responded to the encounter by stationing two ironclads in the Pacific for a couple of years following the incident (1879–81) before reverting to one.

The *Huascar* fight excepted, the service of ironclads on overseas stations was largely uneventful. Following the conclusion of the Second Opium War and the American Civil War, both of which provoked substantial buildups of British naval force on the affected stations, service abroad followed a leisurely routine for those in squadron flagships: fraternizing with personnel from other navies, entertaining fellow officers, making ritual visits to ports, and maintaining contact with British ambassadors and consuls.[47]

This leisurely, unwarlike existence should not, however, obscure the deterrent value possessed by the handful of capital units overseas. There existed no more potent symbol of force in the late nineteenth century than the ironclad or battleship, combining overwhelming firepower and near invulnerability. The deterrent value, unfortunately, is not easily demonstrated; counterfactual constructs of what might have happened had the British not maintained armored units on certain overseas stations would be pointless. Yet given the general placidity of life on most of the foreign stations and the lack of serious naval confrontations—the *Huascar* incident again excepted—one must conclude that by and large the forces stationed abroad, ironclads included, were sufficient to dissuade substantive challenges to British naval hegemony.

Of course, naval force was not the only factor in the equation for the lack of challenges prior at least to the mid-1880s, but there is no doubt that other nations generally accepted Britain's self-designated role as police of the seas. "With the gradual transition from a mercantilist to a free-trade empire," observes Paul Schroeder, "British maritime supremacy became at worst only an irritant and a latent threat to others, and in some ways even an asset."[48] Part of the reason for this general acquiescence may be tied to the largely unthreatening nature of Britain's overseas squadrons. There was little need to deploy massive force on most overseas stations; less-impressive vessels than ironclads were ordinarily capable of performing most of the tasks required of the peacetime navy, in a less provocative manner and much more cheaply. Under ordinary circumstances overseas the power of an ironclad was unnecessary, inappropriate, wasteful of precious resources, or, most likely, a combination of the three. Hence, the existence of the second element that with the battlefleet made up the Royal Navy: the small vessels of the marine constabulary that have become inextricably identified with the Victorian era.

In 1820 there were five overseas commands besides the Mediterranean: the South-East Coast of America (i.e., South America), North America and the West Indies, the Cape of Good Hope, the West Coast of Africa, and the East Indies.[49] There were seventy ships serving on these "foreign" stations, the largest number (twenty-eight) in North American waters, stretching from Halifax and Newfoundland in the north, along the east coast of the United States, through the Caribbean basin. There were a further twelve ships off the east coast of South America, ten in the East Indies, seven off the west coast of Africa, and one at the Cape of Good Hope, in addition to the twelve in the Mediterranean. Almost all of these ships were small.[50] Over the next forty-five years the duties of the overseas squadrons multiplied, prompting an increase in their number. By 1865 there were eight overseas commands besides the Mediterranean; the Pacific station had been established in 1838, the Australian station in 1859, and the China station following the Second Opium War. The Cape of Good Hope and the West Coast of Africa stations had been combined following the diminution of the West African slave trade, but this consolidation was almost simultaneously offset by the creation of a "detached squadron" designed to cruise the world, train officers and seamen, and show the flag and uphold British prestige.

With the multiplication of squadrons came a concurrent increase in the size of most of them.[51] The seventy vessels in service overseas in 1821 had, by 1840, grown to 120. During the 1840s the number was reduced, but it ballooned again during the Crimean War. By the end of the conflict 149 warships were in commission overseas, no less than forty-eight of them in the Mediterranean or the Black Sea. As of 1860 the total had been reduced to 133, but thereafter it climbed again, largely a consequence of the American Civil War—reinforcing the North American station in the event of hostilities with the United

States—and increased involvement in the Far East. Hence, as of 1865 there were 145 warships stationed abroad. Most of these vessels were small; there were but two ironclads overseas (both in the Mediterranean), eight steam ships of the line (four in the Mediterranean and one each in China, North America, the East Indies, and South America), and one sailing ship of the line (in the Mediterranean). There were, however, seventeen steam frigates in service abroad, along with eighteen steam corvettes and thirty-five steam sloops. Last, but by no means least, there were twenty-three gunboats and another twenty-nine gunvessels at sea.[52] The gunboat and its slightly larger kin, the gunvessel, were originally designed and built during the Crimean War for inshore operations against Russian fortresses in the shallow waters of the Baltic, but following the cessation of hostilities the Admiralty quickly discovered that it had large numbers of vessels well suited for the duties of marine policing.[53] By 1865 there were twenty-two gunboats and gunvessels in service on the China station and another twelve off the coast of Africa, where by this juncture they were involved more in protecting British interests and merchants than in combating the slave trade.

The duties of the overseas squadrons were multifarious; gunboats and their larger brethren were employed to fight piracy and the slave trade, to protect British settlements, fisheries, traders, and commercial interests, to survey and chart coastlines, to compile hydrographic data, to support British civil authorities overseas, to transport troops, and to perform virtually any other task of which ships were capable. In mid-1862 an M.P. requested the specifics of "all applications, as far as can be obtained, that have been made by the commercial and other interests, during the last five years, to the government of the day, for ships of war to be sent to foreign stations, for the protection of British interests and commerce."[54] The resulting return reveals the range of British naval operations. From 1857 through 1861 there were ninety-five such applications, forty-nine of them from the foreign office or consular officials, twenty-one from colonial governors, twelve from the colonial office, sixteen from private concerns (usually through the foreign or colonial offices), and seven from other sources, ranging from the board of trade to the trustees of the British Museum and the Archbishop of Canterbury.

Twenty-four applications specifically requested naval force for the protection of British interests. Several others merely asked for "more frequent visits of a ship of war" to show the flag. More seriously,

TABLE I
Ships on Overseas Stations, 1821–1900

Year	Station	Fighting	Non-Fighting[a]	Year	Station	Fighting	Non-Fighting
1821	Mediterranean	12	2		Great Lakes	0	5
	South America[b]	12	0		Particular svce.	8	7
	East Indies	10	2		Total	112	47
	No. Amer./W. Indies	28	7	1850	Mediterranean	25	9
	West Africa	7	2		South America	8	2
	Cape of Good Hope	1	0		East Indies	17	4
	Great Lakes	0	16		No. Amer./W. Indies	11	11
	Particular svce.[c]	0	3		West Africa	23	1
	Total	70	32		Cape of Good Hope	6	3
1826	Mediterranean	13	3		Pacific	10	3
	Lisbon[d]	6	0		Great Lakes	0	3
	South America	12	0		Particular svce.	14	14
	East Indies	14	1		Total	114	50
	No. Amer./W. Indies	29	6	1856	Mediterranean	54	15
	West Africa	6	2		Baltic	10	0
	Cape of Good Hope	4	0		South America	8	2
	Great Lakes	0	16		East Indies	14	1
	Total	84	28		No. Amer./W. Indies	19	3
1830	Mediterranean	17	5		West Africa	15	1
	Lisbon	5	0		Cape of Good Hope	6	1
	South America	14	1		Pacific	11	3
	East Indies	11	1		Australia[g]	4	1
	No. Amer./W. Indies	25	1		Particular svce.	8	3
	West Africa	10	3		Total	149	30
	Cape of Good Hope	7	0	1860	Mediterranean	39	2
	Great Lakes	0	6		South America	8	2
	Particular svce.	6	0		East Indies	32	10
	Total	95	17		No. Amer./W. Indies	16	1
1835	Mediterranean	22	5		West Africa	14	2
	Lisbon	10	0		Cape of Good Hope	6	1
	South America	15	0		Pacific	10	4
	East Indies	11	1		Australia	5	0
	No. Amer./W. Indies	25	10		Particular svce.	3	3
	West Africa[e]	12	3		Total	133	25
	Great Lakes	0	7	1865	Mediterranean	24	6
	Particular svce.	4	2		South America	11	3
	Total	99	28		East Indies	9	2
1840	Mediterranean	30	11		China[h]	35	11
	Lisbon	4	0		No. Amer./W. Indies	25	6
	South America	20	3		West Africa	18	3
	East Indies	12	0		Cape of Good Hope	1	1
	No. Amer./W. Indies	24	18		Pacific	12	2
	West Africa	20	2		Australia	8	0
	Particular svce.	10	8		Particular svce.	2	10
	Total	120	42		Total	145	44
1845	Mediterranean	21	4	1871	Mediterranean	13	2
	South America	9	5		South America	8	1
	East Indies	22	8		East Indies	9	0
	No. Amer./W. Indies	11	14		China	23	4
	West Africa	21	1		No. Amer./W. Indies	16	5
	Cape of Good Hope	8	2		West Africa	7	2
	Pacific[f]	12	1		Pacific	9	1

TABLE 1 (CONTINUED)
Ships on Overseas Stations, 1821–1900

Year	Station	Fighting	Non-Fighting	Year	Station	Fighting	Non-Fighting
	Australia	6	0		China	21	3
	Particular svce.	4	3		No. Amer./W. Indies	11	3
	Detached Squad.[i]	5	0		West Africa	8	1
	Total	100	18		Pacific	7	0
1876	Mediterranean	13	0		Australia	7	4
	Lisbon	5	0		Particular svce.	6	8
	South America	4	0		Detached Squad.	4	0
	East Indies	14	0		Total	101	23
	China	19	2	1890[j]	Mediterranean	22	1
	No. Amer./W. Indies	11	3		South America	4	0
	West Africa	5	2		East Indies	13	0
	Pacific	9	0		China	18	0
	Australia	10	0		No. Amer./W. Indies	11	0
	Particular svce.	2	9		West Africa	8	0
	Detached Squad.	6	0		Pacific	8	0
	Total	98	16		Australia	7	0
1881	Mediterranean	18	2		Total	91	1
	South America	5	0	1895	Mediterranean	29	2
	East Indies	11	0		Atlantic[k]	22	0
	China	21	3		East Indies	8	8
	No. Amer./W. Indies	10	6		China	24	3
	West Africa	9	1		Pacific[l]	22	3
	Pacific	11	0		Total	105	16
	Australia	10	1	1900	Mediterranean	36	3
	Particular svce.	1	9		Atlantic	17	1
	Detached Squad.	5	0		East Indies	10	2
	Total	101	22		East Asia	32	0
1886	Mediterranean	22	4		Pacific	12	1
	South America	4	0		Total	107	7
	East Indies	11	0				

SOURCES: 1821 through 1886, *The Navy List* (published by Admiralty authority, London: John Murray, 1821–81); 1890 through 1900, Thomas Brassey et al., *Naval Annual* (Portsmouth: J. Griffin, 1887–1905).

[a]Including surveying ships, troop ships, receiving ships, tenders, tugs, hospital ships, supply ships, convict ships, hulks, and other support vessels as well as uncommissioned warships.

[b]Properly, the "South-East Coast of America," thus denoting the continent's east coast. Prior to 1838 vessels from this station or the East Indies Squadron were responsible for duties on the west coast of South America or elsewhere in the Pacific, the duties being divided on the basis of geographic proximity.

[c]"Particular service" designated ships operating outside the jurisdiction of the regular station commands; their activities ranged from Arctic exploration to transporting army troops, to surveying, to any conceivable duty requiring the service of a ship or ships for a specific, short-term purpose.

[d]Lisbon was never a permanent foreign command, but naval vessels were frequently stationed there.

[e]For the years 1835–40 and from 1871 onward the Cape of Good Hope and West African Squadrons are combined in the *Navy Lists*.

[f]The Pacific station became a separate command in 1838.

[g]Australia became a separate command in 1858.

[h]China became a separate command (from the East Indies Squadron) following the Second Opium War (1861).

[i]The Detached Squadron was created in 1869, its purpose training officers and sailors, and showing the flag around the world. It was later superseded by the Training Squadron.

[j]Beginning in the late 1880s cruising vessels began to be classified as 1st-, 2nd-, and 3rd-class cruisers, rather than corvettes and sloops. Generally speaking (but not consistently), ships designed before 1880 are designated by the old terms, those designed after 1880 by the new.

[k]By 1895 the North America and West Indies Squadron, the South-East Coast of America Squadron, and the African Squadron were consolidated into the Atlantic Squadron.

[l]The Australian Station was subsumed by the Pacific Station and later incorporated into the East Asian Command.

TABLE 2
Ships in Commission on Overseas Stations, 1821–1900

Year	Ship Type	Number	Year	Ship Type	Number
1821	Ships of the line	2		Steam frigates	6
	Frigates	30		Sloops	28
	Sloops	34		Steam sloops	21
	Brigs	4		Brigs	5
	Nonfighting vessels	32		Schooners	6
	Total	102		Steam vessels	17
1826	Ships of the line	6		Steam gun vessels	3
	Frigates	34		Nonfighting vessels	50
	Sloops	38		Total	164
	Brigs	3	1856	Ships of the line	6
	Schooners[a]	3		Steam ships of the line	11
	Nonfighting vessels	28		Frigates	17
	Total	112		Steam frigates	18
1830	Ships of the line	7		Corvettes	1
	Frigates	35		Steam corvettes	3
	Sloops	35		Sloops	21
	Brigs	6		Steam sloops	24
	Schooners	10		Brigs	3
	Steam vessels[b]	2		Schooners	6
	Nonfighting vessels	17		Steam vessels	35
	Total	112		Steam gun vessels	4
1835	Ships of the line	8		Nonfighting vessels	30
	Frigates	31		Total	179
	Sloops	25	1860	Ships of the line	4
	Brigs	17		Steam ships of the line	15
	Schooners	12		Frigates	4
	Steam vessels	6		Steam frigates	17
	Nonfighting vessels	28		Steam corvettes	13
	Total	127		Sloops	9
1840	Ships of the line	18		Steam sloops	38
	Frigates	26		Brigs	1
	Sloops	31		Schooners	3
	Brigs	23		Steam vessels	20
	Schooners	19		Steam gun vessels	8
	Steam vessels	3		Ironclad batteries	1
	Nonfighting vessels	42		Nonfighting vessels	25
	Total	162		Total	158
1845	Ships of the line	4	1865	Ships of the line	1
	Frigates	27		Steam ships of the line	8
	Steam frigates	2		Ironclads	2
	Sloops	36		Steam frigates	17
	Steam sloops	23		Steam corvettes	18
	Brigs	4		Steam sloops	35
	Schooners	9		Steam vessels	11
	Steam vessels	7		Steam gun vessels	29
	Nonfighting vessels	47		Steam gunboats	23
	Total	159		Ironclad batteries	1
1850	Ships of the line	12		Nonfighting vessels	44
	Steam ships of the line	1		Total	189
	Frigates	15	1871	Ironclads	9
				Steam frigates	9

TABLE 2 (CONTINUED)
Ships in Commission on Overseas Stations, 1821–1900

Year	Ship Type	Number	Year	Ship Type	Number
	Steam corvettes	12		Steam gunboats	24
	Sloops	1		Nonfighting vessels	23
	Steam sloops	18		Total	124
	Steam vessels	7	1890	Ironclads	8
	Steam gun vessels	33		Battleships	3
	Steam gunboats	10		Armored/	
	Ironclad batteries	1		1st-class cruisers	3
	Nonfighting vessels	18		2nd-class cruisers	5
	Total	118		3rd-class cruisers	5
1876	Ironclads	9		Steam frigates	1
	Steam frigates	7		Steam corvettes	18
	Steam corvettes	15		Steam sloops	20
	Sloops	5		Steam gun vessels	10
	Steam sloops	19		Steam gunboats	17
	Brigs	2		Torpedo boats	1
	Schooners	5		Nonfighting vessels	1
	Steam vessels	7		Total	92
	Steam gun vessels	27	1895	Ironclads	2
	Ironclad batteries	1		Battleships	11
	Nonfighting vessels	17		Armored/	
	Total	114		1st-class cruisers	7
1881	Ironclads	10		2nd-class cruisers	10
	Steam frigates	2		3rd-class cruisers	31
	Steam corvettes	23		Steam sloops	25
	Sloops	1		Steam gunboats	9
	Steam sloops	17		Torpedo boats	10
	Schooners	5		Nonfighting vessels	16
	Steam vessels	5		Total	121
	Steam gun vessels	20	1900	Ironclads	3
	Steam gunboats	16		Battleships	13
	Ironclad batteries	1		Armored/	
	Nonfighting vessels	23		1st-class cruisers	9
	Total	123		2nd-class cruisers	18
1886	Ironclads	12		3rd-class cruisers	17
	Steam frigates	2		Steam sloops	25
	Steam corvettes	29		Destroyers	13
	Sloops	1		Torpedo boats	9
	Steam sloops	17		Nonfighting vessels	7
	Steam vessels	5		Total	114
	Steam gun vessels	11			

SOURCES: 1821 through 1886, *The Navy List*; 1890 through 1900, Brassey et al., *Naval Annual*.
[a]Other small vessels, such as brigantines, cutters, and ketches, are included under this head.
[b]Initially a generic term, referring to any type of steam vessel other than tugs. All early steamships were small, lightly armed paddlewheel vessels, used often as dispatch vessels. Gunboats and gun vessels were subsequently classified separately.

vessels were repeatedly summoned to the farthest reaches of the globe to quell disturbances, generally uprisings or civil unrest. On 23 January 1858 the foreign office forwarded a request from the British consul at Lagos (Nigeria), asking for protection "against a threatened attack of [the] King of Dahomey"; four months later the governor of Singapore asked for "a ship of war to accompany him to effect a mediation between hostile chiefs on the Malay coast; in December 1859 the foreign office requested "[n]aval force for [the] suppression of disturbances in Mexico"; earlier that year it had lodged a "[r]equest for [the] presence of a ship of war on the Coast of Ecuador, in consequence of the Peruvian blockade of [the] coasts." And with a familiar, modern ring to it, on 30 May 1860 Her Majesty's consul-general in Syria enjoined the Admiralty to send a "vessel of war to proceed off Beyrout [sic] to protect British subjects and interests, in consequence of a civil war in Mount Lebanon between Christians and Druzes." Such a random sampling can hardly convey the frequency with which such requests were forthcoming. No less than thirty-one of the ninety-five entries referred explicitly to the need for protection against disturbances, riots, uprisings, or other threats of violence. Many other tasks required naval assistance, among them preventing the plunder of shipwrecks or, worse still, the evil practice of "collusive wrecking," halting illegal extractions by customs and revenue authorities abroad, searching for shipwreck survivors, securing the release of incarcerated British subjects, and fighting piracy—not forgetting the campaign against the slave trade, the most famous of the navy's exploits between 1815 and 1914.

The most remarkable aspect about the continual demands made on the overseas squadrons was the degree to which the navy complied with them. When the foreign office asked for a ship to visit an island in the Greek archipelago to prevent the plunder of shipwrecks, the Admiralty responded with "orders . . . to the Admiral in the Mediterranean to send a ship." It was the standard reply. Even the more exotic and less economically imperative requests were almost invariably honored. Thus, when the foreign office asked for "[a]ssistance to Dr. Livingstone on [his] Zambesi Expedition"; when the Board of Trade wanted "[a] ship to assist in [the] erection of a lighthouse at Cay Lobos"; when the Governor of Vancouver desired the "[p]resence of a ship of war at British Columbia, on account of the excitement on the discovery of gold"; or when the trustees of the British Museum asked that "a ship . . . be sent to Mersa Lousa, in Cyrene, to assist in researches after antiquities, &c . . . ." the navy's response was "orders given to that effect," not only in all of these instances, but in the overwhelming majority that came to the Admiralty. Of the ninety-five requests for extraordinary naval assistance between 1857 and 1861, only five were turned down outright, one of these the unreasonable colonial office demand for the establishment of a separate station, commanded by an Admiral, at the Australian colony of Victoria, an entreaty coming a mere year after the creation of the Australian station.[55] In a further nine cases, naval aid was not forthcoming immediately, ordinarily owing either to a clear lack of pressing need or want of available vessels. But in every other case, the navy's compliance was direct and as immediate as the communications of the day permitted, lending considerable credence to the service's boast that nothing was impossible.

It is likewise clear from William Laird Clowes' narrative that the demands made of the squadrons abroad during the 1860s, 1870s, and 1880s were similarly ubiquitous.[56] Naval vessels participated in several colonial campaigns during the period: the Abyssinian expedition of 1867–68, the Ashantee War (1873–74), the Zulu War (1878–79), and the first Boer War (1880–81), generally providing transport for troops and supplies, but often taking a more active role in the hostilities. Of course, the Mediterranean squadron spearheaded the assault on Alexandria in 1882, and was thus a crucial factor in the British occupation of Egypt. Many further instances of the use of naval power in support of colonial or mercantile policies can be cited. For several months in 1866–67 the gunboat *Wizard* was stationed off the coast of Crete owing to local unrest; in 1876 an expedition was dispatched up the Niger in response to interference with navigation on the river; the following year a force ascended the Congo for similar reasons. Over the course of the late 1860s, 1870s, and early 1880s, naval vessels were dispatched to trouble spots as diverse as Samoa, the New Hebrides, Mozambique, Madagascar, and Burma. Likewise, the effective suppression of the Atlantic slave trade did not signal an end to the employment of warships for moral and ethical crusades. Indeed, slaving was pervasive on the east coast of Africa as well as the west, and considerably more difficult to eradicate, in large part because the sultan of Zanzibar, an important British ally, was a beneficiary of the trade. Easier to suppress was the *engagé* trade—the recruitment of indentured workers under conditions tantamont to slavery—between Mozambique and French-held territories in the Indian Ocean.[57] By the late 1860s the navy had five vessels in place to cruise the southeast coast of Africa to lend weight to the efforts of the British consul at Zanzibar to stamp out the practice.

Yet notwithstanding the wide-ranging and numerous demands made of the peacetime navy, the five years from 1868 to 1873 witnessed a large-scale reappraisal of the size, if not the duties, performed by the overseas squadrons.[58] By 1865 the force abroad, owing largely to recent or ongoing hostilities in the Far East, the United States, and Mexico, had swelled to 145 ships, prompting repeated contemporary denunciations of the policy of maintaining so many ships in commission. The vanguard of the attack was led, not surprisingly, by William Gladstone, who as early as December 1864, while chancellor of the exchequer, clashed with First Lord the Duke of Somerset over the range and number of duties demanded of the navy. Gladstone admitted that the traditional practice of maintaining substantial overseas squadrons "was intelligible in the age of canvas, and of slow and uncertain posts, but . . . is wholly antiquated in the age of steam, of mailpackets, of telegraphs, of rapid, certain, continuous communications all over the world."[59]

Over the next several years his refrain would be picked up by other politicians, not only Liberals and Radicals, but also Conservatives, prominent among them Lord Henry Lennox and none other than Benjamin Disraeli, who believed the reduction of the overseas police force to be "the keystone of the position" in the quest for naval economy.[60] The cry for reduction and retrenchment was also echoed by influential organs of the press, in particular the *Times*.[61] Similar demands were made in the Commons by a number of speakers, including Hugh Childers, James Stansfeld, and, most significantly, Lennox, who served as the parliamentary secretary to the Admiralty, the second-ranking civilian on the board, during the Derby-Disraeli Ministry of 1866–68. In the course of moving the navy estimates for 1867–68 Lennox, presumably with Disraeli's blessing, asked "the country to consider what is the absolute necessity or advisability of keeping up large squadrons in all parts of the world of small unarmoured ships, which, when a more formidable ship than they approaches them must, what is vulgarly termed 'cut and run.'"[62]

The first Liberal to reply to Lennox's statements was not Hugh Childers, to whom speeches on naval affairs were usually entrusted, but Gladstone himself, who rarely made his presence known in navy debates. He rose not to condemn, but to congratulate. Indeed, parts of the parliamentary secretary's speech led Gladstone to wish that Lennox "occupied a more prominent and important position [the First Lordship] than the one he actually holds."[63] The following year, after bitter fighting between Lennox and Disraeli on one hand, and Henry Corry and the Naval Lords on the other, the fruits of Lennox's policy, which had been strenuously pushed on Prime Minister Lord Derby by Disraeli, began to be manifested. When Corry moved the estimates for 1868–69 he was able to point to reductions in the forces overseas, from 135 ships to 120, with a consequent diminution of 2,768 seamen.[64]

With the advent of Gladstone's Liberal government, in which Childers was First Lord, the policy of trimming overseas strength was pursued considerably further. But even Childers, who deserves the largest share of credit for reducing the number of ships abroad by about forty percent, did not go far enough to satisfy Gladstone, who expressed the hope to Childers' successor, George J. Goschen, that still further reduction was possible. Aside from "a powerful fleet in & near our own waters," he argued, "nothing is to be maintained except for well-defined & approved purposes of actual service, & in quantities of force properly adjusted."[65] Indeed, Gladstone was the one prominent mid-Victorian politician who confessed doubts regarding the utility of maintaining forces overseas on a permanent basis. This doubt was revealed in his subsequent words to Goschen. They should not operate on the assumption, Gladstone continued, "that there are to be fleets in the various parts of the world ready when a difficulty arises with a foreign country, or an offense to our ships, *then & there* to deal with it by the strong hand." In short, his views were indistinguishable from those of Hutt, Lindsay, Rylands, and other Cobdenite Radicals. The navy, thought Gladstone, should be a defensive force, to be employed in protecting the home islands.

By the time Goschen arrived at the Admiralty, however, the scope for further reductions appeared to him to be exhausted, unless the government was prepared to adopt the radical course of wholly abandoning the overseas stations. Gladstone himself seems to have favored such a policy, but he was evidently alone, even within the cabinet, to say nothing of the larger political and public spheres. Certainly he was opposed by Goschen, who informed him that the public did appear inclined to be "content with less naval force," and who followed this assessment with his own opinion: "[I]n every direction I must frankly say that I think economy has reached its limits in naval administration."[66]

In the end, Goschen's view prevailed, and thus it is important to note that the mid-Victorian "reappraisal" did not extend to the fundamental political, economic, or strategic preconceptions that dictated the deployment of forces overseas to uphold British interests, redress grievances, maintain the peace, combat piracy, avenge outrages, prevent disorder amongst shippers of guano, or any of the myriad other duties demanded of the navy. Despite the substantial reductions that took place during the late 1860s and early 1870s, the police force abroad continued to perform the same functions it had up to that point. Nonetheless, one should not underrate the accomplishments of Gladstone, Childers, Lennox, Goschen, and others who pushed for and achieved significant reductions in the size of the forces overseas. Further reductions, indeed, continued on a small scale until the mid-1870s, and by 1876 the number of ships serving abroad had dropped to ninety-eight, almost fifty fewer than had been in commission eleven years earlier. Moreover, there was no substantial increase in the size of the maritime police force for the remainder of the century. True, ninety-eight was a bit below the minimum number requisite for the performance of the navy's duties: the real bottom figure was about 100. In 1881 the overseas forces numbered 101, and over the next two decades they fluctuated between the low nineties to upwards of 110, as circumstances abroad required.

The reductions of the 1860s and early 1870s thus marked a real and permanent accomplishment. Even with the rise of colonial tensions during the final years of the century and the rapid expansion of the empire and overseas trade, never again did the squadrons abroad climb anywhere near the numbers that had characterized the 1850s and early 1860s. This reduction, however, was not the result of a fundamental reassessment of the duties of the navy; it continued largely to play the role of the police of the seas, and notwithstanding Bartlett's claim that "gunboat diplomacy was no longer employed with Palmerstonian self-confidence as a panacea for British difficulties with weaker and less civilized countries," it is plain from a cursory examination of Clowes that there was still a great deal of activity after 1865 requiring naval assistance.[67] It may not have been applied with Palmerstonian self-confidence, but it was nonetheless applied. The reductions were possible owing chiefly to two factors. The first was that as a consequence of inertia, the overseas squadrons were in many cases larger than necessary by the mid-1860s, as ships dispatched for specific purposes during crises remained behind after the initial reason for their presence had disappeared.

The second was that as communications improved during the second half of the century, fewer vessels could perform the duties of the overseas squadrons. Gladstone hit on a cardinal truth when he stated that the practice of maintaining large squadrons abroad to deal with any likely eventuality was increasingly unnecessary as telegraph cables and regular, prompt steamship services multiplied. The reductions that he, Childers, Lennox, Goschen, and others achieved reflected these changing circumstances, without marking a fundamental shift in Britain's political or strategic framework, a framework within which the navy continued to function as a vital tool for the implementation of policy.

CHAPTER 3

Administration, Politics, and Economics

Admiralty Administration, 1832–68

The structure and operations of the Admiralty attracted much scrutiny from politicians and naval administrators during the nineteenth century, and occasioned repeated frustration for those attempting to reform either its internal arrangements or the method that it dealt with business. The First Lord, due to the nature of British government, had to be answerable to Parliament, but the business conducted by the Admiralty demanded professional knowledge of the navy possessed by few Lords or M.P.s, none of them, arguably excepting Henry Corry, among political elites of the 1860s, 1870s, and 1880s. The First Lord had to be a cabinet minister and had also to be accountable to Parliament and voters, but these necessities meant that the post was repeatedly filled by men who lacked the specialized knowledge necessary to direct the myriad operations of the navy intelligently and competently.

Much the same problem existed in army administration, of course. But there were differences in the natures of the two services that made a First Lord's lack of professional knowledge more critical than was the case if an amateur was at the war office, especially with regard to ship design, which required both professional appreciation for what service a ship was intended and the skill and training of a naval architect to produce a design that satisfied service requirements. Only men who had made careers at sea or in the shipyards were competent to judge such matters, and no Victorian First Lord could lay claim to either, save for the Duke of Northumberland, First Lord in the brief Conservative ministry of 1852.[1]

Hence the existence of a board of Admiralty to provide advice to the First Lord and oversee many of the day-to-day operations of the navy, such as recruiting men, outfitting ships, supervising dockyard operations, and directing the movements of vessels at sea. For all of these tasks naval officers were far better qualified than civilians. Moreover, by relieving the First Lord of such generally trivial duties, the Naval Lords, as they were known, enabled him to spend his time attending to parliamentary matters and to larger questions of policy. In theory, therefore, administration by a board satisfied the need for both parliamentary accountability on the part of the First Lord, and for professional knowledge to oversee naval operations and guide policy competently.

The problem arose due to the board's ambiguous constitutional position. In theory, the First Lord alone was responsible to queen, cabinet, Parliament, and country for the navy. In practice, however, administration by board diluted the First Lord's accountability. As contemporaries complained, the "individual responsibility" of the head of the Admiralty was replaced by "collective responsibility," making it all but impossible to apportion blame or punish the responsible party in the event of an operational debacle or a disaster such as the capsizing of H.M.S. *Captain* in 1870. Not surprisingly, then, repeated attempts were made over the course of the century to ensure that the board operated in a manner consistent with established constitutional principles. In addition, successive naval administrators turned their attention to rationalizing the structure of the Admiralty itself, the goals being the twin Victorian virtues of increased efficiency and greater economy.

First to try his hand at reforming naval administration was Tory-turned-Whig (and future Tory and Peelite), Sir James Graham, who, as First Lord in the Whig administration of Lord Grey, in 1832 abolished the navy and victualling boards—quasi-autonomous bodies that oversaw certain aspects of building, outfitting, and supplying naval vessels—in order to secure "a just division of labour, an undivided control and a due responsibility on the one hand, and, on the other, that unity and simplicity which he held to be the very essence and life of public business."[2] Graham's reforms served two purposes. First, they were intended to establish the principle of "individual responsibility" in naval administration by directly subordinating the service's entire administrative structure to the authority of the First Lord, and, through him, the authority of Parliament. There was, however, an ulterior motive for the reforms, one that turned largely on political partisanship. The long dominance of the Tory party from 1807 to 1830 had resulted in navy and victualling boards composed of staunch Tory officers, chief among them Admiral Sir Thomas Byam Martin, who headed the navy board. By eliminating the two boards, Graham therefore simultaneously ridded the government of a particularly galling Tory thorn in its side.[3]

Although it was simple enough to abolish the navy and victualling boards and the redundancy, divided authority, waste and other administrative evils they engendered, it was less easy to reshape the board of Admiralty to encompass the necessary and useful functions that had hitherto been performed by the defunct bodies. Certainly it presented problems for Graham, who was new to the demands of high political and administrative office, and in his ignorance he apparently relied heavily on the highly experienced permanent secretary of the Admiralty, Sir John Barrow.[4] According to his own account, Barrow devised the administrative arrangements that took the place of the old system of fragmented authority. The new scheme divided the business of the Admiralty into five branches, each to be overseen by a permanent superintending officer: the surveyor (later the controller) of the navy, the accountant general, the storekeeper general, the comptroller of victualling and transport, and the director general of the medical department. Each of the department heads, in turn, was under the charge of one of the Lords Commissioners of the Admiralty, who collectively constituted the board. The surveyor answered to the First Naval Lord, the accountant general to the Second Naval Lord, and so on.[5] And, to ensure the individual responsibility and accountability of the First Lord, the five Lords Commissioners were answerable to him.

Unfortunately, with the passage of time it became apparent even to Graham that the restructuring of naval administration had failed to secure the individual responsibility and efficiency for which he had strived. Although he and like-minded reformers could speak assuredly of individual responsibility and accountability on the theoretical level, the corporate board structure and mode of operation made such responsibility practically "elusive."[6] On paper it was easy to draw a clear distinction between a purely consultative body—the ideal of the reformers—and a policy-making one, but in operation the line between the two quickly blurred.

Aside from this major structural flaw, several lesser ills plagued naval administration, two of which were particularly noteworthy. First, transaction of the navy's business by consultation at the board was often a cumbersome method of proceeding. Much of the Naval Lords' work was routine or trivial, and could be settled by an individual decision or, at most, consultation between two or three Lords independent of a formal board meeting. There still remained, however, a great many matters, both large and small, that came before it, and numerous contemporaries expressed their exasperation at the sluggish transaction of business.[7] Second, and contributing in no small way to administrative sluggishness, was the steady and significant increase in business with which the department had to contend as the century progressed. In the seven years between 1827 and 1833, the Admiralty's incoming correspondence increased from 25,428 letters in the former year to 31,330 in the latter. The jump in the number of outgoing letters was a staggering 22,464: from 25,402 to 47,866.[8] By 1856 the number of incoming letters was 38,170; 68,622 were dispatched.[9] Much, if not most, of the increase, especially after mid-century, related to the rapid technological transformation of the navy as it moved from the age of wood and sails into that of iron and steam.

But the primary problem perceived by public and Parliament remained the First Lord's lack of control over the board and, by extension, the inadequate supervision of board over expenditure, and First Lord over board. By the late 1850s, these deficiencies were evident to no less a figure than Graham himself, who had by that point served a second stint as First Lord during the Aberdeen administration of 1852–55. Questioned at length by the Roebuck Commission on the conduct of the Crimean War, Graham admitted that the First Lord, acting individually, had "no power whatever to overrule the Board's decision." This statement prompted the question, "Supposing there were a majority of the Board against his opinion, would that majority govern?"[10] Graham's reply could hardly have reassured advocates of individual responsibility. "[P]ractically," he told the Commission, he had "never found a Board interfere with the large discretionary power of the First Lord." Of course, decision making on a collective basis, which Graham had described as the method "in which he had always transacted business," was the antithesis of his sought-for goal of individual responsibility, and all the discretionary power at his command was not going to alter the fact.

Given the unimpressive showing of the British army in the Crimean War, it was not surprising that calls for its reform were widespread and insistent in the years following the conflict. The navy's performance had been less disastrous, but lackluster by the standards of Nelson, and during the latter half of the 1850s calls for naval reform were frequent as well, both within and outside of Parliament. Agitation was in no way quelled by the report of a subsequent commission charged with devising more efficient management and more effective control of expenditure in the royal dockyards (1861). Graham was again called as a witness, and by this date he had lost all confidence in his creation, for he informed the commission that administration by board "so far from an example to be followed ... might, on the whole, be regarded as an example to be avoided." In short, he testified, "a Board only works well when the head of it makes it as unlike a Board as possible, and acts as if he alone were responsible," and added that he "would certainly reconsider the whole command of the Navy."[11] The commission largely agreed with Graham and took a direct swipe at Admiralty administration. Although the scope of its inquiry was especially the dockyards, and it "condemned" the system of their control and management "as inefficient," it pointedly added that "the constitution of the Board of Admiralty" was the primary cause of that inefficiency.

By the time its report appeared, in March 1861, the outcry against naval administration was loud and sustained. After considerable maneuvering and opposition by Palmerston's government, a select committee of the House of Commons was appointed to "enquire into the Constitution of the Board of Admiralty."[12] The committee did not lack members experienced with naval administration; it contained no less than three former First Lords: Sir John Pakington, Graham, and Sir Francis Baring. It was, however, saddled with the additional task of examining the system of promotion and retirement in the officer corps. But more than the problem of too many tasks, the existence of too many opinions on the subject of Admiralty administration scuttled its efforts. There was widespread disagreement among the witnesses called before it as to how, or even whether, the Admiralty might advantageously be reformed. Of the five former or current First Lords examined, two (Baring and Sir Charles Wood) were strongly in favor of existing arrangements, one (Pakington) was equally strongly opposed to them, and two (Graham and the Duke of Somerset) were ambivalent.[13]

The difference in opinion was in large part attributable not to the structural details of naval administration but, rather, to the personal characteristics of the men who constituted the board at any given point. The crucial ingredient for ensuring the supremacy of the First Lord was not the wording of the patent, nor the precedent of past usage, nor even his "large discretionary power," but the resolve and strength of character of the First Lord himself. Pakington, in fact, adverted to this point in the course of his testimony, albeit in a somewhat roundabout way: "It seems to me that the best conditions under which the Board of Admiralty could be worked, would be that you should have a very able and determined man as First Lord, and that he should act with compliant and comparatively feeble colleagues."[14] Pakington prefaced this statement with the observation "I certainly do feel that it is in fact hardly possible to regard the First Lord as supreme among his colleagues, to the extent to which some witnesses have said he is, looking to the actual practice of the Board," suggesting that he encountered difficulty exercising authority during his initial stint as First Lord.

Before dismissing Pakington as the weak-willed tool of his naval advisors, however, it is well to review the problems confronting a politician suddenly thrust into an office with which he has no prior acquaintance, who finds himself responsible for the most important line of national defense. In so doing, one returns to the most fundamental, and simultaneously the most insoluble problem of administering the navy. In the formulation of general policy, in particular for crucial decisions regarding the requisite level of naval strength necessary to ensure national security and uphold interests abroad, one in Pakington's position (like the Duke of Somerset, George J. Goschen, George Ward Hunt, and W. H. Smith during the mid-Victorian era alone) had to rely on the advice and recommendations of his professional colleagues. If, as was often the case, they based their calculations on purely naval, as opposed to political or economic, considerations, the First Lord was faced either with the prospect of enforcing his will on the board, thereby ignoring professional advice, or with acquiescing in its assessment, thereby becoming "the compliant and comparatively feeble" mouthpiece of the naval element. Also, one in Pakington's position may have had difficulty discerning whether the advice offered by the board reflected a realistic and pragmatic assessment of the nation's defense requirements (a potential problem, of course, when relying either on purely naval or purely civilian advice). How could one, in consequence, challenge the advice of the board?

Of course, given time to grow familiar with the service, with the demands made upon it, and the existing political and economic restraints on the untempered navalist policy often espoused by professionals, administrators in Pakington's position would soon be able to make their own well-informed assessments, thereby reducing the influence of the Naval Lords in the formulation of general policy, if not necessarily reducing the likelihood of disagreements in the boardroom. Pakington's testimony was as much a reflection of his brief tenure at the Admiralty as it was of the inherent shortcomings of British naval administration.

Faced with a welter of divergent opinions, the select committee was not likely to arrive at any definitive conclusions as to how to resolve the dilemma of formulating general naval policy, nor even to bring forward recommendations as to how the administrative structure might be rationalized to increase efficiency, much less solve the problems of upholding the First Lord's supremacy and "individual responsibility." Indeed, given the burden of addressing not only the subject of naval administration, but also that of promotion and retirement in the officer corps—the consequence of Palmerston's evident desire to scuttle the entire question of naval reform—it is scarcely surprising that the committee produced no report at all. Instead, when it issued its findings to the Commons on 16 July 1861, after five months of labor, the bulky volume consisted entirely of evidence, appendices, and index. Where the report should have been there was only a brief statement indicating that the committee "Have made progress in the Matters to them referred, and have taken evidence upon a portion of the subject, which they have agreed to Report to The House."[15]

Moreover, when Sir James Elphinstone pressed for the reappointment of the committee the following year, Admiral Duncombe, the original sponsor, announced "it was not his intention to make the Motion."[16] He had been unhappy with its composition and with the evident efforts of the government to hamper its investigation. An attempt later in the session to renew enquiry into naval administration was thwarted, once by want of a quorum in the House of Commons, and once by Parliamentary Secretary Lord Clarence Paget's bland observation that although "there might be defects in" the structure and operations of the Admiralty, there were also defects in "all human institutions, [and] it would be very difficult to find a practical substitute" for the system currently in place.[17] There matters stood for the remainder of the session.

In fact, there matters stood for the remainder of Palmerston's ministry. The times were not propitious for large measures of reform, not while 10 Downing Street was occupied by the man who in 1864 observed, "We cannot go on adding to the Statute Book *ad infinitum*. Perhaps we may have a little law reform, or bankruptcy reform; but we cannot go on legislating forever."[18] That is not to say that all segments of Parliament or the press concurred with Palmerston, so far as the Admiralty was concerned, for the issue continued to appear in the course of naval debates over the next three years.[19] But as long as Palmerston was still at the head of the government, would-be naval reformers faced an insurmountable obstacle, and following his death the energies of the administration were turned to parliamentary reform. Nor, as it turned out, were times propitious for Admiralty reform once the Conservatives regained office in the wake of Russell's defeat, despite First Lord Pakington's dislike of administration by board. Pakington was at the Admiralty for less than a year, and despite his personal predilections, the efforts of the cabinet were largely directed toward the Second Reform Bill. In such a climate relatively mundane matters such as naval administration were pushed aside.

During the latter 1860s, though, public criticism of naval administration mounted again, following the relative quiescence of Palmerston's final years. In 1866, defending his administration in an anonymous pamphlet, the Duke of Somerset claimed that dissatisfaction with naval administration was endemic: "The human memory cannot recall the period when the department of the Admiralty was not the subject of accusation and complaint."[20] Certainly, however, the chorus of disapproval was more insistent at some junctures than others. The *Times*, in fact, remarked rather sourly on Somerset's disclaimer: "It might have occurred to the apologist that, under the volume of smoke which he is compelled to recognize, there was probably a considerable basis of fire."[21] "No doubt," it concluded, "the Admiralty, like all other departments, suffers from the attacks of political opposition, but the cry against it has been too loud, too long, and too universal to be explained away by general excess."[22] The cry was echoed in other organs of the press. The *Naval and Military Gazette* bluntly avowed: "It seems almost hopeless to expect that we shall ever be able to get our money's worth out of the Admiralty."

"Of course," concluded the diatribe, "all the fault lies in the system—which is rotten to the core, and not in the men that work that system."[23]

By the late 1860s the grounds for criticism had also grown. No longer were the operations of the board found objectionable solely or largely because of clumsiness, inefficiency, and the diluted authority of the First Lord; insufficient control over dockyard expenditure had also become a frequent complaint. "Never before," trumpeted the *Times* in late 1867, "did the absence of economical management more plainly appear." The following April it asked, "[I]s it not intolerable that our coasts and harbours should remain unprotected while the millions we vote are spent on so rotten a system as this?"[24] The direction of naval policy and the deployment of the fleet, especially ships stationed abroad, were also targets for journalistic attack.[25] The most frequent charge, however, was the Admiralty's perceived hostility to technological innovation. "What we want," proclaimed the *Naval and Military Gazette* in late February 1868, "is an administrator at the Admiralty with strength of mind sufficient to kick this old humbugging spirit out of doors, and to install there in its place the fertile genius of the present day."[26] The *United Service Gazette* likewise decried "[t]he immobility—the stolid 'woodenism' ... inherent in all Boards, and for which the Board of Admiralty is pre-eminently distinguished."[27] The *Times* was even more explicit in its condemnation: "We are of opinion that the Constructive Department of the Navy has failed deplorably in providing us with efficient Ironclads, capable of keeping the sea and fighting their guns."[28] In short, "This is the true and the real excuse for the late and present Boards of Admiralty in leaving us so far behind the strength ... which we ought now to possess."

The sentiment that the Admiralty needed recasting was widespread but there was far less consensus on what shape the mold should take. In the course of denouncing naval administration in 1861, M.P. Sir James Elphinstone argued "it is essential to abolish the Board of Admiralty, and to substitute for it a Minister of Marine, with a Secretary in this House."[29] Other parliamentary critics, in particular George "Big Ben" Bentinck, claimed that only a navy man was capable of administering the service efficiently and effectively. Still others, like Graham, preferred civilian heads and were of opinion what was needed was the clear establishment of the uncontested supremacy of the First Lord and the concomitant essential, individual responsibility.

Administration, Politics, and Economics   47

To most of these schemes cogent objections could be raised. Elphinstone's envisioned system, which called not only for a minister of marine but for a council of navy men, appointed for a fixed term, to assist him, was objectionable on a number of counts, beginning with the fact that the minister—presumably a navy man rather than a politician—would not be directly answerable to Parliament. The expedient of having a parliamentary secretary to act as a liaison was an inadequate safeguard to ensure that legislative control and ministerial accountability remained uncompromised. Much the same objections, moreover, applied to the proposal for a council of advisors appointed for a fixed term. Customary usage at the board held individual ministers responsible for the advice they offered, and the First Lord's right to dismiss naval lords a means of enforcing this responsibility. A council beyond disciplinary control was therefore viewed as a potentially irresponsible body. If the head of the navy, be he designated First Lord, minister of marine, or some other appellation, could not dismiss his advisors, the concept of responsibility, individual or otherwise, vanished and there was no assurance that any matter considered by a council thus constituted would be treated with the gravity and careful consideration it demanded.

Finally, Elphinstone's plan closely resembled the system actually in use in France, and could therefore be criticized on practical, as well as theoretical and constitutional, grounds. The French system had its admirers, to be sure, although none among leading politicians or ex-First Lords, Pakington excepted. Rather, it tended to be extolled by those who advocated enhanced professional—as opposed to civilian—influence in the administration of the service. In other words, it was favored by those who wanted officers to have greater—if not unchallenged—say in how the navy was run. Seen by these men—Elphinstone and a handful of like-minded M.P.s, as well as a number of senior officers—the French system was administrative nirvana.[30] The ministers of marine of the Second Empire and early Third Republic were uniformly navy men. Likewise, the naval element was similarly dominant in the French Council of Admiralty, the ministry's advisory body. Hence, "[t]he navy was essentially run by a small group of the more vigorous senior officers, and the minister was simply the one who was given the thankless task of wringing money from the reluctant cabinet and Chamber." But critics of the French system saw their worst nightmares of ministerial and, especially, conciliar irresponsibility acted out. Legislators urging naval reform were even more impotent in France than in Britain. The minister of marine "had little chance of establishing good relations with Parliament, the cabinet, or public opinion," and the Council of Admiralty was "neither legally nor financially responsible for the results of [its] recommendations," and "often proposed solutions that were technically perfect but financially impossible."[31]

A variation on the theme of naval dominance of Admiralty administration was touted incessantly by Conservative M.P. George Bentinck, this being that only an officer was competent to run the navy. He contended in 1858 (and again for many years thereafter) "that the naval department could never be efficiently conducted until the system of placing civilians in positions with which they could not possibly be conversant was done away with—until the Navy was, like the Army [!], administered by men of competent professional knowledge."[32] Bentinck's pronouncements on this, his pet subject, were virtually annual features of the naval debates in the Commons, even after 1876, when no less a figure than Disraeli took it upon himself to refute Bentinck's arguments point by point, finally dwelling at length on the constitutional difficulties inherent in entrusting the navy to an officer who, like as not, would be beyond the direct control of Parliament.[33]

Hugh Childers, of course, was also an advocate of reform, his interest in naval administration dating back to his stint as Civil Lord in 1864–65, and his appointment as First Lord in the wake of the general election of 1868 held out to many the first real hope for substantive change at the Admiralty after many years of frustrated agitation. "We wish Mr. Childers every success in the introduction of his reforms," wrote the *Times* on 15 December 1868: "Public opinion is prepared for change, and will not be satisfied without it. The inheritance of other men's labours has fallen to him. He has but to enter upon it."[34]

Government Finance

"Let it now, at this epoch of annual reflection," observed the *Times* upon the presentation of the budget in April 1871, "be borne in mind by each taxpayer and reformer and philanthropist that we are rapidly returning to the very highest expenditure on armaments ever known in this country in a time of peace."[35] Noting that the army estimates amounted to almost £16.5 million and those of the navy another £9.75 million, Delane and company concluded "it may be said generally that we have reverted to those gigantic armaments—gigantic financially—which the Liberal party lately prided itself on reducing."[36] This blast's timing was hardly coincidental. The budget unveiled by Chancellor of the Exchequer Robert Lowe in Parliament the previous evening had excited almost universal disapprobation. Foremost on the list of objectionable features was Lowe's novel recourse to a tax on matches as an expedient for raising revenue, a proposal denounced so widely and vehemently that Lowe was forced to abandon it within a few days.[37]

But without increased expenditure, of course, novel expedients for raising revenue would not be necessary, and the presentation of the budget revealed a jump of almost £3 million in government spending from fiscal year 1870 to the proposed expenditure for 1871.[38] Most of the increase, at least as far as defense was concerned, was attributable to military spending—most notably the costs of abolishing purchase of officers' commissions—but the navy estimates for the year also appeared to signal the *de facto* end of a campaign against waste and inefficiency that had been mounted by William Gladstone's Liberal ministry upon its accession to power in late 1868.

The formulation of naval policy hinges, of course, upon several factors aside from security issues, political and economic considerations prominent among them. Although naval spending during the mid-Victorian era did not generally arouse much public concern or media scrutiny, it was one of the major elements of governmental spending. Shifts in fiscal policy, therefore, whether as regards overall outlays or at the departmental level, could and did have a substantial bearing on the fortunes of the navy during the course of the late 1860s and 1870s. Likewise, political pressures often exerted substantial influence on the direction of naval policy, in both the form of party ideology and, in the more mundane, if ultimately no less significant realm of the give and take of everyday political maneuvering. Since defense establishments—borrowing from Clausewitz's well-known dictum, are primarily extensions and tools of the world of politics, the course of British naval policy during this period is better understood in its politicoeconomic context.

Although the policy of financial retrenchment has been associated almost exclusively with the Liberal party in Victorian Britain—and more specifically with Gladstone and "Manchester school" Radicals such as John Bright and Richard Cobden—both major political parties were at one in their desire to keep a firm rein on defense spending.

This desire, however, was not invariably rewarded by success, particularly in the case of the Conservatives. Benjamin Disraeli, Conservative chancellor of the exchequer in 1852, 1858–59, and again from 1866 to early 1868 was, by the last date, no stranger to difficult, even acrimonious relations with the Admiralty. As early as 1852, during his first stint at the treasury, he became embroiled in a quarrel with the First Lord, the Duke of Northumberland, over the distribution of patronage in the Admiralty boroughs, an affair that eventually resulted in a parliamentary enquiry and an embarrassing debate in the House of Commons.[39] Nor was patronage the only source of friction. On the eve of the presentation of Disraeli's first budget, in late 1852, the treasury was informed by chief Conservative whip, Augustus Stafford, that "the Naval Estimates for 1853–54 will be nearly a million more than those of last year." Such an increase was too much for the prime minister, Lord Derby, who drew the line at £350,000. Nonetheless, the frenzied recalculations caused by this and other departmental demands greatly contributed to the haphazard character of the resulting budget. "Seldom," remarks Disraeli biographer Lord Blake, "can a Chancellor of the Exchequer have been faced with such last-minute problems of improvisation."[40] When the budget was exposed to public scrutiny it met a four-night debate in the House of Commons, a scathing condemnation by Gladstone, and, ultimately, defeat. With it collapsed the ministry.

Six years later Disraeli's struggle with the Admiralty resumed, with Pakington his chief antagonist. The latter faced a difficult task at the Admiralty. His board was confronted with Louis Napoleon's decision to build a seagoing ironclad, one of the chief factors driving the invasion scare and naval race of the next half decade. But from Disraeli's perspective, the salient feature of the nascent arms race with France was expense, and in a letter to Lord Derby of 9 October 1858 he roundly accused the board, and especially the surveyor, Sir Baldwin Wake Walker, of incompetence: "All the men that Pakington has chosen . . . are the most inefficient that could be selected. . . . The Admiralty is governed by Sir B Walker who has neither talents, nor science—& as I believe—nor honour—but the last is suspicion, the first are facts."[41] A specific indictment followed. Disraeli accused Walker of panic-mongering and designing large warships "[which] have neither speed nor power, & [which] are immensely expensive from their enormous crews." For the chancellor of the exchequer, the last was Walker's cardinal sin, although in the following months he was also to accuse the surveyor of calculating naval requirements "on the assumption that Britain would have to fight simultaneously all the other powers of the world united."

Lord Derby displayed moderation toward the alleged transgressions of the Admiralty, producing one of the era's few unequivocal statements regarding the basis of British naval policy. "We *must*," he informed Disraeli, "have a naval preponderance over the French, however inconvenient the outlay may be."[42] His solution to the incompatible goals of enlarging the navy while simultaneously reducing expenditure was to raise a loan to finance naval reconstruction. Disraeli refused to resort to this expedient on the principle of opposition to loans in peacetime, and in the belief that the House of Commons would withhold sanction for such a proceeding, unaware that the Liberals would employ precisely that means the following year in financing the construction of land defenses. Nor were the Conservatives to be granted a further opportunity to address the issue of naval expenditure during their administration. On 6 June 1859 Whig leaders Lord Palmerston and Lord John Russell patched up their differences over conduct of the Crimean War. A vote of no confidence in the government, and the accession of a Peelite/Whig coalition, quickly followed. Gladstone, despite significant differences with Palmerston over political franchise at home and the conduct of many aspects of foreign policy, was at one with the prime minister in supporting Italian nationalist aspirations, and accepted the chancellorship of the exchequer.

When the *Times* fulminated over increased service estimates in April 1871, it put the matter in historical perspective, alluding to the French invasion scare of 1858–60. "Some years since, at a time when great distrust of France took possession of the public mind and it was held necessary to create a most formidable navy, the total expenditure was somewhat greater [than at present]."[43] The French threat, of course, prompted increased expenditure upon the nation's defenses, both at sea and on land.[44] By 1865 the ironclad fleet begun by Pakington's board and constructed during Palmerston's final ministry numbered fourteen, with a similar number under construction.[45] Yet the proliferation of ironclads was not viewed favorably by all members of the Liberal cabinet. Palmerston, it is true, as well as the First Lord of the Admiralty, Edward Adolphus Seymour, Twelfth Duke of Somerset, were zealous advocates of naval preparedness, and from 1859 through 1862 they had public opinion behind them.[46] Even as late as 1864, Palmerston was urging that "other Naval Powers are multiplying their Iron Clads, and as we cannot without Danger be left behind, we are obliged to add more to the Building Charges of each Year."[47] But by this point naval expenditure, after reaching a peacetime peak in the early 1860s, was on the way back down, thanks in large part to the zealous economizing of Gladstone.[48]

The chancellor of the exchequer regarded the panic of 1858–60 as a "groundless delusion," and said as much in public.[49] Moreover, he instinctively turned a jaundiced eye on high navy estimates, partly due to his conviction that the service suffered from massive waste and inefficiency, and partly because he—like any responsible politician of the period—was aware that large-scale expenditure on shipbuilding ran the risk of equally large-scale waste of money, owing to next-to-instantaneous obsolescence created by the intrusion of industrialization into ship design and building. By the middle years of the decade, Gladstone's views were making inroads within the cabinet. He was aided by circumstances. By 1863 it was obvious that the French building program, while in terms of numbers superficially impressive—or ominous, depending on one's perspective—was seriously in arrears.[50] As a consequence, British funding for ironclad construction dropped from £630,203 in 1863–64 to only £130,000 two years later, forming a significant portion of the reductions in the service budget during those years.[51] Gladstone's desire to cut naval spending, however, extended beyond reductions in allocations for shipbuilding, and during the latter years of the ministry he turned some of his abundant energy toward the task of convincing his colleagues to reassess the bases upon which British naval policy was founded.

In the short term his proposals bore only modest fruit. Nonetheless, the estimates of 1865 were lower than they had been since 1858, and British forces overseas were cut back slightly in both 1865 and 1866.[52] But the defection of Robert Lowe and the rest of the "Adullamites" over parliamentary reform in October of 1866 drove the Liberals from office, thus denying Gladstone further opportunity to press his economical views on his reluctant colleagues, at least for the time being. The proposals regarding the redistribution of the navy in order to effect reductions in the numbers of men employed overseas did not depart from the political arena, of course, as the subsequent accomplishments of Lennox, Childers, and Goschen demonstrated.

Government Finance and Naval Spending, 1866–80

By present standards British government spending in the nineteenth century was small. Only during the latter years of the second Disraeli administration did the budget top £80 million—a first for peacetime expenditure—and three times during the fourteen years from 1866 through 1880 the government managed to operate on less than £70 million a year. What is today termed social spending was modest during the mid-Victorian era, especially as far as the central government was concerned. There was no government-subsidized medical care, unemployment insurance, housing assistance, or welfare; old age pensions appeared only after the turn of the century. What social spending there was, primarily that sanctioned under the operation of the Poor Law, was both meager by the standards of the modern-day welfare state and collected and administered at the local level. Likewise, in 1866 government expenditure on education, art, and science amounted to only £1.28 million of a total budget of £66.5 million. This figure was to rise steadily in subsequent years, particularly after the Education Act of 1870 provided for government assistance to local school authorities that requested it, but as of 1884–85 it was no more than £5.1 million.[53]

Aside from the costs of tax collection, government spending fell under four major heads: debt servicing, civil service, the army, and the navy. The national debt invariably received the largest share during the post-1815 nineteenth century. In 1869–70, for instance, when the overall budget totaled almost £69.9 million, payment on the debt accounted for £27 million, or 38 percent of the whole. In 1884–85, by which point total outlays had swollen to £88.5 million, the £29 million allocated for payments on the debt still made up 32 percent, a larger proportion than was allocated to any other purpose. Expenditure on the debt remained virtually constant between 1866 and 1885, never falling below £26.5 million in any year nor rising above £29.5 million. These sums directed were not extraordinary. Debt charges remained remarkably stable from 1815 through 1885, fluctuating between £26 million and £33 million yearly.[54]

The army received the second-largest share of the budget between 1866 and 1885. Only in 1869–70 did its budget fall below £14 million: by the early 1880s it consistently consumed more than £15 million, rising to £18.6 million in 1884–85. In contrast, only once during the period did the navy cost more than £12 million. That the army

TABLE 3
Army, Debt Redemption, Civil Service, Navy, and Total Expenditure,
1865–66 to 1880–81

Year	Army[a] Finance accounts	Army[a] Mitchell	Debt redemption Finance accounts	Debt redemption Mitchell
1865–66	13,804,449	14,400,000	27,253,295	26,200,000
1866–67	14,675,549	15,100,000	26,081,775	26,100,000
1867–68	15,418,581	15,900,000	26,571,748	26,600,000
1868–69	15,000,000	15,500,000	26,614,444	26,600,000
1869–70	13,565,900	12,100,000	27,048,316	27,100,000
1870–71	13,430,000	12,100,000	26,826,436	26,800,000
1871–72	15,521,580	14,700,000	26,839,601	26,800,000
1872–73	14,466,700	13,800,000	26,804,852	26,800,000
1873–74	14,426,989	13,500,000	26,656,724	26,700,000
1874–75	14,519,433	14,000,000	27,095,579	27,100,000
1875–76	15,077,466	14,200,000	27,119,848	27,200,000
1876–77	15,251,354	14,500,000	27,075,218	27,400,000
1877–78	14,607,444	14,300,000	27,999,987	27,600,000
1878–79	17,653,472	16,900,000	28,065,842	28,000,000
1879–80	15,645,866	15,000,000	27,999,998	28,100,000
1880–81	15,558,601	14,700,000	28,799,998	29,200,000

SOURCES: *Parliamentary Papers*, "Finance Accounts," 1866, 39:12–13; 1867, 39:12–13; 1867–68, 40:12–13; 1868–69, 34:12–13; 1870, 41:12–13; 1871, 37:10–11; 1872, 36:10–11; 1873, 39:10–11; 1874, 35:10–11; 1875, 42:10–11; 1876, 42:9–10; 1877, 49:10–13; 1878, 42:10–13; 1878–79, 42:10–13; 1880, 40:10–13; 1881, 57:10–13; B. R. Mitchell and Phyllis Deane, *Abstract of British Historical Statistics* (Cambridge, 1962), 397.

[a]Figures for army and navy spending do not include sums provided out of Votes of Credit for extraordinary tasks.

consistently received larger outlays than the navy seems paradoxical. The navy was the first and most important line of defense. The British army, moreover, while acknowledged as a well-trained and disciplined—if not invariably well-officered—corps, was not often favorably compared with its continental counterparts, either in terms of size or of organization. Yet the costs of personnel—wages, clothing, and food—invariably constituted the largest portion of both services' budgets. The army, with manpower ranging between 115,000 and 136,000, therefore cost more to maintain than the navy's 60–65,000 officers, men, and marines, and 15,000 or so dockyard laborers.[55] In addition, the army, although not burdened with the costs of building and maintaining the fleet, was responsible for the royal ordnance installation at Woolwich and other matériel costs.

In 1866 the navy received the third-largest slice of the budget and the broad category of "civil government" the fourth-largest. The latter encompassed numerous allocations, ranging from the salaries

Administration, Politics, and Economics

TABLE 3 (CONTINUED)
Army, Debt Redemption, Civil Service, Navy, and Total Expenditure, 1865–66 to 1880–81

Civil Service[b]		Navy		Total expenditure	
Finance accounts	Mitchell	Finance accounts	Mitchell	Finance accounts	Mitchell
8,956,502	10,300,000	10,259,788	10,300,000	66,474,356	66,500,000
9,667,021	10,500,000	10,676,101	10,700,000	67,230,395	67,200,000
10,385,237	11,200,000	11,168,949	11,200,000	71,766,241	71,800,000
10,870,298	12,000,000	11,366,545	11,400,000	75,497,816	71,800,000
11,039,146	11,000,000	9,757,220	9,400,000	69,064,754	67,100,000
11,959,508	12,000,000	9,456,641	9,000,000	69,698,539	67,800,000
12,160,000	12,200,000	9,900,486	9,500,000	71,860,020	69,900,000
11,810,135	11,800,000	9,543,000	9,300,000	71,022,448	68,800,000
12,728,261	12,700,000	10,279,898	10,100,000	76,966,510	74,600,000
13,377,801	13,600,000	10,680,404	10,500,000	74,928,939	73,000,000
14,676,452	14,800,000	11,063,449	10,800,000	80,871,773	74,700,000
14,929,787	14,900,000	11,364,383	11,000,000	78,565,036	75,700,000
15,624,136	14,900,000	10,978,591	10,800,000	78,703,495	79,600,000
16,599,171	16,600,000	11,962,816	11,800,000	85,399,000	82,800,000
16,923,187	16,900,000	10,416,131	10,200,000	84,105,754	81,500,000
17,356,498	17,400,000	10,702,935	10,500,000	83,107,924	80,600,000

[b]The components of civil service expenditure fell under two different heads. Out of the Consolidated Fund came (1) annuities and pensions, (2) salaries and allowances, (3) courts of justice, and (4) miscellaneous services. Under "Miscellaneous Civil Services" came (1) public works and buildings, (2) public departments, (3) law and justice, (4) education, science, and art, (5) foreign, consular, and colonial services, (6) superannuations, and (7) miscellaneous and special services.

of colonial and diplomatic officers and most civil servants, to the costs of administration of justice and the maintenance and repair of government buildings, plus a host of subheads.[56] In 1866 the total of these various outlays was £9.7 million, about a million less than the navy received. Civil service spending grew substantially over time. This growth owed mostly to the gradual expansion of the responsibilities of the central government through the implementation of social legislation. By the mid-1800s it was in excess of £16.5 million, larger even than the army budget from 1881 through 1884. As a consequence, too, civil spending far outstripped naval expenditure, despite substantial augmentation of the navy estimates during the second half of the 1870s. Even in 1877–78, when an addition of over £1.5 million from a vote of credit pushed naval spending above £12.5 million, combined charges for civil government were higher by almost £4 million. From 1869–70 on the navy consistently received less than the civil service, and the gap between the two widened over time. In sum, throughout the 1870s and early 1880s the "first line of

TABLE 4
Debt Redemption, Civil Service, Army, and Navy Expenditures as a Percentage of Total Expenditures, 1865–66 to 1880–81

Year	Debt redemption	Civil Service	Army	Navy
1865–66	41.34%	13.58%	20.94%	15.56%
1866–67	39.06%	14.49%	21.98%	15.99%
1867–68	37.30%	14.57%	21.64%	15.67%
1868–69	35.49%	14.49%	20.00%	15.16%
1869–70	38.71%	15.80%	19.41%	13.93%
1870–71	38.57%	17.19%	19.31%	13.59%
1871–72	37.54%	17.00%	21.71%	13.84%
1872–73	37.90%	16.70%	20.45%	13.49%
1873–74	34.86%	16.64%	18.86%	13.44%
1874–75	36.45%	17.99%	19.53%	14.36%
1875–76	33.53%	18.14%	18.64%	13.68%
1876–77	34.26%	18.89%	19.29%	14.38%
1877–78	33.65%	18.77%	17.55%	13.19%
1878–79	32.88%	19.44%	20.68%	14.01%
1879–80	33.19%	20.13%	18.54%	12.34%
1880–81	34.65%	20.88%	18.72%	12.87%

SOURCES: All percentages based on figures in *Parliamentary Papers*, "Finance Accounts," 1866, 39:12–13; 1867, 39:12–13; 1867–68, 40:12–13; 1868–69, 34:12–13; 1870, 41:12–13; 1871, 37:10–11; 1872, 36:10–11; 1873, 39:10–11; 1874, 35:10–11; 1875, 42:10–11; 1876, 42:9–10; 1877, 49:10–13; 1878, 42:10–13; 1878–79, 42:10–13; 1880, 40:10–13; 1881, 57:10–13. The remainder of the total was made up by the costs of collection, post office, packet service, telegraphs, and extraordinary expenses, such as Votes of Credit, the costs of fortifications, and the Army Purchase Commission.

defense" received less funding than any of the other principal elements of government.

Contemporaries saw matters in a different light, however. The navy, after all, received between a fifth and a quarter of the national budget, once payment on the debt was deducted. Furthermore, it had not always been as costly. In 1815 the service cost taxpayers nearly £23 million, out of a total budget of almost £113 million. Within two years of the allied triumph at Waterloo, however, naval spending had plummeted to barely £10 million: by 1818 it was below £7 million. It was the beginning of "the long peace." By 1823 the navy's budget had dropped to £5.3 million. This figure, as it turned out, was relatively generous. With the Whigs' return to power in 1830 the service, although perhaps not required to do more, was unquestionably required to do with less. In spite of the intermittent Belgian Crisis, for seven years of the 1830s naval expenditure totaled less than £5 million annually. And through the Eastern Crisis of 1839–41, when the specter of war with Russia, France, or both—to say nothing of the Egyptian forces of Mehemet Ali—loomed ominously, it never

TABLE 5
Naval Estimates and Expenditures, 1865–66 to 1880–81

Year	Estimates[a] Hansard	Estimates[a] Parliamentary Papers	Expenditure[b] Mitchell	Expenditure[b] Finance accounts	Expenditure[b] Navy estimates
1865–66	10,456,139	10,392,224	10,300,000	10,259,788	10,249,840
1866–67	10,434,735	10,388,153	10,700,000	10,676,101	10,340,814
1867–68	10,976,253	10,926,253	11,200,000	11,168,949	11,342,798
1868–69	11,157,290	11,177,290	11,400,000	11,366,545	11,061,703
1869–70	9,996,641	9,996,641	9,400,000	9,757,220	9,781,501
1870–71	9,370,539	9,250,530	9,000,000	9,456,641	9,916,749
1871–72	9,789,956	9,756,356	9,500,000	9,900,486	9,875,981
1872–73	9,526,149	9,508,149	9,300,000	9,543,000	9,531,179
1873–74	9,872,725	9,872,725	10,100,000	10,279,898	10,245,024
1874–75	10,329,485	10,179,885	10,500,000	10,680,404	10,678,372
1875–76	10,784,644	10,784,644	10,800,000	11,063,449	10,900,705
1876–77	11,288,872	11,288,872	11,000,000	11,364,383	11,259,864
1877–78	10,971,829	10,971,829	10,800,000	10,978,591	10,895,660
1878–79	11,053,901	11,053,901	11,800,000	11,962,816	11,787,537
1879–80	10,586,894	10,586,894	10,200,000	10,416,131	10,386,498
1880–81	10,492,935	10,492,935	10,500,000	10,702,935	10,513,468

SOURCES: Estimates: *Hansard*, 1865–66; 180:index; 1866–67, 184:index; 1867–68, 189:index; 1868–69, 193:index; 1869–70, 198:index; 1870–71, 203:index; 1871–72, 208:index; 1872–73, 213:index; 1873–74, 217:index; 1874–75, 221:index; 1875–76, 226:index; 1876–77, 231:index; 1877–78, 236:index; 1878–79, 242:index; 1879–80, 249:index; 1880–81, 256:index; *Parliamentary Papers*, "Navy Estimates," 1866, 45:500; 1867, 44:5; 1867–68, 45:5; 1867–68, 45:5; 1868–69, 38:5; 1870, 44:5; 1871, 40:5; 1872, 39:5; 1873, 42:5; 1874, 38:5; 1875, 45:5; 1876, 45:5; 1877, 52:5; 1878, 39:5; 1878–79, 45:5; 1880, 43:5; 1881, 60:5. Expenditure: *Parliamentary Papers*, "Finance Accounts," 1866, 39, 12–13; 1867, 39:12–13; 1867–68, 40:12–13; 1868–69, 34:12–13; 1870, 41:12–13; 1871, 37:10–11; 1872, 36:10–11; 1873, 39:10–11; 1874, 35:10–11; 1875, 42:10–11; 1876, 42:9–10; 1877, 49:10–13; 1878, 42:10–13; 1878–79, 42:10–13; 1880, 40:10–13; 1881, 57:10–13; *Parliamentary Papers*, "Navy Estimates," 1868–69, 38:5; 1870, 44:5; 1871, 40:5; 1872, 39:5; 1873, 42:5; 1874, 38:5; 1875, 45:5; 1876, 45:5; 1877, 52:5; 1878, 49:5; 1878–79, 45:5; 1880, 43:5; 1881, 60:5; 1882, 40:5; B. R. Mitchell and Phyllis Deane, *Abstract of British Historical Statistics* (Cambridge, 1962), 397.
[a]Figures include all supplementary estimates.
[b]Figures do not include sums provided by Votes of Credit for extraordinary purposes.

crept above £5.4 million yearly. During the 1840s the navy fared slightly better; from 1847 through 1849 it received more than £7 million per annum. But this relative largess was anomalous. Not until the Crimean War (1854) did the estimates again exceed £7 million; following the war—during which spending had peaked at almost £19 million in 1855–56—they edged back toward prewar levels: from £12.7 million in 1856–57 to £9.6 million in 1857–58, and barely £8 million a year later. The downward trend was arrested in 1859–60 thanks to the combined effects of the French invasion scare and the expense of entering the ironclad era. A new epoch had dawned. Never again was the service budget to fall below £9 million, much less drop to the levels commonly witnessed during the 1820s, 1830s, and 1840s.

TABLE 6
Naval Spending as a Percentage of the Total Budget, 1815–1913

Year	Percentage	Year	Percentage	Year	Percentage	Year	Percentage
1815	20.19	1840	9.92	1865	16.24	1890	16.88
1816	16.88	1841	10.15	1866	15.48	1891	16.70
1817	14.30	1842	11.41	1867	15.99	1892	16.25
1818	11.24	1843	11.25	1868	15.67	1893	16.38
1819	11.45	1844	11.19	1869	15.16	1894	15.73
1820	11.13	1845	9.85	1870	13.93	1895	17.34
1821	11.30	1846	11.73	1871	13.59	1896	18.74
1822	10.78	1847	13.17	1872	13.84	1897	20.23
1823	9.20	1848	12.69	1873	13.49	1898	18.61
1824	10.31	1849	12.37	1874	13.44	1899	20.47
1825	11.17	1850	11.17	1875	14.36	1900	18.09
1826	10.72	1851	10.42	1876	13.68	1901	15.26
1827	11.58	1852	9.25	1877	14.38	1902	15.10
1828	11.44	1853	10.48	1878	13.19	1903	16.06
1829	10.65	1854	12.42	1879	14.01	1904	22.85
1830	10.98	1855	18.00	1880	12.34	1905	24.61
1831	10.21	1856	20.30	1881	13.02	1906	22.65
1832	11.06	1857	16.68	1882	12.72	1907	21.85
1833	9.68	1858	14.07	1883	11.82	1908	21.68
1834	9.01	1859	12.65	1884	12.52	1909	22.23
1835	9.20	1860	15.51	1885	12.88	1910	22.81
1836	6.28 (8.45)[a]	1861	18.24	1886	13.77	1911	24.06
1837	7.77 (8.41)[a]	1862	17.42	1887	14.77	1912	24.64
1838	9.39	1863	16.21	1888	14.18	1913	24.13
1839	8.51	1864	15.92	1889	15.02		

SOURCES: Calculated from figures in Mitchell and Deane, *Abstract of British Historical Statistics*, 397, except for the years 1867–80, which are drawn from *Parliamentary Papers*, "Finance Accounts," 1867, 39:12–13; 1867–68, 40:12–13; 1868–69, 34:12–13; 1870, 41:12–13; 1871, 37:10–11; 1872, 36:10–11; 1873, 39:10–11; 1874, 35:10–11; 1875, 4:10–11; 1876, 42:9–10; 1877, 49:10–13; 1878, 42:10–13; 1878–79, 42:10–13; 1880, 40:10–13; 1881, 57:10–13. Prior to 1854, the calendar and fiscal years were synchronous. After 1854 the fiscal year was calculated from April 1 to March 31. The years listed above are the ending year, i.e., 1878 refers to fiscal year 1877–78.

[a] In 1836 and 1837 the level of government spending was swollen by the cost of compensating former slaveholders. The first figure is the percentage calculated on gross expenditure, that in parentheses is calculated on expenditure minus the sums paid in compensation.

When the Liberals came to power in 1859 the level of naval spending bequeathed to them by Derby, Pakington, and the Conservatives was a little less than £12 million. The following year it ballooned by almost a million and a half.[57] From thence, however, the sums allocated crept downward as Gladstone's mania for thriftiness made increasing inroads on Palmerston's liberality, and from 1863–64 through 1866–67—the last four navy estimates brought forward by the Duke of Somerset's administration—spending on the service remained below £11 million. It climbed significantly again between 1866 and 1868, during the Derby-Disraeli Ministry, due mostly to the efforts of First Lords Pakington and Corry. Spending broached the £11 million mark both fiscal years, forming 15.7 percent of overall governmental outlays in 1867–68 and almost 15.2 percent the following year. This increase was matched, it might be added, by higher levels of spending under other heads.

The trend of rising naval and government spending was arrested dramatically, however, with the advent of Gladstone's Liberal government in late 1868. The naval budget unveiled by First Lord Hugh Childers the following March showed a reduction of more than £1 million from the figure announced by Corry the previous year, and the sum expended was more than £200,000 below Childers' estimate. Furthermore, thanks to the efforts of the First Lord and his cabinet colleagues, total government spending for 1869–70, including a vote of credit of £1.3 million for the Abyssinian expedition and £200,000 on Palmerston's "follies" barely topped £69 million, over £5 million less than the previous year.

The first of Childers' budgets was indicative of the Liberals' naval and fiscal policies over the next five years. Government expenditure never exceeded £72 million, save in 1873–74, when a constellation of extraordinary expenditures—notably an £800,000 vote of credit for the Ashantee expedition, £713,973 for the army purchase commission, and £3,196,874 paid to the United States to resolve the *Alabama* claims—swelled the total to almost £77 million. During the same period naval spending topped £10 million only twice, in one instance from the addition of £600,000 allocated to the navy from the vote of credit of 1870 occasioned by the outbreak of the Franco-German war.

Gladstone maintained that naval spending should not exceed £9 million a year: an expectation that remained unfulfilled.[58] Nonetheless, the savings achieved by Childers and his successor George J. Goschen were far from insignificant. Whereas the navy had accounted for almost 15.5 percent of government spending under the preceding administration, it averaged only 13.65 percent, exclusive of the vote of credit in 1870, for the five fiscal years from 1869–70 through 1873–74. Moreover, the years 1869–70, 1871–72, and 1873–74 were the last three times naval spending dropped below eight figures.

The course pursued by the Disraeli ministry from 1874 through 1880 was not significantly different from the five years that preceded it, although the amounts allotted to the service during these years did not match the Liberals' frugality. In six years, naval spending exceeded £11 million three times, topping £12.5 million in 1877–78, during the Eastern Crisis. Yet, in the overall context of government outlays, a different picture emerges. At the same time that naval expenditure was, in Gladstone's words, "walking upwards," so was total spending. The Liberals' budgets, with the exception of 1873–74, hovered around the £70 million mark. Government spending topped £80 million four of Disraeli's six years in power, rising to nearly £86 million in 1878–79. As a consequence, the navy, leaving aside the £1.5 million provided out of the vote of credit in 1878, received an average of 13.66 percent of the budget from 1874 to 1880, a figure virtually identical to that of the previous five years.

The Historical Context

One modern authority remarks, "It is doubtful whether Britain was able at any other time to purchase security at so cheap a price."[59] The situation should, however, be considered in a contemporary context, as well as from the vantage of retrospect. To be sure, the naval budgets from 1867 through 1885, both in terms of actual spending levels and as a percentage of total government outlays, were paragons of thriftiness by comparison with those of the naval-race years of the late nineteenth and early twentieth centuries. From 1901 onward the naval budget exceeded £30 million, climbing above the £40 million plateau during the four years prior to World War I.[60] Moreover, the navy continued to receive a growing percentage of government expenditure despite the fact that these years also witnessed an increasing commitment to social spending on the national level. Whereas the highest level of government spending from 1867 through 1885 was under £89 million, for the first fourteen years of the twentieth century it never sank below £143 million, rising above £190 million in 1913–14. Yet even given this vast expansion of the state's financial obligations, the navy's slice of the pie continued to increase. At no point between 1904 and the outbreak of World War I did it consume less than 20 percent of government expenditures, and on four occasions it received almost a quarter of the entire budget. By these standards the level of naval spending in the late 1860s and 1870s was modest indeed.

But by the standards of earlier years the amounts allocated to the navy during the mid-Victorian era were gargantuan. Between 1835 and 1861 naval spending roughly tripled and nearly half of this increase occurred after 1850. In 1849 the navy received £6.2 million, less than half of the figure for 1860–61. In addition, the navy had routinely spent less than £6 million during the 1840s—to say nothing of the 1830s—and the 1830s and 1840s were well within the collective memory of the ruling class of the 1870s, led by Gladstone, who had entered Parliament in 1833, and Disraeli, who joined him in the House of Commons four years later. For that matter, as recently as the 1850s the navy had managed on less than £6 million a year no fewer than three times.

Total government spending during the 1830s and 1840s was also considerably lower than it was in the 1860s and 1870s. Throughout the 1830s the budget remained below £55 million with the exception of 1835, when £16.7 million paid out in compensation to exslaveholders pushed the figure over £65 million. Over the course of the 1840s the level of government spending never topped £60 million. Nonetheless, the navy's share during these two decades never exceeded 13.2 percent, coming close to that figure only once. For no less than eight straight years, from 1833 through 1840, the service accounted for less than 10 percent of total government spending. By these standards, both in terms of actual spending and in terms of proportion of the whole budget, the navy of the late 1860s and 1870s was very liberally funded.

Furthermore, its superiority over rivals appeared more pronounced in the 1830s and 1840s than after 1859, owing to the vast surplus of matériel left over from the wars against France and that country's unprovocative naval policy during most of the period between 1815 and 1847.[61] And the relatively modest, if nonetheless significant pace of technological development in naval weaponry during the first half of the century enabled costs to be held in check, while simultaneously denying any rival the opportunity to achieve numerical parity through blanket obsolescence, then initiating a building race. But, as the *Times* wistfully observed in 1867, the advent of steam and iron, the former chiefly in the 1850s and the latter after 1859, had destroyed the "respectable and judicious average of naval expenditure" that had been maintained with little apparent difficulty through the years of Melbourne, Peel, and Russell.[62] Modern assessors may conclude that the sums expended on the naval service in the mid-Victorian era constituted a veritable bargain, when compared to the standards of later years, but contemporaries, denied the benefits of foresight, saw matters in a very different light. The *Times* remarked in 1876, upon learning that the estimates for that year were £11 million, "it will be very hard if for this expenditure the country cannot obtain the satisfaction of being assured that it possesses a sufficiently powerful sea-going Navy to render it secure against any reasonable probability of attack."[63] In short, if Britain did not possess a navy worthy of the country's tradition it was not "for the want of paying for it," and the *Times* probably spoke for many of its readers when it stated that while the service should not be allowed to waste away, neither did they "want to spend more than 10 millions" on it.[64]

The Naval Budget

The navy's budget was divided into two principal categories: the "effective" and the "noneffective" services. The former included every cost relating to the conduct of naval operations, the latter covered the expense of pensions, half-pay to unemployed officers, and the cost of transporting army troops. Typically, the "noneffective" services consumed between 17 and 20 percent of the naval budget, rising to a high of slightly over 23 percent in 1878–79. Sums expended usually ranged between £1.8 million and £2.3 million. The crucial figure, though, was not the sum of the "noneffective" services, but what was left for the needs of the "active" navy after those votes were deducted.

Contemporary perceptions notwithstanding, it is hard not to conclude that the navy made do with remarkably little, given its role as the first line of defense for the home islands, to say nothing of its duties worldwide—combating piracy, conducting antislavery patrols, upholding British "honor" and interests, and myriad other tasks. In no year between 1866 and 1885 did the "effective" services receive £10 million, with the sole exception of 1878–79, when they received £1.6 million beyond the initial budget, the windfall from the vote of credit for the Eastern Crisis.[65] Ordinarily, expenditure on the "effective" votes consumed between £7.5 million and £9.5 million, with which the navy had to pay, clothe, and feed its personnel, build and maintain its ships, run its dockyards, buy its materials, cover the cost of its administration, and pay for corollary services such as its scientific branch, hospitals, medicines, and legal expenses. These services, in turn, were classified under three subheads, namely, personnel, matériel, and administration. Personnel expenses included the costs associated with paying, clothing, feeding, and otherwise maintaining sailors and officers. Matériel costs consisted of the purchase of naval stores and other materials, dockyard maintenance

TABLE 7
Navy Estimates and Expenditure, 1865–66 to 1880–81 (£)

Year	Vote 1 Seamen and Marines	Vote 2 Clothing and Victuals	Vote 3 Admiralty Office	Vote 4 Coast Guard/ Reserves	Vote 5 Scientific Branch	Vote 6 Dockyards at Home and Abroad
1865–66[a]	2,945,006[b]	1,325,094	175,957	284,395	70,042	1,304,195
	—	—	—	—	—	—
1866–67	2,866,253	1,235,188	173,655	274,119	63,958	1,376,971
	—	—	—	—	—	—
1867–68[c]	2,950,952	1,241,614	176,018	267,067	65,108	1,375,368
	2,926,557	1,338,667	180,049	238,317	59,399	1,421.629
1868–69	3,036,634	1,335,842	182,364	243,926	63,565	1,223,562
	2,952,847	1,312,688	181,413	236,506	63,059	1,220,016
1869–70	2,762,353	1,172,263	168,704	224,073	62,826	1,036,004
	2,756,067	1,059,655	168,442	218,780	59,431	1,060,904
1870–71	2,692,731	968,857	159,368	196,955	68,794	878,352
	2,714,926	981,939	158,216	184,861	62,638	973,988
1871–72	2,693,336	1,038,202	163,499	187,830	67,103	967,418
	2,696,702	1,052,911	161,410	162,633	60,292	964,870
1872–73	2,674,145	1,062,269	173,767	174,500	72,741	978,983
	2,658.869	1,021,065	173,716	143,679	76,697	958,562
1873–74	2,629,884	1,035,719	174,983	167,575	98,654	1,115,080
	2,612,715	1,105,847	178,201	151,057	103,115	1,148,243
1874–75	2,603,737	1,085,534	178,066	163,311	113,120	1,253,326
	2,590,030	1,123,380	183,128	168,280	127,976	1,253,609
1875–76	2,644,062	1,107,781	183,916	188,505	107,324	1,326,649
	2,609,355	1,142,670	187,809	183,602	107,262	1,356,368
1876–77	2,634,904	1,158,367	189,820	210,230	109,194	1,328,750
	2,680,947	1,115,917	189,693	196,702	102,929	1,338,243
1877–78	2,384,048	1,178,819	203,890	207,900	109,602	1,341,680
	2,682,375	1,110,800	193,737	193,328	99,996	1,349,104
1878–79	2,702,240	1,146,192	200,760	207,510	106,041	1,350,140
	2,744,383	1,039,025	197,200	186,987	99,133	1,464,510
1879–80	2,708,695	1,003,375	185,400	193,870	105,576	1,355,000
	2,724,457	965,027	183,764	190,564	98,933	1,357,738
1880–81	2,721,536	1,013,524	179,485	194,273	113,107	1,363,585
	2,655,421	952,285	174,406	192,342	103,256	1,360,353

[a]Prior to 1868–69 Navy estimates did not contain expenditure figures for previous years.
[b]The upper figure is the original estimate with no additions owing to supplements. The lower figure is the amount expended, save in noted cases.
[c]Expenditure figures do not include sums provided from Votes of Credit.

and building costs, and dockyard wages. Administrative and miscellaneous expenses covered the Admiralty and its clerical staff as well as other obligations such as legal costs.

The expense of paying, clothing, feeding, and otherwise maintaining the navy's personnel invariably consumed the largest part of the naval budget during the period.[66] Reductions in the number of seamen did allow some concurrent reductions in Vote 1 (wages to seamen and

TABLE 7 (CONTINUED)
Navy Estimates and Expenditure, 1865–66 to 1880–81 (£)

Year	Vote 7 Victualing and Transport	Vote 8 Medical Establishments	Vote 9 Marine Divisions	Vote 10/1 Naval Stores	Vote 10/2 Steam Machinery, Contracts	Voye 11 New Works and Building
1865–66	84,712	55,347	14,133	1,134,572	564,700	527,985
	—	—	—	—	—	—
1866–67	85,624	59,299	15,550	1,003,501	338,000	892,865
	—	—	—	—	—	—
1867–68	86,395	62,686	17,448	855,511	860,559	888,588
	85,903	61,337	17,580	1,085,926	860,559	862,197
1868–69	87,179	64,824	20,709	892,908	1,092,500	814,237
	83,289	62,317	19,306	926,231	1,060,571	809,791
1869–70	80,671	54,757	16,566	801,572	767,076	749,816
	76,614	51,953	16,192	766,561	745,278	737,510
1870–71	69,267	57,730	18,122	779,090	466,173	744,232
	66,809	57,082	16,890	971,284	690,002	855,945
1871–72	68,334	57,906	18,021	837,965	751,716	780,994
	67,221	57.428	16,961	915,320	665,675	823,751
1872–73	68,344	59,926	18,728	928,510	477,116	716,691
	67,704	59,945	18,084	1,049,527	375,256	755,516
1873–74	70,935	62,214	18,863	1,072,380	609,336	682,218
	71,655	62,232	18,341	1,327,871	636,871	678.865
1874–75	73,385	63,701	18,720	1,175,159	828,679	682,061
	72,416	64,676	18,514	1,376,712	823,657	614,712
1875–76	75,548	64,644	18,868	1,285,770	903,608	644,751
	74,339	65,193	18,204	1,270,048	913,675	625,086
1876–77	76,400	65,830	20,053	1,261,320	1,353,600	569,249
	75,323	85,810	20,609	1,235,213	1,355,382	508,022
1877–78	76,930	66,150	21,316	1,207,300	1,042,000	537,715
	75,280	65,522	20,486	1,172,622	1,041,340	455,540
1878–79	76,740	66,400	21,139	1,199,300	1,042,000	539,115
	75.499	66,857	20,817	1,338,084	1,008,142	530,261
1879–80	76,570	87,030	21,408	1,030,000	842,000	566,749
	73,060	65,861	20,620	965,266	783,528	546,589
1880–81	71,166	63,415	21,402	1,011,060	749,000	558,950
	69,052	62,573	20,377	1,043,266	670,082	520,965

marines), but the savings were surprisingly small given the inroads made on the navy's manpower. In 1860–61 Vote 1 had provided for wages for 85,000 men, boys, and marines.[67] By 1866–67 the number had dropped to 68,000.[68] The zealous economizing of Hugh Childers cut manpower to 61,000 in 1870.[69] Three years later Goschen, prodded by Gladstone, managed to effect a further reduction of 1,000, but maintained that this was the limit.[70] For the following nine years the navy's manpower did not vary, until W. H. Smith implemented a further reduction of 1,200 men in 1879.[71] These reductions, incidentally, had little impact on the overall strength of the navy, due largely

Administration, Politics, and Economics 65

TABLE 7 (CONTINUED)
Navy Estimates and Expenditure, 1865–66 to 1880–81 (£)

Vote 12 Medicines, etc.	Vote 13 Martial Law, etc.	Vote 14 Misc. Services	Vote 15 Half Pay/ Retired Pay	Vote 16/1 Military CPensions	Vote 16/2 Civil Pensions	Conveyance of Troops[d]
64,800	2,742	103,925	698,195	507,211	208,033	320,580
—	—	—	—	—	—	—
75,664	20,605	105,950	701,708	528,904	213,837	402,788
—	—	—	—	—	—	—
21,332	21,332	168,450	704,937	528,667	218,915	450,976
87,736	17,811	193,996	690,776	532,165	209,429	469,351
78,164	20,365	174,800	700,166	550,447	223,498	350,600
88,021	18,470	183,950	688,074	545,634	208,401	396,273
79,300	18,144	120,650	723,231	589,728	222,566	316,348
76,746	15,356	141,684	713,846	571,577	247,945	292,643
73,150	16,678	118,791	902,100	635,066	287,134	237,340
65,068	17,140	135,127	803,355	606,324	303,452	247,844
67,600	16,005	125,617	829,238	633,785	312,237	173,150
68,318	15,303	159,012	793,463	622,692	308,413	256,557
70,800	16,110	117,297	818,626	638,341	309,185	156,700
68,151	15,958	128,665	820,571	642,222	308,607	156,875
70,800	16,080	105,288	862,462	643,216	296,448	167,740
70,171	15,869	117,047	846,097	658,176	298,543	141,425
70,745	15,605	123,410	870,166	657,090	238,670	175,690
73,054	15,372	138,712	876,633	680,016	289,809	182,198
73,530	15,904	156,423	889,511	681,781	254,529	172,090
74,746	15,815	203,530	881,171	703,855	284,423	178,364
76,230	15,114	135,547	888,472	726,136	282,176	197,480
77,759	14,741	178,895	734,203	734,203	284,771	219,906
78,010	8,147	130,134	880,796	759,940	279,931	168,280
76,064	8,124	150,021	870,649	761,546	278,711	245,777
77,230	7,994	134,725	891,605	790,297	284,223	210,250
76,587	7,708	144,241	877,889	781,505	282,052	844,890
75,710	7,985	140,530	891,615	803,920	301,211	210,250
65,954	7,816	145,221	891,623	810,893	332,991	184,926
75,150	9,250	135,760	895,156	823,219	322,428	245,500
65,937	10,478	128,077	897,814	882,900	328,584	398,294

SOURCES: Estimates: *Parliamentary Papers*, "Navy Estimates," 1866, 45:500; 1867, 44:5; 1867–68, 45:5; 1868–69, 38:5; 1870, 44:5; 1871, 40:5; 1872, 39:5; 1873, 42:5; 1874, 38:5; 1875, 45:5; 1876, 45:5; 1877, 52:5; 1878, 39:5; 1878–79, 45:5; 1880, 43:5; 1881, 60:5. Expenditure: *Parliamentary Papers*, "Navy Estimates," 1868–69, 38:5; 1870, 44:5; 1871, 40:5; 1872, 39:5; 1873, 42:5; 1874, 38:5; 1875, 45:5; 1876, 45:5; 1877, 52:5; 1878, 39:5; 1878–79, 49:5; 1880, 43:5; 1881, 60:5; 1882, 40:5.
[d] Conveyance of Troops did not have a vote number and the cost of transporting army troops was calculated separately from the rest of the estimates.

to changing technology. The shift from sail to steam, and from broadside to turret ships resulted in a fleet requiring fewer crewmen to man it.[72]

Yet the diminution of manpower did not lead to a commensurate reduction in the sums applied to wages. In 1867–68 Vote 1 totaled slightly in excess of £2.9 million. Thirteen years later it was only

£200,000 less, despite the reduction of manpower by almost 10,000. The wages paid those who remained increased. From 1867–68 through 1874–75 the figure spent on wages decreased steadily: from £2.9 million in the former year to less than £2.6 million by the latter. In 1876, however, George Ward Hunt found that the incentives held out to encourage boys to enlist were "not sufficient."[73] As a consequence he was compelled to raise wages and increase enlistment inducements to attract recruits. For the next three years the expense of wages crept steadily upward, reaching £2.74 million by 1878–79 before falling off slightly the following year, when Smith managed to reduce manpower.

The costs of food and clothing, too, were prone to fluctuation, but here the blessings to naval administrators and politicians were less mixed. In 1866–67 Vote 2 (clothing and victuals) required an outlay of over £1.2 million. Thanks to the efforts of Childers the figure was less than £1 million by 1870–71. This proved to be an ephemeral accomplishment, as the figure climbed gradually, reaching £1.14 million by 1875–76. But the effects of deflation in the agricultural sector, apparent after 1873, were reflected in Vote 2 from 1876 onward. By 1879–80 spending on victuals and clothing had fallen to £965,027, less even than the figure achieved by Childers' administration nine years earlier. Hence, while an across-the-board rise of prices for industrial goods during the early and mid-1870s pushed matériel costs upward, the influence of the Victorian great depression permitted substantial, if not entirely commensurate, savings on victuals.

The votes for personnel were relatively "inelastic"; those of matériel far less so. Three of the five matériel costs were much more capable of short-term reduction than those relating to seagoing personnel. First of all, dockyards wages (Vote 6) were much more susceptible to short-term reductions than those paid to seamen. At their peak, in 1878–79, they accounted for £1.46 million, or almost 12.25 percent of the year's budget. But from 1870–71 through 1872–73 they fell below £1 million per annum, reaching a low of £958,562 the latter year. This achievement was a short-term anomaly, since allocations for Vote 6 did not drop below £1.2 million for nine of the remaining eleven years between 1866 and 1880. Not surprisingly, the other two exceptions occurred in 1869–70 and 1873–74, also under the stewardship of the Liberals.

The swing between extremes was still more pronounced under the two sections of Vote 10, the first devoted to purchase of naval stores,

Administration, Politics, and Economics 67

the second to contract shipbuilding—construction in private shipyards—and furnishing steam engines and boilers. In 1874–75 Hunt's administration spent £1,376,712 on naval stores. In 1869–70 the Childers regime made do with £766,561, over £630,000 less. There was no consistent pattern to expenditure on stores. Henry Corry, whose administration embarked upon a major building program, spent under £1 million on Vote 10 Section 1 in 1868–69; Ward Hunt's board never allocated less than £1.17 million. Fluctuations in Vote 10 Section 2 were similarly marked. Ward Hunt's administration undertook an ambitious unarmored shipbuilding program in 1876–77, primarily fulfilled by contract building. In consequence, Vote 10 Section 2 climbed above £1.3 million. At the other extreme, Goschen's reluctance to enter into contracts in 1872–73 because of rising industrial prices resulted in an expenditure of only £375,256 on contract building and machinery, almost a million less.

The cost of new works and dockyard extensions displayed no more consistency, ranging from £477,116 in 1877–78 to more than £850,000 a year in 1866–67 and 1870–71. The remaining element of matériel spending, pensions to former dockyard workers, increased from about £200,000 to £330,000 a year during the period. Finally, the costs of administration and miscellaneous services varied substantially. The cost of transporting troops was especially prone to fluctuation. Expenditure on administration and miscellaneous costs reached £1,186,331 on one occasion, but ordinarily ranged from £500,000 to £800,000. In short, the greatest variation in the sums spent yearly on the navy usually came under the heading of matériel. Exclusive of the votes of credit of 1870 and 1878, the greatest outlay on matériel occurred in 1876–77, when Votes 6, 10, 11, and 16 Section 2 totaled £4,721,631. The lowest figure—that of 1872–73—was over a million and a quarter less. As Goschen observed to Gladstone in 1871, the only way to achieve large reductions in the estimates was "by building fewer ships."[74]

Consequently, there was a marked correlation between outlays for Votes 6 and 10 and ups and downs in overall spending. A total increase of £713,845 in 1873–74 was virtually duplicated by a jump of £729,640 in construction and repair funding. In 1876–77 the figures were £359,159 and £388,747, respectively. And, as if to illustrate Goschen's dictum, from 1876–77 to 1877–78 total spending declined by £364,209. Outlays on Votes 6 and 10 dropped by £365,772. The shipbuilding and repairing votes were more susceptible to manipulation in order to achieve savings than any other expenditure heading. Moreover, there is abundant evidence that naval administrators were frequently prepared to utilize this manipulability in pursuit of more economical estimates. Conversely, increases in shipbuilding and repair outlays were likely to be reflected in higher overall spending, owing to the difficulty of offsetting them through substantial reductions on the other votes.

Thus, the complexion of the matériel votes—and indeed of the estimates as a whole—often turned largely on economic considerations. But these considerations were themselves manifestations of other perceptions: contemporary assessments of rival navies, the political necessity of framing policy to appeal to electors, the state of the economy, and differing views regarding what the navy should be and what it was supposed to do. It was the interaction of these factors and others that shaped the course of British naval policy during the era of Gladstone and Disraeli, and it is to a consideration of them that we must turn to comprehend that course.

CHAPTER 4

Derby, Disraeli, and a Mutinous Admiralty, 1866–1868

The 14th Earl of Derby, heading a minority government, became prime minister for a third time in June 1866, with Disraeli again at the treasury and Sir John Pakington as First Lord. The latter two were quickly at loggerheads. Less than a month after coming to office Pakington wrote Derby, urging an immediate start on building six ironclads while charging *"Disraeli does not understand the subject . . . [and] distrusts me & my motives in this matter."*[1] This last was a considerable understatement. Disraeli wrote confidentially to Derby a month later, "The maladministration, not to say malversation, of the Admiralty has struck deep into the public mind, & is, at this moment, the predominant feeling of the nation."[2] Specifically, he charged that the dockyards employed far more laborers than required and maintained huge and wasteful surpluses of naval stores. Further great waste stemmed from "the obstinacy with [which] the [Admiralty] had declined building iron ships, & the vast sums they have vainly expended in cobbling up old wooden vessels." In both accusations there was a solid core of truth, surrounded by substantial embellishment.

Throughout the 1860s and 1870s the charge that the dockyards sorely required efficient and frugal management was commonly aired. A succession of parliamentary committees and royal commissions condemned the navy's management of its building and repair facilities, most notably an 1861 royal commission on shipbuilding, and later investigations into naval expenditure and accounting chaired by M.P. Charles Seely.[3] Disraeli's critique, however, was based on a comparison of royal yards, with a total workforce of about 18,000, and stores worth slightly less than £5,000,000, with the shipbuilding facilities of Lairds at Birkenhead, where only 4,000 men were employed and where the value of stores on hand was about £60,000.[4] Superficially, the stark contrast of the figures implied wholesale inefficiency and waste—not to say corruption—in the government yards, but a few crucial points, overlooked or omitted by Disraeli, explained much of the difference.

The navy undertook much larger shipbuilding and repair operations than Lairds; there were building facilities at Chatham, Portsmouth, Pembroke, and Sheerness, although little activity took place at the last of these. Government yards could not conveniently lay off workers during slow times as Lairds could; a skilled workforce could not be improvised in the event of a national emergency. Lairds' responsibility for their ships, moreover, ended when clients took delivery; the navy, in contrast, maintained upwards of 250 ships in commission at a time, and vessels were continually being made ready to replace those whose commissions were about to expire. Furthermore, as arsenals and depots in time of war, the royal yards had to maintain amounts of stores that would have led to economic suicide in a yard run solely for profit. Finally, government yards also boasted self-contained manufacturing or fabricating facilities for many of the items used in construction and repair—rope, sails, lumber, and ultimately ironwork, to list the most notable. These facilities, naturally, contributed to the large numbers employed. As to the accusation that the Admiralty wasted huge amounts by patching up old wooden vessels instead of building new iron ones, cogent technological factors prevented a wholesale shift to iron construction during the 1860s and 1870s, and the policy of "cobbling up" old wooden vessels was to a great extent the consequence of naval funding that was often insufficient to permit major overhauls, much less the construction of new vessels. None of these considerations, however, deterred the zealous chancellor of the exchequer. Finishing his condemnation of naval administration, Disraeli urged Derby not to succumb to Pakington's entreaties, arguing "increased expenditure will aggravate, not cure the disease" and that the prime minster himself must deal with the matter: "All extraordinary motion in the great Departments [should] come from you. . . . A First Lord is surrounded by the criminals [i.e., the Naval Lords], & it requires intellectual grasp, & a pre-emptory firmness to deal with them."

Pakington maintained that the reductions of expenditure achieved by Gladstone during the latter years of the Liberal administration had left the navy, especially the ironclad fleet, in poor shape: "[T]he Navy has been neglected & hardly anything done, & ... France has made a *fresh* start. She is building both armour [plated ships] & no armour [i.e., unarmored ships], with great vigour, & I have inherited the navy *again in a state of great relative inferiority.*"[5] The First Lord certainly lent too much credence to the alarmist proclamations of the board, Naval Lords Admiral Sir Alexander Milne and Rear-Admiral John C. D. Hay, and Controller Rear-Admiral Robert Spencer Robinson. One recent study on the navy of the 1860s and early 1870s, places the ratio of British to French ironclads in 1866 at twenty-one to fourteen, figures difficult to reconcile with claims of "great relative inferiority," whatever Pakington might have meant by that ambiguous phrase.[6]

Forced to mediate between Disraeli and Pakington, Lord Derby hedged. In mid-September 1866 he informed Pakington that "our object must be to increase efficiency without increasing, &, if possible, while diminishing expense; & this can only be done by cutting down *unnecessary* expenditure, for which, I am convinced, there is ample room."[7] Yet it is equally clear that Derby's support for Disraeli stemmed from political and fiscal expediency, rather than personal conviction, for when the navy estimates were being drawn up and debated by the government in early 1867, he confessed to the First Lord, "In the sense of the Admiralty, & in the sense of the Public Service, the [Navy's] case is very strong, & personally I am very unwilling to throw any obstacle in the way of your Estimates." But, he continued, as a "Ministry on sufferance," the Conservatives could not "*command* a majority on any subject, [therefore] we must not venture on so hazardous an experiment as that of a largely increased expenditure." Finance was clearly the arbiter of naval policy. "Our potential surplus on the year is a Million," he stated to Pakington, but "the demands from the various departments show an increase of 4 1/2 *millions*; of which your Estimates furnish not far short of 1 1/2 [Million].... Are we prepared in our first Budget, to propose an additional 2d in the Income Tax?" he asked the First Lord, "or must we not cut down *all* our Estimates so as to be at least within our Income, if we cannot show a surplus?"[8]

In the face of such arguments Pakington could do little. His surrender, however, was hardly unconditional. Nine days after Derby's plea he announced to Disraeli, "I have reduced the excess on the Navy Estimates, as first prepared, from £1,330,000 to £615,000. Towards this excess I hope to receive from sale of [old] ships and ballast iron, £300,000."[9] A deficit of £315,000 remained, of which slightly over £100,000 was caused by ongoing expenditure on Palmerston's forts. Over the remaining £207,000 Pakington remained resolute. It was to be devoted to the construction of new ships which, he maintained, were "so necessary." The First Lord carried his point. The estimates, slightly under £10.5 million in 1866–67 jumped by almost half a million the following year, the bulk of the increase being attributable to the votes for stores and contract shipbuilding.[10]

It is not entirely clear why the cabinet sanctioned such a substantial increase in the face of Disraeli's intransigence and Derby's pragmatism. Certainly the estimates question had not been resolved, at least not to Disraeli's satisfaction, when he wrote to the prime minister on the 2nd of February, 1867:

> My Dear Lord:
> The Admiralty is beyond the control of a [Chancellor] of the [Exchequer] or any other subordinate Minister. It is the Prime Minister that can alone deal with that department....
> It is useless to attempt to reason with them: you must command. The whole system of administration is palsied by their mutinous spirit. Not another four and twenty hours ought to elapse without the estimates being settled.[11]

Equally clear, Disraeli's outburst regarding the board's "mutinous spirit" was not a gratuitous slur. Board member Rear-Admiral Sir John Hay, M.P., recounted the incident in his autobiography: "When the estimates were prepared in November 1866, it was found that no provision was made for building armour-clad ships.... [George] Seymour [another Naval Lord and M.P.] and I both... [stated] that we could not support estimates of the character which we were invited to sign,... and tendered our resignation."[12] Hay then claimed, "A few days later I was surprised by a visit from Mr. Henry Corry.... He came to tell me that he was to be First Lord[,]... that Lord Derby had told him of our resignation, and that it had been of great use in enabling him to get the Treasury to consent to building four armour-clads." Hay's account lacks corroboration, but without it Disraeli's retreat is inexplicable. The Naval Lord reflected that "if Seymour and I had not been members of the House of Commons we could not have forced the hand of the Government," which probably illuminates the crucial consideration. With a minority in the Commons, the Conservatives, as Derby admitted, could ill afford to embark on expensive shipbuilding programs. But, conversely, the resignation of two members of the government might have sown the seeds of discord among the more hawkish Conservatives and given the opposition a possible point of attack. The ministry was already shaky and could hardly risk alienating any of its supporters. Hay and Seymour doubtless would have been ignored had they not been M.P.s. But they were, the estimates rose by nearly a half million, and in the absence of information to the contrary, Hay's account remains the sole explanation for that outcome.

Disraeli minced no words when writing to Derby regarding the "mutineers": "The more I see and hear about the [Admiralty], the more I feel the feebleness & absurdity of the Department. Power is exercised there by individuals who have no responsibility.... Fancy a [Secretary] of the Treasury, or an [Under Secretary] of State threatening to resign because he did not approve of his chief's policy!"[13] It was but another straw, though hardly the last one, to be loaded onto the camel's back. As far as Disraeli was concerned, there must have already been enough to have caused severe anatomical damage, and he proposed to the prime minister that "[t]he [Admiralty] [should] be remodelled on the general scheme: a [Secretary] of State with Under-Secretaries." He must have favored the idea even more strongly a year later.

Henry Thomas Lowry Corry (1803–73), First Lord of the Admiralty since the transferal of Pakington to the war office in March 1867, was a naval administrator of long experience, having been appointed Junior Civil Lord as far back as 1841, in Sir Robert Peel's ministry. He served another stint on the board during the 1858–59 Conservative administration and, owing to the resignations and reshufflings in the cabinet over the Second Reform Bill, found himself in charge of the navy in early 1867. Doubtless his experience stood him in good stead.[14] Unfortunately, at least from Disraeli's standpoint, Corry's own predilections regarding naval policy placed him squarely in the camp of Hay and the other Naval Lords and, hence, at odds with the chancellor of the exchequer who, not surprisingly, was hardly prepared to sanction a large increase in shipbuilding, or anything else that might drive up expenditure. In late November 1867 Corry prepared a statement for the cabinet based on his board's assessment of the state of the fleet. He alleged that "[n]umerically, the two Navies [i.e., English and French], in respect of First and Second class armour-clads afloat, are on exact equality, which, in relation to her wants, must be a dangerous inequality to England."[15] He claimed furthermore that the French had no less than forty-six ironclads built or under construction, against England's thirty-nine.

For more than a month, however, this memorandum remained uncirculated. As Corry admitted to Disraeli on 11 January, although his "conviction was so strong as to the absolute necessity ... of increased expenditure on the building and outfit of ships," he was simultaneously "convinced that it would be perfectly idle" to bring his views before the cabinet.[16] His conviction was well-founded. Indeed, Disraeli, attempting to prevent a repeat of the struggles of 1867 had already dictated the figure the navy would receive, a course of action that prompted Corry to protest that although "a novice in the Cabinet" and "ignorant of the mode in which it has been the practice to determine the amount of the Navy Estimates, [he had been] under the impression that it was usual to consult the First Lord of the Admiralty on the subject."[17] Such was not the case, and he confessed "a little surprise to learn that it had been irrevocably determined without any reference to me." But despite his "belief that there is no business ... which can be more deserving of your attention, and that of Lord Derby," he candidly acknowledged "I am satisfied that I should only be wasting your time and his if I were to attempt to induce you to alter your decision."

Here, one might presume, the matter rested. But like the previous year there was an epilogue. The parliamentary secretary to the Admiralty, Lord Henry Lennox (1821–86), was also, probably not coincidentally, a close confidante of Disraeli's, who had ample reason to appreciate the information passed along to him. Indeed, Lennox acted as the chancellor of the exchequer's spy at the Admiralty, keeping his friend abreast of the machinations of the admirals. In this role Lennox informed Disraeli on 5 January 1868 of the tenor of the forthcoming naval budget: "[T]he Estimates are ordered to be prepared as if you were going to sanction a large increase in shipbuilding, even over & above that of last year."[18] Further bad news arrived on the 11th, when Corry informed Disraeli that despite his apprehension of "provoking ... barren controversy," he had resolved to "let my paper go forward."[19]

In addition to his warning, Lennox also dispatched a lengthy missive to Disraeli, detailing not only the intentions of the First Lord but possible alternative policies. Corry, he stated, "wishes to see a large increase in the Armour-Clad Fleet, & so do I—but he offers no plan or scheme by which this can be effected, except the crude one, of a large increase to the Naval Estimates." Lennox offered a critique of this policy, noting that the First Lord wanted, in addition to the ironclad fleet, a large force of wooden vessels, primarily for service on overseas stations and this, he argued, was "the *key stone* of the position.... [I]t is impossible to progress, as one may desire, with Armour Clads at the same time & keep up these costly squadrons without increased estimates." Lennox admitted that this was a matter of "Imperial policy," best left to the cabinet, but simultaneously charged that Corry and the Naval Lords could advance no defense for the practice other than that the numerous vessels overseas provided "employment & practice for your officers & men" and served to protect the interests of British colonists and merchants.

Sounding strikingly Gladstonian, Lennox demolished these arguments. "I know not *why* we should keep up more men & [officers] than we have employment for." Moreover, the days when independent action by an officer on the spot was needed, he maintained, were past. "Suppose that some insult is offered or some grievance inflicted, on one of our Merchants settled in Peru, the Brazils, Chile, or the River Plate. Would the naval officer [commanding that station] venture to take upon himself to redress this insult[?] [N]o, he would send home for orders before acting." Furthermore, he argued, the British force on the station would find its hands tied, even if ordered to act, "& for this simple reason, that each of these Powers have one or more English-built Iron Clads in their waters, which would sink our small unarmoured Vessels with little or no trouble." Instead, claiming his opinion was "shared cordially" by Rear-Admiral Robert Spencer Robinson, the controller, and "in large measure" by the Second Sea Lord, Admiral Sir Sydney Dacres, Lennox proposed

> that our honour & the interests of our merchants would be perfectly safe were this system of numerous Squadrons exchanged for Flying Squadrons, composed of ships of a calibre worthy of the Country. Those of which they are now composed *can neither fight nor run away.* If Flying Squadrons were established, the numbers of ships would be greatly reduced, & the vast sums now spent annually in their building & repair could be diverted to the building of Iron Clad Ships.[20]

So taken was Disraeli with Lennox's line of reasoning that he repeated it to Derby, borrowing ideas—and often words as well—

wholesale when he wrote the latter—less than two months from retirement and already in poor health—on 28 January.[21] Naturally, too, Disraeli also added his own arguments to sway the prime minister. He wrote emphatically, "The state of our finances will not permit any increase in our expenditure, but if the state of our finances [would] do so, the requisitions of the Admiralty are unwise & unnecessary."[22] Moreover, he charged, the Admiralty's assessments of French naval strength were "marked by the usual exaggeration & false colouring, [which] always accompanies these estimates," a tolerably accurate assessment.[23] And even if its figures were correct, "the management of the Admiralty, with regard to shipbuilding, is at this moment so decried & distrusted, that even if the [House] of Commons wished to increase its naval expenditure it would not entrust the office to a department constituted as at present. . . . We must prepare for an increase of taxation," warned Disraeli ominously, "[which] can no longer be limited to an additional two pence to the income tax." The cost of the then-raging Abyssinian war—ultimately some £8,300,000—would inexorably drive up expenditures, quite aside from the demands of the navy.[24] But "[w]hen a [Chancellor] of the Exchequer has to contemplate increasing the duties on Tea & Malt the wild suggestions of these ignorant & narrow minded Admirals are doubly distressing."[25] Therefore, he concluded, "I hope . . . I may count on your decisive disapproval of these objectionable requirements."

If he anticipated decisive disapproval, Disraeli must have been disappointed. Displaying characteristic caution, Derby replied "I must confess that for the last few years the comparative strength of the British Navy . . . has not been altogether of a satisfactory character & without yielding to panic . . . it must be admitted that we do not possess the preponderance of Power which used to be considered as essential for our safety." On the other hand, the prime minister admitted that "there has been a continual increase of expenditure upon our Naval Estimates, which it is very difficult to justify or explain," adding, "the Cabinet will be found unanimous in their decision, that in the present financial condition of the Country, we could not apply to Parliament for a largely increased Naval vote, with any hope of success." Hence, despite any misgivings, Derby assured Disraeli, "You may rely upon my giving you every support in my power in maintaining the strictest economy, the necessity for which indeed becomes the more evident when you are compelled to look forward, not only to an increase of Taxation but to an increase on such articles as Tea and Malt."[26]

Yet Derby's verdict failed to quell the struggle. On 28 January—the very day that Disraeli wrote Derby—Lennox forwarded another warning. The naval members of the board, evidently bent on employing the same tactics used by Hay and Seymour the previous year, had formed what the parliamentary secretary derisively termed a "combination." Their intent, according to him, was to force Corry to deliver their own memorandum to the prime minister stating "their fears of the French Navy & their insistence for more money for shipbuilding."[27] The communiqué, entitled "Memorandum of the Naval Members of the Board, For the Consideration of the First Lord of the Admiralty," appears to have been the culmination of a series of exchanges between the Naval Lords in the autumn of 1867, probably instigated by the First Sea Lord, Sir Alexander Milne.[28] Using the same statistics cited in Corry's memorandum, the "combination" justified their insubordination on the ground that "they would not be fulfilling their duty, if, holding these convictions, they were to keep silence."[29] With the existing balance of ironclad strength, they claimed, "If France was to collect her Iron Clads in her Atlantic ports she would command the Channel." The threat of invasion, according to Milne, Dacres, Hay, Seymour, and Robinson, all of whom affixed their signatures to the document, was not the only peril. The "mere assembling of such a [French] fleet in troubled times, without actual war, would by its effect on trade, be in itself a disgrace and a disaster."

The memorandum's appearance generated fresh paroxysms of rage from Lennox and Disraeli. Lennox denied any knowledge of the contents: both he and the chancellor of the exchequer again dismissed the Admiralty's calculations as exaggerated, if not altogether specious. Derby was puzzled by the missive. "I cannot but look upon the memo of the Admiral[s] . . . as a most unusual proceeding. It is addressed to the 1st Lord of the Admiralty, & consequently is framed without his concurrence, nor does the Secretary of the [Admiralty] appear to have been consulted upon a matter for which, in dealing with the finances of the Navy, he is in a great measure responsible."[30] As to how it should be received, Derby doubted "the expediency of taking any official cognizance of it," even though it had been sent to the cabinet. Furthermore, the prime minister, for once without a hint of caution, stated "the 1st Lord of the Admiralty should be informed distinctly that a further increase in the Naval Estimates cannot be sanctioned, & that he, & his Naval Colleagues, must use to the best advantage the sum with which Parliament may think fit to entrust them." Disraeli had earlier made this abundantly clear to Corry, who replied that although he could not "pretend to accept your ultimatum either cordially or cheerfully," he nonetheless "frankly accept[ed]" the situation, and that the chancellor of the exchequer "need be under no apprehension of the scenes of last year being renewed by me."[31] Following hard upon Corry's assurance, the conspiracy of the Naval Lords must have seemed to Disraeli nothing short of treachery.

Given the impasse, the proposal made by Lennox to redistribute expenditure via reducing the size and expense of overseas squadrons, hitherto evidently rejected by the First Lord, offered a possible solution. Indeed, the parliamentary secretary reported to Disraeli on 1 February that Corry had informed the board "he wished to revise the number of our small unarmoured ships on Foreign Stations."[32] At this "monstrous proposal," Lennox reported, the Naval Lords "did not attempt to conceal their indignation," but he claimed that he "fired off a strong shot in approval and appealed directly for support to Admiral Robinson, the enlightened Controller of the Navy, [who] hotly seconded my views." Lennox claimed such a reversal of policy would be "reasonable and popular" in public and political circles. Indeed, he had sounded parliamentary opinion on the matter when introducing the estimates the previous year, and had earned the plaudits of Gladstone, among others. Thus, his views could not have been novel to Corry by early 1868. Indeed, it seems doubtful that Lennox would have broached the subject to the House—his claims to the contrary notwithstanding—without the approval of a higher-up, probably Disraeli himself.

As it turned out, Lennox's expedient was sufficient to placate, if not entirely satisfy, both sides. Lennox formally wrote to Corry (the letter is undated but was certainly written prior to 15 February) advocating the adoption of a "bold and vigorous policy [namely, his] by which we could reduce the Navy Estimates and with that saving add considerably to our Iron Clad Fleet."[33] The salient points of Lennox's recommendations were reducing the marines from 16,000 to 15,000, cutting the number of shipboard servants from 4,000 to 2,500 or 3,000, decommissioning ten old coast guard ships, and deferring the repair of wooden vessels in favor of building new ironclads. This last proposal might, he readily admitted the following year, "make reliefs of our Foreign Stations more difficult [to furnish]," but such a situation might, he also maintained, "lead to their reduction, a consummation which in some parts of the world would be much to be desired."

According to Lennox, Corry went along with enough of the proposals that the former could boast to Disraeli on 15 February that "we have struck off £124,000 today [from the existing estimates] which will [when reappropriated] give us 3 additional Iron Clads."[34] Furthermore, enthused the parliamentary secretary, "By cheese-paring the other day we got £50,000 i.e. another Iron Clad. Therefore we have four more Iron Clads than when the Admirals struck, & with the same Estimates."[35] Hence, when the First Lord presented the navy estimates for the upcoming financial year, he was able to claim that, although the figure upon first examination seemed to be £201,037 higher than that of the preceding twelve months, the increase was entirely owing to a change in bookkeeping methods, and that, in reality, the estimates amounted to only £10,973,998, a decrease of £2,255.[36] Furthermore, he was able to point to reductions in the forces overseas. With the savings thus achieved he proposed to step up the construction of ironclads, stating in his opening remarks that "it was the unanimous opinion of my Colleagues and myself that as large an amount as could be possibly spared from the other departments of the naval service, without disregard to their proper efficiency, ought to be appropriated to the construction of armour-plated ships." Offering no clue as to the acrimonious exchanges that had accompanied the preparation of the estimates, Corry pointed proudly to an increase of almost £120,000 overall in the amount allocated for building, repair, stores, contract building, and purchase of machinery; enough, in fact, to permit the commencement of work on six new ironclads, in addition to the six already under construction.

The ambitious building programs put in motion by Pakington in 1867 and by Corry the following year were the direct consequence of the ability of the Naval Lords to convince their superiors that the ironclad fleet had suffered from neglect and underfunding during the latter years of the 1859–66 Liberal government. They were equally successful in convincing the two First Lords that concurrently the French had been making "redoubled efforts" to increase the size of their ironclad fleet. Of course, it was crucial that the pleas of Corry and Pakington found support in the cabinet—from Lords Malmesbury and Carnarvon, and, with ambivalence, Derby himself—or they doubtless would have been quashed by Disraeli, who indeed managed to curb Corry's excesses in 1868.[37] The Chancellor's efforts notwithstanding, however, construction funding jumped by almost £600,000 between 1866–67 and 1867–68, and dropped only moderately the subsequent year. In short, more than purely financial considerations came into play when formulating the yearly shipbuilding programs, a fact Disraeli may well have rued when reflecting on Conservative fortunes at the polls in 1868. By the time the next occasion to present the estimates rolled around the party was no longer in power, having been soundly defeated in the general election of 1868.

Disraeli has more than once been taken to task by historians for his niggardly treatment of the navy. Indeed, he has been accused of palpable hostility to the service and its duties and needs.[38] Certainly this conclusion seems warranted in light of his response to the challenge from France in 1858–59 and the technological threat posed by the *Gloire*. But circumstances were much different when he began his third stint at the treasury in 1866 and his appraisal of French naval strength was more accurate than the numerous alarmist memoranda generated by the board between 1866 and 1868.[39] Besides, to focus solely on the Naval Lords' view is to consider only the external dimension of defense policy, whereas Disraeli, as manifested by his preoccupation with finance, taxation, and the mood of the country, never lost sight of the fact that national security—particularly in countries with a substantial electorate to which statesmen and politicians must answer—has an important internal dimension as well. Disraeli may have erred in his preoccupation with that dimension to the exclusion of other factors, but the circumstances of his position and his official responsibilities made such preoccupation entirely natural. As his successor Lord Salisbury admitted many years later when testifying before a commission on naval and military administration, "The Chancellor of the Exchequer, little familiar with the defensive services, is rightly the spokesman of economy."[40]

Finally, if one accepts the view put forward, among others, by William Gladstone, that one of the primary issues over which the election of 1868 was fought was government finance, Disraeli was downright prescient in judging the mood of the electorate toward "bloated" armaments expenditures.[41] On 23 October 1868—less than three weeks prior to the dissolution of Parliament and only a month from the election—the *Times* proclaimed, "We are neither so prosperous, nor so rich, nor so well able to pay taxes as we were five years ago, and the revenue accounts show as much on the face of the returns."[42] The remedy it suggested was "that retrenchment should be taken in hand before the difficulty becomes greater still," but the newspaper further charged that the "Conservatives, when they wanted money, got it by adding to the Estimates; the Liberals in the same predicament [presumably referring to 1863–66] found it in new economies." As if the hint were not already broad enough, the editors added, portentously, "We suspect that will be about enough for the public." An earlier editorial was no less explicit: "We have to pay more for the Army. We have to pay more for the Navy. . . . Instead of a dragon of economy with lidless eyes guarding the Exchequer, there has been a watch-dog snoring hard by command. Extravagance has been winked at right and left."[43]

In 1868 an organization called the Financial Reform Union issued a series of pamphlets entitled *Papers on Taxation and Expenditure*.[44] Significantly, the first of the series dealt with "Naval Mal-Administration," the authors charging that the Admiralty administrative system "would not be tolerated in any private commercial establishment. If it were, there would be but one result—speedy bankruptcy. It is only possible because the Admiralty deals with the resources of the nation, and is able to make up its deficiencies by heavy and oppressive taxation."[45] Furthermore, in its third pamphlet the organization claimed that "[t]he departments are masters alike of the Treasury, the House of Commons, and the people."[46] Yet, as is obvious from a perusal of the Derby and Disraeli Papers, the *Times* was very much wide of the mark in accusing Treasury officers of sanctioning this extravagance. Had it been left entirely up to Disraeli, the navy would have received considerably less than it did, and when actually permitted by prime minister and cabinet to put his foot down, as in 1868–69, he quashed all attempts by Corry and the rest of the board to push through a second straight substantial increase. Ironically, in doing so he forced the Admiralty to adopt the very policy advocated by the *Times* and other journals.[47] The *Pall Mall Gazette* noted early in 1868 that "we are spending less than one twelfth our annual outlay on the Navy upon the increase of our Ironclads [and it is] . . . alarming that of the ten or eleven millions devoted annually to the navy, much less than a million is expended upon the increase of the Ironclad fleet on which we all know perfectly well our supreme reliance must be placed if England goes to war."[48] Of course, the policy suggested by Lennox and forced upon a reluctant Admiralty by Disraeli in February 1868 addressed this very shortcoming.

But Disraeli's economical endeavors were of little avail when it came to placating press or public opinion. Even a service journal, the *Naval and Military Gazette*, roundly condemned the waste and inefficiency of naval administration: "It seems almost hopeless to expect that we shall ever be able to get our money's worth out of the Admiralty. Neither Parliament, nor the opinion of the public, nor the Press—not even a hostile vote in the House—can move the gigantic, blundering, ship-tinkering National Company out of its old groove."[49] Insofar as voters in 1868 were recording a verdict on Conservative fiscal policy, they clearly judged it a failure. Disraeli had hoped the election would reduce the Liberal majority in the House of Commons or, ideally, transform it into a small Conservative majority. Instead, the Conservatives wound up losing about 20 seats, and faced a Liberal majority of over 100 when Parliament opened the following year.[50] With a commanding position Gladstone thus embarked on his first premiership, with Hugh Childers delegated to administer the navy.[51] Finally, noted several organs of the press, loomed the promise of reform at the Admiralty. Even before 1868 came to a close, Childers had unveiled plans for a wholesale shakeup of the service, with the avowed goals of making it both more efficient and less expensive. Noted the *Times* approvingly, "This is precisely what the country wants, it is precisely what the country has been told, time after time, is perfectly practicable; but it is what, for all that, we have never seen accomplished yet. Most heartily do we wish that Mr. Childers may be the first to solve the problem."[52]

CHAPTER 5

Hugh Childers at the Admiralty, 1868–1870

Reform

Hugh Culling Eardley Childers (1827–95) was no novice at the labyrinth of naval administration when William Gladstone offered him the post of First Lord in December 1868. He had served a modest stint as Civil Lord—the most junior civilian on the board—during the latter days of the 1859–66 Liberal ministry.[1] The expertise he then acquired was probably not the qualification foremost in Gladstone's mind, however, when he selected Childers to head the Admiralty. More important was the concurrence of the two men's views when it came to matters of finance and expenditure. "[S]ince I have been in Parliament," wrote Childers to Gladstone in August 1865, "it has been my most sincere desire to support your financial policy both in regard to the incidence of taxation and to the reduction of expenditure."[2] Childers furthermore supplemented his commitment to retrenchment with a deep loyalty to Gladstone.[3] Indeed—in stark contrast to the voluminous and often acrimonious correspondence between the First Lords of the Admiralty, Lord Derby, and Disraeli during the Conservative ministry of 1866–68—the absence of any indication of tension or disagreement between Childers and Gladstone in their letters serves as an eloquent testimonial to their singleness of purpose. The latter could count on a reliable, zealous and sympathetic lieutenant at the Admiralty, one who needed little in the way of overseeing, much less guidance.

Childers wasted little time in making his presence felt at Whitehall. Within three months of the government's appointment he had implemented a barrage of reforms: a substantial alteration in the administrative structure of the board, the rudiments of an expanded program of promotion and retirement for the officer corps (to be implemented the following year), and further redistribution and reduction of the overseas squadrons. Moreover, Childers had "determined on a distinct policy to be followed in shipbuilding, . . . has just touched, by way of beginning, the management of the Dockyards, and gives fair promise of doing much more."[4]

The last estimates presented by the Liberal government of 1859–66 authorized the construction of 18,253 tons of warships during the ensuing fiscal year. Sir John Pakington's program the following year jumped to 33,206 tons: Henry Corry called for 29,688 tons in 1868–69. To meet these building quotas the Conservatives increased the dockyards' labor force substantially. By February 1868 the size of the yard establishment had swelled to 20,690 men, more than 2,300 above the figure sanctioned in the 1867–68 estimates. At that point, however, Corry's policy, influenced in no small way by the cabinet's refusal to permit another large increase in the navy's budget, underwent a dramatic reversal. The 1868–69 estimates authorized a dockyard workforce of only 15,272.[5] Admiralty policy in the dockyards, in short, lacked consistency from year to year.

Lack of consistency, in turn, generated wasteful expenditure, itself guaranteed to attract the attention of a fiscal reformer like Childers. Even after Corry's substantial reduction of the dockyard workforce in early 1868, Childers considered the size of the establishment far larger than necessary. "After careful consideration," he informed the Commons in 1870, "we have arrived at the conclusion that 6,000 men will suffice for all the shipbuilding . . . and as to repairing and refitting, we are of opinion that 5,000 men will suffice for that purpose."[6] Since the establishment for 1869–70 was pegged at 14,000, achieving Childers' figure meant discharging a further 3,000 men. His calculations regarding dockyard workforce were, however, only one aspect of an overarching scheme comprehending yearly building and repair demands, expenditure and, ultimately, the navy's requisite level of matériel strength. "We have come to the conclusion, having regard to the present state of the Navy, and to the point at which it ought to be kept up, that we should annually build between 19,000 and 20,000 tons of shipping; of these about 12,000 being armoured and 7,500 unarmoured." This tonnage would give the navy "nearly three new ironclads, one frigate, one corvette, and six small vessels annually." Basing these calculations on the assumption that an ironclad would furnish two decades of useful service, his steady building program would, the First Lord claimed, "produce and keep up a force of from 50 to 60 ironclads, which would be ample for our requirements." This assessment was indisputable, assuming no foreign rival reacted to this consistent augmentation by escalating its own construction program, and assuming twenty years' service was realistic.[7] Childers' proposed shipbuilding program, in sum, seemingly offered a firm foundation on which to establish a stable, long-term building program. Not only, he hoped, would it bring coherence and consistency to an aspect of British naval policy sorely lacking both, it would also lead to greater efficiency and economy in the dockyards, prominent Liberal party objectives. Finally, it would result in an unmatched level of armored naval strength. As such, construction policy formed a significant part of Childers' comprehensive naval reforms.

The First Lord naturally stressed the envisioned economic benefits. Maintenance of the navy's existing vessels, as well as the 19,000–20,000 tons of shipping to be added yearly could, he promised, be achieved on an annual expenditure of £2,400,000.[8] This figure was not plucked from thin air. The controller of the navy, Rear Admiral Sir Robert Spencer Robinson, who, under Childers' division of responsibilities at the Admiralty, oversaw all aspects of business relating to the service's matériel, prepared for his superior a review of naval expenditure over the previous half decade that pointed to the "want of system in regulating [the expenditure] of past years." It concluded that "about two and a half million [was] wanted annually for ships and dockyards."[9] In practice, however, these estimates, even the slightly higher figure of Spencer Robinson, were little more than flights of fancy. Only in 1872–73 did shipbuilding expenditure—even exclusive of pensions to superannuated dockyard laborers—drop below the £2.4 million level, and only on two other occasions during the decade did it come within £100,000 of Spencer Robinson's ideal of £2.5 million. In fact, only twice during the 1870s did construction and repair costs dip below the much higher figure of £3 million. Average yearly expenditure for the decade, including votes of credit, was £3,423,871, a full million higher than Childers' wildly optimistic calculation. Even leaving aside the extraordinary outlays of 1870 and 1878, the average was still in excess of £3.2 million.[10]

Yet despite spending an average of 33 percent more a year than

TABLE 8
Shipbuilding Programs versus Tonnage Completed, 1865–80

Year	Armored Tonnage Proposed	Armored Tonnage Completed	Armored Tonnage Difference	Unarmored Tonnage Proposed	Unarmored Tonnage Completed	Unarmored Tonnage Difference	Total Tonnage Proposed	Total Tonnage Completed	Total Tonnage Difference
1865–66	16,692	11,538	−5,154	4,766	4,351	−415	21,458	15,889	−5,569
1866–67	10,434	7,453	−2,981	6,170	6,113	−57	16,604	13,566	−3,038
1867–68	12,392	13,568	+1,176	14,217	13,855	−364	26,609	27,423	+814
1868–69	19,951	16,414	−3,537	7,830	7,726	−104	27,781	24,140	−3,641
1869–70	19,411	21,460	+2,049	3,535	3,713	+178	22,946	25,173	+2,227
1870–71	17,899	15,962	−1,937	5,746	4,569	−1,177	23,645	20,531	−3,114
1871–72	12,726	13,920	+1,194	8,553	7,538	−1,015	21,279	21,458	+179
1872–73	5,812	6,353	+541	12,196	8,178	−4,018	18,008	14,531	−3,477
1873–74	7,504	5,003	−2,501	10,010	9,701	−309	17,514	14,704	−2,810
1874–75	10,705	8,457	−2,248	9,092	8,023	−1,069	19,797	16,480	−3,317
1875–76	13,494	14,276	+782	6,171	5,440	−731	19,665	19,716	+51
1876–77	11,393	11,448	+55	12,369	12,782	+413	23,762	24,230	+468
1877–78[a]	9,676	7,113	−2,563	8,972	9,450	+478	18,648	16,563	−2,085
1878–79	10,295	8,429	−1,866	7,812	9,461	+1,649	18,107	17,890	−217
1879–80	7,732	7,427	−305	7,546	7,800	+254	15,278	15,227	−51
Total	186,116	168,821	−17,295	124,985	118,698	−6,287	311,101	287,519	−23,582
Yearly Average	12,407.7	11,254.7	−1,153	8,332.3	7,913.2	−419.1	20,740.1	19,167.9	−1,572.2

SOURCE: "Return of the Amount of Shipping—Tons Weight of Hull—Estimated for and calculated to have been actually Built for the Year 1865–66 to the Year 1884–85, together with Appendix, showing the Amount of Money proposed by Programme to be Expended for Labour and that actually Spent on the several Ships building in Her Majesty's Dockyards during the Year 1884–85, with Tonnage corresponding thereto:—Also see a similar Return for Ships Building by Contract, based on Payments to Contractors. [In continuation of Parliamentary Paper No. 329 of Session 1884]," *Parliamentary Papers*, 1884–5, 48:565–67.

[a] Does not include vessels purchased through the Vote of Credit. "The 'Neptune,' 'Superb,' 'Belleisle,' and 'Orion' (iron-clads), the 'Hecla' (torpedo depot ship), 'Tyne' (transport), and 'Mint' (tug), and two lighters and six iron barges, for torpedo service, were purchased and mainly paid for in 1877–78, out of Vote of Credit, but are not included in the above. ... The net tonnage added thereby in 1877–78, exclusive of the barges and lighters, the tonnage of which is unknown, was, for iron-clads, 14,808 weight of hull, and unarmoured, 4,839 registered tonnage; total 19,647 tons." (Ibid., 1884–85, 48:566).

Childers had envisioned, the dockyards routinely failed to achieve his annual tonnage target. From 1870–71 through 1879–80, yearly building programs ranged from 18,000 to 24,000 tons, with the exception of 1879–80. With the further exceptions of 1870–71 and 1876–77, the average was 18,000–21,700 tons, close to Childers' figure of 19,000–20,000 tons.[11] Only twice during the decade did estimated construction reach the stated quota. A further three times it came within a thousand tons of the yearly provision. Of the remaining five years, deficits ranged from 2,085 tons to 5,175 tons, the latter figure almost a quarter of the year's building program.[12]

The recurring shortfalls hardly escaped the notice of contemporaries. In introducing the shipbuilding program for 1876–77, First Lord George Ward Hunt admitted that "the tonnage programme for many years had not been fulfilled; about 20,000 tons had been intended to be built, and the amount accomplished had for a long time fallen short by 4,000 or 5,000 tons."[13] He exaggerated; the deficit from 1870–71 through 1874–75 amounted to 15,089 tons, or slightly more than 3,000 tons annually. A significant shortfall it was, nonetheless. Failure on the part of private shipbuilders to meet contracts was, of course, beyond the control of the Admiralty, and could result from a variety of factors. Ward Hunt stated vaguely in 1875, "With regard to the work done by contractors . . . in many cases strikes and difficulties with their workmen prevented them from making so much progress as was expected."[14] Failure to build the specified amount in the government dockyards was another matter, however, and indeed the state establishments failed to come within 1,000 tons of their allotted tonnage for seven of the ten years of the 1870s. Over the decade the cumulative shortfall in the government yards was almost 1,400 tons a year, despite the yearly program being substantially exceeded twice.[15] The lion's share of the construction deficit, in other words, was being run up in the royal yards.

One might suspect Childers' reduced dockyard establishment was the cause, but investigation reveals that the ideal of 11,000 dockyard workers came near to realization only during 1870, and then for only a matter of months. In a revised construction program concocted by Spencer Robinson as a response to the Franco-German War, the dockyard workforce was increased to 13,500, at virtually the precise moment when Childers' gradual reductions were to have been completed.[16] The following year, moreover, George J. Goschen's estimates called for an establishment of 12,707 men, more than 1,500 above

Childers' figure. By 1873 the workforce in the dockyards numbered almost 14,000, and Ward Hunt increased it to 16,000 men in 1875, a full 1,000 above the level denounced as extravagant by Childers in 1870.[17] A workforce of 16,000 was maintained for the remainder of the decade. The assumptions informing Childers' steady building program, then, were based on several fallacious premises. Not only was it impossible to build 20,000 tons of shipping a year for £2.4–2.5 million; it was impossible to build 20,000 tons of shipping a year for £3.2–3.4 million. And not only was it impossible to build 14,000 tons a year in the dockyards with an establishment of 11,000 workers; it was also evidently impossible to do so with 16,000 men.

Although numerous factors came into play, one was of central importance in this chronic—not to mention potentially serious—shortfall in the navy's yearly building programs: an equally continuous underestimation by successive naval administrations of the amount of repair work required of the dockyards, where virtually all such work was performed. Childers had assumed that by lowering the number of ships in commission through reductions on foreign stations, and by keeping those that remained at sea in commission for longer periods, 5,000 men would be adequate for repairing and refitting the existing fleet.[18] Of the sanguine assumptions that contributed to his optimistic vision of future dockyard policy, in which efficiency would be combined with economy, this was Childers' most erroneous.

In mitigation it is worth reiterating that the perception of wholesale waste and inefficiency in dockyard management was common in political and public spheres during the 1860s and 1870s. It was not restricted to the economic Radicals below the gangway, or even to the Gladstonian Liberal party.[19] Disraeli had also denounced the management of shipbuilding and repair facilities during his tenure as chancellor of the exchequer from 1866 through early 1868, and the more hawkish Lord Derby agreed with his subordinate that there was "ample room" for cutting down "unnecessary expenditure" via reductions in the scope and cost of repairs and, for that matter, by discontinuing the practice of repairing old and useless ships. "Can't some of them be sold, or at least broken up," he wrote to Sir John Pakington in September 1866, his exasperation almost tangible, "to spare us the cost of maintenance?"[20] He suggested, furthermore, that proper superintendence of the dockyards was wanting, and that the quantity of work done in them was not commensurate with the number of men employed.[21] The *Times* also denounced alleged dockyard waste repeatedly during the late 1860s.[22] With an understanding of their background, therefore, Childers' proposals regarding the size and duties of the dockyard workforce, radical though they appear, were merely attempts to confront what contemporaries viewed as a major source of inefficiency and needless expense.

But whether well laid or not, the First Lord's scheme very quickly ran aground. The increased establishment prompted by the Franco-German War was intended, it is true, to speed the completion of ships then under construction as well as to provide a workforce for building new vessels. In other words, it was intended as a temporary measure. But Goschen's 1871–72 estimates amounted to a tacit admission that Childers' ambitious scheme for dockyard reform and building policy was a failure, at least insofar as the size of the establishment and the division of its duties was concerned. The new First Lord enlarged the workforce to 12,700; moreover, he allocated 5,200 men for new construction. The remaining 7,500 were to be engaged in repairs.[23] And when some months later Goschen expressed his hope that the yearly building quota would be met, his optimism was lampooned by Lord Henry Lennox. "The right honourable Gentleman proposed," Lennox observed, "with 400 [more] men to build, and 400 less for repairs, to give the country 16,741 tons, or nearly 17,000 tons. . . . [I]f he did he would certainly be something of a conjuror."[24] Lennox was right. The following year Goschen admitted that there had been "delays in the dockyards," and that "comparatively little progress had been made in the building program." He then confessed "that he was not a conjuror, and he had not succeeded in accomplishing his task."[25] The reason was not far to seek. "They were, no doubt, behind in their shipbuilding," Goschen continued, because of "not being able to employ so many by 1,000 men as they had hoped to be able to do at the beginning of the year."

There was but one solution. Goschen expressed disappointment that many men had been diverted from building to repairs, but wear and tear were, after all, inherent in life at sea, and failure to take them and other contingencies into consideration was apt to lead to complications. He decided, therefore, that for the forthcoming year he would "employ 650 more men in the dockyards, but not so many in shipbuilding." This was to be an oft-repeated refrain. An attack by Ward Hunt in 1874 on the preceding naval administration hinged on the alleged unsatisfactory state of the fleet. "Representations have been made to me," he insisted, "by the responsible member of the Department [i.e., the controller, William Houston Stewart] that the number of men taken for the dockyards is not sufficient to keep up the present establishments."[26] His remedy, naturally, was to increase the "number of men taken for the dockyards," to 16,000 in 1875–76, but to little avail. The workforce assigned to repairs climbed from 9,500 to 10,700: the number engaged in building rose by only 500. Nonetheless, upon presentation of the estimates the following year the First Lord admitted "a great many ships appeared as part of the Fleet, but he was sorry to say that many of them were entirely unserviceable."[27]

Clearly, much of the volume of repairs that drew so much contemporary attention was a result of lack of familiarity with the maintenance requirements of a machine-age navy. The first warships dependent on steam alone for motive power were products of the 1860s, and only in the following decade did naval administrators fully confront the complexities and maintenance costs attendant upon technological sophistication. Modern rifled ordnance, hydraulic steering and gun-loading apparatus, even electricity—all of these and other innovations led to increasing demand on the navy's repair facilities.

The biggest problem was boilers. The almost simultaneous adoption of two inventions in the late 1860s—the surface condenser, which collected the steam exhaust from the cylinders, condensed it, and returned it to the boiler, and the evaporator, which distilled feed water—permitted marine boilers to run on fresh, rather than salt, water. This change, it was anticipated, would increase the service life of machinery and, especially, of boilers. Expectations were soon dashed. By 1865 it was apparent in the merchant marine that "the use of 'fresh' water, which was continuously circulated through the system, was having the opposite effect to that which had been anticipated.... [T]he insides of boilers were now subject to corrosive attack from the recirculated water which became... 'excessively foul.'"[28] Before the enforced reliance on steam, the navy's ships as a rule employed sails far more often than engines. Boiler deterioration was consequently fairly gradual. Once steam became the sole, or even the primary source of power, the rate of deterioration and the need for frequent boiler repair and replacement became, in the judgment of contemporaries, distressingly common. And headaches with boilers themselves were exacerbated by the difficulty of replacing them. As W. H. Smith observed in 1878, the problem involved "much more than the mere cost of repairing or replacing them; it involves the laying-up of the ship and the[n] pulling her to pieces, and this leads not only to considerable expense, but to the presence of a certain number of absolutely unusable ships at all times in Her Majesty's Dockyards."[29]

Prior to the early 1870s the subject attracted little attention. By 1873, however, Goschen informed the Commons a "cause of increased expenditure . . . was the necessity of replacing a number of boilers in our ironclads that had run out their ordinary time of wear and tear."[30] He added a note of alarm, confessing that this phenomenon "gave the Admiralty some anxiety, not so much in regard to the state of the boilers as regarded the expense in the future." The following year Ward Hunt announced the appointment of an Admiralty committee to investigate the matter.[31] The committee, in turn, sat for the duration of Hunt's tenure at the Admiralty, studying the problem without discovering solutions. In 1878 former secretary to the Admiralty George John Shaw-Lefevre pointedly criticized its apparent inactivity: "[B]oilers . . . did not last more than five or six years; and it was clear, therefore, that nearly a whole set of boilers for the Navy had been worn out while the Committee was making its investigations."[32] Ward Hunt's successor, W. H. Smith, could merely agree with Shaw-Lefevre "in thinking that delay has certainly been excessive." Smith explained, however, that Ward Hunt "did everything in his power, short of physical force, to induce the Committee to conclude its operations and present a final Report."[33] The boiler problem defied solution, however. Contemporaries ultimately had to face the realization that boilers wore out faster than they liked. The boiler committee finally recommended useful methods for slowing the rate of deterioration, but throughout the 1870s the problem of corrosion "remained acute."[34]

On the larger subject of maintenance costs, Ward Hunt succinctly summarized matters in 1874: "[T]he cost of repairs of ironclads, according to the experience we have obtained, is far greater than had been anticipated."[35] The *Warrior* had, after seven and a half years in commission, cost £121,000 for repairs, a bit more than a third of her original price tag. Over the course of nine years £65,000 had been spent on the *Defence* and £68,678 on the *Resistance*. Hunt cited further examples, winding up with the *Black Prince*, which, during ten years in commission, accumulated repair costs of "the very large sum of £108,495," with yet another £61,000 anticipated. The First

Lord concluded his grim survey by lamenting, "This seems to be a rather alarming account of what we must expect to have to spend upon repairs of our ironclads."

The ramifications of this alarming prospect were indelibly stamped on the yearly navy estimates from 1871 onward. While the number of workmen engaged in building during the 1870s fluctuated between 4,700 and 6,300, the number assigned to repairs, refitting, and yard manufactures increased steadily from 4,800 in 1870–71 to 10,700 by 1875–76. Furthermore, as the numbers involved in repairs and refitments climbed from 4,800 to 7,500, 8,700, 9,500, and 10,700, the numbers assigned to construction dropped from Childers' ideal of 6,400 to 5,200, to 4,700, before climbing back to 5,200 in 1875–76. Most of the increases in the size of the dockyard workforce during the 1870s provided additional manpower for repairs, rather than shipbuilding. Aside from 1870–71, only in 1877–78 were as many as 6,000 employed on construction. Hence, despite all the virtues of Childers' program as he and his contemporaries envisioned it, it remained a goal to be strived for rather than attained during the ensuing decade. Yet notwithstanding all-but-chronic inability to meet yearly construction quotas, Childers' policy was to have considerable influence on construction policy over the course of the following decade. Although 19,000–20,000 tons of construction annually was ordinarily unattainable, it became the target at which successive yearly programs aimed, so consistently that it might fairly be labeled "the Childers standard."

Retrenchment

Since the expense of repairs and the need to augment the dockyard workforce did not become apparent until after Childers had left the Admiralty, his wide-ranging reforms initially attracted little other than fulsome praise. By no means the least-praised achievement, as might be expected, was the amount of money saved. The *Daily News*, a journal of Liberal sentiments, struck an almost celebratory note upon the presentation of the 1869 estimates, lauding Childers' pleasant manner, business expertise, and capacity for work, concluding that with this combination of virtues "we ought to have the stuff of such a First Lord as the nation and the Navy have long desired."[36] But, stressed the journal's editor, although "the first thought of the new Chief has been to secure greater efficiency; [and] to secure it at less cost . . . there has been no indiscriminate cutting down."

Indiscriminate it may not have been. There was nonetheless a great deal of cutting down. Childers announced that he had reduced the estimates from 1868–69's £10.9 million to less than £10 million, a drop of £1,027,357.[37] For this accomplishment he was, at least according to the *Daily News*, "heartily and deservedly cheered on both sides of the House."[38] Even the Conservative-leaning *Standard* grudgingly admitted the First Lord's "statement last night in bringing forward the naval estimates is fairly entitled to the credit of being at once clear, candid, and comprehensive."[39] It was less generous in describing his policy, claiming it differed "in no material respect from the policy which we ourselves have maintained, and which, so far as the pressure of public business would allow, was initiated by the Conservative Government."

There was more than mere sour grapes to this claim. Corry's draft estimate for 1868–69 showed a savings of almost £660,000 over those of the previous year. He candidly confessed to the Commons "this large reduction of £658,000 was forced on us by public opinion—that we were compelled to be economical on account of the feeling of the country in favour of retrenchment," thus simultaneously trying to undercut Liberal charges of extravagance and, ironically, lending considerable credence to Disraeli's views both on naval spending and the mood of the public. Thus, maintained Corry, Childers' achievement "was not the reduction of £1,000,000 in the Navy Estimates, but only of £356,000."[40] But even the *Standard* observed that regardless of who deserved greater praise for his economical attainments, the cuts were judicious. "There is to be a reduction both in ships and men," it noted, "but the reduction, if we admit its necessity, has been made in the manner least injurious to the efficiency of our fleets, and least damaging to the national prestige."[41] Childers' initial naval budget, indeed, met with across-the-board satisfaction, aside from several laborers at Woolwich dockyard who, presumably motivated by impending unemployment—Childers had scheduled the yard to be closed—were reported to have hanged an effigy of the First Lord.[42]

In most quarters the reception of his budget the following year was, if anything, more rapturous still. "The year 1870," enthused the *Times*, "will form an era in our modern naval history, and people will remember it as the date of the first earnest attempt at economy after a season of unparalleled wastefulness."[43] The editors shared no doubts as to the tenor of public opinion: "It has been a long time since there has been a speech on the Navy Estimates so fitted to interest and satisfy the nation as that which was made last night." The *Daily News* was moved to even more graphic paeans: "There is as much difference between the British navy as it figures in this year's Estimates, and as it figured in the Estimates of a few years since, as between puffy corpulence and the finest muscular training and condition of wind and limb."[44] Even the *Naval and Military Gazette*, which had in 1868 charged Childers with "reckless haste" in his reforms and had likened his policy to "the uncertain, inconsistent, unintelligent, blind, and gusty hurryings to and fro of a straw driven hither and thither by the wind," acknowledged, "No one will hesitate to say that the First Lord of the Admiralty is an able and hard-working servant of the Crown."[45]

The praise was inspired largely by Childers' revelation that the estimates, "while providing for what I believe to be a thoroughly efficient Navy, ... exhibit the lowest charge under this head since the year 1858–9." Yet, he claimed, the sum was "sufficient to provide the country with a thoroughly efficient naval force, unless some disturbing causes, such as a great war, or the reconstruction of our ships, should intervene."[46] The exact figure was £9,250,530, almost £750,000 less than that of the previous year and, as Childers stressed, "just £1,700,000 less than those of 1867–8." Corry, as might be expected, took issue with both Childers' speech and his policies, charging that the latter stemmed from political expediency and Liberal campaign promises rather than from frank assessments of national security needs. "[T]here is," said Corry, "a broad distinction between economy within the limits of what is due to efficiency and economy carried out in fulfilment of a pledge given on the hustings for party purposes, and I cannot doubt that it is under this influence that these Estimates have been prepared."[47] Furthermore, he charged that Childers' claim that naval strength had been left unimpaired by the reductions was suspect. The First Lord claimed that "his economy is regulated by a due regard for efficiency," but Corry, perhaps drawing on his long experience as a naval administrator, added a postscript to Childers' bold statements, observing he had "never known a low Estimate that did not make ample provision for efficiency, nor a high one over which the genius of economy did not preside." The *Standard*, as befit its party affiliation, echoed Corry's critique, charging that the First Lord seemed to "have no other idea than that the British fleet is kept afloat in order to illustrate and defend the principles of economy."[48]

Childers claimed that his estimates were sufficient to maintain a navy commensurate with the needs of the country "unless some disturbing causes should intervene."[49] Ironically, only four months after his speech, such a disturbance did intervene in the form of the Franco-German War. His initial reaction to the mounting tension between the two powers in the midsummer of 1870, however, betrayed little anxiety regarding the strength and state of the navy. On 11 July, with war barely a week away, Childers informed the foreign secretary, Lord Granville, "Our Fleet is in admirable condition & we shall shew in the Channel seven ironclads this month & at Gibraltar about twelve next."[50] This optimistic, if impressionistic, appraisal was quickly reinforced. Childers assured the cabinet upon the outbreak of hostilities that the ratio of British to French ironclads was three to two.[51] Gladstone sounded a similar note in an epistle of 16 July to the queen. "[H]e would be justified," wrote Gladstone, "in stating that the defensive means of this country are greater than they have been at any period since the peace of 1815, except in the year 1856 before the War Establishments had been reduced." Yet there lurked within this letter a curious ambiguity, for the prime minister added that the cabinet had also discussed the question of supplementing the armed forces, but concluded that "it would be impolitic in a high degree to make any proposal at this moment to Parliament respecting the Army and Navy, on account of the shock it would give to public confidence with regard to the position of this country."[52]

Any doubts regarding national security received a substantial boost from a pair of memoranda composed in early August by Childers' chief naval advisors, First Naval Lord Sir Sydney Dacres and Controller Sir Robert Spencer Robinson. The latter, indeed, claimed that the British ironclad fleet was *inferior* to that of France, and, owing to repairs and other problems, the British ironclad force immediately available for service in European waters was but thirty-two ships, six fewer than the minimum he held to be necessary "to maintain a Naval Position suitable for a secure neutrality."[53] To rectify this alleged ironclad gap, the controller recommended a "crash" building program of one seagoing and four coastal defense ironclads, claiming the latter could be ready for sea within a year and a half. These recommendations were staunchly supported by Dacres, who added that even counting Spencer Robinson's proposed additions, "we should not . . . be in a condition such as England, depending alone on her navy for her safety, ought to be in."[54] The controller, incidentally, got around his earlier enthusiastic endorsement of Childers' reforms and economies by claiming he had sanctioned the estimates as suitable *only* for a period of "profound peace."[55] That condition having vanished, so did the approbation he had formerly entertained for them.

Whether due to the urging of the naval members of the board or not, by the end of July the government had changed tacks. Gladstone informed the queen that the cabinet had "determined to lay on the Table an Estimate for a Vote of Credit of Two Millions to increase our Naval and Military strength."[56] Of this sum, £600,000 would be directed toward the navy, to be used primarily, as Goschen put it the following year, "to produce more ships, and for hastening towards completion the dockyard [enlargement] at Chatham."[57] Spencer Robinson's program, plus half a dozen gunboats, were authorized. With this supplement, the final expenditure on the navy for 1870–71 was £9,876,000, rather than the £9,250,000 originally moved by Childers.[58] Even with a £600,000 augmentation, however, it was almost a million less than the lower of the two Conservative naval budgets of 1866–68. Yet it was not low enough to placate Gladstone, as would presently become evident.

Naval Administration

In keeping with his other reform efforts, Childers wasted little time in turning his attention to naval administration. Barely two weeks after his appointment the *Times* reported proposed changes in the structure and working of the board: changes set forth in a memorandum of 22 December 1868 and, ultimately, embodied in a 14 January 1869 order in council. As Childers inherited it, the board of Admiralty was structurally unaltered from the days of Graham. Each of the Naval Lords and the Civil Lord were "assigned a share of the general business [of the navy], which he transacts at the Board," the duties entrusted to the First Naval Lord being "of a more confidential and important character than those of the other three."[59] Of this arrangement Childers observed, "there can be no doubt that the administration of the Board of Admiralty was practically in the hands of four or five distinguished naval officers, presided over by the Minister, those naval officers dividing the departmental business among them, and approaching to the action of a committee."[60] The board itself met "daily, and almost all of the business of the Admiralty is brought before it by the several Lords for discussion and consideration."[61]

Childers found several features of the system objectionable. He acknowledged that "so far as the management and discipline of the fleet were concerned, the arrangements of the Board were not unsatisfactory." In other respects, however, the case was quite different, especially with regard to "those great public establishments: the dockyards."[62] "The practical superintendence of them," he explained, "was divided between three Lords of the Admiralty . . . and under such arrangement it is hopeless to expect distinct efficient responsibility." Moreover, as he pointed out in his memorandum, the position of the controller of the navy, the man directly responsible for the dockyards, was "the most anomalous feature of the present system." "He acts under the supervision of the First Naval Lord . . . and no civilian can be said effectually to control his expenditure." Furthermore, "the double subordination of the Dockyards to the Board," the result of the controller's subordination to the First Naval Lord, "is full of inconvenience." A further consequence, as Childers saw it, was that "the only member of the Board in a position to enforce economy in shipbuilding [the First Naval Lord] is the person most interested in increased expenditure." Of equal importance, especially to a zealous advocate of retrenchment like the First Lord, "no Lord or Secretary is considered specially charged with the finance of the department, i.e., with continuous supervision and control of the expenditure."[63]

Childers' reforms, therefore, aimed principally at correcting these perceived deficiencies: the tangled chain of authority and divided responsibility over the dockyards and the overall lack of financial supervision. But he wished to reform the system "without in other respects disturbing the constitution of the Board of Admiralty."[64] Consequently, no major alteration of the outward form of the board was undertaken—no radical change such as the installation of a minister of marine or, heaven forbid, the implementation of a Bentinckian scheme. Extensive internal restructuring, however, was mandated. First, the "confusion of responsibility" that arose from the anomalous position of the controller was resolved by elevating that officer to board membership and by "putting him in charge of all the matériel departments connected with the building, repairing, and fitting out of our ships." These moves simultaneously relieved the First Naval Lord of the duties that related to the dockyards hitherto performed by him, thereby, it was hoped, reducing his workload. Moreover, the major task of the Fourth Naval Lord—overseeing the supply of naval stores—was eliminated, enabling Childers to abolish the position entirely. Childers also transferred most of the duties of the Third Naval Lord, and those of the Fourth Naval Lord that did not relate to naval stores, to the First Naval Lord. To enable the latter to cope with his increased administrative burden, he assigned a Junior Naval Lord to assist him.

Childers clearly envisioned rationalizing the structure of naval administration through this redistribution: "[T]he First Sea Lord will take charge of all the business connected with the personnel of the Navy[;] . . . the Controller [now titled Third Lord and Controller] will take charge of all the business connected with the *matériel*." The duties of the First Naval Lord pertained to manning, deployment, and fleet operations, those of the controller shipbuilding and repair and the management of the dockyards. This administrative redistribution was accompanied by a physical consolidation of Admiralty offices. Prior to Childers' accession the board was housed at Whitehall, but the coast guard branch and several other offices were in Somerset House, a mile down the Thames Embankment, off the Strand, "a thoroughfare," as the First Lord put it, "constantly blocked up."[65] This division had existed since 1786. The navy board had led a separate existence from the Admiralty and the departments under its direction had followed suit. The navy board's elimination in 1832 had not been accompanied by wholesale administrative consolidation, despite obvious inconvenience—not to say waste—caused by a substantial redundancy in clerks needed to staff the office.[66] The physical division also generated a great deal of needless and time-consuming correspondence between the two offices.

Childers' initiative in transferring the outlying offices to Whitehall was motivated by economic considerations as well as by his desire to rationalize administration. "I found," he informed the Commons, "that two departments were preparing precisely the same books in precisely the same form, and that neither department knew that the other was so employed." He anticipated that the consolidation would result in a savings of "not less than £20,000 a year," to say nothing of "increasing the efficiency of the service." Whatever his motives, the consolidation was long overdue and the chief wonder was that it had not been undertaken by a previous administration. The restructuring was additionally designed to correct a further "great defect of the former system," namely, "the absence of sufficient financial control over the expenditure."[67] During his stint as Civil Lord in

Somerset's administration Childers was especially charged with overseeing the department's expenditure and receipts and, indeed, was styled the "Financial Lord." Evidently he was impressed by the innovation, for on returning to the Admiralty in 1868 he reestablished the position, entrusting it to Edward Baxter, the parliamentary secretary. Henceforth, Baxter was to be "called the Financial Secretary, and all matters connected with expenditure, whether in the fleet or in the dockyards, whether relating to men or ships or stores, will come under his review."

Thus, the Admiralty's business was now divided under three heads—personnel, matériel, and finance—the first to be overseen by the First Naval Lord, the second by the controller, the last by the financial secretary. The First Naval Lord was, in turn, to be assisted by the Junior Naval Lord, the controller, as hitherto, by the chief constructor and his staff, and the Financial Lord by the Civil Lord.[68] Two Naval Lords had been eliminated. Along with this administrative rationalization, Childers eliminated two of the "principal officers" who oversaw departments under the system established by Sir James Graham. The controller, obviously, was retained and, indeed, promoted, but the storekeeper general and the controller of victualling and transport were abolished and their duties assumed by the new department heads, assisted by lower-status permanent officials: the superintendent of stores, the superintendent of contracts and the superintendent of victualling. Finally, all of the department heads were directly answerable to the First Lord, whose supremacy and individual responsibility were explicitly set forth in the order in council.[69]

One further innovation, although not embodied in writing, was to prove the most controversial of Childers' reforms. He introduced a significant alteration in the manner the board conducted its daily business. Traditionally it met almost daily to discuss the general business of the department. In 1866, for instance, there were no less than 244 meetings. Under Childers' system, however, the board meeting became an endangered species. In 1870 there were but thirty-three formal gatherings, most of which sat for only a few minutes.[70] The alteration did not stem from Childers' disdain for his colleagues' advice, the chief commodity of board meetings. Instead, it aimed at increasing the efficiency of the department and at the same time firmly fixing individual responsibility. "Under the former system," Childers testified to a royal commission in 1872, "for two, and

I have even known for three hours a day, when during the six months of the year the parliamentary members of the board hardly had on the average three hours a day for their ordinary business, the lords and secretaries were collected round the table, not discussing grave questions of importance which were settled practically outside, but hearing the recital of the business of others ... a waste of mind which to my mind was appalling." Therefore, "from the very first day of the new arrangements, discussions at the board came to an end, and this was the distinct understanding with those who with me formed the new Admiralty." As for the crucial question of how the First Lord was to avail himself of professional counsel if the board was "practically abolished," Childers conducted informal discussions in his private office with the relevant members of the board on any given matter.[71]

By eliminating formal board meetings, however, Childers also eliminated one undeniable virtue along with the perceived drawbacks. Wasteful, inefficient, and unconducive to establishing individual responsibility the conduct of business in the boardroom may have been, but if nothing else, daily discussions enabled the members of the board to remain abreast of the general business of the Admiralty, beyond the specific duties with which they were charged, thus facilitating coordination of action. To keep the lords informed of the general goings on in the office, Childers' remedy was compiling, printing, and distributing daily synopses.

Despite the speed with which Childers implemented his reforms, they were hardly the product of hasty and ill-considered reforming zeal. Indeed, every significant innovation, with the exception of the de facto elimination of the board as an agent of administration and policy making, sprang from previous suggestions, many of them long-standing. The consolidation of all business relating to the dockyards under one supervisor, answering directly to the First Lord, had been recommended in the report of the royal commission on control and management of the dockyards (1861). It further pointed to the need for "all the departments of the Admiralty connected with the dockyards [to be] brought under one roof."[72] The elevation of the controller to board membership also had numerous advocates, not least of whom was the controller himself, Robert Spencer Robinson, who, by his own admission, "more than once" during his eight years in office brought forward the "question whether the Controller of the Navy was not better at the Admiralty Board than outside it."[73] Childers himself had firsthand acquaintance with the want of overall financial supervision at the Admiralty from his stint as Civil Lord in 1864–65. "I became aware," he testified in 1872, "that practically under the then system there was very little financial control over the operations of the Admiralty.... I determined, therefore," Childers concluded, "to carry out to the best of my powers an entire system of reform in the Admiralty which, during the time that I had been more free and out of office between 1866 and 1868, I had taken every means carefully to study."[74]

CHAPTER 6

Of Captains *and Lords*

Chaos

While the government was responding to the perceived threat posed by the Franco-German War, a conjunction of other circumstances and events during the summer and fall of 1870 brought the Admiralty, by the end of the year, to a state of virtual paralysis, and pushed Childers himself to the verge of nervous collapse.

The initial development was an unexpectedly hostile reaction to Childers' promotion and retirement scheme by the controller, Robert Spencer Robinson. Indeed, from the spring of 1870 to his forced resignation a year later, Spencer Robinson was a disruptive and, ultimately, destructive element at the Admiralty.[1] In early 1870 Childers took the bold step of instituting mandatory age retirement for flag officers, following up on a series of earlier reforms that had applied the practice to the lower ranks.[2] By so doing he earned the undying enmity of many of the service's senior officers, who saw their position and privileges unceremoniously stripped from them.[3] The response of those forcibly retired was, for the most part, no surprise to Childers. What was unexpected was the indignant reaction of his trusted and valued subordinate, the controller of the navy. Spencer Robinson was not retired from the Admiralty; since the controllership was a civil position, his removal from the navy's active list—the wellspring of his discontent—did not force him to relinquish his post. Nor was he mandatorily retired on account of age. Rather, he was removed from the active list because Childers also stipulated enforced superannuation for flag officers who had not served at sea for ten or more years.[4]

Spencer Robinson had not served afloat since the 1850s; he was appointed to the Admiralty in 1861 and had subsequently been there without interruption. The controller maintained that his Admiralty service—despite being a civil appointment—should count as "sea time," pointing out that it had been counted thus by the Duke of Somerset when an earlier retirement scheme had been implemented in 1866.[5] He was correct, but Childers' plan of 1870 eliminated the dispensation that had allowed Admiralty service to count as sea time, probably on the recommendations of First Naval Lord Sir Sydney Dacres, Junior Naval Lord Sir John Hay, and Civil Lord the Earl of Camperdown.[6]

At the best of times Spencer Robinson was a difficult man with whom to deal. Dacres wrote Sir Alexander Milne privately in March 1870: "Robinson is furious, that is his 'normal' state so it does not matter if he has an additional reason or not."[7] But goaded by his involuntary retirement, from March through early June he bombarded Childers with "repeated remonstrances" that he be spared the working of the retirement scheme. The First Lord's action "appeared to me," he wrote, "to involve injury to the Public Service for the future . . . and a direct and needless breach of faith as regards the past."[8] Moreover, he claimed Childers himself had led him to believe "for some time past" that he would strive "to make some arrangement which should remove from my mind the feeling that I have been unjustly treated."[9] Childers refused to make an exception, aware that to do so would be denounced as favoritism.[10] But it was clearly a difficult decision for the First Lord. He described Spencer Robinson to Gladstone in March, when trouble first loomed, as "a most valuable officer in the management of the Dockyard & construction business; and nothing could be more painful to me than any difference with him."[11] In fact, Childers went out of his way to accommodate Spencer Robinson's wish to avoid removal from the active list, offering to appoint him to the then vacant command of Sheerness Dockyard, a move that would fulfill the ten-year clause, although it would also mean relinquishing the controller's post.[12] For the sake of fairness Spencer Robinson could be offered only one or the other, and Childers made no secret of the fact that he hoped the controller would remain at the Admiralty: "because the entire confidence placed in you by Her Majesty's Government, and by no member of it more than myself, justifies me in anticipating great public advantage from your continued advice and assistance in the office of Lord of the Admiralty and Controller of the Navy; the duties of which you discharge with such conspicuous ability and success."[13] Should Spencer Robinson choose to stay at Whitehall, he was assured, he would be classed as a "Supernumerary Vice Admiral" and would "retain, in full, the position and authority of any other Flag Officer on the Active List, except that you would not be eligible to hoist your Flag."[14]

The controller wanted the best of both worlds, however: to remain on the active list *and* to stay at the Admiralty. On 1 June he addressed a confidential letter to the First Lord, asking to be exempted from enforced retirement.[15] Childers' refusal then sparked an indignant follow-up letter, in which the designation of "Supernumerary Vice Admiral" was derided: "[I]t leaves me de facto retired, stamps me as incapable of command and . . . offers me an official assurance which on reading over again I am sure you must see is wholly illusory and of no value whatever."[16] Moreover, he again reminded Childers of Somerset's promise that service at the Admiralty would count as sea time, while at the same time heaping scorn on the offer of the Sheerness command. Childers' response to this insubordinate and intemperate missive was astonishingly mild, a measure of how highly he valued Spencer Robinson's abilities. Indeed, he merely requested further information on the guarantee that Spencer Robinson claimed had been given him by Somerset. Had the controller been able to produce concrete evidence of such a promise, Childers, doubtless in search of any expedient by which to resolve the dispute, might well have honored it. Spencer Robinson never produced the evidence, evidently because an explicit individual promise was never given by Somerset. Instead, Spencer Robinson replied "I can find nothing in my letter referring to a personal guarantee from the Duke of Somerset."[17] Since Childers steadfastly refused to make an exception to his order in council on the basis of superseded regulations, the impasse continued.

Nor, for that matter, was Spencer Robinson content to harangue only the First Lord. Beginning in April and continuing for almost three months, he badgered Gladstone and his private secretary, Algernon West, sending them unsolicited memoranda and requesting interviews with the former. His object, not surprisingly, was to have Childers overruled.[18] Worse still, at least for the sake of naval administration, the controller's pique spurred outright disruptive behavior at the Admiralty. Admiral Sir Sydney Dacres, the First Sea Lord, wrote privately to his colleague, Admiral Sir Alexander Milne—then in command of the Mediterranean squadron: "Robinson has been in open rebellion ever since he heard that he would be retired under the ten year clause.... [H]e goes in to annoy harass and inconvenience every act of the First Lord's and does his best to obstruct me in every way he can.... Robinson thinks it [his forced retirement] personal and is immersed in his opposition to all that is done or doing."[19]

Meanwhile, naval administration was beset with additional problems. As if the obstructionism and petulance of Spencer Robinson were not by themselves plenty for Childers and the rest of the board to cope with, they were also confronted with overt disaffection from the controller's subordinate, Chief Constructor Edward James Reed. Reed was a highly talented and original naval architect, and an important innovator in iron shipbuilding. But even his admirers admitted him to be a remarkably difficult man with whom to get along.[20] Childers' private secretary, Captain Beauchamp Seymour, somewhat of a gossip, wrote Sir Alexander Milne in May 1870: "Mr. Reed, I believe, is about to tender his resignation (for the 14th time) because we have declined to arm the British Navy with untried Whitworth Guns!"[21] Possessed of an exceedingly caustic tongue, the chief constructor also actively relished controversy and argument, and while many—though by no means all—of his contemporaries were willing to acknowledge his professional brilliance, many more doubtless wished it was accompanied by a somewhat less acerbic personality.

Curiously enough, despite Spencer Robinson's easily wounded vanity and Reed's abrasiveness, the two men worked together closely and often successfully, with no evident friction, producing and building some of the most revolutionary warships of the 1860s. Hence, it was no cause for surprise that when the Controller fell out with Childers in the spring of 1870, Reed eagerly pitched into the fray as well, partly, one suspects, out of loyalty to Spencer Robinson, and partly because of his bellicose nature. The controller repeatedly threatened resignation during the course of his campaign to be restored to the active list, and Reed followed suit, support for Spencer Robinson his stated motive. Seymour reported to Milne in midsummer: "There was an idea here the other day that Robinson & Reed really meant going as the Controller was violent beyond measure. C[hilders] was all prepared with people to replace them, but Robinson remains & so I firmly believe will Reed, though he is trying to make terms such as no one with an atom of self respect could listen for an instant, in which he is backed by Robinson."[22] Childers felt it necessary on 27 June to warn the prime minister of this development: "[S]ome one [in Parliament] may ask you whether it is true that Mr. Reed has resigned."[23] Presuming that Gladstone knew nothing of the matter, Childers added that although Reed "has said nothing to me either in writing or verbally about resignation," Spencer Robinson himself had alluded to the threat, and it was, moreover, a poorly kept secret at the Admiralty, owing to the chief constructor's "open-mouthed statements to half the gentlemen of the office."

Yet another factor plaguing naval administration from the spring of 1870 onward, and one more critical to Admiralty operations than even the behavior of the controller and chief constructor was Childers' health. Concurrent with the Spencer Robinson contretemps the First Lord was stricken by illness. He wrote Sir Alexander Milne in early May that he had been incapacitated "with a rather sharp attack of what might have been inflammation of the kidneys," but hoped to be back at work quickly.[24] The hope was forlorn. A month and a half later Gladstone, in connection with the controller's continued hectoring, instructed the chief secretary for Ireland, Chichester Fortesque, to call on Childers, since "you know he moves with difficulty."[25] Nor was the illness simply physically incapacitating; Childers informed Milne, "It produces great depression & physical weakness, & the proper treatment is *absolute* rest.... All of this is not easy or pleasant for a hard-worked First Lord," he lamented.[26] Thus, by June 1870, personal relations between Childers and two of his most valuable subordinates were badly strained, and the conduct of Admiralty business was further hampered by the illness of the First Lord.

Matters reached the crisis stage late in the month. On the 21st, Beauchamp Seymour sent his counterpart Algernon West an alarming communiqué:

Strictly Private
My dear Algy
Pray let me express in writing to you what I would ask you to do.
1. To have this matter [of Spencer Robinson's insubordination] settled one way or another as soon as possible; it is killing Childers.
2. To remember that if this business is patched up now it will only be a temporary relief, and it will break out again as sure as fate. How can a department go on when a constant threatening of resignations is taking place?

> Yours most sincerely, BLS
> Do not on any account mention the names.[27]

The following day Seymour wrote again, reporting the situation to be even more dire than he had earlier said:

> Since I saw you this morning I find a fresh complication and that is if [Robinson] stays Dacres will go.—he says that it is perfectly impossible for him to work with a man who always throws every obstacle in his way, and who gives him no support in the business of the Admiralty. I may add that his health is evidently giving way. He says that he never felt so ill in his life and attributes his illness to worry, the result is that public business is delayed, in fact, not going on.[28]

Seymour's alarm was shared by the Civil Lord, the Earl of Camperdown. The business of the Admiralty was nearly at a standstill.[29]

Moreover, the ire of the controller had by this point become public knowledge. On the 27th the *Times* took cognizance of the situation in a leading article, noting that the "sole ground of complaint" appeared to be Robinson's forced retirement.[30] The journal sided firmly with Childers, proclaiming that Spencer Robinson had, "by reason of a certain hastiness of temper and intolerance of criticism upon his ships, given great offense to naval officers who have been brought into contact with him." Moreover, in threatening his and Reed's resignations unless the retirement scheme was modified, he had "adopted a course which no public services can altogether excuse." As for the chief constructor, not one of the *Times*' favorites, the judgment was harsh: "[I]f he cannot cultivate the lowly virtues of a public servant we think he would do better to retire at once from a position for which he is too great. There are many avenues open to him in private life, through some of which, if he is to be always resigning and never resigned, he would do well to select his course." Such airing of dirty linen can have done little to improve the board's standing in the public view.

The sovereign remedy, as Beauchamp Seymour implied, would have been the dismissal of Spencer Robinson, the wellspring of disruption and insubordination. Instead, the government attempted to placate him. Childers, although tormented in his personal dealings with the controller, remained convinced that he was irreplaceable at his post, which required a great grasp of myriad technical matters. Therefore, Gladstone, to whom Spencer Robinson had repeatedly appealed over the previous weeks, intervened in the affair. The controller's petition that he be exempted from retirement was emphatically and finally put to rest on 23 June.[31] Simultaneously, however, Gladstone attempted to smooth his ruffled feathers, "[Y]our services at the [Admiralty] have been most valuable to the nation, & . . . their cessation [would] be very injurious to the [public] interest. I trust that your disapproval of that portion of the Order [against] [which] you have so strongly protested, will not induce you to resign the duties of the important office [which] you now occupy." The prime minister made a similar statement in Parliament on 27 June.[32] Although he wrote no more than what Childers had repeatedly stated, perhaps hearing it from the prime minister carried greater weight for the latter. For the short term, Gladstone's words of praise had a salutary effect. Spencer Robinson replied with "warm acknowledgments, and sincere thanks [for the] manner in which you have referred to my services," and assured the prime minister "they will be continued so long as you consider their employment to be for the public advantage."[33] The respite was short-lived, however. By fall the obstreperous controller was again at loggerheads with the First Lord and matters would continue thus until the former was finally dismissed, by Gladstone himself, early the following year.

The matter of Reed was resolved much more quickly and permanently. By 4 July Childers could inform Gladstone, "I hear (though I have no official knowledge on the subject) that Sir J[oseph] Whitworth will tempt Reed from us."[34] Whitworth was one of the most successful private armaments manufacturers in Great Britain. To Childers, this information demonstrated that Reed's proclaimed "adherence to Robinson's fortunes was clearly a pretense, not creditable to him." Reed himself admitted in his official letter of resignation that he had "accepted a valuable offer which has been made to me by Sir Joseph Whitworth," but added "I have no desire to discuss, or even to mention, those circumstances which make the office I have held less desirable than it might otherwise be."[35] Whatever the true reason, Reed left the Admiralty on 8 July 1870, to become a vociferous critic of Britain's naval and, especially, shipbuilding policies in the press and, after 1874, in Parliament.

With Reed gone and Spencer Robinson temporary mollified, the Admiralty's coherent and forceful response to the outbreak of the Franco-German War in late July was no surprise. Indeed, Beauchamp Seymour had observed to Milne immediately prior to the chief constructor's exit, "if we can only get rid of Reed, whose impudence passes all belief, we may have a chance of getting on."[36] Presumably the sense of urgency that the crisis engendered induced Dacres and Spencer Robinson to put aside their differences and cooperate for the good of the service. Much credit, however, was undoubtedly due Dacres individually. During Childers' lengthy illness, it was he who supervised the day-to-day operations of the navy. Moreover, the First Lord himself was well enough to attend the cabinet meeting of 23 July, at which he assured his colleagues of the adequacy of the navy's strength and condition. Still, it appears that the memoranda by Dacres and Spencer Robinson advocating the supplementary building program eventually adopted by the government were generated voluntarily, rather than at Childers' specific request. Furthermore, it seems that the program was conceived by the controller, and merely approved *ex post facto*.

Possibly Admiralty affairs would have returned to the unhappy and unproductive status quo antebellum once the war scare receded, or, perhaps Childers' health would have improved during the waning months of 1870, enabling him to reassert his authority over the department and thereby restore a semblance of order and efficiency. Fate was not cooperative, however. Instead, as Beauchamp Seymour predicted, personal antagonisms resurfaced with increased fury in the wake of the most dramatic and costly tragedy to befall the Victorian navy. On the morning of 7 September 1870, the Admiralty received a telegram from the commander of the Mediterranean Squadron, Sir Alexander Milne: "I very much regret to send painful intelligence. Her Majesty's Ship "Captain" must have foundered during the night. . . . All have unfortunately perished."[37] Behind the *Captain* disaster lay a lengthy and twisted saga that, in turn, sowed the seeds of discord that would reduce the Admiralty to paralysis and by year's end cause the complete collapse of Childers' health.

The Captain

Years earlier, during the siege of Sevastopol, a junior navy officer, Cowper Phipps Coles, conceived the idea of mounting a heavy gun or two on a turntable, covered by an armored "cupola" and situated on a flat raft, so as to allow the guns—themselves impervious behind armor—an uninterrupted arc of fire. Contained in Coles' flash of inspiration was the genesis of the turret design, although it might be noted that Swedish inventor John Ericsson came up with a strikingly similar notion independent of Coles. Following his return from the Crimean War, Coles lost little time trying to drum up interest in his novel design. A tireless publicist and self-promoter, he eventually enlisted the support of no less than Prince Albert, who was not above personal intervention on behalf of the inventor. The prince wrote then First Lord of the Admiralty, the Duke of Somerset, in December 1860, "I hope you will take the resolution and give the order to build one of Captain Coles's ships *at once*, with such modifications as may be suggested by him.... Should Captain Coles's plan succeed, his ships will be vastly superior to those we are now building."[38]

The Admiralty, however, was far less enthusiastic than the prince consort. First, as long as ships continued to rely largely on sail power, a seagoing Coles-style turret ship was unattainable, owing to the impediments to unrestricted fire posed by masts and rigging. Second, even after improvements in steam technology enabled designers to dispense with masts and sails in some classes of warships, the navy remained lukewarm to Coles' schemes. The reluctance largely stemmed from doubts as to the seaworthiness of a seagoing turret ship, and were shared by Spencer Robinson and, after he was hired in 1863, Edward Reed. The weight of the gun, turntable, and surrounding turret could easily compromise the stability of any contemporary vessel—typically no larger than 10,000 tons displacement—if placed more than a few feet above the waterline. Mounting on a low-lying raft would ensure stability but, like Ericsson's *Monitor* design, render the resulting vessel unfit for anything but coastal and riverine operations.

Coles was no naval architect, to be sure. Indeed, Spencer Robinson, who boasted a considerable grasp of the principles of warship design, at one point informed the board of Admiralty, "Captain Coles is completely ignorant of the very first principles of Naval Architecture as a science and from want of knowledge proposes designs which are utterly impracticable."[39] Yet notwithstanding the soundness of this appraisal—and events were to show it very sound indeed—the commonsense stubbornness of Spencer Robinson and Reed in resisting Coles' lobbying triggered a vicious journalistic campaign. Throughout the mid- and latter 1860s several organs of the press, the *Times* prominent among them, carried out a vehement, often scurrilous, war of words with the Admiralty, the chief aim of which was to bludgeon reluctant naval administrators into adopting Coles' design.

Whatever his shortcomings as ship designer, Coles was a master at enlisting popular support. The *Times*, relatively late to enter the fray, typified the stance, if not the tone of the press when, in May 1868, it charged that "although the turret-system, combined with low freeboard, is the only method known of carrying with steadiness heavy guns at sea, the Admiralty have hitherto persistently set their face against it."[40] Two days later the journal further claimed that "the Admiralty, undeterred by all the former blunders of the Chief Constructor, are rushing blindly on" in the wrong direction.[41] The *Naval and Military Gazette* was equally caustic: "A benighted traveller wandering along ill-defined and intricate bye-paths, which lead in every direction across a vast open plain, and not knowing which would take him to his journey's end, fitly represents the present pitiable position of the Constructive Department of the Admiralty."[42]

Ironically, by the time the *Naval and Military Gazette* asked "when all this would end," the Admiralty had bowed to the pressure of political, press, and public opinion, and taken the unprecedented step of allowing Coles, in conjunction with Lairds shipbuilding firm, to design and build a vessel for the navy to his own specifications.[43] The Duke of Somerset's administration first agreed to the project before the Liberals fell from power in mid-1866, and their Conservative successors set the terms under which Coles and Lairds were to share responsibility for the resulting vessel. The design that emerged had not only turrets and low freeboard, but also a full sailing rig, despite being a significant departure from Coles' original conception. The inventor would stop at nothing to best any ship designed by the Admiralty, sails or no. The board did nothing to interfere. Unveiling the navy estimates in 1867, Secretary to the Admiralty Lord Henry Lennox assured the Commons that Coles had "been allowed to chose his own tonnage, his own specification, and his own builder, in order to give the country a fair trial of his system, on the results of which we may be able to rely with safety."[44] Hence, the *Naval and Military Gazette* grudgingly acknowledged, "At last a feeble attempt has been made to interfere with the tyrannical monopoly exercised by the Controller's Office, and one solitary ship on the Turret principle of Captain Coles has been permitted to be built in a private yard."[45] The journal continued, however, to bemoan "until this ship shall be completed the control of the Controller and the preponderance of the antiquated broadside system remain intact." And it remained dubious whether Coles' ship would be given a fair trial. "Even when the *Captain* shall be completed, we have the almost certain prospect of seeing the same system of jockeyism applied to her, as was so perseveringly used to keep the *Royal Sovereign* in the background."

The *Royal Sovereign* was an earlier Coles design, intended and employed as a harbor defense vessel, but the Admiralty's wholly reasonable refusal to try the ship at sea was widely seen as confirmation of Spencer Robinson's and Reed's pernicious influence, denying Coles an opportunity for triumph and vindication.[46] Unfortunately, the result of public, press, and political pressure on the Admiralty was to bear out their objections to Coles' combining full sailing rig and low freeboard in his design in a particularly spectacular and tragic fashion. Barely six months after being commissioned, the *Captain* was struck by a squall in the Bay of Biscay and capsized.

At first glance there would appear to be nothing in the horrifying tale of the *Captain* to fuel renewed—and heightened—acrimony at the Admiralty. The ship had been authorized and its design sanctioned by previous administrations, and of the three men who were at the Admiralty both in 1866 and in 1870, all three—Dacres, Spencer Robinson, and Reed—had been unswervingly hostile to the proposal from the start.[47] Yet the country was soon treated to the unseemly spectacle of fingerpointing, accusations, counter-accusations, implications, and exculpations by most of the principals.

Coles himself took no part in the mudslinging, having gone down with his creation. Along with him went all but eighteen of the crew of 490, among them the sons and nephews of several leading politicians, including Sidney Herbert, Sir John Pakington, Lord Northbrook, and, significantly, Hugh Childers himself, whose second son, Leonard, sailed as a midshipman on the ill-fated ship. Thus, Childers, both for personal and professional reasons, was crushed by the disaster. A week after the *Captain*'s disappearance he wrote Sir Alexander Milne from the continent, where he was attempting to recover from his persistent illness: "I shall remain here for a few days longer, as I am hardly equal to much just now."[48] He was to remain away from London, moreover, until mid-October, and in his absence the business of the navy was entrusted to Sir Sydney Dacres, assisted by two former naval administrators, Viscount Halifax (who as Sir Charles Wood had served as First Lord from 1855 to 1858) and Lord Northbrook.[49]

But even prior to his return, insinuations that Childers had sent the *Captain* to sea despite the misgivings of his advisors were aired in public. Reed, taking advantage of his severed relations with the Admiralty, lost little time in proclaiming that he knew the *Captain* to be unsafe, but that the First Lord refused to be swayed from his bias in favor of Coles' design. Taking its cue from the former chief constructor, the *Times* baldly stated, "The *Captain* was unfit for sea, exactly as Mr. Reed said she would be. She could not swim, which was just what he prophesied."[50] Further damaging statements were made by Reed at the court martial held to probe the circumstances of the *Captain*'s loss.[51] On 3 October he claimed, "As soon as the news of the *Captain*'s disappearance came to this country, I concluded that she had capsized under the pressure of her canvas; and while I believe from such information as one can gather, that it might have been quite practicable so as to spare the canvas on the night of her loss, my conviction is that the evil day would only have been deferred."[52] Moreover, when asked point-blank by the court if he had "from the first mention of the *Captain*'s construction up to the time of her loss any misgiving as to her stability and seaworthiness," Reed replied, "[U]ndoubtedly." Finally, the former chief constructor explained his departure from the Admiralty in terms that implicated Childers in the disaster.

It was, of course, beyond dispute that Reed and Spencer Robinson "from the beginning believed the characteristic feature of the ship [its low freeboard] to be wrong." Reed, indeed, went to considerable lengths to emphasize his lack of responsibility for the design, claiming (after the fact) he felt "that the time would come when it would be necessary for us to prove our exemption from ... responsibility." Reed's claim that the *Captain* had its zealous partisans at the Admiralty was equally true, especially with regard to Childers himself. As Dacres informed Milne in August 1870, when the Admiralty was contemplating enlargement of the shipbuilding program, "Childers ... is all for more *Captains*."[53] Yet Reed's testimony at the court martial was a disingenuous blurring of truth and falsehood. Although convinced from the start that the *Captain* would prove unseaworthy, there is no indication that he or Spencer Robinson—the latter of whom was on board for one of the vessel's trial cruises—ever suspected the ship to be downright unsafe. The distinction may appear little more than semantic, but it is crucial to understanding subsequent actions, especially those of Childers.

If Reed thought the *Captain* dangerously unstable, he never gave tongue to his thoughts prior to the disaster, regardless of his claim to the court martial. As Dacres reported to Northbrook following Reed's testimony, "You must take Mr. Reed's evidence with a great deal of dilution; he never in his life expressed fears of the *Captain*'s safety to anyone, unless it was to Childers in reference to a proposal of the First Lord's to build a ship something like her, nor can I find a line in the office giving even a shadow of an apprehension of danger."[54] More damning to his case, prior to the disaster Reed publicly attempted to claim partial credit for the ship, which was then being hailed as the best and most powerful ironclad in the fleet: "I now come to the assumption," he informed the *Times*' readership, "that the turret ship *Captain* has proved Captain Coles right, and the Controller of the Navy and myself wrong; and I state with the utmost confidence that the *Captain* proves precisely the contrary, for she is in flat and open contradiction of all the crude ideas and early contentions of Captain Coles, and is a vindication of what the Admiralty have always believed and acted upon."[55] Reed's opinion all along was, at worst, that the *Captain* would prove unseaworthy and, indeed, he elaborated such sentiment at one point in his testimony.[56] His subordinate and eventual successor as chief constructor, Nathaniel Barnaby, spoke more generally for the entire controller's department in the course of his testimony: "The Controller of the Navy never supposed, I understand from the correspondence I have seen, and from what I know of the facts, that the *Captain* would be in danger of capsizing; his objections to her on the grounds of want of seaworthiness were, as I understand it, never pushed to this point."[57] In addition, remarked Barnaby, even after experiments had confirmed that the ship had a fairly narrow range of stability, the department still "saw nothing ... to cause us to apprehend, in the face of the reports of the officers who had tried the ship at sea, that she was in danger of capsizing."[58]

For Childers, however, and for the government and navy, the crucial point was less what Reed knew or thought prior to the disaster, than what impression his testimony created in the public mind. His pronouncements strongly implied, if they did not explicitly state, that not only had the *Captain* been built in defiance of his and Spencer Robinson's misgivings and objections—which was beyond dispute—but that it had been sent to sea by the Admiralty, and in particular by Hugh Childers, in defiance of Reed's expressed opinion that the ship was not merely unseaworthy but downright dangerous. The impression thus created cannot have been weakened by the official verdict of the court martial: "[T]he *Captain* was built in deference to public opinion expressed in Parliament, and through other channels, and in opposition to the views and opinions of the Controller and his Department, and ... the evidence all tends to show that they generally disapproved of her construction."[59] In short, Reed's charges gave rise to widespread public doubts as to the competence—not to mention the objectivity—of the board of Admiralty, in particular the First Lord.[60] And these doubts, in the wake of the fierce controversy surrounding many of the Admiralty's ironclad designs, also led to a crisis of confidence in the safety of much of the fleet. By early 1871 the *Times* was denouncing a new class of six ironclads—designed by Reed—as "a strange freak of the Constructive Department, which is now the derision of Naval officers, and has been attended by miscalculations of displacement almost as great as those of the unfortunate *Captain*."[61] In the House of Lords, the Earl of Lauderdale charged that two ironclads then under construction were equally unsafe, contending that they "were not fit for general sea service—that if forced out against a very heavy head sea they would founder."[62]

The peril to the Admiralty's—and indeed the ministry's—standing in the public view could hardly escape the notice of the cabinet. Hard on the heels of Reed's testimony to the Court, Northbrook wrote Dacres,

> It appears to me to be essential, for yourself especially [Dacres had given the specific order attaching the *Captain* to the Mediterranean squadron], as well as for the Board of Admiralty, that the impression conveyed by Mr. Reed's evidence should be removed.
>
> He should, I think, be recalled and asked distinctly whether he did or did not communicate the facts of calculations in his possession, as well as his opinions, formally and officially to his superior officer Sir Spencer Robinson.
>
> If he did, the reports should be produced; and Sir Spencer Robinson should be examined to ascertain whether he brought them before the Board of Admiralty....
>
> I must urge upon you in the strongest manner the responsibility which will rest upon the Board of Admiralty if they can interpose now to render the inquiry complete, and omit to do so.... Be assured that it is quite as much in your interest as that of the Public that the inquiry should be full, searching, & complete.[63]

Northbrook's warning came too late; on the same day he wrote Dacres urging haste, the court completed its inquiry and adjourned. Reed was not recalled to the stand, nor was Spencer Robinson ever called to testify.[64] Consequently, the former's remarks went unchallenged. Moreover, the court's expressed opinion, which reinforced the impression created by Reed's testimony, was followed by a further indictment of the Admiralty. The *Captain*'s stability, it was stated, "proved to be dangerously small," and its spread of canvas "excessive." Moreover, the verdict inferred that the Admiralty was at best precipitate and at worst criminally negligent in sending the *Captain* to sea: "[T]he Court deeply regret that if these facts were duly known and appreciated, they were not communicated to the officer in command of the ship, or that, if otherwise, the ship was allowed to be employed in the ordinary service of the Fleet before they had been sufficiently ascertained by calculation and experiment."[65]

Under the circumstances, government action to stem loss of public confidence in the navy was a forgone conclusion. Indeed, on the same day he urged Dacres to have Reed recalled to the stand, Northbrook wrote Algernon West, setting forth his views as to the critical need for action:

> My dear West
> I am sorry to say that my anticipation that the Court Martial on the loss of the *Captain* would not fully investigate the case has not proved to be unfounded. . . .
> I feel that it is essential to make this inquiry complete. . . .
> The point is very precise—
> Were the Constructors' Dept of the Admiralty in possession of mathematical calculations proving the Captain to be dangerous under sail?
> Did Mr. Reed, chief constructor, entertain that opinion?
> If so, did he make a report to his superior officer Sir Spencer Robinson?
> Did Sir Spencer Robinson make any report to the Board?
> Did he report his own opinion of the *Captain* to the Board after his cruise, and if so, what was it?
> If any Reports were made to the Board, how were they dealt with?
> What instructions were given to Captain Commerell, Sir T. Symonds, Sir A Milne, & Captain Burgoyne as to the trials of the *Captain* at sea?
> If I had supposed that all this would not have been fully investigated by the Court Martial, I should have tried to secure a full investigation by employing counsel, and even now, if I fail to induce the Admiralty to interpose, I think I shall make an attempt.
> I told you my feelings which are most truly in no way to desire to punish any one for the calamity but to insist, if no one else does (and I have the greatest repugnance to appearing in the matter) for the protection of others who may be employed in experimental ships that the terrible responsibility, which appears from Mr. Reed's evidence to rest somewhere, should be brought home.
> I should be much obliged to you to show this letter to Mr. Gladstone, for in the absence of the 1st Lord I almost think the decision, whether the inquiry should be completed or not, ought to rest with him.[66]

Childers shared Northbrook's desire to clear the air of the misconceptions generated by Reed's statements, and to assign the "terrible responsibility" to the proper parties. On 18 October, the First Lord, freshly returned from the Continent, addressed the matter himself in a missive to the prime minister, setting forth his views as to what should be done to restore faith in both Admiralty administration and—equally important—the safety of the navy's ironclad fleet. His first task, he informed Gladstone, "has been to make myself thoroughly [the] master of everything done or said about the Captain.... There are," he continued, "two distinct questions (1) What has been done by successive Boards of Admiralty, which on very imperfect evidence, has been the subject of remark & etc by the Court Martial; and (2) What ought to be done to obtain the best scientific opinions on the questions which this calamity has reopened." As a solution to the first he proposed to draft an official statement setting forth the history of the *Captain* from its ordering to the ill-fated decision to send it to sea. As for the equally crucial matter of restoring public confidence in the safety of the ironclad fleet, he thought the appointment of a commission made up of professional and scientific authorities "may be desirable."[67]

The initial step was taken on 15 November, with the issuance of an Admiralty minute on the findings of the court martial. It took exception to several of the court's verdicts, not the least of which being that the latter passed "so grave a reflection upon 'public opinion,' upon 'Parliament,' and upon the 'Board of Admiralty,' [without ever having] examine[d] any member or Secretary of either the present or late Boards of Admiralty, or even the officer who then as now held the appointment of Controller of the Navy." "Thus," it continued, "the 'conviction' which the Court-Martial has felt it necessary to record as to the motives of Parliament and the Board of Admiralty, in failing to comply with the views of the Controller and his Department, is based on the evidence given by two subordinates of that Department, and by the late Constructor of the Navy." Further criticism was leveled at the conclusion that the danger of the *Captain*'s design was either unknown, or withheld from those on board the *Captain*: "My Lords regret that this part of the finding which imputes blame to parties who are not named, should have been expressed in language obscure ... and also conditional instead of positive." Most crucially, however, "It was in the competence of the Court, and indeed was its duty ... to have clearly established by evidence when and by whom the fact of her stability being 'dangerously small' ... was ascertained, to whom the fact was reported, and what action was taken." In short, the board minute criticized the court for not having definitively determined who bore responsibility for the disaster, and "[t]heir Lordships may add that an official Minute is in course of preparation which ... will, so far as is possible, make good this deficiency."[68]

The official minute—Childers' work entirely—was completed by the end of the month and published in mid-December.[69] In it the First Lord laid out the entire correspondence that led to the Admiralty's decision to allow Coles free rein in building the *Captain*, and all subsequent papers relative to the ship's construction, the Admiralty's acceptance of it, reports of sea trials, and experiments as to its stability, right up to the disaster.[70] Following this lengthy recitation, Childers added his own judgments as to who bore responsibility for the *Captain*'s loss. Initially, wrote the First Lord, "Captain Coles and Messrs. Laird accepted entire responsibility for [the *Captain*'s] design, and ... the Controller of the Navy and his officers were for the time relieved from any responsibility."[71] But, he added, at the point that the vessel was ready to be tried at sea, "the Controller of the Navy and his officers became responsible for the *Captain*'s fitness to go to sea; so if they had reason to apprehend danger from her trials, it was their duty to make representations accordingly." The responsibility imputed stemmed from Spencer Robinson's office passing judgment on the ship before it entered service (and before the Admiralty would pay Lairds); were it not fit to go to sea or otherwise defective, Spencer Robinson should have alerted the board.

Curiously, in mid-March 1870 Reed advised withholding the final installment of Lairds' payment on the grounds that the ship had been designed with a freeboard of 8.5 feet, but, owing to overbuilding and careless supervision of the weight of materials worked into the hull, the freeboard upon completion was only 6.5 feet. Reed therefore expressed the "strong conviction that a ship of her size, with this height of freeboard only ... cannot possibly prove a satisfactory sea-going ship for Her Majesty's Navy." Yet rather than advising the rejection of the *Captain*, Reed recommended only withholding the final payment "until the ship has been thoroughly tried at sea." Spencer Robinson did not go so far. "Considering all the clauses of the contract," he added to Reed's report, "and the speed the ship has attained [in trials], it is very doubtful whether, at any future time, if the *Captain* should prove an indifferent sea-boat ... the Admiralty could refuse to receive the ship, as being unfit for Her Majesty's

Service, and in consequence, demand repayment of the monies paid to the Contractors." Therefore, he concluded, "unless it is clearly the opinion of the Admiralty Solicitor that the contract enables us to do this, I do not see any advantage in postponing the final payment until after the ship has been tried at sea." The controller's advice was based primarily on the Admiralty's contractual obligation, yet it is clear that he entertained no doubts as to the *Captain*'s stability. Hence, Childers' minute stated that "[t]hroughout the voluminous reports that were made by the Controller, who watched her first trial at sea, the Chief Constructor, and his assistants . . . no fears were expressed, or even hinted at, that she would be capsized from want of stability."[72]

Furthermore, charged the First Lord, the very fact that the *Captain* emerged from the shipyard with so little freeboard should have prompted the controller's department to calculate immediately its center of gravity and curve of stability. Again, Reed himself had suggested the desirability of undertaking the experiments that would provide this information, writing Spencer Robinson on 26 February 1870 "steps should be taken for ascertaining the vertical height of the *Captain*'s centre of gravity when an opportunity offers." Yet the chief constructor attached no urgency to the procedure, for he added "it is not considered desirable to carry out the experiment before the [*Captain*'s] forthcoming steam trials are completed, or while the weather is so unsettled."[73] Nor did Spencer Robinson perceive any reason for haste. Not until late July 1870 was the experiment carried out. Nor did the results, when finally ascertained, give rise to alarm on the part of the controller.

The report, written by Assistant Constructor Frederick Barnes did point out that "with the coals, provisions, water and ammunition consumed, and boilers empty, the stability is very small, and would not be sufficient to enable [the Captain] to carry a moderate amount of canvas without excessive inclination." But, he added, the expedient of filling compartments in the ship's double bottom with seawater—a simple process—would alleviate the danger. Thus, wrote Barnes, "it is considered that this deficiency is of no practical importance." The assistant constructor did warn of a further hazard, almost sketching out the circumstances under which the vessel actually capsized. Should a sudden gust of wind incline the ship to 15 or 16 degrees while it was in the trough of a wave "and the crest of the wave on the inclined side . . . there would be some danger of the ship foundering." But in this scenario Barnes also presupposed that the sides of the poop deck and forecastle (both of which helped impart stability) had been "shot away" in action. Nothing in the report hinted at any danger under ordinary conditions. When he received the preliminary report on 23 August, Spencer Robinson saw no reason to warn the ship's commander, Captain Burgoyne, or Milne, the commander of the Mediterranean squadron, of the findings.

As for the implication in Reed's testimony that he was cognizant of the danger prior to the *Captain*'s loss, Childers stated "if they correctly describe his anticipations, a heavy responsibility rests upon him, in never having warned the Controller of the Navy of the danger he apprehended, and in having, on the contrary, recommended that the ship should be tried at sea." In sum, despite the "anomalous position" of the controller's department, in which the design and construction of the ship was beyond its control—upon which he laid great emphasis—Childers concluded that "the duty of the Professional Officers to report and advise the Admiralty, as to the fitness for trials at sea of the ship . . . was left undiminished." Therefore, as the *Times* summarized the minute's judgment, "if the Admiralty authorities did not know of the ship's unseaworthiness, they ought to have known it; if they did know it they ought either not to have sent her to sea at all or not to have left her commander unacquainted with the fact."[74]

With the latter part of this verdict there could be no disagreement. Had the Admiralty been aware of the risk of capsizing, as Dacres assured Northbrook, the ship would never have been sent to sea, and if Reed had withheld his apprehensions that it was unsafe from Spencer Robinson and the board, then he bore, as Childers put it, "heavy responsibility" for not having taken steps that would have averted the tragedy. To condemn the controller's department for its failure to recognize the inherent instability of the ship was, however, less fair. With the advantage of hindsight it might seem that the danger should have been ascertained, and the vessel never put into active service. But this was an extremely novel and largely experimental design, and practical knowledge of the seagoing qualities of low-freeboard, masted turret ships was practically nonexistent in 1870. Moreover, it is clear that both Coles and Burgoyne were determined that the ship would outsail its consorts in the squadron, and by crowding on sail—Coles told a friend that he intended to sail the ship "like a witch"—to achieve this end, they contributed in no small way to their own doom.[75] Their actions could not be forecast, nor could they be attributed to the Admiralty. For that matter, as Reed noted, there was no guarantee that any warning from the board would have been heeded by the impetuous, fiercely proud, and megalomaniacal inventor. Finally, the science of determining ships' stability by experiment was all but unknown in 1870. As Assistant Constructor Barnaby—himself responsible for much of the pioneering work on determining stability—testified at the court martial, "Mr. Barnes who made the experiment for the *Captain*, first showed how to perform the operation in a proper and simple manner, and before his time not one ship in a thousand in Her Majesty's navy had the centre of gravity obtained by experiment, and out[side] of Her Majesty's service such experiments are still as rare."[76]

Again, for Childers and the government, the crucial dimension was not whether responsibility had been objectively apportioned, but, rather, whether the public perceived it to have been. The reputations of the Admiralty and the navy both took severe drubbings in the wake of the *Captain* fiasco, first for the disaster itself, then for Reed's allegation that the ship was known to be unsafe prior to its loss. His remarks were followed by the court martial verdict that, as Childers put it, held "unnamed persons" responsible. On top of this judgment, came the board minute of 15 November, followed a month later by Childers' lengthy minute, in which two of his subordinates—Reed and Spencer Robinson—were assigned much of the blame.

Worse yet was to come. The publication of Childers' minute prompted a savage counterattack by Reed in the *Times*: "I learn, for the first time, from Mr. Childers' Minute, three months after the ship's loss, that Sir Spencer Robinson and I were responsible for her safety."[77] For the record, Childers explicitly stated, "[I]n my opinion great allowance ought to be made for the anomalous position . . . [of] the Professional Advisers of the Admiralty."[78] Moreover, Reed himself confessed, amidst his torrent of invective, that he and Spencer Robinson entertained no more than "vague apprehensions" about the *Captain*'s stability, although he pointedly added that had they been aware of their responsibility at that time, they would have made "searching investigations and saved 500 precious lives from that death of horror into which a shameful agitation precipitated them."[79]

Judging public reaction to the Childers minute—indeed, judging any aspect of the tragic tale of the *Captain*—is fraught with difficulty. The acrimonious circumstances surrounding the vessel's construction so polarized press and Parliament that by September 1870 there were few, if any, unbiased observers. The polarization was accentuated by the ship's fate and the subsequent mudslinging by those involved. Captain Sherard Osborn, a close friend and staunch advocate of Coles, who had railed at the alleged obstructionism of the Admiralty throughout the 1860s, did an astonishing about-face in the wake of the disaster, and went so far as to charge the controller's department with manslaughter: "[O]ne of the [Admiralty's] departments has inflicted on the British Navy a loss. . . . In this case 500 lives have been disastrously sacrificed, and a disgrace lies at the door of Whitehall." Nor did Osborn merely urge Childers to identify and punish the guilty parties: "[A] Royal Commission ought to be assembled to consider the lamentable position into which the Controller's Department of the Navy is drifting us."[80]

Reed and Spencer Robinson were not without their own partisans, however. Among them was the ordinarily pro-Liberal *Daily News* which, upon the First Lord's minute, remarked, "Mr. Childers exerted himself with natural anxiety to shift the burden of liability to any shoulders but his own. . . . We are afraid that, on the face of things as they appear, Mr. Childers' eagerness to put himself right touching on the disaster to the *Captain* got the better, not only of his discretion, but of his sense of justice and fair play."[81] The *Pall Mall Gazette*, another journal of Liberal sympathies, termed the minute a "damaging defence." "He [Childers] says it is clear that no danger was apprehended by the Controller or his officers, and we have seen that they were one and all deeply suspicious of the ship. . . . Mr. Childers says that in the absence of warning from Mr. Reed, the First Lord was justified in sending the *Captain* to sea. . . . We cannot see that Mr. Reed's neglect can exculpate Mr. Childers in a case of such notoriety."[82] In contrast, the violently anti-Reed and Spencer Robinson *United Service Gazette* labeled Childers' minute "the most complete, lucid, and fair document we have ever known to issue from the Admiralty. . . . [W]e doubt," it continued, "if that despotic and obstinate opposition which Captain Coles had to endure had not more to do with the fate of the *Captain* than circumstances which seem more immediately connected with it," and Childers was praised for the courage and determination to "resist the bullying of his colleagues."[83]

The *Times* magisterially pronounced Childers' minute "impartial," but the leading journal was itself far from impartial, having been arrayed on the side of Coles, and in opposition to the controller and chief constructor, during the controversy surrounding the *Captain*'s construction.[84] Its verdict supporting the First Lord's findings was therefore not rendered objectively. "The Minute," it stated, showed "conclusively that the Constructors of the Navy failed to recognize the particular danger [of instability]."[85] But despite these and similar pronouncements, Childers, it was widely perceived, in an attempt at self-exculpation, had made Spencer Robinson and Reed the scapegoats for his own blunder in sending the vessel to sea, a perception heightened by the fact that he had repeatedly stressed to the House of Commons the sole responsibility of the First Lord to Parliament and, by extension, to the country.[86]

Regardless of where observers stood with regard to Childers' and Reed's war of words, the ongoing squabble did nothing to improve the standing of the Admiralty, or to bolster public confidence in the navy as a whole. Moreover, steps needed to be taken to put an end to alarming reports about the safety of the navy's remaining ironclads.[87] In mid-October Childers had mentioned to Gladstone the possibility of appointing a commission to pass judgment on the safety and utility of the ironclad fleet, but the idea seems to have originated a few weeks earlier, and not with the First Lord.[88] Gladstone himself, despite his preoccupation with the course of the Franco-German War, suggested a wide-ranging investigation into design and shipbuilding. On 13 October he told Lord Halifax, "I think the time has now come when Childers himself will have to consider the question of an inquiry by Commission respecting iron[clad] ships for naval purposes."[89] Therefore, Childers' reference five days later to a "commission half professional, half scientific," was presumably an acknowledgment of Gladstone's suggestion.[90]

It is likely too that the prime minister's foremost consideration was restoring public confidence in the navy's vessels, rather than getting to the bottom of the tangled *Captain* mess. In short, the inquiry was motivated largely, if not wholly, by political considerations, especially the need to allay public doubts as to the government's naval policy, and fears as to the safety of the battlefleet. The Admiralty's reputation had been so badly battered by the *Captain* fiasco and by the ensuing insinuations by Reed, that only the findings of a clearly impartial, independent, and expert committee could restore public— and parliamentary—faith in the country's first line of defense.[91] It is equally evident that none of the cabinet members who discussed the appointment of a committee (it was decided to employ an independent Admiralty committee rather than a royal commission) on shipbuilding and design in October 1870 had any doubts about the verdict—printed in the parliamentary papers in 1872—such a committee would render.[92] All of the navy's ironclads were safe—at least in terms of intended roles—with the tragic exception of the *Captain*, and on this question neither Gladstone nor Childers, Halifax, and Northbrook entertained any serious qualms, for the committee appointed by the First Lord—concurrent with the publication of his minute in mid-December—was clearly no rubber-stamp for the government. Although chaired by Liberal peer Lord Dufferin, its members were largely distinguished men of science, including the Reverend Dr. Joseph Woolley, Professor William J. Rankine, William Froude, and Sir William Thomson (later Lord Kelvin), and equally prominent naval officers, among them Admiral George Elliot, Rear Admirals A. P. Ryder and Geoffrey Phipps Hornby (related by marriage to both Coles and Conservative politicians the 14th and 15th Earls of Derby), and Captain James Goodenough. "The Committee to examine the Designs upon which Ships of War have recently been constructed," as it was styled—although popularly shortened to the Committee on Designs—was appointed for the express purpose of restoring public confidence in the navy, a purpose that George J. Goschen, Childers' successor as First Lord, bluntly acknowledged in the House of Commons immediately prior to publication of the committee's report in the spring of 1872.[93]

CHAPTER 7

Collapse and Recovery, 1870–1874

Collapse

Although the committee on the designs of recent ships of war was created to satisfy the pressing need to restore public confidence in the navy, its appointment had the unpleasant—although certainly not surprising—effect of further inflaming relations between Hugh Childers and Robert Spencer Robinson. Affairs between the two men remained in a state of uneasy truce in the wake of Gladstone's letter to the controller in late June, but by early November, even prior to the board minute criticizing the court martial verdict, the peace was shattered, and Spencer Robinson was again on the rampage. He first produced his own paper on the loss of the *Captain* and the findings of the court martial in late October, a paper that, naturally, absolved him of any responsibility for the disaster.[1] On Guy Fawkes Day, moreover, the controller requested an interview with Gladstone, to which the prime minister warily responded, "[A]s I presume it may have reference to some aspect of the questions lately raised with regard to the *Captain* & our [ironclad] fleet, I should be very glad to know what you propose should be the subject of our conversation that I may consider it with Mr. Childers."[2] Childers had received no intimation from Spencer Robinson as to what he wanted to discuss with the prime minister, but informed Gladstone, "I had some conversation with him today about the Committee on Construction, & he was to let me have his ideas on Monday. He does not like it."[3]

By mid-December Childers had resolved to do that from which he had shied away during the earlier fracas with his difficult subordinate, namely, to force him to resign. According to a report sent to Lord Halifax and Gladstone by the First Lord, at a meeting between him and Spencer Robinson on 14 December 1870 the latter was induced to relinquish his post at the end of his five-year term, which would be completed on 7 February 1871.[4] This agreement, however, was made immediately prior to the publication of Childers' minute on the *Captain*, and the appointment of the committee on designs. Spencer Robinson reacted violently to the publication of the former, complaining to Childers: "This Minute affects very materially both me and my department, and I was distinctly informed by you that I should see it before it was published. . . . [H]ad I known that your opinion differed from mine as to my duties and position respecting the *Captain*, I could, I believe, without difficulty, have removed the misconceptions under which, as I think, you wrote, and which are embodied in the Minute of the 30th of November."[5]

The appointment of the committee on designs, moreover, occasioned a fresh paroxysm of indignation from the controller, who denounced the step as "an act of accusation against all the public officers who had administered the Naval Service during the period of which the Committee was to extend its investigation, and it was specially appointed against the Controller and the Chief Constructor of the Navy . . . who were both more responsible than the Board of Admiralty for these designs."[6] In his wrath, Spencer Robinson was incapable of perceiving the factors impelling not just Childers (as he was convinced), but Gladstone and the cabinet, to appoint a committee. Such was his vanity that he took it as a personal attack, rather than as a stroke of policy. Had he cared to consider the issue rationally, he would have realized that the government was hardly about to carry out a public inquiry on its own policy unless it was confident of a favorable outcome, an outcome that would, of course, exonerate both the controller's department and the designs it had produced over the previous half decade. Yet owing to pride or political naiveté, Spencer Robinson remained blind to the public dimension of the matter.

Whether or not he was taking a reasoned and rational view of Childers' policies, Spencer Robinson's response to the *Captain* minute and the appointment of the committee on designs had the predictable result of further confounding Admiralty administration. Not content simply to file protests about the First Lord's alleged highhanded actions, the obstreperous controller was, by early 1871, refusing to honor the agreement he and Childers had reached in mid-December. Lord Halifax informed Gladstone in late January, "I understand from Lord Camperdown, Sir S. Dacres, Mr. Baxter, and Mr. Lushington [the permanent secretary] that he does not intend to go. ... This change of purpose," added Halifax, "is more or less owing to Mr. Childers' minute on 'the *Captain*' having been made public, which Sir S. Robinson considers as imputing blame to him individually, & which he considers it necessary for him to answer & that in order to have the command of the papers necessary to enable him to do this he must remain at his present position at the Admiralty."[7] Were there any doubts remaining as to his intentions, the controller laid them to rest in a letter to the prime minister: "I feel that it would be a dereliction of duty to abandon the care of the department before it has been fairly and truthfully placed before the public. ... I do not wish to resign my office, or to take any steps about it, until the committee has made its report."[8] Spencer Robinson assured Gladstone that he felt himself "honour bound to consult your wishes in the matter, to go or stay as you think best," but only after the committee had issued its report.

By this point the beleaguered Childers was incapable of acting on the deteriorating situation at Whitehall. On 30 December the *Times* reported that he had suffered "an ordinary bilious attack" while visiting his banker, but was expected to be back to work by week's end.[9] The expectation was wildly optimistic. A week later Childers informed Gladstone that his illness had returned, adding that were he not better within a few days he should resign.[10] On the 9th his resignation was submitted, but the prime minister, evidently moved by kindness and loath to lose such a zealous and conscientious subordinate, replied, "I hope ... that you will not scruple to take a liberal allowance of time for your recovery before coming to any such conclusion as [your] expressions indicate."[11] To Childers' physician, Dr. Robert Ellis, Gladstone revealed the specifics of his offer: "Let him take 4 [weeks] of absolute rest trusting to others to open his [letters]. ... At the end of the 4 [weeks] let his state be reconsidered. It would then have to be decided whether he was likely to be in a condition of strength and health in [which] he might prudently after some further rest move the [navy estimates] [in Parliament]."[12] Childers ruminated on his chief's offer until 21 January, at which point he accepted, although he warned Gladstone that Ellis specified three months for recovery, and even after that time there was no guarantee of his being able to return to the Admiralty.[13]

On 19 January the *Times* erroneously reported the First Lord's resignation, and although this notice was quickly contradicted by the government, a note reprinted from the *Lancet* the following day left no doubt that Childers had suffered, at minimum, a nervous collapse: "It appears that Mr. Childers is suffering from a great depression of nerve-power, rendering any exertion, either of mind or body, disproportionately exhausting to him.... The heavy pressures of public duties might alone have prostrated a stronger constitution, but when to these is added the grievous domestic trial involved in the loss of the *Captain*, his condition is very fully explained."[14]

It was thus left to Gladstone to effect Spencer Robinson's removal from the Admiralty. Indeed, Halifax maintained that only the prime minister could perform the unpleasant task: "If he ... refuses to resign, Mr. Gladstone is the only person who can say with authority that he as the head of the [government] considers it essential for the Public Service that he [should] no longer continue in his present position."[15] Accordingly, Gladstone wrote the controller at the end of January that, by Childers' account, it had been "arranged ... that you [should] at the expiration of [your] term, [which] I believe is the 7th [February], quit the office in [which] you have earned so much [distinction] as a [public] [servant]."[16] In an attempt to mollify the controller's sensitive feelings, he added, "I need not dilate upon the regret [which] in common with Mr. [Childers] I feel that [circumstances should] have brought about the [termination] of our official [connection] with you: but I wish with these few lines to say that it was Mr. Childers wish (a wish [which] I cordially share) that [your] convenience [should] be consulted as to the precise time & mode for the execution of this [arrangement], in every way compatible with the demands of the [public] service." It was a tactical error. Spencer Robinson, as Halifax had predicted, refused to resign his post until the committee on designs issued its report.

Gladstone flatly refused this demand. Spencer Robinson would certainly have "freest access" to the papers of the controller's department "for the purpose of dealing with the [questions] before the [Committee]." Such access, the prime minister admitted, was "obviously just & right." But, he continued, "I fear it [would] not be possible for me to depart in any degree fr[om] the grounds ... on [which] my recent [letter] was founded."[17] A copy of this ultimatum was also sent to Lord Halifax, who was again overseeing the Admiralty in Childers' absence.

So Spencer Robinson departed the Admiralty in early February.[18] The reaction of the press was mixed. The *United Service Gazette*, long a vocal foe of the controller, was exultant: "[N]o man within the knowledge of its oldest inhabitant ever left the Admiralty less regretted."[19] Likewise, the *Times*, recalling Spencer Robinson's repeated threats of resignation the previous spring and summer, thought it "a lamentable error that the resignation was not accepted the first time it was tendered," since the continued presence of both Spencer Robinson and Childers at Whitehall created "a schism [that] became worse and worse and has ended in positive hostility." For this state of affairs, the journal held, the controller was principally to blame: "[A]fter eight years of undisputed rule in the Constructive Department of the Navy, Mr. Childers was the first to thwart him . . . and his was a temper which could not brook to be thwarted. . . . Neither as a Naval Constructor nor as a Dockyard administrator can we pretend to regret his loss," the editors concluded: "His rule had become a tyranny, and it was well he should retire."[20]

Yet the ex-controller was not without his partisans, including the pro-Liberal *Daily News*, which charged that Childers had hounded Spencer Robinson out of office and had, furthermore, shirked his responsibility by having Gladstone do the dirty work. "Unless the case has some features which have not yet been disclosed, he [Spencer Robinson] has been treated with singular injustice and indiscretion."[21] Even the *Times*, although expressing no regret at Spencer Robinson's departure, was critical of the manner in which it was accomplished.[22]

Administrative Paralysis

> I presume that it is evident that Admiralty reform is more or less on its trial, and that in pushing it forward the First Lord will be subjected to the keenest and most malevolent criticism, both for what he has done and what he intends to do.
> —Robert Spencer Robinson to Hugh Childers, 1870[23]

From their introduction until the *Captain*'s loss, Childers' far-reaching administrative reforms received little commentary aside from glowing praise. The *Times*' initial response was cautious, but unmistakably positive: "Experience only can show how far his reforms are salutary," wrote the editors shortly after the presentation of the navy estimates in March 1869. There was, however, no question in their minds but that "Mr. Childers deserves the praise of great energy and success since he has been at Whitehall," for, among other reasons, "recasting the supreme administrative machinery."[24] The *Times* was not alone. A few days earlier the *United Service Gazette* remarked, "It is with great pleasure that we found ourselves able to acknowledge that our confidence in the intentions and in the judgment of our new First Lord increases from day to day."[25] Even the generally hostile *Standard* mildly observed, "The old board was neither efficient nor responsible. It has been replaced by one on which every member has a distinctive function and a separate responsibility."[26]

By early 1870 the *Times* was singing Childers' praises. "A beginning, and a bold beginning, has been made in that thorough examination and reform of our naval system which has been sought, but sought in vain, from so many Administrations.... This year the British Navy is, as we firmly believe, in a greater state of efficiency ... than at any time within the last quarter of a century."[27] Even in the wake of the *Captain* disaster and the subsequent unsavory public quarrel over blame for the tragedy, the "leading journal" termed the incapacity of the First Lord "almost as much a national as it is an individual calamity."[28] The sentiment was echoed in the *United Service Gazette*: "[W]hatever our feelings might or might not be at seeing the backs of the Gladstone Ministry, we should consider the departure of Mr. Childers from the Admiralty as a serious loss to the Navy and to the country."[29]

The accolades of the public were fleeting, however. By March 1871 perceptions had swung around completely, and Childers' administrative reforms, so recently the subject of nearly unanimous praise, had become almost as widely vilified.[30] The *United Service Gazette*, which in January and February had been unstinting in its praise for the First Lord and his efforts, had, by 25 March, concluded that his regime had been a failure, owing to his disregard for naval opinion, and that he had further erred in failing to hold board meetings.[31] The perceived flaws were as numerous as the criticism was widespread; among the more prominent were the evident underrepresentation of professional opinion in policy decisions, the abolition of board meetings, and the reduction of the number of permanent officials, as well as complaints that the system could not function in the absence of the First Lord, that the First Naval Lord was badly overworked, that the members of the board were ill-informed of the doings of their colleagues, and that there was a want of continuity in administration and policy-making. Finally, the elevation of the controller to board membership, which, along with the tripartite division of Admiralty business, had been the centerpiece of Childers' reforms, was, by the spring of 1871, roundly condemned.

The *United Service Gazette,* rarely a journal to mince words, opined that "[t]he introduction of the Controller of the Navy [to the board] has had its natural effect of intensifying all the evils of the Admiralty, and has made the last state of that house infinitely worse than it was at the very beginning."[32] More reasoned, if no less explicit, was the report of a Lords' committee on Admiralty administration chaired by ex-First Lord the Duke of Somerset, that noted simply that "[a]lmost every witness gave his opinion that the union of a seat at the Board with the office of Controller had been a mistake." "The results of this arrangement have not been altogether successful."[33]

But more than the apparent folly of giving the controller a seat at the board or the chaos that, down to simple matters like filing correspondence, seemed to have followed from Childers' structural reorganization, the main wellspring of discontent with the system he had installed was that the cumulative effect of the "reduction of the naval element" and the practical abolition of board meetings had evidently resulted in "the unmodified supremacy of a civilian First Lord."[34] As the Duke of Somerset put it, "a civilian must have naval men round him. If he tries to go without their advice, he will get into continual difficulties, the public interest will suffer, and the profession of the Navy will be discontented with its management."[35] The public perception was that this was precisely what had happened under Childers' regime. "Especially in the introduction of changes and novelties," wrote the *Times,* "the advantage to be derived from the deliberative action of a Board must be great. If Mr. Childers has not in practice called his Board together, whenever such a matter arose for consultation, we think he has carried his theory too far."[36] Significantly, Somerset's committee, after observing that "[t]he witnesses are ... unanimous in their opinion that the present constitution of the Board of Admiralty is not satisfactory," devoted no less than ten paragraphs to the subject, remarking among other things that Childers' Order in Council (January 1869) had "so far disabled the Board that it is no longer fitted for consultation or for the review of naval affairs"; that "[a] civilian at the head of the Admiralty must ... have advice and assistance from naval men"; and that if the consultative function of the board were to be discarded, "some arrangement must be substituted in order to furnish the information that the Board meetings had hitherto supplied." The article concluded: "The First Lord of the Admiralty can only be acquainted with such [professional] matters through daily intercourse and friendly communication with officers of the Navy. It is therefore of primary importance that the naval service should be adequately represented in the department which regulates naval affairs."[37]

Much of the criticism stemmed, not surprisingly, from the apparent failure of the Admiralty—both in its individual departments and in the actions of the entire board—to detect the fatal flaws in the *Captain* and warn the officers in charge of the vessel of the doubts entertained as to its seaworthiness. Spencer Robinson's departure served only to heighten the public's sense that naval administration was paralyzed. The First Lord, trying to recover from a nervous breakdown, was on a cruise in the Mediterranean; the chief constructor had resigned the previous June; the controller had just been fired; and the navy's newest ironclad had gone down, carrying almost 500 souls with it. Worse yet, the charges and countercharges of blame and responsibility that followed the disaster had been hurled back and forth in full view of the public.[38] In the press, virtually every aspect of recent naval administration, and of Childers' attempts to reform the system, was held up for critical scrutiny, usually with unflattering results. On 19 February the *Times* observed, "[I]t seems to be now assumed that Mr. Childers was rash and ill-advised in introducing into the governing body [the board] alterations which had long been clamoured for," and added some weeks later that despite Childers' successes in other aspects of naval administration, "[T]he Board, like an arch without a crown, fell to pieces when he withdrew."[39] More succinctly, the *United Service Gazette* stated, "The present Board of Admiralty may be described in one word:—Chaos." Moreover, although the journal had staunchly supported Childers' reforms up to this point, it now concluded it was "patent to all that our present Admiralty Administration has not the confidence of the nation."[40]

Attacks on the navy and the government's management of it were equally sharp in Parliament. On 16 February, when Somerset moved for the appointment of his committee "to inquire into the present state of the Board of Admiralty with reference to the recent changes in the constitution of the Board and the practical working of the Department," Lord Halifax, replying for the government, answered, "Although the committee would be inconvenient, he offered no opposition to its appointment."[41] The following day Lord Henry Lennox initiated a debate in the Commons on the state of naval administration, in the course of which he asked "[h]ow long was the chaos and confusion and weakness now patent to all in the councils of the Admiralty to be endured by Parliament and the country?"[42] On 18 April it was Lennox again who sparked a lengthy debate on naval administration by his motion for a select committee to "inquire into the circumstances which led to the dismissal of Vice Admiral Sir Spencer Robinson from the post of Third Lord of the Admiralty by the Prime Minister."[43] Under assault from all quarters, the government's naval administration was, by early spring 1871, badly battered and in need of salvage.

The perception of want of competence, of confusion, of mismanagement, and of lack of responsibility—the very evils that reformers from Graham onward had striven to eradicate—received a substantial boost nine months after the loss of the *Captain* when, on 19 June 1871 the troopship *Megaera* was intentionally beached on St. Paul's Island, "a little-known speck on the charts of the Indian Ocean," to prevent it from foundering.[44] The *Megaera*'s hull was badly corroded, a state that should have been ascertained by dockyard inspectors, should have been reported to the controller's department, and should have prevented the Admiralty from employing the vessel without first undertaking repairs.

Again the Admiralty appeared culpable. As early as 1866 Edward Reed had remarked that some of the *Megaera*'s hull plates were very thin, and in January 1870 the ship's carpenter "explicitly warned" the dockyard authorities at Sheerness "that some of the hull plates were in his opinion dangerously thin."[45] The publication of this information, along with the revelation that the warnings from the dockyards had been "misplaced" in the controller's office, only seemed to provide another indication—were any needed—of the glaring shortcomings of Childers' administrative reforms. As the *Times* scathingly remarked on 8 August, "[E]nough has transpired to show that from undue economy, or simple stupidity, a vessel was sent to sea under conditions which filled people at the time with apprehension, that the warnings given to the Admiralty were disregarded, and that there is good reason for supposing the disaster to be the direct and almost necessary consequence of the state of the ship."[46]

Worse yet was to come, for the scandalous circumstances surrounding the loss of the *Megaera* allowed parliamentary critics of the

Liberals' naval administration—by this point these were numerous indeed—a field day. Lord Henry Lennox led the assault, initiating a full-scale debate on 7 August from which, as a recent authority notes, "Admiralty and government did not emerge with much credit."[47] The upshot was the government's decision, following the *de rigueur* court martial—which fully acquitted the vessel's captain—to appoint a royal commission, chaired by Lord Lawrence, to investigate the circumstances that led to the fateful decision to send the ship to sea.

Still more damaging, were it possible, was the evidence taken by the commission and the report it produced. Especially notorious was the testimony of the Admiralty's permanent secretary, Vernon Lushington, who, in describing the administrative arrangements at Whitehall, informed the commission, "I am called Secretary to the Board of Admiralty, but the Board of Admiralty does not exist, and the business of the Admiralty is all transacted here and there in various compartments, as I may say."[48] He followed this pronouncement with the observation that although outwardly "the machinery of the Admiralty is a board," it was only "the phantom of the old board," a choice of words that created a minor furor in the press.[49] Moreover, the report stated, among other things, "it has been clearly shown to us that the system of administration at the Admiralty is defective in some important points."[50]

Hugh Childers, however, was no longer at the Admiralty when the *Megaera* was lost. As late as 27 February Gladstone held out hopes that the ailing First Lord would be able to remain at his post, going so far as excusing him from regular attendance in Parliament until fully recovered.[51] On 1 March, however, the prime minister informed Lord Halifax "I am afraid the question as to Childers continuance in office must now be considered as decided in the negative."[52] In time, Childers would recover, returning finally to the House of Commons almost a year later. Subsequently he would serve as chancellor of the Duchy of Lancaster during the latter stages of the first Gladstone ministry, as secretary for war and then chancellor of the exchequer in the 1880–85 Liberal government, and as home secretary in the brief Gladstone ministry of 1886. For the moment, however, he was, as the *Times* reported, "[i]n a state which renders it impossible that he should resume the duties of his office. . . . [I]f the cruel kindness of his colleagues had permitted him an earlier relief he might before this have been able to return to the Admiralty with the prospect of a long and useful career in the public service."[53] The prospects that had appeared so bright upon his appointment as First Lord in 1868 were, by early 1871, tarnished, and his system of naval administration, the product of immense exertion and dedication, seemed to have shattered and collapsed in ruins. The promises made three years earlier now rang hollow, and the fruits of his labor were almost universally lambasted. Daunting, therefore, was the prospect facing his successor as First Lord. "It must be universally acknowledged," the *Times* stated in March 1871, "that the Admiralty never required a strong hand to guide it more than at this moment. The ship is at sea and in distress."[54]

Recovery

Gladstone's choice to succeed Childers fell upon George Joachim Goschen (1831–1907), a selection that moved the editors of the *Times* to incredulity, mingled with mirth. "It is Mr. Goschen!" they exclaimed, when the choice was made public. "It is just possible that there may be some surprise at this announcement." Readers were then asked to picture "Mr. Goschen embarking on board an Admiralty tender; Mr. Goschen on the quarterdeck, with spyglass under his arm and the Admiralty pennant aloft, saluted by officers and crew; Mr. Goschen instructed by the Navigating Lieutenant in the mysteries of boxing the compass; Mr. Goschen in the Bay of Biscay; the most sluggish of imaginations can picture a series of tableaux such as these with fresh exhilaration as each successive scene rises on the fancy."[55] The *Naval and Military Gazette* was more puzzled and disquieted than amused by the selection of Goschen. "To us it is no laughing matter, but a very serious calamity, that in the present critical state of affairs at the Admiralty, a gentleman should be appointed First Lord, to whom his best friends can only give the negative praise that besides being a good Liberal and a consistent supporter of Mr. Gladstone, he worked with efficiency and credit to himself at the Poor Law Board."[56] The humor and perceived impropriety of his choice were lost on Gladstone, who, when asked if the reported appointment were true, replied with typical terseness: "Whether the report is credible is a matter of opinion, whether it is true is a matter of fact. It is true, and I am glad of it."[57] Unlike Sir John Pakington in 1866, Henry Corry in 1867, or Hugh Childers in 1868, Goschen could boast no prior firsthand acquaintance with naval administration when tapped as First Lord. Goschen was serving as president of the Poor Law Board at the time of his transferral. But the new First Lord had a formidable reputation for expertise in matters of finance and expenditure, having been made a director of the Bank of England at age 27.[58] These qualities may well have influenced the prime minister's choice.

Goschen's most important task was the restoration of public confidence in the government's naval administration and in the service's ships. By the time he took office the navy's public standing was at a lower level than at any point since the invasion scare of 1858–60, and its administration in greater disrepute than at any previous juncture during the century, save perhaps 1827. And, as the revelations about the *Megaera*'s loss and administrative chaos at the Admiralty became public, it was to sink lower still. It was left to the new First Lord to set matters right, to polish the navy's badly tarnished image, and to convince public and press that the Admiralty could function smoothly and harmoniously.

Goschen himself was fully aware of the pressure surrounding his task, and the scrutiny focused on his performance. Indeed, a note of complaint about the onerous circumstances under which he labored surfaced in a letter to Gladstone in late 1871. "The difficulties in administering a service like the Navy," he stated, "is [sic] immensely enhanced and almost made insufferable by the withdrawal of all confidence from the Board of Admiralty on the part of the public."[59] Doubtless mindful of charges that his predecessor had moved with "reckless haste," Goschen proceeded very cautiously during the early months of his administration. Indeed, he resisted public pressure to set right the Admiralty's machinery supposedly wrecked by Childers' tinkering until the following spring, the principal reason, it would appear, why parliamentary calls for inquiry and reform continued unabated through the remainder of the session and why, as the *Times* put it in early 1873, "We are not surprised that, even with more exciting topics to discuss, the important question of Admiralty organization should maintain its hold on the public mind."[60]

Lack of perceptible action, however, did not connote want of study. Indeed, Goschen gave the subject very careful consideration, and on 6 March 1872 produced a lengthy confidential memorandum for the cabinet that summarized a year's observations of Childers' system, its evident flaws, and proposed remedies. "The experience gained in the three years which have elapsed since Mr. Childers passed his Order in Council ... have been sufficient to show both the merits and the weaknesses of his scheme." Goschen contended that the merits were numerous, but also conceded "the uneasiness which the public feels as to the present condition of the Admiralty, and as to the conduct of its business ... [renders it] clearly indispensable to make at once such changes as have been shown to be necessary by the experience of the last three years, and by the further light thrown on Admiralty administration by the various enquiries and discussions which have taken place."

Goschen recognized six principal "defects" in Childers' system "which have been mainly insisted on [in the press and public debates] and with which I think it expedient to deal to a certain extent":

1. The placing of the Controller on the Board, instead of leaving him as a high officer under the Board.
2. The abolition of two Naval Lords.
3. The discontinuance of Board meetings for any save formal purposes.
4. The limitation of the business of the Parliamentary Secretary to financial matters only.
5. The rigid definition of the duties of the various Lords.
6. The subordination of the Junior Naval Lord to the First Sea Lord as his assistant.[61]

His decision to remove the controller from the board was motivated by the amount of adverse commentary Childers' scheme had generated on this score.[62] "The combination of the two offices of a Lord of the Admiralty and Controller of the Navy," remarked the Somerset Committee, placed Spencer Robinson "in an anomalous position, since he was at once a member of the Board of Admiralty and also serving under the Board of Admiralty."[63] Goschen's remedy was designed to eliminate the anomaly. The controller would no longer have a seat on the board, but neither would he be returned to his old position of subordination to the First Naval Lord: "the Controller should be immediately under the First Lord, without the intervention of a Superintending Lord."[64] Moreover, when the board dealt with business that fell within the controller's sphere of responsibility, he would be able to participate in the discussion, although he could not vote.

Public sentiment also played a role in Goschen's decision to increase the number of Naval Lords. "The feeling is very prevalent," he acknowledged, "that the Naval element is unduly reduced in Mr. Childers' scheme. . . . In that criticism I do not entirely concur," he informed the Cabinet, "but it doubtless would be an advantage to meet that feeling to a certain extent." Simultaneously, though, the

First Lord acknowledged that two Naval Lords could not cope with the burden of duties that devolved upon them. Therefore, the appointment of an additional Naval Lord, quite aside from its effect on public opinion, "appears to me very necessary on administrative grounds, the Naval Lords . . . having no time to give sufficient attention to large and important questions."

To further lighten the Naval Lords' workload, Goschen recommended the creation of the post of naval secretary in place of the chief of staff, one of Childers' innovations. The alteration was not simply nominal. The chief of staff's responsibilities had been ill-defined—Goschen himself termed him an "anomalous officer"—but the naval secretary would have specific duties, being charged with overseeing personnel in much the same way that the controller's staff oversaw matériel. He was to be, like the controller, a permanent officer, and would thus bolster administrative continuity. And to fortify further the professional element at the Admiralty, Goschen proposed appointing a deputy controller "whose special province should be to direct and manage the dockyards," adding that the controller himself was already so busy that "he cannot give that continuous and daily attention to the administration proper which I think essential to their efficient and economical working."

The resurrection of board meetings was practically mandated by the amount of criticism generated by Childers' decision to dispense with them. Goschen's observations on the subject, however, were not those of a man who considered constant discussions by the full board crucial for the proper functioning of naval administration. "I propose to revive the meetings of the Board for consultative purposes," he told the cabinet, "and to submit all important questions where professional considerations are involved, to the Board for discussion." But, he added, "I am not clear in my mind whether any fixed rule should be laid down as to what questions should be submitted, or whether it should be left entirely to the discretion of the First Lord of the Admiralty."

In his introductory speech to Parliament twelve days later he enumerated the considerations impelling his reforms. Only "a very foolish First Lord," he began, would "not avail himself to the full of all the professional advice at his command," adding pointedly, "I doubt whether there ever has been one."[65] As for his own administration, Goschen hastened to assure his listeners, "I frankly say that I consult my naval advisers now every day and on all occasions I consult them as I would consult partners in business, and they consult each other, and we have no difficulty in making ourselves acquainted with all that goes on. . . . [L]ooking," however, "to the fact that constant consultation should be guaranteed—I think it expedient to have regular meetings of the Board for consultation on all the important questions that may arise connected with professional and technical matters." Likewise, to facilitate harmony of action and purpose, and to prevent a recurrence of the administrative paralysis that had accompanied Childers' incapacitation, Goschen proposed "that the Parliamentary Secretary should once again be the 'alter ego' of the First Lord, and make himself, as far as possible, acquainted with the whole business of the Department."[66] He added that this change would "to a certain extent, take his attention from finance," but proposed to meet this difficulty by making the Civil Lord—under Childers' system the assistant of the financial secretary—chiefly responsible for the financial division of Admiralty business: "I should greatly prefer that a *Financial* Lord of the Admiralty should be appointed in the room of the present office of Civil Lord."[67]

Finally, the First Lord saw no reason to alter Childers' tripartite division of Admiralty business under the heads of personnel, matériel, and finance, but he did "not think it advisable to define, so rigidly . . . the duties to be performed by the different Lords. . . . I am entirely of [the] opinion," he elaborated, "that each Lord should have his separate work; but the actual distribution of business between them may, I think, be varied, according to the aptitude of the different Naval Lords composing the Board at different times." Likewise, there was to be a distribution between the three Naval Lords of the duties relating to personnel hitherto performed by the First Naval Lord and his assistant, the Junior Naval Lord. The First Naval Lord's place of precedence as the First Lord's chief advisor remained intact, but the Second and Third Naval Lords were not directly subordinated to him: "[T]he work is too heavy for him to be able to exercise more than a nominal control over it."

Such was the sum of Goschen's reforms, as unveiled to the cabinet and subsequently embodied in his order in council of 19 March 1872. And such was their efficacy that once implemented they rapidly dissipated the furor over naval administration that had raged for more than a year. By the final months of 1872 the storm had completely subsided, to be replaced by a fierce debate over the proper direction of future naval designs and construction.

The Struggle Renewed

Restoration of the Admiralty's reputation aside, Gladstone expected Goschen to take up where Childers had left off, especially in terms of retrenchment. He wrote the former on 16 September 1871, "I have been writing to Cardwell [the secretary for war] [about] the [Estimates], to the effect that we ought in the next Session to present them, [between] Army and Navy, [circumstances] continuing as they are now, with a [diminution] of not less than two [millions]."[68] As for the increased expenditure in 1870 occasioned by the war on the Continent, Gladstone entertained hopes that matters would quickly return to normal, and that it might even aid Goschen's economical endeavors: "From Childers I used to understand that, when the extended or accelerated building [operations] to [which] the Vote of Credit was applied, [should] have been concluded, matters [could] without [valient] effort return to their old course." The prime minister's obsession with frugality was equally evident in a letter written to the queen three months later, in which he maintained that the "reduction of a million and a half in round numbers from the very high [Army and Navy] Estimates of last year would be considered insufficient by a large portion of the Liberal party."[69] No doubt he numbered himself among that portion.

If Gladstone anticipated that Goschen would follow the same economical path taken by Childers, he may well have regretted his choice. The new First Lord's reply to his letter of 16 September was long, involved, and hardly encouraging. While he professed himself reasonably content with the strength of the ironclad fleet, and therefore felt safe to proceed with caution and minimal expenditure on that head, the picture elsewhere was far less rosy. Childers, he noted, had "effected great things by departmental changes; & he had done more. He has impregnated the Department to a very considerable extent with the spirit of economy." This accomplishment, naturally, was all to the good, but one of the side effects, as Goschen pointedly remarked, was that "his successors have less scope for economic reform." Elaborating on this theme, he said, "In the six months during which I have been at the Admiralty and during which I have constantly had my eye on the possibility of further changes in the direction of economy, I must candidly say that in many directions it appears to me that the limit has been reached & that further reductions are almost impossible." Furthermore, he maintained, "I do not see that the public in any given direction is prepared to be content with less naval force. On the contrary, demands are being made for more ships in every quarter."

The First Lord then furnished Gladstone with a detailed summary of the worldwide scope of the navy's duties, aimed at demonstrating that "half our expenditure is not for war service in the strict sense, but for keeping the police of the seas and protecting commerce during times of peace, and for carrying out our views as to protecting semi-barbarous and barbarous races against kidnapping and various forms of outrage.... Philanthropy," he concluded, "decidedly costs money." Of course, he also admitted, there was the possibility of reduction through a further diminution of naval strength. "If the Estimates are to be largely reduced, I feel sure (though of course I can only form a very general opinion at present) that it is only to be done by building fewer ships, and we can only afford to build fewer ships if we make up our minds to reduce our squadrons and to undertake less duties in every part of the world." This, however, was a matter for the cabinet, rather than the First Lord of the Admiralty, to decide. As for his own views, Goschen minced no words. "I quite concur," he assured the prime minister, "in the view that it is most important to us that we should present economical estimates next year.... On the other hand, taking even the grounds of political expediency, it seems to me equally important that there should be no disasters owing to economical pressure ... and, in every direction I must frankly say that I think economy has reached its limits in naval administration."[70]

Gladstone's response to this gloomy prognosis was temperate. "I can well believe," he wrote, "that in many portions of the field Childers has left you little harvest to gather in." Still, he suspected that there was excessive expenditure on repairs, and that advances in the shipbuilding program made possible by the vote of credit "went to anticipate the work of coming years; & in so far as to relieve those years." Under the circumstances, therefore, the prime minister hoped that "the [Estimates] of 1870 [would] be the natural *prima facie* basis for those of 1872."[71]

Gladstone's hopes were dashed. Goschen promised to do his best to "get back to the point of 1870–71," but noted, "That year was in some respects a favoured year as a reduction was made by reducing stocks, an operation that cannot be repeated."[72] The estimates for 1870–71 had originally been £9.25 million; those for 1871–72 showed an increase of some £500,000.[73] As for those of 1872–73, over which

Gladstone and he argued, Goschen apologetically announced a figure of £9.5 million—higher than that of 1870–71, but lower than that of 1871–72.[74] Employing the same arguments in Parliament he had with Gladstone the previous September, he maintained defensively, "Much is spent on the performance of those expensive duties in every part of the world, which consist in keeping the peace, in preserving our commerce secure, and in carrying civilization to the most distant shores."

Such noble sentiments notwithstanding, the ensuing debate suggested that his defensiveness was not misplaced. Radical M.P. Peter Rylands charged that Goschen "had reversed the policy of his predecessor, and by so doing had reverted to the old ways of waste, extravagance, and inefficiency." As for the peacetime duties upon which the First Lord laid such stress, Rylands was sarcastic. "What were these ubiquitous duties?" he queried. "Occasionally there was evidence of some of them in the Civil Service Estimates, when Votes were taken to cover charges of conveying a Bishop on his visitation to the Sandwich Islands, or of entertaining Royal and distinguished personages on board of men-of-war. But it was scarcely necessary to keep up foreign squadrons for such purposes as those." Furthermore, maintained Rylands, by committing outrages and atrocities, the forces stationed overseas did more harm than good and, anyway, he "entirely protested against the doctrine that the taxpayers of this country should be burdened to keep up a Navy 'not for ourselves alone, but for the benefit of the world at large.'"[75] The situation faced by Goschen could not have been comfortable, with Gladstone and the economy-minded Radicals disapproving of his policy on one side, and navalists such as Sir John Hay and Sir James Elphinstone equally critical on the other.

Soon thereafter the First Lord confronted a further headache. In July 1872 he wrote Gladstone on the question of bringing forward a supplementary estimate to cover rising matériel costs.[76] As Goschen put it, "The immense rise of prices is contributing in one way to the revenue while it costs us a great deal of money at the Admiralty." The prime minister opposed the suggested remedy. Supplementary estimates, he maintained, "disturb the annual reckoning with the [House] of [Commons]," although he did admit that "the facts in relation to the rise in prices are very strong."[77] Gladstone's decision carried the day, but additional confirmation of the problem—were any needed—came to him in early December with a long memorandum from George John Shaw-Lefevre, the parliamentary secretary to the Admiralty. It detailed a thirty percent increase in the price of bar iron over the previous twelve months, thirty-five percent in the price of sheet iron, thirty-three percent for copper, and thirty-five to forty-five percent in the price of coal (dependent on type), among the commodities required by the navy. The upshot, according to Shaw-Lefevre, would be a substantial increase in the stores vote for the coming year, "amounting as far as can be ascertained to £140,000."[78] Such news no doubt made unpleasant reading for Gladstone, but worse still was to come. The upcoming estimates, according to the parliamentary secretary, would also reflect a higher-than-ordinary cost for contract shipbuilding and steam engines. Because of these increases, plus the increase in the stores vote, and higher salaries for some dockyard laborers, Shaw-Lefevre warned Gladstone to expect estimates for 1873–74 to be some £480,000 higher than those of the previous year.[79] As the final straw, he informed the prime minister, "It is not possible to reduce materially any other Votes in the Estimates."[80]

Gladstone, of course, was no stranger to disputes with the Admiralty over spending. Although lacking Disraeli's gift for invective, he conveyed his sentiments no less forcefully. "The question of finance," he wrote Goschen on 9 November, "is rather a sore & critical one with [reference] to the coming year. . . . For two years I have given consideration to the [wishes] of the Cabinet; but I must own we do not at present stand four-square with the (very reasonable) Election pledges of 1868." The prime minister saw no reason why these pledges might not be redeemed. The states of the navies of Europe, as well as that of the United States, were such, he maintained, that circumstances were "now favorable [for a reduction of Britain's naval expenditure] in a degree & with a clearness impossible for alarmism itself to overlook or misapprehend."[81]

Goschen's perception was markedly different. Although claiming to be equally keen on effecting savings, he saw many obstacles in the way. Early in 1873 he informed Gladstone he had managed to strike another 1,000 men and boys from the manpower of the navy, but although this accomplishment looked "well on paper," it would have little impact on expenditure. The rest of his news was still less palatable. "I have had," he wrote, "a great disappointment on the vote for transport of troops. . . . I had calculated on £30,000 reduction & now have an excess of £12,000—Difference £40,000, a dreadful amount to make up." Nor was it the only source of increase. Owing primarily to rises in the cost of pensions and half pay for officers (over which he had no control), Goschen was facing an increase of £370,000 from the estimates for 1872–73. "I have been closely over all the items again," he assured Gladstone, "& have with the greatest reluctance struck off £30,000, partly from the vote for men, & partly from other votes, but I am now at the end of my tether with an excess of £340,000."[82]

At the end of his tether he remained, for 1873–74's estimates amounted to £9,873,000, or an increase of exactly £340,000 over those of the previous year.[83] The blame for most of the jump fell on the rise in prices, the phenomenon being sufficiently notorious by this point to have rated mention in the speech from the throne opening Parliament. As for savings under other headings, the First Lord was emphatic: "We might be able to reduce them by some few thousands, but the most rigid economist could not effect any such reduction there as would make up for increased prices."[84] His explanation carried conviction, for the *Times*, editorializing on his introductory speech, suggested that the promises of wholesale reduction made at the outset of Gladstone's administration had been illusory: "Are we to believe that we were misled . . . when we listened to the promises of Radical retrenchment, and expected them to be fulfilled?" The journal supplied its own answer. "We must own that our last knowledge is in this matter our best, that there is not that great gain to be realized by parsimony which we were led to expect, and our only consolation is to be found in a resolution not to suffer ourselves to be deceived again."[85]

One could easily believe, upon reading the *Times*' sorrowful epitaph for naval retrenchment, that the Liberals had accomplished almost nothing during the course of their administration. In this context it is well to bear in mind that Gladstone's two First Lords had, between them, brought in estimates of less than £10 million for four successive years, a feat unparalleled since before the Crimean War. Indeed, between 1859 and 1868 not a *single* naval budget had dropped below eight figures and during those eleven years the estimates exceeded £13 million once, £12 million once, and £11 million a further four years.[86] By this standard the Liberal "failure" to reduce naval spending was no failure at all. Possibly public and press had been led to expect greater accomplishments via retrenchment, but from the perspective of more than a century after the event, it is very difficult to fathom why there should have been dissatisfaction with the financial accomplishments of Childers and Goschen.

Gladstone, however, remained steadfastly unconvinced that "there is not that great gain to be realized by parsimony," and continued to maintain that the campaign promises made in 1868 remained unfulfilled. The following November, when the service estimates for the next financial year began to be considered, he started gathering ammunition for a full-scale assault on the level of army and navy expenditure. From Goschen he requested figures for shipbuilding expenditure, on a yearly basis, all the way back to 1840. "I [should] very much like to see the figures," he wrote, in the process revealing a studied indifference to—one might almost say disdain for—matters of naval technology and terminology, "both for Estimate & outlay year by year, & it [would] increase their interest & value if the paper showed the kind of ship built as wooden, sailing—Paddle Steamers—Screw Steamers, Iron coated & true iron, [though] this I believe is called Ironclad."[87] In addition, the prime minister had Robert Welby, one of the permanent officers at the treasury, prepare an elaborate memorandum detailing military and naval expenditure by ministry since 1859. These tactics were reminiscent of those employed in his battles with Somerset and Palmerston over naval spending in the early and mid-1860s and presaged those to be used in his last political battle, some twenty years later, again over the level of naval spending.

As he accumulated his figures, Gladstone's letters to Goschen and other correspondents in late 1873 and early 1874 were sprinkled with hints that circumstances were favorable for substantial reductions in the estimates. Regarding the state of prices, he wrote Goschen on 1 December, "I hope and believe we are upon falling not rising markets," and three weeks later added, "The course of the markets for coal & iron is I hope favorable to [your] Estimates."[88] He remonstrated with Foreign Secretary Lord Granville over foreign-office demands for ships to uphold British interests around the world. "Goschen feels the great pressure of demands for ships at this & that place in all parts." At the same time, he dropped a broad hint that the threat from their closest rival was minimal. "The French Navy Estimates are nearly 1 [million] below those of /69."[89]

Five days later he addressed a further missive to Granville, on the subjects of party policy and the government's future. Tacitly admitting that the twin fires of retrenchment and reform that had kindled the party's enthusiasm five years earlier were burning low, he asked

Granville "can we make out such a course of policy for the Session ... as will with reasonable likelihood reanimate some portion of that sentiment in our favour which carried us in a manner so remarkable through the election of 1868?"[90] Gladstone suggested three possibilities; local taxation, the county voting franchise, and finance. The first two he quickly dismissed. As for the third, "my opinion is that we *can* do it: can frame a budget large enough and palpably beneficial enough, not only to do much good to the country, but to sensibly lift the party in the public view & estimation." There was but one small sticking point; both army and navy expenditures would have to be cut. "If we can get from three-quarters of a million upwards towards a million off the naval & military estimates jointly, then as far as I can judge we shall have left the country no reason to complain, and may proceed cheerily with our work."[91]

A major struggle over the service estimates was brewing. Goschen informed Gladstone on 11 January, "I am sure you know how gladly I would strain every nerve to meet your wishes as regards reductions but a combination of circumstances have baffled all my efforts."[92] Gladstone would not accept this state of affairs tamely. He replied to Goschen on 17 January, "The reason for treating Estimates is now so close & the subject is one of such great importance generally ... that I should very much like to see you upon them, at least in a preliminary way, with 2 or 3 of our colleagues—Granville, Cardwell, Bright—whom I have invited to come to my house at 11:30 on Monday [19 January]."[93] Edward Cardwell, of course, was the secretary for war, with whom Gladstone had reached a similar impasse regarding the army estimates.[94] Granville was a close friend of the prime minister and shared his views on retrenchment. Bright was a pacifist.[95] Both could be expected to adhere to Gladstone's position regarding defense expenditures. The prime minister was marshalling his forces for a showdown with the service chiefs.

Among Gladstone's papers is a memorandum dated 19 January 1874, containing the position for which he argued in that day's meeting. He calculated that a minimum of £600,000 would have to be cut from the service estimates, of which "the larger part should be furnished (as far as I can judge) by the Admiralty, and a good deal from the [Ship] Building vote."[96] At this point the sequence of events becomes partially obscured in the mists of secrecy. Certainly the meeting was a failure, at least from Gladstone's standpoint. He wrote Cardwell and Goschen cryptically on the 22nd, "I would propose to consider the point raised between us as one adjourned though with a perfect knowledge in each of our minds as to the views of the others."[97] The "point raised between us" must have concerned military and naval spending. Further confirmation of a rift between the prime minister and his subordinates was evident in Goschen's reply, in which he assured Gladstone, "I had proposed myself to ask you whether what had passed between us had better not remain entirely confidential for the present as it is best not to state differences where the statement of them is not indispensable."[98] The persons from whom knowledge was to be withheld were the remainder of the cabinet and the queen, for the upshot of the impasse over the estimates was a decision to raise the possibility, when the former next met, of a dissolution of Parliament with a general election to follow.[99] In the cabinet meeting of 23 January the prime minister raised the subject, stating both his motives for so doing and his sentiment in favor of dissolution "on the grounds of general advantage."[100] The response was positive: "Granville concurred, All agreed."[101]

Gladstone's struggle with Goschen and Cardwell has been largely ignored as the critical factor in the decision to dissolve Parliament.[102] Clearly, however, the impasse over naval and military spending accounted for the timing of the dissolution, and figured heavily in the tenor and content of the prime minister's subsequent appeal to the country. But voters took little notice of promises of still greater savings. Despite the government's achievements the electorate appeared indifferent to the point of ingratitude. Notwithstanding his offer to abolish the income tax—the linchpin of Gladstone's appeal—the election of 1874 turned on issues other than retrenchment and finance and when the dust had settled Liberals were out of office.

Nonetheless, the successes achieved by Gladstone, Childers, and Goschen in reducing the level of Britain's worldwide naval presence and the concomitant reduction of expenditure were noteworthy on more than one level, not least of which was the first's deeply held belief that they could and should have been carried still further. In his Gladstone biography, John Morley, who attributed the reductions primarily to the prime minister's exertions, delivered a eulogy on the policy and accomplishments of his late friend. The tone is scarcely surprising in view of Morley's own pacificism and the European naval race under way when he wrote. The hagiographical tone, however, cannot detract from the force of the figures cited. Gladstone, he wrote, "fought with all his strength for a reduction of the public burdens, and in at least one of these persistent battles with colleagues of a less economizing mind than himself, he came near to a breach within the walls of his Cabinet. In this thankless region he was not always zealously seconded." Still, argued Morley, the cost of army, navy, and civil expenditures, which had reached £34.75 million during the final year of the Derby-Disraeli ministry had, by 1873, "been brought down again to little more than 32 millions and a quarter."[103] Of this reduction, as a more recent author has noted, the navy provided the largest sum.[104] This savings was the most quantifiable accomplishment of Childers' and Goschen's stints at the Admiralty, and serves as a further reminder that although Goschen's estimates did not match the ruthless economizing of Childers', they were nonetheless paragons of thriftiness by the standards of the previous administration or, for that matter, the first three years of the Duke of Somerset's. What Gladstone viewed as Goschen's manifest failure to slay the dragon of naval extravagance is more charitably and fairly seen in retrospect simply as his inability to match Childers' spectacular reductions. There can be no doubt that Goschen labored under more difficult circumstances than had his predecessor. By the time he arrived at Whitehall there was little left to exploit in terms of additional reductions. Indeed, in some instances he was faced with replenishing stocks depleted over the previous two years.[105] Moreover, Goschen was the victim of circumstances. Rising materials costs coincided almost perfectly with his tenure at the Admiralty. Childers faced no comparable problem and it was rather unfair to judge, as Gladstone did, Goschen's performance by Childers' standards.

It is equally clear, however, that Goschen was not suffused with the spirit of radical retrenchment to the degree that Gladstone or Childers were. True, the ongoing reductions of British forces on distant stations, under way since the mid-1860s, continued on a modest scale into the mid-1870s.[106] Yet, Goschen and Gladstone ended up at loggerheads over the bottom-line requirements for British naval strength, something that never occurred between the latter and Childers. As Goschen once observed, he did not perceive that the public was prepared to sanction a further reduction in naval power beyond that already made by Childers and others.[107] In this conflict the two men illustrated ultimately crucial differences of opinion within the Liberal party over economy, defense, imperial, and foreign policies. Gladstone and other economy-minded radicals were prepared to go much further than Goschen and Cardwell in striving for savings, while the latter two—and doubtless others as well—put greater emphasis on upholding interests abroad. In sum, they placed economy second to efficiency.

Ironically, the financial dimension of defense policy, upon which both Gladstone and Disraeli placed such emphasis, and which figured in the Conservative disappointment of 1868, had minimal significance in the electoral misfortunes of the Liberals in 1874. Disraeli's administration failed to increase its base of support because, among other reasons, it had manifestly failed to achieve the level of economy in government expenditure that the country seems to have demanded.[108] As a consequence, in 1868 Gladstone was able to pick up where he had left off two years earlier, and had, by 1874, achieved noteworthy success where his predecessor's fortunes had been so mixed. He then learned, to his chagrin, after five-plus years of economical government, that the issue had temporarily lost its political resonance. Sounding the trumpets of nationalism and revived imperial glory, Disraeli and the Conservatives converted a 100-seat deficit in the Commons into roughly a forty-seat surplus in the general election, giving the party its first majority since 1846. Ironically, thus, Disraeli reaped some of the benefits of Gladstone's economy, in the form of a £6 million treasury surplus left by the Liberals.

CHAPTER 8

Politics, Finance, and the Navy, 1874–1880

> The present Government has shown a strong disposition to make things pleasant all round by the lavish distribution of public money. A strict and jealous exercise of the functions of the opposition was never more needed in this respect than it is just now.
> — The *Daily News*, 2 March 1876, 4.

The ongoing contretemps over naval funding between Gladstone and Goschen during the latter years of the Liberal administration set the tone for the ensuing decade. Finance dominated public discourse on the navy, both within the walls of Westminster Palace and in the editorial columns of the mainstream press. From the Admiralty came repeated demands—one might say pleas—for more ships and, by implication, more money, but the Conservative government that took office in 1874 was generally more concerned with the state of the revenue than with claims that the service was inadequate even for a period of "profound peace." Indicative of the mood within the cabinet, in the wake of the Conservative victory at the polls, the newly appointed foreign secretary, the 15th Earl of Derby, took the opportunity to address a few words of caution to the chancellor of the exchequer, Sir Stafford Northcote. Were Northcote to maintain a large surplus, he warned, then "the military and naval departments, which have destroyed every Conservative budget in my recollection, will begin the old game of extravagance again."[1]

When constructing his cabinet in February of 1874, Disraeli's options for First Lord of the Admiralty were limited. Henry Corry had passed away the previous year, and Sir John Pakington, the other Tory with experience at the head of the navy, had lost his seat in the election. Pakington's elevation to the peerage as Baron Hampden, it is true, made him again available for office, but Disraeli wanted the heads of the service departments in the House of Commons.[2] Lord Henry Lennox was therefore the leading candidate. Following Corry's death he had become the chief party spokesman in the Commons on naval matters. But Disraeli's choice fell elsewhere. Lennox was offered—and accepted—the post of first commissioner of works, which did not carry with it a seat in the cabinet, and we are left to speculate why he was not appointed First Lord. Certainly his earlier stint at Whitehall, in particular his activities as Disraeli's mole, had poisoned his relations with the naval members of the board.[3] Moreover, Sir Alexander Milne, First Naval Lord between 1866 and 1868, was serving another stint at that post in 1874, and the incoming ministry decided to retain his services, a situation that might well have led to stormy relations between him and Lennox had the latter returned to the Admiralty.

So Lennox was passed over, and as First Lord Disraeli selected George Ward Hunt (1825–77). Ward Hunt had no prior experience in naval administration. In 1866 he had been named secretary to the treasury and had succeeded Disraeli as chancellor of the exchequer when the latter became prime minister in March 1868.[4] His ignorance of naval matters doubtless seemed a boon to Disraeli, given the disputes that had arisen between the exchequer and Corry and Pakington, both of them experienced naval administrators. Furthermore, while at the treasury, Ward Hunt had pursued a policy regarding naval and military spending that essentially duplicated Disraeli's. "The very disappointing yield of the Revenue induced me," he wrote the prime minister in 1868, "to write strongly to the [Secretary] of State for War and First Lord of the Admiralty as to the necessity of their expenditure being kept at the lowest possible point."[5] He also advocated the policy of reducing squadrons abroad to lower costs and labeled Corry "a difficult one to watch," a cryptic observation, but one that, it may safely be assumed, was not complimentary.[6] Disraeli's choice of Ward Hunt was therefore probably motivated by the belief that their views on naval spending policy were in fundamental agreement, and that there would be no repetition of the continual demands for increased funding that had marred the three previous Conservative administrations.

If so, the prime minister suffered a rude shock in April 1874, for the man who when at the treasury had advocated keeping the navy and the army on a tight leash displayed a wholly different face when appointed to the Admiralty. First, Ward Hunt submitted a memorandum stating the views of the professional members of the board as to the state of the navy.[7] This tactic presented the cabinet with a tougher problem than did the "combination" of the admirals in 1868; their views had been forwarded without the official sanction of the First Lord and could therefore be ignored for having circumvented proper channels. Ward Hunt pointedly solicited the naval members' views. Second, although he made it clear to the Naval Lords that he sought their opinions as to the necessary level of naval strength for "a state of European peace with no sign of a likelihood of war in the immediate future," the admirals, presented with a convenient forum, made the most of the opportunity. Indeed, Milne stood the request on its head. "This question would imply a state of war, and opens up the larger question of what would be required of the Navy in a state of hostilities: it is to this state that the Admiralty have [sic] to look."[8] Having thus conveniently dispensed with the parameters of Ward Hunt's query, the First Naval Lord surveyed the demands that would be made of the service in terms of home defense, offensive operations against an enemy's coast and commerce, defense of British commerce, and defense of the empire, before arriving at a conclusion that could hardly have been surprising, given this practically limitless context. "[I]t is evident," he stated, "that we have no fleet, either of iron-clads or fast unarmoured ships to meet any such demand." His colleagues were scarcely less alarmist. Admiral John Walter Tarleton, indeed, went as far as to assert that the Mediterranean Squadron was at that instant "below what it ought to be, even in profound peace."[9] The ludicrousness of maintaining the navy on war footing at all times, with the consequent financial burden this policy must have entailed, seems not to have entered their minds. They were asked for their opinions as administrators, but replied as naval officers.

Ward Hunt, of course, was ultimately to blame for this navalist excrescence. Slightly less than a year earlier, Milne had apparently written a similarly alarmist—although this time unsolicited—memorandum to George J. Goschen. His paper is no longer extant, but the reply survives. Noting that the First Naval Lord had sent him a list "of 27 ships which you say require repair," Goschen's tone bordered on incredulity when he turned to Milne's proposal to build "20 corvettes and sloops!"[10] The First Lord's response to this suggestion was blunt and unmistakable. To be presented, he wrote, "with a proposition to build 20 corvettes and sloops is utterly out of the question. No government could do it." Furthermore, the course advocated by the First Sea Lord was "one which I cannot contemplate in a time of peace, with our chief naval rival France disabled [by its defeat at the hands of Germany] and doing very little, & which, if I did contemplate, I could not carry either with the House of Commons or with the Government." The First Lord then closed with a veiled threat to his subordinate to keep the exchange confidential. Aside from lending credence to Goschen's protestations that he was a zealous advocate of economy, the contrast between the course he steered in May 1873 and Ward Hunt's eleven months later is illuminating. Of course the latter was still new to his post in April 1874, whereas Goschen had been over two years at Whitehall when he rejected Milne's plea. But ample evidence exists that Ward Hunt, like Corry and Pakington before him, was more susceptible to accepting without question the alarmist views of the Naval Lords. Indeed, his policy did not alter significantly over the ensuing three years. Finally, Milne, who appears to have instigated the "combination" of 1868, was a continuing source of such pronouncements whenever he served at the Admiralty.

Regardless of the First Lord's lack of experience, Disraeli cannot have been pleased to receive his memorandum. No evidence exists that he or the rest of the cabinet took any cognizance of the Naval Lords' panic-mongering. Ward Hunt, however, had another arrow in his quiver, and he loosed it on 20 April 1874, while presenting the estimates for 1874–75. His comments on the votes and the sums allotted them—largely inherited from Goschen—were not extraordinary, but having dispensed with the introductory portion of his statement, he launched into a review of naval policy over the previous half dozen years, praising Corry's administration and castigating those of Childers and Goschen.[11] Blatant partisanship, naturally, was hardly a novelty in the House of Commons, and certainly not surprising in the wake of the Conservative triumph at the polls. What followed, however, was to create a serious furor. While insisting that he had "come to the Admiralty with Treasury views," Hunt charged that the level of expenditure sanctioned by Goschen's estimates was inadequate, and that he could not, nor did he want to "conceal . . . that I shall have to submit to my Colleagues in the Cabinet some further demands for the service for the year." Still more provocative was his parting salvo. "As long as I remain at the Admiralty," he declaimed, "it must be understood that I do not mean to have a fleet on paper; that whatever ships appear as forming a part of the strength of the Navy must be real and effective ships and not dummies." The implication was unmistakable: this policy marked a striking reversal from the retrenchment of the Liberal administration.

Partisan mudslinging aside, there were observable ways in which Liberal and Conservative naval, especially construction, policies differed. Gladstone, of course, took issue with the traditional policy of maintaining squadrons worldwide, but was unique in this respect, at least in the upper reaches of the British political world. Hugh Childers' views were more representative of "mainstream" Liberal naval policy, although as far as the role of the battlefleet was concerned he, Gladstone, and many others were at one. The navy was the most important *defensive* bulwark of the country.[12] Through Childers' policy of steadily augmenting the strength of the battlefleet, the nation's defensive powers were enhanced, and the concentration of its most powerful units in home waters had deterrent value. At the same time, his avowed desire to discourage "as much as possible repairs and unnecessary alterations, especially to ships of the old type," went hand in hand with the goal of reducing "the foreign squadrons to the minimum amount necessary for the maintenance of the honour of the country, the protection of our commerce, and for effecting those other objects for which the squadrons are maintained."[13] The yearly construction ratio of 12,000 ironclad tons to 7,500 of other vessels envisioned by Childers likewise left no doubt as to where his emphasis lay. Aside from reducing the potential for intervention, Liberal naval policy placed the greatest weight on long-range planning and augmentation of the battlefleet. Ironclads, moreover, had a higher long-term than immediate value, partly owing to their lengthy construction time and partly because the bulk of the battlefleet was held in reserve—in readiness for a future conflict—rather than maintained continually at sea. The Liberal fleet, in short, was built largely in the expectation of future crises and, equally important, for deterrence. Less energy and resources were devoted to more immediate concerns, such as policing the seas.

A pronounced shift in emphasis accompanied Ward Hunt to the Admiralty. Noting the country had fifty-five ironclads built or building, he announced "the state of many of those ships, not to put it too strongly, is anything but satisfactory."[14] This was an oft-iterated theme in his and W. H. Smith's departmental statements over the next six years. In 1875 he informed Parliament, "The principal work undertaken by the Government this year was the repairing rather than the building of ships."[15] Three years later Smith proclaimed, "I lay great stress upon the necessity for repairing existing ships . . . and it will be my duty, so long as I am at the Admiralty, to see that every ship which is worth repairing—and I shall not have any ship repaired that is not worth repairing—shall be repaired at once."[16] He sounded a similar theme the following year.[17]

Whereas Childers saw the reduction of squadrons abroad as a matter of great importance and Gladstone strongly deprecated the tactic of employing the navy to deal with altercations "by the strong hand," both Ward Hunt and Smith emphasized the necessity of maintaining a force afloat capable of intervention in troubled waters at a moment's notice. This approach, of course, accorded well with Disraeli's "forward" foreign and imperial policies, and indeed the prime minister evinced no hesitation about using the navy as an agent of British policy during the Eastern Crisis of 1876–78. As early as May 1876—a full year and a half before Russia menaced Constantinople and the Straits—he suggested that the Mediterranean squadron should be "greatly strengthened" and sent to the Dardanelles.[18] This ideological divergence between the two parties extended to the realm of construction policy, too. Childers advocated building 12,000 ironclad tons per annum to maintain the requisite strength of the battlefleet. Of the six years of Conservative stewardship of the navy during the second Disraeli ministry, only in 1875–76 and 1876–77 was that figure approached by the yearly building programs. In 1877–78 only 9,676 tons of ironclads were slated for construction: two years later the figure dropped to 7,732 tons.

There were some exceptions to this general rule. First, while the Conservatives generally displayed a greater willingness to employ the navy as a tool to enforce British policies or as an agent of intimidation, the Liberals furnished the most spectacular instance of naval intervention during the era: the bombardment of Alexandria in 1882. Likewise, the views expressed by Childers, Ward Hunt, Smith, and others were not always faithfully reflected in the yearly programs, and the smallest yearly ironclad building programs—those of 1872–73 and 1873–74—were conducted under Liberal auspices. Conversely, the most ambitious ironclad building programs, in terms of vessels laid down, if not tonnage built, were those of 1867–68 and 1868–69, when no less than twelve ironclads were commenced. These programs were instigated by the Conservative boards of Pakington and Corry.

Yet the Liberal/Conservative policy dichotomy was ordinarily clearly evident in the sums spent on shipbuilding. During the Gladstone administration the money allotted for wages in the dockyards to men employed in shipbuilding averaged over 70 percent of Vote 6. By contrast, under Conservative leadership (1874–80) wages to men employed in shipbuilding averaged 46.4 percent of Vote 6, and fell below 30 percent the last three years. The difference in the sums voted was not great; the Conservatives generally allocated larger sums to Vote 6.[19] But although they spent more in the dockyards overall, they spent less of it on shipbuilding. Likewise, they ordinarily attached greater importance to unarmored shipbuilding than did their political rivals. The augmentation of the dockyard workforce under Ward Hunt and the continuation of the enlarged establishment by Smith served principally to improve repair and refitting arrangements for the existing fleet, rather than to enlarge the fleet of the future via the yearly building programs. Finally, Conservative building programs from 1874 through 1880 were about 1,500 tons a year smaller than those of the preceding administration, despite the substantial augmentation of the dockyard workforce.

In April 1874, though, Ward Hunt's attack on his administration was so unexpected that Goschen was unable to offer a convincing rebuttal.[20] As a consequence, the *Times*, which had disapprovingly noted the estimates' modest increase upon their publication and which had also recently stated that the last few years had seen "broad improvements" in the state of the navy, was moved to observe "[a] more disquieting debate than that ... on the Navy Estimates has seldom been known. The ... ominous remarks of the First Lord of the Admiralty give us reason to fear that we may be on the verge of a new period of naval outlay more unlimited and more indefinite than any we have before experienced."[21] Only a day earlier Ward Hunt's claims had been discounted, and the newspaper urged Northcote to "resist the demands that will be made on him. . . . [I]t would never do to allow the first year of Conservative administration to end in a deficit."[22]

By 25 April, however, Ward Hunt's charges were accepted unquestioningly. "Does the country wish to retain the supremacy of the seas?" the *Times* queried rhetorically. "If so, the Navy Estimates must, we fear, be increased considerably more than the Chancellor of the Exchequer now likes to contemplate."[23] The *Standard* made considerably more of Hunt's speech, "pregnant with instruction and suggestive of grave reflection." Furthermore, the press latched onto an infelicitous phrase dropped by former chief constructor of the navy and newly elected Liberal M.P. Edward J. Reed, who urged Hunt to greater exertions in shipbuilding, so that the country might have more than a "phantom fleet." "A phantom fleet indeed," editorialized the *Standard*, "it may be called without exaggeration, in every respect other than in expense." Finding irresistible the temptation to level a few partisan shots, it charged "the continuance in the policy of reduction for the mere sake of savings and out of political motives has brought about one of those crises which we are accustomed to find at the close of a Liberal administration." Rather than having "done their duty" by increasing defense spending instead of accumulating a sizable surplus, the Liberals were accused of having acquired the latter to "debauch the constituencies when all other claims upon the country had been exhausted." Therefore, both the *Standard* and the *Times* speculated, the country would learn the cost of framing the estimates with "the sole aim of satisfying the clamours for retrenchment," courtesy of the lesson that Ward Hunt would "be compelled to give us when he submits his further estimates for the Navy, to supplement those which the late Government had proposed with a view to a surplus, and to prevent our fleet from melting away altogether."[24] As of the 25th, to judge by the tenor of leading articles, the First Lord had triggered a full-scale navy panic. He had conveyed, the *Times* observed, "the impression that utter ruin, concealed for a time by official dishonesty, had fallen on the British Navy.... A ministerial speech pervaded by such a tone naturally produces a great effect."[25]

Yet by 1 May the storm had completely blown over. On 30 April Hugh Childers made a lengthy speech in the Commons defending Liberal naval policy, in the course of which he bluntly termed it "unpardonable ... that the First Lord of the Admiralty should come down and give to the country and to Europe, in a speech composed for political purposes and replete with party phrases, these deprecating descriptions of the Navy."[26] Furthermore, said the ex-First Lord, "it was unpardonable to create that 'scare' which his speech, his references to dummy ships and paper fleets, produced throughout the country." Ward Hunt responded defensively, claiming "he was merely discharging his duty as the person charged with the Administration of the Navy." More significantly, he denied that a large supplementary demand was forthcoming. "He had not contemplated, and he did not contemplate, any very large addition to the Estimates as he had found them." His defense was technically true. He had said only that he would present "some further demands for the service" to the cabinet. The tone of his remarks, however, had created the impression on both sides of the House, to say nothing of the *Times* and other journals, that these "further demands" would be considerable.

They were not. When the supplementary estimate arrived on 7 May, Parliament discovered that it amounted to the modest sum of £150,000, prompting a sarcastic outburst from Liberal M.P. Sir William Harcourt. "The First Lord," he stated, "had given them Supplementary Estimates for a ruined Navy—Estimates to replace a 'paper fleet,' and yet they only included an addition of £55,000 for Dockyards, of which £47,000 were for workmens' wages, £5,000 for repairing a depot ship at Hong Kong, which could hardly establish our European influence, and £3,000 for repairing a tug at Chatham." He added, "nothing could be more consolatory . . . than the character of the Supplementary Estimates for the Navy, for they would satisfy the country that a 'paper fleet of dummy ships' could be replaced by an efficient one at the moderate cost of £40,000."[27] The *Times* sounded a similar note, minus the sarcasm, although it, too, chided Ward Hunt for the ruckus he had created. "If new Cabinet Ministers will indulge in sensational speeches, if Heads of Departments will take it in hand to damage their predecessors, instead of following the honourable tradition which forbids Ministers to drag official chiefs through the dirt by the help of their subordinates, they must expect that their expressions will be criticized in proportion to the effect they produce."[28]

The First Lord's hasty retreat, coupled with the modest character of the supplementary estimate, suggest that his charges had not received cabinet sanction prior to their delivery. Given Disraeli's history with navy funding, it is scarcely plausible that he lent his blessing either to Ward Hunt's alarmist tone or to his call for "further financial demands." Retired Admiralty clerk John Briggs also termed his demand "highly inconsistent and the reverse of agreeable," regardless of its merit, since Disraeli had lately excoriated "bloated armaments expenditures" in Parliament. "Mr. Ward Hunt was consequently compelled to back out as adroitly as he could, and make the best of a very insignificant addition."[29] The *Times* offered a post mortem on the incident, noting, "Mr. Hunt, being placed by the exigencies of politics in a Department of which he had no experience or scientific knowledge, has echoed more loudly and faithfully than usual the professional representations which are always ready to be poured into a new ear.... If he holds his office for a twelve-month, he will find that no liberality and no public spirit will ever be able to satisfy the ingenuity and zeal which distinguish naval projectors."[30] Furthermore, the journal suggested that the First Lord "will now, we trust, be better employed in spending his supplementary £150,000 ... and during the next twelve months he may study with effect the Department committed to him. We shall be much surprised if the result be not to moderate the zeal of his novitiate."[31] As it turned out, the *Times'* prognosis was wide of the mark.

The process of framing the estimates for 1875–76 provoked another prolonged struggle reminiscent of both 1866–68 and the latter years of the first Gladstone ministry. Both Disraeli and Northcote pushed vigorously for economy, while both of the service chiefs—Ward Hunt and Secretary for War Gathorne Hardy—urged increases for their departments. Disraeli revealed his traditional distaste for Admiralty demands in writing the queen in November 1875 about a proposed Arctic exploration expedition. "When the proposal was first made by the First Lord of the Admiralty," Disraeli informed Victoria, "the Chancellor of the Exchequer objected to it, on the ground of expense, and, Mr. Disraeli supporting the Chancellor of the Exchequer, the subject was allowed to drop, though all the other Ministers were in its favour." Alas for the prime minister, there was a postscript to the tale. "[T]he next day, the Chancellor of the Exchequer withdrew his opposition, in consequence of the state of public opinion, and, after this, any resistance was impossible."[32] Northcote gave way in this instance, but was ordinarily at one with his chief on the subject of naval and military expenditure. On 6 January 1875 he warned Gathorne Hardy of "difficulties about Estimates." A week later the secretary for war learned "that at the Cabinet yesterday great pressure was made for Army & Navy reduction of expenditure." He steadfastly defended his ground: "[T]here is a limit to reduction."[33]

Ward Hunt shared his sentiment. On 4 January he addressed the prime minister on the state of the navy. Calculating that thirty-two ironclads were required to meet the needs of the service, he claimed that Britain possessed thirty, only nineteen of which were available for immediate duty.[34] Furthermore, nine unarmored vessels were urgently needed. "Mr Childers in 1868 considerably reduced the several [Overseas] Squadrons but [though] he set the numbers at a minimum we are considerably short of them." The First Lord also advocated an increase in pay to warrant officers and increased inducements to stimulate enlistment; he also noted that "the rapid progress of Torpedo inventions destined to play a most important part in the next naval war opens an expanding vista of expenditure," an observation that, it may be imagined, scarcely went over well with Disraeli. "[I]n considering the financial arrangements for the coming year," Ward Hunt urged, "the state of things I have described cannot be disregarded."[35] Nor did he lack persistence. Gathorne Hardy recorded on the 14th, "Hunt called on me last night & warns me of the unpleasant conflict on Estimates which is before me. He says he cannot & will not give way."[36]

This dispute between Disraeli and the Admiralty lacks the voluminous documentation that makes it possible to recount the struggles of 1866–68 in such vivid fashion. Yet it was no less hard-fought on both sides than its predecessors, lasting the better part of a month. Only on 6 February were the navy estimates finally approved, since at the same time as Hunt was defending his turf so staunchly, Northcote was making gloomy predictions about the state of the government's finances. "The chance of getting through [the next year] without any addition to taxation," he wrote to Disraeli on 28 January, "appears to me very remote, though not *quite visionary*."[37] Surprisingly, especially in light of Disraeli's ingrained hostility to "bloated expenditures," Ward Hunt, without having been aided by another "mutiny" of the Naval Lords, managed to carry the cabinet and win his increase. Gathorne Hardy's *Diary* recorded on 7 February that there was "a long Cabinet yesterday afternoon, [during which] Hunt . . . had his way at last."[38] Curiously, Disraeli resigned himself to the increase well before the cabinet gave its sanction. He wrote to the queen on 14 January, "There must be an increase, probably between £5 & 600,000, on the Army and Navy."[39] The prime minister was quite sensitive on the subject, since Tory defense expenditures were a favored target for Liberal attack. He admitted, "It is to be regretted that it [should] take place this year, but it cannot be helped, & Mr. Disraeli will be satisfied if the expenditure, tho' increased, is not accompanied by fresh taxation."[40]

In this hope, at least, he was not disappointed. Northcote, his financial position bolstered by the surplus inherited from the Liberals, had been able to reduce the income tax from three to two pence on the pound in 1874, and managed to avoid reimposing the additional penny the following year, although he did increase the duty on spirits. He also embarked upon a new scheme for reduction of the

Politics, Finance, and the Navy 161

national debt, which at that point stood at £775,000,000. But with or without an increase in taxation, government expenditure rose almost £3,000,000 between fiscal year 1874 and its successor and, regardless of the benefits accruing from the chancellor of the exchequer's "New Sinking Fund," one contemporary judged the budget of 1875 "a pitiful contrast to that of 1874." It was also charged that much of the blame for this state of affairs rested on increased spending by the navy and army, especially the former: "Mr. Ward Hunt's unnecessary declaration that he did not mean to have a fleet on paper had made it impossible to avoid some increase in the Navy Estimates."[41]

Yet, when the estimates made their appearance, the increase, like the supplementary estimate of the previous year, seemed modest enough. The *Times* noted that while increased, which was not of itself "altogether agreeable," they were, at the same time "composed of very moderate augmentations in detail. [Therefore,] we may draw from the Estimates the satisfactory conclusion that the Navy is at length placed upon a sound footing."[42] The increase was £344,539 over the total—including Supplementary Estimate—for 1874–75. Hunt's explanatory statement confirmed the *Times'* observations. He pointed to increased pay for warrant officers and enlistment inducements, for which he had so tirelessly campaigned, as well as 800 of 1,000 additional dockyard workers for which he had lobbied. Finally, he managed modest increases in the votes for naval stores and contract shipbuilding.[43]

This victory was inadequate for Ward Hunt. The following November, in anticipation of the preparation of the estimates for 1875–76, he repeated his tactic of 1874 by producing another detailed memorandum on the state of the navy in an attempt to sway his colleagues.[44] Indeed, it shared more with its predecessor, for its tone was similarly alarmist. First Naval Lord Milne, naturally, furnished a gloomy assessment. "We have not a single spare vessel at home," he maintained, "none in reserve, and this in a period of peace, and year by year we are getting worse." His solution had a familiar ring: "It appears to me some extreme measures must be taken to meet this serious difficulty which is before us, by an increase in the Dockyard Establishment, and a large increase in the rate of shipbuilding."[45] His pronouncements were echoed by his colleagues on the board, Admiral Lord Gilford and Admiral Geoffrey Phipps Hornby. The latter sounded a note of despair: "I do not know how long the Government may think fit to continue in our present utterly unprepared state.... [I]f they are determined to do the least that could be thought reasonable by any naval officer," then they should at once embark upon building ten sloops and corvettes a year for the next nine years. Only then would Britain have an adequate force of unarmored vessels.[46]

The tone of Ward Hunt's own comments was indistinguishable from those of his naval advisors. Were the construction of ironclads maintained at the present pace, he admitted, within five years they should be "in a pretty good condition," but his views on the state of the unarmored fleet were quite the opposite. "It is evident," he claimed, "that we are sadly deficient in ships to furnish reliefs to those on foreign stations and that (speaking of unarmoured ships) *we have no reserve whatsoever*. . . . The *very least*," he continued, "that, in my opinion, ought to be done is to order by contract twelve gun-boats for China; also six gunboats and two sloops . . . and also six fast cruisers, say corvettes." Of course, there was a price, which Hunt estimated at £600,000, £187,000 of which could be met by reallocating the amounts voted for the previous estimates. The remaining £413,000 would have to be met by increased spending.[47] A month later the First Lord wrote directly to Disraeli. "My demands for increased shipbuilding are," he argued, "the least that any one occupying my position and acquainted with the present state of things could make, and this I must impress seriously on the Cabinet."[48]

Northcote had, however, already addressed himself to his colleague at the Admiralty on the subject of expenditure. Neither in 1874–75 nor 1875–76 had the navy managed to stay within its budget, a precedent that, the chancellor of the exchequer confessed, "rather takes away my courage for more expenditure." Also pointing to "very uncertain" revenue production, he ended by pleading with Ward Hunt: "Can you do anything to reduce your expenditure for 1875–6[?]"[49] The answer was no. There was an unmistakable note of dismay in the *Times'* tone upon the discovery that the navy estimates for 1876–77 showed yet another increase. "On one point [they] leave no doubt," it observed on 2 March 1876. "If we do not possess an efficient Navy, it will not be for the want of paying for it. . . . In round numbers," continued the editors, the estimates were "suddenly increased from ten and a half to eleven millions," the bulk of the increase going to building the ships for which Hunt had argued. The *Times* termed it "an immense addition to the ships to be built by contract."[50]

"Immense addition" was hyperbolic. Nonetheless, Ward Hunt had won a sizable building program, having received cabinet sanction for his entire demand.[51] His estimates, moreover, had repercussions in Northcote's budget, prompting the *Daily News* to note ominously, "The Government seem to be running somewhat of a risk with its general policy of swollen expenditure."[52] The *Times*' dissatisfaction was equally evident. "Sir Stafford Northcote has to provide for an expenditure exceeding £78,000,000. It is an enormous sum—a sum exceeding anything that has been known in our time—a sum excusing, if not justifying, the accusation Sir Stafford tried to parry [in Parliament] ... that the present is an extravagant Government.... [W]e have difficulty in believing that the accusation is not in some degree well-founded."[53] In consequence of rising expenditure, the chancellor was also compelled to reimpose the additional penny he had managed to strike off the income tax two years previously.

Some of the government's financial woes were not of its own making. By the mid-1870s revenue production was dropping, owing largely to the onset of the Victorian "Great Depression," that set in first in agriculture in 1873, gradually extending to other sectors of the economy. Northcote mournfully noted in 1877 that "he could not see any signs of a revival of trade, for the ill years were fairly begun.... Thus he could not treat the revenue as a thing necessarily bound to keep on increasing."[54] The same year, the *Times* bewailed the "absolute loss of elasticity" of revenue and two years later noted with unconcealed wistfulness there were "some faint signs of improvement in some directions.... [Yet] [s]ince the beginning of the year [1879] all the figures have been those of a trade more contracted than it was a year ago," and—"faint signs of improvement" notwithstanding—there was "no indication of any spring in business." As a consequence, Northcote "would be foolish to expect better revenue than last year."[55] The impact of the depression upon government finance during the latter half of the 1870s cannot be ignored.

Government expenditures, however, were on the rise at the same time that revenue production was declining, and the Tories' fiscal policy came in for some very harsh criticism. One contemporary observer noted "in two years [1874–76] the expenditure of the country had increased by £5,500,000," and of the increase some £2,000,000 "was due to the army and the navy."[56] In three years Ward Hunt had managed to reverse the policy of his predecessors. Naval expenditure in 1876–77 was almost £2 million above what it had been in 1870–71—a 20 percent increase—and more than £1 million above

Goschen's less draconian naval budget of 1873–74. Given concurrent increases in army and civil service spending, it was expenditure, rather than the depression, that caused Northcote to resort to the increase in the income tax.

Under such circumstances it was no surprise that the navy estimates for 1877–78 showed no increase. Perhaps criticism of lavish government expenditure had made a point with the Admiralty. The First Lord maintained that "the state of the fleet is so far advanced ... that it is quite safe for me to make some reduction in the sums required for the coming year."[57] This admission prompted the *Daily News* to observe sarcastically that the First Lord had "toned down a good deal since the somewhat arrogant days when fresh to office.... [H]e boasted himself as a great regenerator come to do away with phantom ships and navies on paper."[58] The presentation of the 1877–78 estimates, however, was to be virtually Ward Hunt's last official act. His health was failing during the spring, and he spent much of the summer abroad attempting to recover. He passed away at the end of July and Disraeli, after initially offering the First Lordship to Viscount Sandon, chose William Henry Smith (1825–91), hitherto a subordinate officer at the treasury, to replace him.[59]

Smith was an anomalous creature in the mid-Victorian Conservative party, which was at that time still—Disraeli himself notwithstanding—largely dominated by the landed interest. Smith, instead, came from a commercial background. His grandfather founded the firm that was to become W. H. Smith and Son, the newspaper distributors and booksellers. Smith himself entered Parliament in 1868 and Disraeli, never averse to recruiting fresh talent from nontraditional sources, had offered him the secretaryship to the treasury only six years later. He came to his new post in 1877 under ominous circumstances. The specter of Russian intervention in what had started in 1875 as a revolt among the Ottoman Empire's Balkan subjects had, by late 1876, begun to cast a long shadow over British foreign and military policies.[60] By March 1877 the *Times* had abandoned its traditional approbation for economy and, on presentation of the navy estimates, commented, "The country and the House, we fear, take but a languid interest in the fact that the Estimates [for 1877–78] are £309,000 less than they were last year; for everybody feels that, in the critical state of the Continent, such a saving may be an uncertain gain."[61] Indeed, the Eastern Crisis of 1875–78 was to baffle Conservative fiscal policy for most of the remainder of the

Politics, Finance, and the Navy 165

administration. Spending had risen significantly during the first three years of the ministry, a period of peace abroad. Now, as Northcote tried to rein it in, the situation in the East provided a fresh impetus for increased outlays. He would not surrender without a fight, however. His budget for 1877 managed to avoid another increase in taxation, and while total expenditure was up, an increase of only £750,000 overall was modest by the standards of the previous three years.[62]

Indeed, at the outset it appeared that the government was trying its best to ignore the military implications of the situation in the Levant. Smith's first estimates, introduced in March 1878, contained no intimation that Britain was at that moment on the brink of war with Russia. The First Lord, in fact, went out of his way to stress the pacific qualities of his navy budget.[63] His figures showed an increase of all of £74,072, prompting the *Times* to note with unconcealed approval, "[W]e cannot but recognize the almost anxious care of the Government to keep the Estimates for the Navy rigidly within their normal limits, as a wholesome and useful feature in the present threatening aspect of affairs."[64] Yet the impression of frugality given by the estimates was belied by events by the time they were presented to Parliament.

The Russian advance on Constantinople, following the fall of the Turkish fortress of Plevna in late 1877 had, by January 1878, aroused the government to request a vote of credit of £6 million with which to augment the army and navy. This request encountered strenuous opposition in the House of Commons, not least from Gladstone, owing largely to his revulsion at Turkish misrule in the Balkans.[65] But resistance to the proposal effectively ended when word of the terms of the Treaty of San Stephano, between victorious Russia and the defeated Turks, reached Britain, for they appeared to pose a serious threat to British lines of communication and interests in the eastern Mediterranean. The most ominous terms of the treaty called for the creation of a large, independent Bulgarian state with access to the Aegean Sea—Disraeli's cabinet feared it would be a Russian client—and the agreement of Russia and Turkey to settle the question of access to the Straits of Constantinople by Russian warships between themselves, rather than in concert with the other powers. This last proviso was a direct contravention of the Treaty of Paris (1856).

Of the £6 million, £1,434,070 was spent purchasing ironclads under construction in private British shipyards for other countries—the so-called "war scare purchases." The idea of supplementing the navy in the event of war with Russia was not novel. In the autumn of 1875 Ward Hunt had broached to Northcote the possibility of purchasing three ironclads then being built in private shipyards for the Ottoman Empire, as well as one being built for Brazil.[66] The Turks were short of cash and needed funds to crush the Bulgarian revolt. In contrast to his usual attitude towards naval expenditure, Disraeli was, according to the chancellor of the exchequer, "rather taken" with the idea. Northcote further reported, however, that both he and the prime minister thought "that there is no immediate hurry, as there are not likely to be many purchasers." The scheme was mooted again the following year, for Disraeli wrote to the queen on 10 June, "The Cabinet today resolved *not* to purchase the Three Ironclads building in England and belonging to the Porte."[67]

Another enthusiast for the idea was W. H. Smith, who wrote to Northcote endorsing the purchase of one of the vessels in November 1876. But Smith, at this point, was in no way connected to the Admiralty. In fact, as secretary to the treasury he was Northcote's immediate subordinate, and the latter replied to his missive with shock: "I am rather staggered by your commendation of . . . the purchase of the Turkish Ironclad, and shall much like to talk it over with you." The chancellor then recited a number of reasons for not buying the ship, most crucial being the state of finance, which would not be "able to stand a pull of some £400,000 additional expenditure."[68]

With £6 million available, however, the circumstances were considerably altered, and during the spring and summer of 1878 the battlefleet was enlarged by the three former Turkish vessels, and the ex-Brazilian *Independência*. Another £140,000 was spent on unarmored vessels. Several supplementary estimates followed: £688,000 was allocated for transporting troops—especially a contingent of sepoys shipped to Malta during the height of the crisis—and another £443,000 for dockyards and stores. In an instance of creative bookkeeping, however, the sums provided out of the vote of credit were added neither to the figures for fiscal year 1877–78, during which they were voted, nor 1878–79, during which they were largely spent. If added to the former, naval spending that year was over £12.5 million, and if to the latter it was over £13.5 million, instead of £11.97 million.[69]

The "war scare purchases" may have caught the fancy of Disraeli, reassured the British public, and helped to convey to Russia the impression that the government meant business. Along with the sums spent on the army, however, they drove up expenditure despite Northcote's efforts to keep it in check. Nor was the Eastern Crisis the only source of worry for the increasingly harried chancellor of the exchequer, since the colonial government of India had become embroiled in a conflict with Afghan rebels hard on the heels of the resolution of affairs with Russia. With a gloomy outlook, therefore, Northcote wrote his colleague at the foreign office, Lord Salisbury, in late September 1878. "My revenue is coming in very badly," complained the chancellor, "and I am warned that I must expect a heavy deficiency at the end of the year."[70] He addressed W. H. Smith at about the same time in a similar tone. "The prospects of the Revenue are I am sorry to say, most gloomy.... On the other hand, the Expenditure is going on merrily, and we fear it will be considerably over the Estimate. Something desperate must be done or we shall find ourselves landed in a big deficit."[71] Northcote predicted that the government's financial quandary would cause discontent in Conservative ranks: "[O]ur friends are beginning to grumble at the expenditure; and I fear that when the results of the year are before Parliament we shall be subjected to some highly disagreeable criticism."[72] Nor would the criticism be confined to Parliament. As a consequence of imperial demands, Northcote had been forced in his 1878–79 budget to raise the income tax not one penny, but two, up to five pence on the pound. Gladstone denounced it as "the painful Budget," and displeasure was by no means confined to the ranks of economists in the Commons.[73] Noting that even staunch Tory M.P. Charles Newdegate objected to the budget, the *Times* observed, "A Conservative Ministry which has succeeded in giving offense to Mr. Newdegate has accomplished a feat which is neither very easy nor very safe."[74]

Unsurprisingly, Northcote's aim in writing Salisbury was to sound the latter out on spending cuts, in particular in the army and navy budgets. By this point the situation in the East looked far less ominous. The Congress of Berlin, which met in June and July of 1878, had abrogated the Treaty of San Stephano and replaced it with one whose terms were acceptable to Britain.[75] "Is it safe," wrote Northcote, "to consider a reduction of armaments?"[76] The foreign secretary saw "little or no objection to considerable reduction" in the army. But he added that he "should be sorry to see the navy much reduced," and other than suggesting that the North America and West Indies and West African Squadrons might be reduced—"furnish material for the knife," as he put it—Salisbury could make no substantive recommendations.[77]

When Smith presented the estimates in March 1879, however, he was able to point proudly to a figure of £10,586,894, almost half a million below the original estimates for the previous year, and over £2 million below the final expenditure for 1878–79. Smith announced that his figures had been framed "with a very considerable regard, though I trust not an undue regard, to economy." The better part of £400,000 of the reduction was furnished by the votes for naval stores and shipbuilding by contract, for, as Smith observed, "looking to the expenditure last year on armoured, and also, to some extent, on unarmoured vessels, I do not think that I should be justified in asking for the full amount usually spent on shipbuilding by contract." Moreover, he maintained, the supply of naval stores was adequate for any demands likely to be made on it. Despite the tones of optimism and economy that pervaded Smith's statement, he was forced to confess that his figure did not include any "abnormal charge for transport [of troops], which may be occasioned by the Zulu war."[78] This expense would require another vote of credit—of £3 million—which came on top of the £1.5 million voted for South Africa the previous year, to say nothing of the £6 million for the Eastern Crisis.[79]

The consequences of the government's policy abroad were brought into sharp focus by the havoc wrought on Northcote's budgets. Despite his efforts to balance expenditure with income, the finances of the Conservative government were torpedoed. The treasury recorded a surplus of £4,658,936 in 1876–77, but the final three years of the ministry were beset with large deficits.[80] Thus, one contemporary remarked, "The financial history of England, during the years in which Sir Stafford Northcote occupied the Chancellorship of the Exchequer, is melancholy reading. . . . His predecessor had enabled him to reduce the income tax to 2d. in the pound; his own necessities compelled him to increase it to 5d."[81] Such a harsh appraisal was not entirely fair to Northcote. The "inelasticity" of revenue resulting from the depression was beyond his control, and was a factor of considerable significance in the formulation of fiscal policy during the late 1870s. Under the circumstances the fiscally prudent course would have been to curtail expenditure to match income, but such a course was impossible given the government's foreign and imperial policies and the crises that confronted it.

Politics, Finance, and the Navy

The following year Smith termed the navy budget "peace Estimates and economical Estimates [that had] been prepared to impose as small a charge on the Exchequer as possible" while still remaining commensurate with the need of the service.[82] Smith's fine words aside, economizing had produced a reduction of less than £100,000 from the previous year. Still, the *Times* welcomed such a savings, "in view of the depressed appearance of the revenue at the present time."[83] But the pleasing appearance of the estimates for 1880–81 was overshadowed by more momentous news, for the same day Smith made his presentation (8 March), Northcote announced to the House of Commons the government's decision to dissolve Parliament prior to Easter. Like Gladstone's action in January 1874, this was virtually a spur-of-the-moment decision, prompted largely by Conservative success in two recent by-elections.[84] It was, however, a mistake of considerable magnitude, as the Liberals swept the Tories from power in the subsequent general election, winning 353 seats to the Tories' 258. After attempting to persuade the Marquess of Hartington to form a Liberal government, the queen faced up to political realities—despite her distaste—and sent for Gladstone, who thus embarked upon his second premiership.

The expensive and not wholly successful foreign and imperial policies of the second Disraeli ministry following the Congress of Berlin were probably the largest contributors to Conservative misfortune at the polls in 1880, but the financial woes of the government did nothing to improve its chances.[85] True, the chancellor of the exchequer managed to avoid another increase in taxation, but at the cost of plundering resources from his own "sinking fund" to reduce the deficit, which by that point exceeded £8 million. Certainly the *Times* sounded a note of unease upon the presentation of the budget: "The condition of the finances disclosed in Sir Stafford Northcote's budget speech . . . cannot, indeed, be contemplated with pleasure."[86]

Gladstone, not surprisingly, lost little time in making political capital of Northcote's budget woes. One of his speeches in the course of the Midlothian campaign of 1879 addressed the Disraeli government's financial policy.[87] It was not a flattering portrayal. "If all the millions bestowed upon giving effect to the warlike policy of the Government had, instead of being so applied, been thrown down to the bottom of the sea, you would have been better off, with such a mode of disposing of the funds, than you are now." He charged that the Tories were extravagant from the outset, offering examples of naval and military expenditure. But the situation had worsened, he charged, when the government initiated its "vigorous" foreign and imperial policy. Army and navy spending was £25.9 million in 1874–75: by 1878–79 it had reached £32.25 million. Curiously enough, Gladstone had words of praise for none other than W. H. Smith, although not on account of his administration of the navy: "[T]here has been, I must say, one member of the present Government—let me do him justice—Mr. Smith, the First Lord of the Admiralty, who, when he was Secretary of the Treasury, fought like a man for the public purse." As for Smith's superior at the treasury, Gladstone's own former private secretary, the verdict was unsparing. "I am bound to say hardly ever in the six years that Sir Stafford Northcote has been in office have I heard him speak a resolute word on behalf of economy. ... As to speaking irresolute words, gentlemen, I assure you they are all worthless."

Yet there is no lack of evidence that Northcote, whatever Gladstone may have thought of his resolution, doggedly tried to check expenditure. Indeed, the chief enigma surrounding the second Disraeli administration's stance towards the navy is the attitude of Disraeli himself. Here, evidence is frustratingly sparse, especially when contrasted to his voluminous correspondence on the subject during his previous stints on the treasury bench. Of course, the prime minister no longer faced the necessity of convincing a superior of the wisdom of his opinions. He was thus left few occasions requiring that he commit his views to paper. He did, it is true, inform the sovereign in 1875 of the impending increase in the service estimates, but offered no commentary beyond the observation that it could not be helped.[88] Aside from this instance, there is the scanty information gleaned from Gathorne Hardy's diary that Disraeli sided with Northcote in the battle over naval spending in 1875, and the prime minister's objection to funding the Arctic expedition later the same year. Presumably, Disraeli realized the possible costs of his active foreign and imperial policies. On the other hand, there is no evidence to support this presumption and against it must be balanced his well-documented hostility towards "bloated" navy estimates during each of the previous three Tory administrations. Moreover, although it would appear logical that Disraeli should have realized the possible ramifications of "restoring Britain's prestige," there is no dispensation rendering statesmen less fallible than ordinary mortals.

CHAPTER 9

Admiralty Administration: Childers, Goschen, and the Historians

George J. Goschen's system of Admiralty administration was subjected to subsequent tinkering—the number of Naval Lords and their and the secretaries' functions varied over the years, and the controller oscillated between board membership and back again—but it is seen in retrospect as the foundation for modern British naval administration.[1] To be sure, significant structural problems remained or subsequently surfaced. Admiral Sir Alexander Milne, whose experience and abilities combined to make him an unusually perceptive and well-informed critic, addressed a lengthy memorandum on his workload to Goschen in September 1873: "There is no *cohesion* between the *Naval Element in the Board*. Admirals Tarleton and Seymour [the Second and Third Naval Lords] are nominally ignorant of what is done by the Senior [Naval] Lord, great questions may be decided without their knowing what is being done.[2] In addition, he complained of the burden of work he had to undertake, Goschen's redistribution of business notwithstanding. He was confronted, Milne stated, with a "mass of papers of all descriptions to be read, considered, and minuted. He takes one after the other to get through them. Some paper of more importance than another turns up. He makes a minute in the hurry, an erroneous one and it goes away." The First Naval Lord, he emphasized, "has no one to consult with and the minute which has left his room may be executed without any check and unknown to any other Naval Member." Milne assured his superior that it was not his purpose "to compare the present system of Admiralty work with former arrangements," but to reduce the First Naval Lord's workload, "while at the same time ensuring greater cooperation amongst the members of the Board."[3] Goschen replied in a spirit of cooperation, assuring Milne "I should like . . . to look into the subject with you, and to see of what details the Senior Naval Lord can be permanently relieved. I am greatly opposed to his being overworked."[4]

Milne also drew up a memorandum that suggested one way "the work at the Board Room might be very much lightened," both for Goschen and the rest of the board, "and the work more quickly done."[5] Much of the correspondence to the board, the First Naval Lord pointed out, was of routine nature or dealt with minor matters and did not, in either case, require minute perusal by the board, much less minuting. Let these letters, he therefore suggested, simply be read at the daily meetings and acknowledgment or consent given verbally on the spot. The Admiralty's reply could then be drafted by the clerical staff. Perhaps this innovation went some way toward easing the administrative burden on the First Naval Lord, as well as on the rest of the board. There is no indication from Milne's papers that he felt it necessary to make a further complaint about the level of work during the remainder of his tenure at the Admiralty.

But Milne's difficulty in coping with the administrative burden that confronted the First Naval Lord was symptomatic of a larger problem, one that Goschen's enlargement of the naval element on the board barely began to address and one that would persist at least into the late 1880s. There were not enough naval men at the Admiralty—as opposed to on the board itself—to give adequate consideration to all the professional questions confronting it.[6] The controller's department was better off in this respect, for that official had a staff to assist him, including the chief constructor (who, in turn, had several subordinates to deal with routine matters), the director of naval ordnance, a similar officer to supervise the purchase of steam machinery, and, after Goschen's reform, the deputy controller. What was needed was a naval staff that could serve the First Naval Lord and First Lord as the controller's staff served the controller.

True, the navy had existed for centuries with a central administrative structure within which the naval element was surprisingly small. But it was also true that Graham's abolition of the navy and victualling boards, however much it may have done to rationalize the administrative structure, reduced the number of professionals in decision-making positions, a reduction that was not fully offset by the creation of the five principal officers, and which was furthered by Childers' subsequent elimination of two of those official positions.[7] The real problem, however, was not reduction of the naval element so much as it was the vast increase of business whose transaction or resolution required professional expertise. As long as the navy relied on largely traditional technology and operated within a similarly traditional strategic framework, the naval element did not need to be especially numerous, because the number of novel questions or problems needing professional opinion was limited. With the passage of the wooden sailing navy and the concurrent revolutions in weapons, strategy, and tactics, however, the need for professional judgment and appraisal escalated geometrically.

The proper solution for this shortcoming was neither tinkering with the administrative structure nor even increasing the naval element on the board, an expedient that would have probably done little other than make the system more unwieldy and less efficient than it already was. Rather, it was simply the creation of a naval staff that could assist the board by relieving it of some of the routine administrative duties that nonetheless demanded professional knowledge, and by considering larger matters such as strategy, wartime planning, and design policy.

There had been agitation both inside and outside Whitehall for the creation of such a body since the mid-1870s. Admiral Geoffrey Phipps Hornby, Second Naval Lord during the early years of the second Disraeli ministry, explicitly addressed the want of a naval staff in a letter of late 1876 to future First Naval Lord Sir Astley Cooper Key: "Under its present organization the Service is not, and cannot be properly worked.... [T]here is no time or staff to enable fitting arrangements to be made for war, & thus the outbreak of one will go far to ruin our naval reputation.... The great fault is the absence of any qualified—i.e. professional—assistance to the naval Lords. The clerks are unable to assist them in naval matters, and keep them smothered in paper, so that they shall have no time for reorganization."[8] Hornby himself attempted to remedy the perceived deficiency. When invited to join Ward Hunt's board in 1874, he made his acceptance of the offer contingent on being provided a professional assistant and "an enquiry into the state of the Navy."[9] The First Lord could not accede to these demands and Hornby refused the post. He would, however, bow to the urging of friends and join the board as

Second Naval Lord in early 1875, this time without conditions.

Upon Milne's retirement in 1876, Hornby was offered the post of First Naval Lord and took this occasion to renew his attempts to create a naval staff. Once again the moment was not propitious, but this time, rather than acquiesce, Hornby refused the offer and left Ward Hunt to find another candidate. Simultaneously, however, he tried another tactic. Calculating that the three officers most likely to be offered the post of First Naval Lord were himself, Frederick Beauchamp Seymour, and Cooper Key, Hornby attempted to create another "combination": "[I]f we three agree that certain reforms are necessary for the efficiency of the service, and refuse to accept the position of First Sea Lord unless they are carried out, we must carry our point." They did not. Ward Hunt tapped another officer, Admiral Sir Hastings Yelverton, and when a second opportunity arose in 1879, Cooper Key declined to join the combination.[10] The initial efforts to augment the professional staff at the Admiralty thus fell by the wayside during the 1870s.

The call for a naval staff was renewed, however, by the Carnarvon Commission on Colonial Defense, whose second report (March 1882) stated that "the creation of an intelligence department" was a "matter of urgency"; as a consequence of this unequivocal observation, the Admiralty established a foreign intelligence committee the following December. Moreover, its organization and influence developed quickly; by the time of the Penjdeh incident and subsequent Russian war scare (1884–85) "less than three years after its creation, it had already become something like a naval staff" and had prepared "detailed war plans."[11] Its development was, in turn, symbolically acknowledged in 1886, when it was renamed the naval intelligence division.

The creation and development of a naval staff was, to be sure, hesitant, piecemeal, and opposed by some influential elements in naval administration. But it is also worthwhile to point out that expecting the Admiralty, in response to the myriad technological, strategic, and tactical upheavals that transformed the navy from a traditional to a modern force, to have evolved overnight, or even in the short space of two decades, from the largely traditional policy-making structure of the 1860s to a sophisticated and thoroughly professionalized modern department is rather akin to expecting modern business management techniques and cost-accounting procedures to have evolved concurrently with the invention of the water frame and power loom. It is anachronistic to assume that the early ironclad era should have witnessed the rapid implementation of a modernized system of naval administration. As in the case of many, if not most, revolutions, there was a considerable lag between the revolution itself and complete—or even partial—comprehension and appreciation of its implications by those who lived through it. The mid-Victorian Admiralty, and indeed the British government as a whole, was hardly unique in this respect.

On the purely administrative level, or perhaps more accurately, on the level of structure and administrative organization, there is little question that the system set forth in Goschen's order in council, and as it subsequently functioned, remedied the fundamental defects—Milne's strictures notwithstanding—that had hitherto attracted the attention of contemporaries. Whereas the administration of the navy had garnered repeated, and generally critical, scrutiny by parliamentary committees and royal commissions prior to 1872, thereafter the story was quite different. The royal commission on civil establishments (1887) was unstinting in its praise of naval administration: "The constitution of the Board of Admiralty appears to us well-designed, and to be placed, under present regulations, on a satisfactory footing."[12] Likewise, the report of the royal commission on the civil and professional administration of the naval and military departments (Hartington Commission, 1890) while recommending minor changes to bring the Admiralty patent into conformity with usage and while also noting the continued shortage of "naval assistants to the Lords," extended its general approbation to the existing administrative structure.[13] As a final commentary on the enduring worth of the mid-Victorian reform of naval administration, in 1904 the Esher Committee was appointed "with the specific object of modeling a new system of Army administration" on the Admiralty system. Matters had thus "come full circle" from 1860, when "Sir James Graham's Committee [on Military Organization] reported that to model the higher administration of the Army on that of the Navy would be 'a retrograde measure which could not be recommended.'"[14]

Modern assessments of Childers' efforts at Admiralty reform have uniformly been unsparingly critical.[15] To be sure, his system was flawed in several respects. Most critical was the overburdening of the First Naval Lord. Milne's complaints about his workload, even in the wake of Goschen's restoration of an additional Naval Lord to deal with matters have been noted and the situation was in this respect considerably worse during the lifespan of Childers' system. In his zeal to concentrate the entire business of personnel—including every matter concerning the fleet in commission—in the hands of one administrator, Childers subjected Dacres to an administrative nightmare. He took the duties that had hitherto been performed by three Naval Lords and reassigned them to the First Naval Lord alone. As a sop he gave Dacres an assistant in the person of the Junior Naval Lord, but the latter had no independent authority; the First Naval Lord alone was responsible for every matter relating to personnel. Prior to Childers' order in council he had been directly responsible for ten subjects. The new arrangement raised the number to forty-two. The burden was far too great for anyone to manage, save perhaps a man of boundless enthusiasm and capacity for work. In a letter of 1870 to Milne, Beauchamp Seymour wrote: "One thing I am quite sure of and that is that no human being can stand the work that Dacres is trying to get [through] and if he lasts another twelvemonth I shall indeed be surprised."[16] Dacres himself provided confirmation: "I see every day how the changes here have completely upset the working efficiency of the Admiralty. . . . [If] the slightest additional pressure be put on us or either Childers or myself fall sick . . . the whole would come to a stand still."[17] The evidence taken by Somerset's committee was equally unequivocal. Vernon Lushington declared, "In my opinion the Senior Naval Lord is an overworked man." Lord John Hay, Dacres' subordinate, remarked, "I think he has more work than it is at all necessary that he should have," and Dacres, when asked whether he could cope with the myriad administrative responsibilities entrusted to him, replied forthrightly "It is impossible."[18] Were this testimony not sufficiently convincing—and the committee found it convincing enough to cite in its report—John Briggs made similar observations in his memoirs.[19]

Childers did not initially perceive the problem when he distributed the business of the department in late 1868, but he soon recognized it. In late 1869 Dacres informed Milne, "Every day shows to me more and more the fatal error it was doing away with the two Naval Lords . . . and I suspect Childers is much of my opinion."[20] By November 1870 the First Lord had certainly reached the same conclusion, for when announcement of the Russian renunciation of the Black Sea neutrality clauses of the Treaty of Paris (1856) reached the Admiralty, he remarked to Dacres, "[T]he first thing which must be done is to put another Naval Lord into the Admiralty."[21] By so doing, therefore,

Goschen was carrying out a modification that Childers himself was on the verge of implementing when his health collapsed.

Two further problems of naval administration, at least as seen by Goschen, were not directly addressed by Childers' reforms. These were the "weakness of the permanent staff working under the Naval Lords" and the "anomalous and unsatisfactory position of many of the professional and scientific officers of the Board." Goschen proposed to resolve the first problem by removing the controller from the board and making him once again a permanent officer and by creating the positions of naval secretary and deputy controller (also permanent appointments). The second was addressed through improved pay and status for the naval architects, engineers, and other professional staff of the Admiralty, a solution that Goschen hoped would enhance their position and authority over the clerical staff.[22]

Aside from these specific flaws in Childers' system, however, there is little evidence to suggest that his reforms failed, disastrously or otherwise. Indeed, most modern accounts of his work are inaccurate on several counts, starting with the authorship of much of the system attributed to the controversial First Lord, and concluding with how much of it survived his tenure at the Admiralty, and the fierce and widespread denunciations he and it aroused. First, with the furor that surrounded the system's perceived collapse in 1870-71, it is easy to forget how widely vilified the previous arrangement had been. Under Childers' scheme the First Naval Lord was grossly overworked, to be sure, but the same had been true prior to 1868. When asked if he thought the First Naval Lord was "rather overworked," Vernon Lushington replied: "[Y]es," but added, "and I should say still more so under the old system."[23] Despite the lengthy list of duties assigned to the First Naval Lord under Childers' system, he had been relieved of one particularly weighty burden when the supervision of the dockyards was transferred to the Third Lord and Controller.

Furthermore, Childers had been uniformly condemned for the practical abolition of the board, on the grounds that this innovation destroyed any chance for "collective discussion," and hampered unity of action amongst the heads of departments.[24] The evidence taken on this point by Somerset's committee is not convincing, however. Dacres stated that "a Board is of great value, and it gives an opportunity to all members of the Board to know every subject under discussion," but immediately prior to this observation he admitted that much time in the boardroom was wasted on extremely trivial matters. Spencer Robinson, it is true, was highly critical of Childers' innovation. Yet the only examples the former controller could adduce in support of his contention that the public service had suffered involved instances in which he personally had been overruled by what he seemed to regard as a cabal of Childers and Dacres.[25]

In contrast, Lushington testified that from his own observation it was "the practice of the First Lord to continually confer with his colleagues in his own room," and when asked specifically whether, in the case of "any question which touches two departments, or the spheres of two officers, the First Lord would invariably consult both those officers," the permanent secretary replied: "I should think invariably; it would be the merest inadvertence if he did not." Lushington's testimony was corroborated by Lord John Hay. "I think that it is impossible," he informed the committee, "to have had more access to the First Lord; the First Naval Lord seemed to be constantly there, and the Third Lord [and Controller] constantly there." When asked if he thought "any measure of importance has been adopted without ample consultation with everyone concerned," Hay was unequivocal: "I think he saw more constantly the Lords of the Admiralty than has been common, or I might almost say possible, with another man; he was a very long time at business, and saw them constantly."[26] Briggs made much the same observation. Childers, he wrote, wished "to be accessible at all times, and the consequence was that the members of his Board were in and out of his private room all day long."[27]

Faced with contradictory evidence, Somerset's committee hedged on the subject in its report. Spencer Robinson was quoted to the effect that Childers "so entirely changed [the] constitution and character of the Board . . . that affairs were more embarrassed than before, and the inconvenience to the public service was greatly increased."[28] Yet the observation that followed, that "decisions were arrived at seriously affecting the Controller's business in his absence, so that his objections were not heard," was demonstrably false, since Spencer Robinson's testimony stated nothing of the sort. It provided only examples in which his objections were heard and overruled. Furthermore, the committee's observation that "[w]hether the members of a department meet in one room or another, they cannot properly conduct the public service unless they can act cordially together in the arrangement of innumerable details requiring agreement and harmony of action" was hardly to the point, since Childers' structural alterations had no direct effect on whether the board was to "act cordially together," and had only limited influence on the matter of "harmony of action," assuming the Lords took the time to familiarize themselves with the daily minutes.

With these points in mind, it is worth considering observations printed in the *Times* in February 1871, at the height of parliamentary criticism of Childers' work. The old system of naval administration was, it baldly stated, "proverbial for its inefficiency.... It was costly [and] cumbrous, it was unready, it was always in arrear of the improvements required by the times." Quoting testimony by Spencer Robinson and his predecessor as controller, Sir Baldwin Walker, as to the defects of the previous system, the paper added, "We have cited these testimonies as to the actual working of the old Board, because it now seems to be assumed that Mr. Childers was rash and ill-advised in introducing into the governing body alterations which had long been clamoured for."[29]

Five months later, while commenting on a debate in the House of Lords, in which the Duke of Somerset, among others, harshly criticized Childers' innovations, the *Times* admitted, "The general impression produced by the debate was damaging and unsatisfactory," but pointedly added that "it may surprise one to be told that no instance was alleged by the assailants in which the Admiralty had failed, unless it was in the building of the turret ship *Captain*—a ship which was contemplated by the Duke of Somerset and ordered by Sir John Pakington under the old *regime*, before Mr. Childers or his changes had ever tainted the Administration." From the observations of Somerset, one might think that the previous system was "a model of administrative success," and the *Times* felt obliged to list the many charges against it in order to supply "the necessary corrective to the one-sided sketches in the House of Lords debates."[30] In short, there is no conclusive contemporary evidence to suggest that Childers' system was worse than the one it supplanted, and, as will be noted presently, much evidence that suggests, on the contrary, that in many respects it marked a considerable improvement.

Second, it is inaccurate to attribute to Childers himself the whole of the administrative reforms introduced at the Admiralty in 1868–69. He was the engineer, to be sure, and deserves credit or blame for implementing the system, but it is clear that several crucial innovations were conceived by none other than Spencer Robinson, particularly the consolidation of all matters relating to the dockyards, ship construction, and repairs under the authority of the controller and his elevation to the board.[31] From the evidence the ex-controller gave Somerset's committee and Childers gave the *Megaera* commission, it is indisputable that the former was the source of and the prime mover in this innovation. As early as 1861 Spencer Robinson was pointing out the problems stemming from divided authority over the dockyards, most notably in a paper presented to the committee on management of the dockyards and subsequently printed in its report. Moreover, by his own admission he tried to convince the Duke of Somerset that making the controller one of the members of the board "might be an advantageous change."[32] When the Duke left office in 1866 without having been convinced of its utility, Spencer Robinson attempted to sway Pakington and Corry. In 1867 he produced a lengthy memorandum that laid stress on the evils arising, as he saw it, from both the controller's incomplete authority over the dockyards and from his subordination to the First Naval Lord. "[I]n a word," wrote Spencer Robinson in a glaring instance of understatement, "the management of the dockyard[s] is vested in the Board of Admiralty, in the Senior Naval Lord, in the one or two Junior Naval Lords, in the Controller of the Navy, in the Storekeeper General, and in some respects . . . the Secretary of the Admiralty. How, then, can there be unity of purpose, forethought, or method, in conducting these establishments?" Moreover, added the controller, in a remark likely to catch the attention of an economy-minded reformer like Childers, "It is equally clear that it is impossible under such management to know whether the expenditure is judiciously made, or to get work, with certainty, performed economically." Only if the controller were "a member, and a permanent and influential member," of the board of Admiralty, would satisfactory supervision over the dockyards be obtained. Were this change implemented, claimed Spencer Robinson grandiosely, a whole welter of weaknesses, ranging from divided authority over the dockyards and wasteful correspondence to the overall coordination of naval administration and "a thousand other impediments to the due dispatch of business, to economy, and to responsibility would disappear at once."[33] Again, however, Spencer Robinson failed to achieve his aim; both Pakington and Corry remained unconvinced of the need to enhance the controller's authority and position.

Significantly, however, it is clear that he did succeed in winning Childers over to his views at about the same time that his memorandum was rebuffed by the Conservative First Lords. Childers forthrightly informed the *Megaera* commission that by 1867 he "was on terms of personal friendship" with Spencer Robinson, and that the controller's views "much influenced me."[34] In fact, he testified, the two men "had many conversations on the subject [of naval administration] before I took office."[35] There was no doubt, in the *Times'* view, as to the authorship of these parts of the administrative reform. On 20 April 1872 the newspaper devoted a leader to the subject of the Admiralty, remarking, "It appears from the testimony which has just been taken before the Duke of Somerset's Committee that the changes in the Board of Admiralty which were introduced by Mr. Childers were largely in accordance with the suggestions of Sir Spencer Robinson himself."[36] The Childers reforms, therefore, were the joint efforts of the First Lord and Spencer Robinson.

But at the same time the controller's important role in the innovation of the reforms of 1868–69 is acknowledged, his equally crucial role in their apparent collapse two years later must also be stressed. Childers and his allegedly autocratic personality have traditionally been blamed for the want of harmony and unity of action that contributed heavily to the failure of his reforms.[37] But the *Times* drew a strikingly different picture of the First Lord's personality in January 1871. "The weak part of Mr. Childers' nature was his excessive gentleness, which shrank from inflicting a wound, and suffered his subalterns almost to mutiny against him rather than deprive them of their positions and prospective pensions."[38] Briggs, who could claim firsthand knowledge, stated that Childers always treated him with "kindness and consideration" and gave no hint that he behaved otherwise to the members of the board.[39] The *United Service Gazette*, it is true, did raise the charge of autocracy against Childers, but this occurred in late March 1871, at which time Spencer Robinson's damaging but not altogether reliable testimony before Somerset's committee was fresh in the public mind.[40] It is likely that anyone attempting, as Childers did, to reform the Admiralty thoroughly, plus the system of promotion and retirement of officers and the service's overseas deployment—as well as other matters—was doomed to be charged with autocratic and high-handed behavior, since the bulk of these reforms, in particular those relating to the officer corps, would be carried out in the face of professional inertia, if not outright opposition. This likelihood, in turn, suggests that it was primarily Childers' measures, rather than his manner, that soured his relations with the service. And there is no indication that any of his subordinates, other than Spencer Robinson and Edward J. Reed, had difficulties in their personal dealings with him.[41]

On the other hand, there is a great deal of contemporary evidence to suggest that Reed and especially Spencer Robinson were extremely difficult to get along with. Indeed, the terms used by modern authors to describe Childers—autocratic, high-handed, offensive, and brusque—may, along with others—intemperate, intolerant, insubordinate, and uncooperative—be applied far more accurately and deservingly to the controller. The observations of both Dacres and Beauchamp Seymour on the difficulty—the virtual impossibility—of working harmoniously with Spencer Robinson have been noted in conjunction with the breakdown of Admiralty administration in mid- to late 1870. Others shared their sentiments. Briggs left no doubt as to the source of disharmony and friction at the Admiralty during Childers' regime. The contest between Dacres and Spencer Robinson for the ear of the First Lord led, he wrote, "to warm discussions and to much that was unpleasant, which was followed by constant threats of resignation—one day from the Controller, the next day from the Constructor, and not infrequently from both at once. . . . I was daily shocked and annoyed," Briggs stated primly, "to find that the general topic of conversation among the gentlemen of the office was about the 'rows' in the First Lord's room, and the resignation of this person and that." He furthermore singled out Spencer Robinson as the leading disruptive element, and even made suggestions to Childers' private secretary as to how the controller's fractious behavior might be curbed.[42] Moreover, the evidence given to Somerset's committee prompted the *Times* to remark that Gladstone's government was "amply justified in asserting the incompatibility of Sir Spencer Robinson was felt by his colleagues quite as much as by his immediate chief."[43] Yet the controller had, by that point, been almost a decade in his office and had evidently worked with three previous administrations without the friction and disputes that so marred his relations with Childers' board. What had happened to alter the situation so dramatically?

The crucial transformation was the elevation of the controller to a position on the board. As long as Spencer Robinson remained subordinate to both the board collectively and the First Naval Lord individually, he was a governable, if argumentative, officer. Elevated to a position of parity with the First Naval Lord, he became unmanageable. The controller's office became, Briggs wrote, "an *imperium in imperio*. The business which had been and ought to belong to the First Sea Lord was usurped by the Controller, and the papers rapidly transferred to his office."[44] He added, rather unnecessarily, "This, as a matter of course, led to serious personal differences between the First Sea Lord and Second Sea Lord [controller], as well as to grave departmental inconvenience."

Confirmation of Briggs' charges came from no less a source than Spencer Robinson himself, who informed Somerset's committee that the naval element at the Admiralty "has been reduced to too low a pitch very considerably," and maintained "that arises entirely from the mistaken view which has been taken of cutting off the Controller from all purely administrative business, excepting what relates to his own department, namely the matériel. I think it absolutely necessary that more than one naval officer should advise the First Lord on the many professional points of naval policy, [and] on the general duties of men and officers in the Navy."[45] Not content with undisputed authority over the dockyards for which he had long agitated, Spencer Robinson, it is clear, sought to dominate all aspects of naval administration. "It is clear from the evidence of Sir Spencer Robinson," the *Times* remarked, "that he was never satisfied with the position of comparative independence which he enjoyed in Mr. Childers' board. He not only complains of being overruled by Mr. Childers in matters of shipbuilding, but he complains of not being allowed, as a member of the Board of Admiralty, to interfere with the personnel of the Navy, which was under the control of the First Sea Lord."[46]

Most telling, however, were observations made by the shrewd Alexander Milne several years earlier. In 1867, when Spencer Robinson composed his memorandum urging the Conservative board of Admiralty to promote the controller, he submitted a draft of it to the First Naval Lord. Milne's remarks are worth quoting, for they served not only as a remarkably accurate prediction of what occurred when Spencer Robinson's scheme was carried out, but also highlighted the crucial differences in perspective and insight between a seasoned naval administrator like Milne and a relative novice (and civilian) like Childers. "If this is the view which the Controller is to take of the Public Service," wrote Milne, "and he is[,] as he proposes to be[,] supreme at the Board, it is very evident that the Senior Naval Lord and Controller could never act together. In fact, Admiral Robinson wishes to place the Controller of the Navy in a position of greater power and authority than the Board of [Admiralty]."[47] It was ironic that the man responsible for devising much of the system introduced by Childers should have been, at the same time, the chief agent of its collapse.

Yet, as subsequent developments would reveal, the problem was not the elevation of the controller to the board per se; rather, it was the manner in which the controller had been given unchecked authority over the dockyards, coupled with the more crucial factor of the personality of the man who was elevated. For if it was such a mistake to make the controller a Naval Lord in 1869, why, then, did Northbrook's administration repeat it in 1882?[48] And if, in 1869, it had been such a mistake to elevate the controller that the promotion was reversed only three years later, why, then, did the subsequent elevation of that officer persist from 1882 to 1917, despite the fact that during those thirty-five years the post was held by such formidable— not to say domineering—officers as Sir Arthur Knyvett Wilson, Sir John Jellicoe, and, certainly not least of all, Sir John Fisher?[49] The answer lay partly in Goschen's method of conducting business at the board, and in his less rigid insistence on separation of responsibilities among the Naval Lords, but at least as much of the reason can be attributed to the personality and ambitions of Spencer Robinson, a man who, as Northbrook himself remarked privately, "is very difficult to deal with, & requires great calmness & good temper."[50]

The paralysis and disharmony at the Admiralty were created largely through the actions of one man, in turn suggesting that both Childers and his critics—contemporary and subsequent—failed to perceive the extent to which the problems of naval administration were the consequence of individual actions, rather than of flaws in the system. Childers resolved, "from the first day" of his administration, that "discussions at the board [would come] to an end," owing to the "appalling waste of time" he had witnessed as a junior member of Somerset's administration, and, more critically, because the conduct of business around the boardroom table "produced a great weakening of [personal] responsibility."[51] The waste of time and dispersion of responsibility could have been eliminated by a far less drastic expedient. The First Lord had only to exercise his recognized authority to control both what subjects came before the notice of the board and the extent to which those that did were discussed. This is no idle speculation, for it was precisely the system adopted by Goschen and praised by subsequent committees and commissions of inquiry. The revival of board meetings placated the Naval Lords and satisfied public opinion, while at the same time the fact that the business brought to the board was, in Goschen's words, "left to the discretion" of the First Lord greatly reduced, if it did not entirely eliminate, "the appalling waste of time" that had so troubled Childers. And with the First Lord supreme at the board it became "impossible for the principle of the personal responsibility of the various members of the Board for their respective spheres of duty to be replaced by a loose system of collective Board administration."[52] The crucial factor was not the system but, rather, the character of the man who directed it. Ironically, Childers may have preferred to dispense with formal board meetings in favor of informal discussions with the Naval Lords so as not to appear too domineering—too autocratic—in exercising his authority at the board.

Likewise, the shortcomings of subsequent boards, especially those of the late 1870s and 1880s, that, according to one critic, arose partly from "administrative inefficiency," can be seen perhaps more appropriately as having followed from the weaknesses of the individuals who made up those administrations.[53] To be sure, it is acknowledged that much of the trouble with naval administration in the final years of the "pax Britannica" sprang from the men who ran the system rather than from it itself. The rapid turnover of personnel in the late 1870s—between 1876 and 1879 there were no fewer than four First Naval Lords—contributed its share to the shortcomings of naval administration.[54]

More crucially, however, the character and talents of Sir Astley Cooper Key, First Naval Lord from 1879 to 1885, and Sir Arthur Hood, who succeeded Key and remained in office until 1889, hampered the navy's response to a rapidly changing technological and strategic scene. Cooper Key was, even his generally sympathetic biographer Philip Colomb admitted, a cautious and conservative man, traits that would have served him well in more stable circumstances, but which were actively detrimental in times of great upheaval.[55] Hood, it seems, was little better.[56] In addition, the First Lords of the late 1870s and early 1880s—W. H. Smith (1877–80) and Lord Northbrook (1880–85)—were less effective administrators, at least from a strictly naval point of view, than their immediate predecessors, Goschen and George Ward Hunt: Smith owing to his concentration on domestic political and economic considerations (he was one of the Conservatives' leaders in the House of Commons) and his relative lack of influence in Beaconsfield's cabinet, and Northbrook because of Gladstone's reliance on him as a colonial troubleshooter.[57] Also, the lack of adequate professional assistance for the Naval Lords doubtless left them immersed in administrative duties, to the detriment of the consideration of larger issues of policy and strategy, and this situation was probably not much relieved at first by the creation of the foreign intelligence committee in 1882. Yet even given the increasing administrative burden on the Naval Lords throughout the 1870s and 1880s, Cooper Key and Hood could have, had they been so inclined, given some consideration to general matters of naval policy, as Milne had done between 1872 and 1876. That they did not resulted more from their individual characters than from the structural flaws of British naval administration. Once again, the crucial element was not the system, but the men who ran it. As the *Times* perceptively noted in July 1871, "There may be persons who consider our naval affairs to be susceptible of more successful handling; but it is a mistake to attribute their deficiencies altogether to the system, and in no degree to the men."[58]

Last, but certainly not least, there has been a general failure to recognize to what a considerable extent the Childers system survived the furor that engulfed it in 1870–71; to what extent it emerged substantively intact from Goschen's subsequent modifications; and, most significantly, to what extent it may be accounted a success. "It may be fairly questioned," observed the *Times* in the wake of the publication of the damaging report of Somerset's committee, if Childers' attempt to rationalize the structure of naval administration "was fairly tried, owing to personal disagreements and peculiarities which could hardly fail to impede the working of the machine."[59] There could be no doubt on this point. But Somerset's committee itself could find little to praise aside from the physical consolidation of the departments at Whitehall.[60] Subsequent writers have largely taken their cue from the committee, or else from the generally hostile response of the navy itself to Childers' innovations.[61]

Bearing this view in mind, it is instructive to turn to that of Goschen, after he had completed his survey of Childers' system. He was quick to admit that it was by no means perfect: "[S]ome of his changes were avowedly compromises, and tentative in their nature, and it was certain, from the beginning, that further changes would be made." Moreover, Goschen, like the *Times*, recognized that "the new system has scarcely had a fair trial, owing to the prejudice and hostility with which many of his [sic] changes were received, and to the immense difficulty of working the system with unwilling elements." Most crucially, however, Childers' successor realized that the scrutiny and criticism that had been heaped on the reforms in the wake of the *Captain* and *Megaera* disasters, and the resulting "uneasiness which the public feels as to the present constitution of the Admiralty, and as to the conduct of its business, render it impossible to allow the system to work itself into order gradually."[62] In other words, Goschen's reforms were to a considerable extent motivated by the necessity of placating public opinion, rather than by the conviction that they were administratively imperative.

There was, furthermore, much that Goschen was quite content to leave untouched. "I entirely adhere," he informed his cabinet colleagues, "[t]o his separation of the work into three great divisions corresponding to the 'personnel,' the 'matériel,' and finance." Goschen's approbation also extended to Childers' "substitution of personal action and responsibility for the action and nominal responsibility of the Board." In short, Goschen chose to retain the central structural feature of Childers' Admiralty organization—the tripartite division of business—as well as the crucial principle guiding its operation: the concept of individual responsibility. Yet many contemporaries and most subsequent writers have overlooked these critical points.[63]

Their importance cannot be overstated. The rationalization of the Admiralty's administrative structure went a long way towards streamlining a clumsy, inefficient, often byzantine administrative apparatus, one that had accreted over the course of centuries and had remained in place, to a considerable extent, even in the wake of Graham's reforms. To convey some idea of the complexity of the old structure, in 1863 Rear Admiral Sir John Hay, Conservative M.P., future Naval Lord and, eventually, one of Childers' harshest parliamentary critics, eloquently denounced the administrative chaos that engulfed the Admiralty: "The cardinal defect of the Board of Admiralty, as at present constituted, was the want of responsibility that pervaded, not only the Board, but every one of the thirteen branches of administration conducted by the Board. . . . It was practically impossible to fix the responsibility on any one officer," continued the indignant Rear Admiral. "The officers who really did the practical work of the Admiralty in its various branches were not responsible to the House or the public, and the superior authorities, who were supposed to be responsible, were shielded by the fact that they had no practical knowledge of what was done in the different branches."[64] Compared to the system denounced by Hay, that with which Childers supplanted it was a model of administrative rationalization and efficiency. The *Times*, to its credit, recognized the importance of Childers' accomplishment. Describing the old structure of six departments, each answerable to one of the Lords, who might be largely ignorant of the business under their charge, "but who had and exercised large powers of interference with the ordinary action of the permanent officials," the editors added, "It was a control in petty details of the more instructed by the less instructed."[65] "Previously to the accession of Mr. Childers," the newspaper remarked almost a year later, "there was a great want of simple distribution in the business of the Admiralty."[66]

Moreover, although the professional element was underrepresented in the Admiralty both before and after Childers' reforms, the rationalization of the administrative structure made it possible, as would be demonstrated, to augment the naval presence with the assurance that it would have a clearly assigned role in a coherent structure. Prior to 1869 the addition of more staff ran a considerable risk of further cluttering an administrative machine already beset with clutter, a machine "proverbial for inefficiency."[67] There can be no question either that the Childers reforms remedied the want of individual responsibility. Up to 1869, as the royal commission on civil establishments (1887) noted, "all important business had been transacted by the joint action of the Board at their daily meetings."[68] As "[t]his procedure [was] found to be ill-adapted to the altered condition of things, the method ... was adopted [by Childers] of conducting the majority of the business by minute, reserving for the consideration of the Board certain specified subjects only." This method, added the commission, "still remains in force."

The commission's findings, in turn, suggest a further point, that being the considerable extent to which Goschen's modifications of the system were cosmetic rather than substantive. Take, for instance, the revival of board meetings. On the surface the change appears to be a major departure from Childers' method of informal discussion, but by placing the decision of what business was to be brought before the board entirely in the hand of the First Lord, Goschen just as thoroughly circumscribed freedom of discussion as Childers had by dispensing with the board outright. Indeed, Childers, who wished "to be accessible at all times," and who had the "members of the Board ... in and out of his private room all day long" was quite possibly exposed to more professional opinion than was Goschen, despite his "humane and considerate character."[69] Moreover, as the commission on civil establishments noted, the resurrection of board meetings did not alter Childers' method of "conducting the majority of the business by minute."

Similar observations can be made with regard to Goschen's removal of the controller from the board. He was removed de jure, but to a great extent remained a de facto member. After all, wrote Goschen, "[d]esigns of ships, and other large questions of that nature connected with his department should be submitted to the Board for discussion; and on those occasions the Controller should be present at the Board to explain and defend his plans." When it is recalled that under Childers' system the only business in which the controller would participate was that relating to his department, the practical difference between his treatment of the controller and Goschen's seems even less significant. Moreover, the rest of Childers' reforms that touched on the controller, namely, making him directly answerable to the First Lord, rather than to the First Naval Lord, and giving him authority over all business relating to matériel, remained unaltered. Finally, the re-elevation of the controller to board membership a decade later suggests to what a great extent Goschen's action had merely been a sop to public opinion. The same was undoubtedly true of the decision to revive board meetings. And while Goschen noted "the feeling is very prevalent that the Naval element is unduly reduced in Mr. Childers' scheme," he added, "I do not entirely concur, but it would doubtless be an advantage to meet that feeling to a certain extent."[70]

In the end, therefore, only Goschen's addition of a Naval Lord, his reacquainting the parliamentary secretary with the general business of the department, adopting a less rigid division of duties between the Naval Lords, and removing the Junior Naval Lord from direct subordination to the First Naval Lord marked substantial departures from Childers' system. Goschen's other reforms were largely superficial. Childers' major structural innovations survived untouched, or only slightly altered, the guiding principle of individual responsibility remained unimpaired, and the First Lord's supremacy unchallenged. The system that garnered such praise from the commission on civil establishments and served as the model for the Esher Committee was largely the work of Hugh Childers, although he has received scant recognition for his achievement and a barrage of criticism for his alleged failures.[71]

On this score, contemporaries were more cognizant of Childers' accomplishments than most subsequent commentators have been. Although his reforms were subject to unrelenting criticism, especially in the wake of the *Captain* tragedy, by 1872 it was recognized how much he had achieved. The unveiling of Goschen's order in council in March "reasserted," wrote the *Times*, "the principles of the reforms initiated by Mr. Childers, and thus vindicated the substantial wisdom of the administration which has of late been so severely challenged."[72] Moreover, Childers' concurrent defense of his reforms to the House of Commons (his first parliamentary speech in almost two years) prompted the "leading journal" to conclude "it cannot be doubted that Mr. Childers was not merely right in his principles, but substantially correct in his application of them. He did what had to be done, and the country will always be indebted to him for the firmness and decision with which he did it."

Similar praise came from Briggs, a man with extensive knowledge of the Admiralty and its workings. He did not shrink from criticizing Childers for overburdening the First Naval Lord, for making the controller a member of the board, and for dispensing with board meetings, but he nonetheless stated that "[n]o First Lord has ever done more for the good of the Navy than Mr. Childers, and that in spite of all difficulties."[73] Briggs then enumerated his achievements: the redistribution of the fleet, the promotion and retirement scheme, extensive dockyard improvements, and, last but by no means least, "the consolidation of the Admiralty departments, are all . . . important measures, each bearing lasting testimony to his herculean labours. . . . Mr. Childers' merits as a statesman stand very high," finished Briggs, "and have hitherto been very inadequately appreciated," but the former Admiralty clerk believed "the time cannot be far distant when ample justice will be accorded to so able and judicious a reformer as Mr. Childers proved himself to be." Almost a century has passed since Briggs' eulogy was published, and Childers still awaits proper recognition for his achievements.

CHAPTER 10

Rivals

One frequently encounters a paradox when assessing the strength of the nineteenth-century British navy vis-à-vis that of its rivals. It has been conventional for historians to regard Nelson's victory at Trafalgar, along with the commanding naval position in which Britain emerged from the lengthy struggle with France and its allies, as having settled the question of maritime hegemony for the ensuing century.[1] Most general historical works that address the nineteenth-century European balance of power assume, either implicitly or explicitly, that Britain faced no challenges to its naval hegemony prior to the 1890s, when the addition of Germany, the United States, and Japan to the list of potential maritime rivals—hitherto restricted to France and Russia—marked the beginning of the end of the "pax Britannia" and the near-monopoly of naval power to which it was in large part attributed.[2]

But a closer examination of Britain's naval standing relative to other powers during the long nineteenth century has convinced others that British naval supremacy was often a facade. Perhaps most common has been the assertion that Britain was both relatively and absolutely under strength at sea during the three decades prior to the passage of the Naval Defence Act (1889), legislation that, in part a response to contemporary perceptions of weakness, legally committed the country to the maintenance of a "two-power standard" of naval strength. Oscar Parkes, longtime editor of *Jane's Fighting Ships* and widely cited authority on the British fleet, writes that as of 1880 Britain could not "claim even a One-Power Standard!"[3] Another author has stated that the navy between 1869 and 1885 was "small

TABLE 9
Naval Spending, 1860–90 (£)

Year	Austria	France	Germany	Italy	Russia	United States	Great Britain
1860	—	8,106,247	—	—	3,057,142	2,484,200	13,331,668
1861	1,023,926	8,400,047	—	—	3,057,142	8,533,600	12,598,042
1862	1,511,881	8,871,865	328,327	—	2,800,000	12,644,400	11,370,588
1863	1,726,444	8,058,717	328,327	—	2,575,714	17,145,200	10,821,596
1864	—	7,886,123	341,853	2,522,505	2,871,428	24,522,266	10,898,253
1865	—	6,918,569	—	2,356,162	2,871,428	8,644,800	10,259,788
1866	785,000	6,893,472	—	1,904,520	3,442,857	6,206,800	10,676,101
1867	—	8,078,914	275,486	—	2,500,000	5,155,200	11,168,949
1868	750,000	7,093,816	744,974	1,405,127	2,585,714	4,000,200	11,366,545
1869	875,016	6,496,110	812,440	—	2,685,714	4,356,000	9,757,220
1870	—	7,435,516	812,440	949,484	2,871,428	3,886,200	10,056,641
1871	1,135,370	5,817,240	1,199,428	—	3,022,857	4,250,000	9,900,486
1872	—	4,859,372	1,562,085	1,779,998	3,185,714	4,705,200	9,543,000
1873	—	5,197,671	1,306,820	1,779,998	3,257,142	6,186,600	10,279,898
1874	1,014,081	5,118,032	1,945,910	—	3,628,571	4,299,600	10,680,404
1875	—	5,199,040	2,471,085	—	3,685,714	3,972,600	11,063,449
1876	1,094,948	5,684,747	2,065,510	1,912,946	3,871,428	2,292,000	11,364,383
1877	941,019	6,491,642	3,031,090	1,983,948	4,628,571	3,473,000	12,536,591
1878	1,084,526	6,655,756	3,102,630	1,901,956	4,671,428	3,025,000	11,962,816
1879	1,084,526	6,652,550	2,210,225	1,805,069	4,428,571	2,707,000	10,416,131
1880	870,978	7,220,031	2,006,840	1,707,359	4,200,000	3,137,400	10,702,935
1881	—	7,681,980	1,922,945	1,845,386	4,385,714	3,006,400	10,576,453
1882	—	8,102,285	1,944,319	1,986,708	4,385,714	3,056,600	10,408,904
1883	917,782	8,864,186	2,016,365	2,287,200	4,857,142	3,458,600	10,728,781
1884	947,097	7,796,929	2,449,540	2,305,941	4,885,714	3,204,200	11,427,064
1885	1,073,858	7,873,812	2,633,730	2,338,985	5,500,000	2,871,600	12,660,509
1886	1,119,481	9,323,884	2,559,715	3,413,266	6,371,428	3,028,200	13,265,401
1887	1,131,603	8,454,685	2,661,005	4,176,326	5,714,285	3,385,200	12,325,357
1888	1,132,322	7,775,582	2,603,165	4,920,519	5,842,857	4,275,800	12,999,895
1889	1,131,822	7,963,900	2,800,450	4,962,388	5,828,571	4,401,200	15,270,812
1890	1,111,440	8,062,100	3,647,995	4,858,608	5,842,857	5,222,800	15,553,929

SOURCES: Austria: Frederick Martin, ed. *Statesman's Yearbook* (London: Macmillan and Co., 1864–90); France: Figures for 1860 through 1866, Ministère de la Marine et des Colonies, *Revue Maritime et Coloniale* (Paris: Imprimerie Administrative de Paul Dupont), 28 (1869): 456–57; 1867–90: Ministère des Finances, *Compte Générale de l'Administration des Finances* (Paris: Imprimerie Nationale), 1871, 162–63; 1872, 166–67; 1873, 162–63; 1874, 164–65; 1875, 164–65; 1876, 170–71; 1877, 172–73, 426; 1878, 178–79; 1879, 183–84; 1880, 178–79, 200–201, 208–209, 630–33, 658–61; 1881, 507–508; 1882, 519–20; 1883, 198–201, 230–31, 238–39, 535–36; 1884, 200–203, 232–33, 240–41, 537–38; 1885, 220–23, 254–55, 260–61, 559–60; 1886, 190–93, 224–25, 230–31; 1887, 200–203, 235, 240–41; 1888, 194–96, 234–35, 240; 1889, 194–95, 230; 1890, 194–95; 1891, 200–201, 203, 241, 524; 1892, 198–99, 219; Germany, 1860–71, Martin, *Statesman's Yearbook* (London: Macmillan, 1864–72); 1872–90, S. Cohn, *Die Finanzen des Deutschen Reich seit seiner Begründung* (Berlin: J. Guttentag, 1899), 186–88, 190–92, 194–96; Italy, Martin, *Statesman's Yearbook* (London: Macmillan, 1864–91) and France, Ministère des Finances, *Bulletin de Statistique* (Paris: Imprimerie Nationale), 4 (1878): 297; 5 (1879): 65; 7 (1880): 62; 9 (1881): 158; 16 (1884): 448; 21 (1887), 216–17; 22 (1887): 107; 24 (1888): 121; 25 (1889): 445; 26 (1889): 88; 28 (1890): 97; Russia: George Modelski and William Thompson, *Seapower in Global Politics, 1494–1993* (Seattle: University of Washington Press, 1988), 340–42, and Donald Mitchell, *A History of Russian and Soviet Seapower* (New York: Macmillan, 1974), 340–42; United States: William Lerner, et al., *Historical Statistics of the United States* (Washington: U.S. Government Printing Office, 1975), 2:1114; Great Britain: "Finance Accounts," Great Britain, Parliament, *Parliamentary Papers* (London, H.M.S.O., 1860–91). Exchange rates stable during the mid- and late nineteenth century. Austria: £1 = 10 Florins or Gulden; France: £1 = 25 Francs; Prussia/Germany: £1 = 6.67 Thalers (1860–70), £1 = 20 Goldmarks (1871–90); Italy: £1 = 25 Lire; Russia: £1 = 7 Roubles; United States: £1 = 5 Dollars.

TABLE 10
Naval Spending, 1860–90: Percentage of British Outlays

Year	Austria	France	Germany	Italy	Russia	United States
1860	—	61.2	—	—	22.9	18.6
1861	8.1	65.7	—	—	24.2	67.7
1862	13.2	77.0	2.8	—	24.6	111.2
1863	15.9	73.1	3.0	—	23.8	158.4
1864	—	71.2	3.1	23.1	26.3	225.0
1865	—	66.1	—	22.9	27.9	84.4
1866	7.3	63.1	—	17.8	32.2	58.1
1867	—	71.2	2.4	—	22.3	46.1
1868	6.5	61.3	6.5	12.3	22.7	35.1
1869	8.9	65.3	8.3	—	27.5	44.6
1870	—	73.9	8.0	9.4	28.5	38.6
1871	11.4	58.7	12.1	—	30.5	42.9
1872	—	50.9	16.3	18.6	33.3	49.3
1873	—	50.5	12.7	17.3	31.6	60.1
1874	9.4	47.9	18.2	—	33.9	40.2
1875	—	46.9	22.3	—	33.3	34.2
1876	9.6	50.0	18.1	16.8	34.0	26.3
1877	7.5	51.7	24.1	15.8	36.9	27.7
1878	9.0	55.6	25.9	15.8	39.0	25.2
1879	10.4	63.8	21.2	17.3	42.5	25.9
1880	8.1	67.4	18.7	15.9	39.2	29.3
1881	—	72.6	18.1	17.4	41.4	28.4
1882	—	77.8	18.6	19.0	42.1	29.3
1883	8.5	82.6	18.7	21.3	45.2	32.2
1884	8.2	68.2	21.4	20.1	42.7	28.0
1885	8.4	62.1	20.8	18.4	43.4	21.9
1886	8.4	70.2	19.2	25.7	48.0	22.8
1887	9.1	68.5	21.5	33.8	46.3	27.4
1888	8.7	59.8	20.0	37.8	44.9	32.8
1889	7.4	52.1	18.3	32.4	38.1	28.8
1890	7.1	59.2	23.4	31.2	37.5	33.6

SOURCES: See Table 9.

in size, by comparison either with its potential enemies or its potential duties," and the standard reference work, *Conway's All the World's Warships*, remarks that between 1860 and 1905 "France was unquestionably the second naval power to Britain and there were times in the 1860s and again in the late 1870s and early 1880s when it seemed that the French navy might be the first."[4]

In one respect, however, commentators have fundamentally agreed: In terms of expense the mid-Victorian navy constituted a veritable bargain for British taxpayers.[5] Yet to contemporaries the picture was very different. "[A]ny Ministry which declares that the Navy cannot be kept in efficiency with ten millions a year," grumbled the *Times* in April 1874, "must expect to have its statements very seriously criticized."[6] The £10–12 million ordinarily allotted to the senior service was one of the principal elements of a defense establishment that, excluding the cost of debt servicing, accounted for 45 percent to more than 60 percent of the total budget.[7] Contemporaries also had a further perspective by which to judge the matter: comparison. In complaining of the naval budget in 1874, the *Times* added that £10 million should be an ample sum to build and maintain an unrivaled navy, since "[i]t seems to be about as much as the united navies of France, Germany, and Russia cost to maintain."[8] The newspaper was not far from the truth: The combined naval expenditures of those three countries in 1874 totaled £10,810,112, £480,627 more than the British navy's budget. During the years 1860–80, Great Britain, with the sole exception of the wartime United States, spent larger sums on its navy than did any other maritime power. In fact, only France consistently spent even half as much on its navy as did its cross-Channel rival.

British planners could altogether dismiss the threat from several states. The Netherlands, for instance, had once been a formidable naval power, but its days of glory were long since past, and although it could boast an ironclad force of nineteen ships in the latter years of the 1870s, only one was as large as 5,000 tons displacement and capable of fighting on the high seas.[9] The remainder of the Dutch armored fleet consisted of coastal-defense vessels, virtually all of them low-freeboard ships, eighteen of them less than 3,000 tons displacement and no fewer than twelve less than 2,000 tons. This was not a force about which the British navy needed to trouble itself. As of 1878 the British fleet numbered thirteen first-class, seagoing ironclads, plus another seven up-to-date coastal-defense vessels and a further twenty-six armored vessels of varying descriptions, to say nothing of ships then under construction. None of the first-class British ships, it might be added, were as small as 3,000 tons displacement.

Likewise, none of the Scandinavian powers, either individually or collectively, could pose a significant naval challenge to Britain, for between them they mustered a force of sixteen ironclads, none as large as 5,000 tons displacement, and only three among them capable of service on the high seas. Such was not a force to intimidate the British navy, with thirty-three ironclads of more than 5,000 tons displacement. Nor were the Iberian countries any better equipped to threaten British naval supremacy: As of 1880 Portugal possessed one ironclad—built in Britain, it might be added—while Spain had built

Rivals

or purchased the slightly more formidable total of seven, two of which had been blown up or scrapped by 1880. Similar appraisals could be made of the Greek, Argentine, Brazilian, Peruvian, and Chilean navies: all possessed a handful of ironclads; none was capable of arousing any alarm at Whitehall.

Austria, on the other hand, demonstrated by its triumph over the hapless Italian navy at Lissa in 1866 that it outclassed at least one other maritime power, and that it was capable of becoming a force worthy of respect in the Mediterranean, or at minimum the Adriatic. Austria's moment of naval glory was fleeting, however. First, the Austro-Hungarian army received the lion's share of attention and funding following the debacle of 1866. The *Ausgleich*, moreover, worsened matters for the navy, which was often held hostage by Hungarian politicians who "considered the navy a purely Austrian interest undeserving of common funds." Hence, the Austro-Hungarian navy received only a pittance in the way of funding compared to its British counterpart. The yearly naval budgets authorized by the Dual Monarchy in the late 1860s and the 1870s never rose above £1.13 million pounds, and on at least three occasions dropped below £1 million. At its highest point, in 1863, the Austro-Hungarian navy's budget was only 16 percent of Britain's. After 1866 the Austrian navy "once again became technologically backward and increasingly weaker in comparison to the other fleets of Europe," and after 1871 it "gave up all pretense of being a first-class naval force and lapsed into a semi-dormant state."[10] Austria-Hungary built seven ironclads between 1866 and 1880 and began work on one more, but four were rebuilt wooden warships. This modest augmentation provoked no alarm in Britain.

Nor did the naval forces of the Ottoman Empire arouse British apprehension. The matériel of the Sultan's forces was not unimpressive: four 6,400-ton seagoing ironclads had been built by English firms for the Turkish navy during the 1860s, augmented by ten smaller armored vessels. The Turks, moreover, ordered five additional ironclads from foreign shipbuilders during the late 1860s and the 1870s, three of them clearly formidable ships. Yet the fate of these vessels indicates why the Ottoman Empire's maritime forces were frequently scorned abroad. Four of the five ended up in the hands of other powers, three of them wearing British colors. The frequent, virtually chronic, insolvency of the Turkish government forced the sale of one of the ships to Germany in 1867.[11] Ten years later the Turks, at war with

Russia and strapped for cash, tried to unload four vessels being built in Britain. No takers were found until 1878, when the Disraeli government bought three of them. Turkish seamanship, it might be added, was held in low esteem by the British.[12]

Prior to German unification, the Prussian navy was scarcely worthy of notice, consisting of five steam corvettes and frigates, plus a handful of sailing ships and gunboats and, by 1865, two small coastal ironclads.[13] Prussian navy budgets hovered around £330,000 a year in the early 1860s, barely 3 percent of the British navy's. A decade later, however, the German ironclad fleet consisted of nine sizable vessels, with a further four being built.[14] Likewise, by the late 1870s spending crept above £3 million a year. In 1881 the *Statesman's Yearbook* noted that the German navy had made "rapid progress" over the previous decade.[15] It was, however, hardly mounting an incipient challenge for mastery of the seas. First, the German naval budget during the latter years of the decade was barely a quarter of the Royal Navy's. Second, front-line German battlefleet strength in the late 1870s was no more than six ships, five after the *Grosser Kurfürst* was rammed and sunk by a squadron mate on its maiden voyage.

Of equal significance, neither Germany nor its navy was regarded as a potential foe by Britain during the 1870s. Indeed, in 1874 the *Times* commented, with understandable lack of prescience, that the excitement caused in Germany by the launch of an ironclad was "a healthy and promising sign for the new German nationality.... England," it added, "will be the last country to view such a spectacle with anything like jealousy, [and] [t]here is nothing to make us view with less approval the naval advances of a Power whose territorial consolidation we are still watching with satisfaction."[16] Nor was any alarm to be aroused by German naval ambitions for many years. Bismarck's general preoccupation with continental affairs throughout the 1870s and much of the 1880s ensured that Britain would have little to fear from Germany as long as the Iron Chancellor remained in control and Admiral Tirpitz out of earshot of Wilhelm II.[17] Indeed, such was the insignificance of the German navy—as compared to the army—during the mid-Victorian period that from its inception until 1888 it was "commanded by army officers."[18]

On superficial examination, the Italian navy was still less impressive than that of Germany. Of Italy's twenty ironclads in 1881, twelve dated from the early 1860s and were small, poorly protected, and weakly armed.[19] A further four were of slightly more recent vintage, and roughly comparable to second-class ironclads in the British fleet.[20] The remaining four vessels, however, made the Italian navy an object of intense interest, not to say apprehension, to naval observers abroad—the British included—during the 1870s. The ironclads in question were designed by Benedetto Brin, the most creative and daring, if not the most brilliant, naval designer of the decade.[21] The first two of these ironclads—the *Duilio* and *Dandolo*—combined huge 18-inch guns weighing 100 tons (manufactured by Armstrong) with remarkable speed for big ships. The largest guns mounted on a British ironclad during the 1870s were 16.25-inch caliber muzzleloaders weighing 81 tons. The Italian ships were designed to reach fifteen knots; few British ironclads managed to top fourteen, except under the favorable conditions of speed trials. But to achieve such speed and offensive power Brin reduced the area and weight of armor coverage and ended up with ships lacking any horizontal armor protection at the stem and stern. Yet despite this omission, J. W. King, chief engineer of the U.S. navy, remarked in 1877 that the *Duilio*, "if completed and successful in all respects, . . . will be the most formidable fighting machine, both for offense and defense, ever set afloat in the waters of continental Europe."[22] So impressed were the British that they produced a near-copy in the *Inflexible*. The second pair of Italian ironclads, the *Italia* and *Lepanto*, were even more audacious in conception, being far larger (14,000 tons) and faster (eighteen knots) than any contemporary capital ships. They were too radical, however, to attract imitators. Moreover, they were completed only in the mid-1880s, and thus omitted from Admiralty calculations during the 1870s.[23]

Regardless of the power of individual ships, contemporaries realized that the Italian navy as a whole was in no position to challenge Britain for maritime supremacy, even in the narrow confines of the Mediterranean. During the 1870s, moreover, the Italian navy was further hamstrung, since none of its provocative capital ships was commissioned prior to 1880. The Italian battlefleet of the 1870s consisted essentially of the ships routed by the Austrians at Lissa. Nor was the navy's funding sufficient to permit a large-scale construction program. Following the debacle at Lissa it plummeted: from over 60 million lire (£2,500,000) in 1864, to less than 25 million (£949,000) by 1870. During the early 1870s funding crept upward, but not until the early 1880s did it match the levels of two decades earlier. Furthermore, even the outlays of the early 1860s were

TABLE 11
Battlefleets, 1860–90

Year	Great Britain	France	Russia	United States	Italy	Prussia/ Germany	Austria-Hungary
1860	0/0/0	1/0/0	0/0/0	0/0/0	0/0/0	0/0/0	0/0/0
1861	2/0/0	1/0/0	0/0/0	0/0/0	0/1/0	0/0/0	0/0/0
1862	4/0/0	6/0/0	0/0/0	0/1/4	0/2/0	0/0/0	0/2/0
1863	5/0/0	6/0/0	0/0/0	0/1/10	0/2/0	0/0/0	0/5/0
1864	8/2/1	6/0/0	0/0/1	0/1/23	2/5/0	0/0/0	0/5/0
1865	10/4/1	11/0/0	2/0/12	0/1/42	2/6/0	0/2/0	0/5/0
1866	13/6/2	12/1/1	2/0/13	0/1/46	3/7/1	2/2/0	2/5/0
1867	16/6/2	16/2/3	2/0/13	0/0/46	1/8/1	0/2/0	2/5/0
1868	19/7/2	16/4/4	2/0/15	0/0/45	1/8/1	2/2/0	2/5/0
1869	20/7/2	16/8/4	2/0/16	0/0/43	2/8/1	3/2/0	2/5/0
1870	22/10/5	17/8/4	2/1/19	0/0/43	2/8/1	3/2/0	2/5/0
1871	22/11/6	16/8/4	2/1/19	0/0/43	2/9/1	3/2/0	3/5/0
1872	22/13/7	16/8/4	2/1/19	0/0/43	2/9/1	3/2/0	3/5/0
1873	23/13/7	16/8/5	2/1/19	0/0/43	3/9/1	3/2/0	3/3/0
1874	23/13/9	16/9/6	2/1/20	0/0/28	4/9/1	3/2/0	4/3/0
1875	22/12/9	16/9/6	2/2/20	0/0/16	4/8/1	5/3/0	5/2/0
1876	22/12/10	18/9/6	3/2/20	0/0/16	4/8/1	6/3/0	5/4/0
1877	25/13/12	19/10/6	3/3/21	0/0/16	4/8/1	7/3/0	5/4/0
1878	25/14/13	21/10/6	3/4/21	0/0/16	4/8/1	9/2/0	5/5/0
1879	26/14/13	20/11/8	3/4/21	0/0/16	4/8/1	8/2/0	5/5/0
1880	24/16/13	20/11/8	3/4/21	0/0/16	5/6/1	8/2/0	5/5/0
1881	26/17/13	19/11/8	3/4/21	0/0/16	4/6/1	9/2/0	6/5/0
1882	24/17/14	17/13/10	3/4/21	0/0/16	5/6/1	10/2/0	6/5/0
1883	26/17/14	17/12/10	3/4/21	0/0/14	5/6/1	11/2/0	6/4/0
1884	26/16/14	16/12/11	3/4/21	0/0/14	5/6/1	11/2/0	6/4/0
1885	20/16/13	16/14/11	2/6/21	0/0/14	6/6/1	11/2/0	6/4/0
1886	19/13/14	15/11/11	2/6/21	0/0/14	6/6/1	11/3/0	5/4/0
1887	21/14/14	17/9/12	1/6/21	0/0/14	7/6/1	11/3/0	5/4/0
1888	23/17/15	19/9/12	1/7/21	0/0/14	8/6/1	11/3/0	5/4/0
1889	24/22/15	20/7/12	3/7/21	0/0/14	9/6/1	11/3/0	6/5/0
1890	26/22/15	20/9/11	4/8/21	0/0/14	9/6/1	11/3/0	6/6/0

SOURCE: Roger Chesneau and Eugene Kolesnik, eds., *Conway's All the World's Fighting Ships, 1860–1905*.
NOTE: The first number indicates first-class ironclads (later battleships), the second indicates second-class ironclads (later armored cruisers), and the third indicates coastal defense ironclads.

insignificant compared to Britain's naval expenditure. The Italian naval budget of 1864, for instance, was less than a quarter the size of the Royal Navy's. Equally important, to British calculations, at no point during the 1870s does Italian naval spending appear to have topped 18.6 percent of Britain's.

Far more formidable than the Austrian, German, or Italian navies during the 1860s and 1870s, at least in terms of numbers, was that of the United States. During the Civil War, in fact, the American navy's budget had dwarfed that of the Royal Navy, reaching $122 million (£24,500,000) in 1864–65, or about 2.25 times what the British spent. The exigencies of maintaining a massive coastal blockade, moreover, coupled with assaults on Confederate strongholds such as New Orleans, Mobile, and Charleston, had spurred the creation of a huge wartime navy. During the course of the conflict the U.S. navy was enlarged to 674 vessels. Most of these, it is true, were insignificant as fighting ships, useful for foiling blockade-running by merchant ships, but unsuited for more demanding roles. The substantial—if hastily constructed—U.S. ironclad fleet should, one might suppose, have been another matter. By the end of the Civil War it had amassed an armored force that outnumbered Britain's. It had, for that matter, caused considerable consternation at Westminster during the early 1860s.[24] And the possibility of hostilities with the United States continued to haunt British politicians for much of the rest of the conflict, owing to tension over British sympathies toward the Confederacy and, especially, the Laird ironclads affair.[25]

The immediate alarm over the U.S. threat was short-lived, however, for a number of reasons. It soon became evident that the American ironclad fleet, though impressive in numbers, consisted of virtually nothing aside from monitors and was designed almost exclusively for coastal and riverain operations. Monitors could, in a pinch, go to sea, and following the war a few were sent on long voyages, but these were hazardous undertakings. All hatches had to be battened down in any sort of rough weather, which brought sweltering temperatures below and the near-asphyxiation of crews.[26] Even thus prepared, the design was not proof against the sea; the *Monitor* itself foundered in a gale off Cape Hatteras. The Duke of Somerset remarked with unintentional accuracy, "This *Monitor* is something between a raft and a diving bell."[27] Moreover, American armor plate and ordnance were both clearly inferior to those of British manufacture. Lacking the capacity to roll thick iron plates, the U.S. navy adopted the expedient of bolting together several one-inch layers, but this laminated product lacked the structural integrity of solid plate, and was much more easily pierced than British armor. Finally, smoothbore U.S. naval ordnance, impressive in terms of caliber and weight of projectile, had such a low muzzle velocity that it was ineffective against even the thin armor of first-generation British ironclads.[28]

Of equal significance, as far as the Admiralty was concerned, following the end of the Civil War most of the huge U.S. wartime navy was hastily demobilized and scrapped or laid up.[29] Although tensions between the two countries remained high—largely as a result of the unresolved *Alabama* claims—by the late 1860s the ability of the United States to carry out a maritime war, quite aside from the shortcomings of monitors as seagoing ships, was highly problematic.[30] The navy's budget fell from $122 million in 1864–65 to $43 million (£8,700,000) a year later, and plunged to less than $20 million (£3,900,000) by 1870–71. By the latter fiscal year it was less than 40 percent of Britain's, during an epoch of zealous economy at the Admiralty, no less. After a brief surge in spending in 1873–74, a consequence of the *Virginius* affair, the U.S. naval budget sank still further, to barely a third of Britain's by 1876. It was not to reach even that modest proportion again until the 1890s. For twelve of the fourteen years from 1876–77 to 1889–90 the American navy received less than 30 percent of the amount lavished on its British counterpart.

Not surprisingly, fiscal policy was reflected in other spheres too. By January 1870 the Admiralty's controller, Rear-Admiral Robert Spencer Robinson, whose naval alarmism generally knew few bounds, reported, "[W]e may declare with tolerable certainty that as an aggressive Navy, capable of making serious attacks on . . . other powers, the Naval force of the United States is not very formidable."[31] Chief constructor Edward J. Reed supplied the details: Of fifty-two American ironclads, no fewer than forty-six were laid up in March 1869, thirty-two of them condemned for sale, while twenty-six—half the total number—had never been commissioned in the first place.[32] True to form, Spencer Robinson envisioned a seaborne threat from the United States, but in the form of fast unarmored ships for commerce raiding—the *guerre de course*, rather that the *guerre d'escadre*. During the latter years of the war the Americans built a class of very fast ships—prototype cruisers—"with which to sweep the ocean, and hunt down the ships of the enemy," as Secretary of the Navy Gideon Welles phrased it.[33] But by the time Spencer Robinson's *Inconstant*—designed to counter the American vessels—was complete (1869), they had been acknowledged as failures. Robinson's apprehensions were groundless. The perceived threat from the other side of the Atlantic receded rapidly, and the United States undertook only one further vessel—the *Trenton*—before the authorization of the "ABCD" vessels in 1883.

In 1872 Royal Navy Captain E. A. Inglefield, touring the United States, reported, "[I]t is acknowledged by all American Naval authorities, that the present condition of their Navy is at a lamentably low ebb, and this opinion is supported by the reports of the Secretary of the Navy [in] 1870, 71, [and] 72."[34] Moreover, although he too raised the commerce-raiding bogey, Inglefield added, "All my observations during a visit to America of some months . . . tend in a great manner to confirm these views." The U.S. ironclad fleet, which putatively numbered fifty-one in 1870, had within five years shrunk to thirty-seven, with a further ten vessels slated for the shipbreakers.[35] Later that year the British naval attaché, Captain Gore Jones, quoted U.S. Admiral of the Navy, David Dixon Porter, who compared "their navy in relation to European Navies as being like a man on foot armed with a pistol encountering a mounted man clad in armor and carrying a rifle." Porter might have added that the pistol was unloaded, for the report of the secretary of the navy for 1873 divulged that no less than thirty-six of the American ironclads were "laid up"—unable to go to sea—a further four were "repairing," two were "in ordinary," and four more were "on the stocks" or otherwise unfinished.[36] In short, the effective armored force of the United States in 1873 was two ships, neither of them suited for service on the high seas. Even the most dogmatic navalist could not regard the American navy as a significant factor in British political or Admiralty calculations for the whole of the 1870s, and this lack of concern was certainly not undermined by the peaceful resolution of the *Alabama* claims in 1872.

The Russian navy was of greater import, if for no other reason than geographic proximity. In addition, throughout the nineteenth century the British were continually apprehensive that Russia, taking advantage of the deterioration of Ottoman power, might gain access to the Straits of Constantinople and threaten the British line of communications to India that ran through the eastern Mediterranean. Indeed, it was this strategic concern that largely shaped the Disraeli government's policy toward Russia and Turkey, which culminated in the Mediterranean squadron's intervention at Constantinople in early 1878. From a casual examination it would appear that British concern was warranted. The Russian ironclad fleet numbered twenty ships in 1869 and grew to twenty-nine by 1877.[37]

Even bearing in mind Britain's hasty purchase of four ironclads at the height of the Eastern Crisis of 1876–78, however, the Russian navy did not pose a significant menace at any time during the 1860s and 1870s. Although figures for Russian expenditure are notoriously unreliable, it appears that the navy typically received between £2.5 million and £3.1 million during the 1860s, and £3 million to £3.6 million during the 1870s, until the Russo-Turkish war pushed expenditures to more than £4.5 million during the final years of the decade. If these figures are roughly accurate, during the 1860s Russian naval spending hovered around 23 to 28 percent of Britain's, climbing to over 32 percent in 1866. During the subsequent decade the British generally spent about three times as much on their navy as did the Russians until 1877, when the latter's percentage began to creep upward, topping 42 percent in 1879. Even at the latter date, though, the Russians clearly were not in the same league as the British.

Nor were they in terms of matériel. In 1871 British naval attaché Captain James Goodenough reported, "There is now no turret vessel [which type accounted for seventeen of the twenty-four Russian ironclads] fit to leave the Baltic, and the broadside vessels are inferior to the *Warrior* & *Defence,* the first broadside vessels built in England."[38] Furthermore, Goodenough noted, "Unless very extraordinary exertions are made, no addition of consequence can be made to the fleet till 1874." To this assessment Director of Naval Construction Nathaniel Barnaby added his own comments: "[I]t appears that . . . with very few exceptions these vessels are small, slow, & weakly armoured as compared with the ships of the Royal navy. No less than 20 . . . have only 4 1/2-inch armour."[39] Only three had plating of nine or more inches thick. Owning no ironclad larger than the British second-class ship *Audacious* and only five armored ships capable of service abroad—all lacking adequate armor protection—the Russian navy could not be regarded as an offensive threat. And even its defensive powers were considerably undercut by the weak armor and guns of the coastal-defense turret ships.

The Russian battlefleet was strengthened over the course of the 1870s, particularly by the *Peter the Great,* a breastwork monitor similar to the powerful British ironclad *Devastation.*[40] The construction of the former generated significant consternation in British political circles during the 1870s, but the threat was much exaggerated. First Lord of the Admiralty George J. Goschen pointed out the fallacy of fearing "that a single vessel of extraordinary power would be sufficient to harm the ascendancy of any other country."[41] Even after its completion in 1876 the Russian navy remained overwhelmingly geared toward coastal defense, rather than offensive operations. In 1877 American naval engineer King surveyed the state of Europe's navies, and dismissed Russia's: "Except for coast defense, the Russian fleet is rather numerous than powerful. The *Peter the Great* and the *Minin* [an armored cruiser] are the only two vessels on the list which approach the modern standard of fighting efficiency."[42] The Eastern crisis, therefore, generated no alarm at the Admiralty. British complacency was doubtless enhanced by the state the Russian Black Sea fleet, which consisted primarily of two curious circular ironclads. In 1871 Barnaby remarked, "[I]t would appear proper to regard them as floating forts possessing the power of locomotion, rather than as warships capable of proceeding to sea and fighting in heavy weather."[43] In none of the surviving correspondence regarding the "war scare" purchases of 1878 is there any indication that Admiralty or cabinet was motivated by a sense of urgency, much less necessity. The British were more concerned they not fall into others' hands, than with the size of their own force.[44] As with the post–Civil War U.S. fleet, the Admiralty perceived the most serious threat from Russia to be in the form of commerce raiders, but the numerous reports of naval attaché Gore Jones detailing Russian attempts to purchase American merchant ships for conversion to auxiliary cruisers underscored the Russian poverty in such vessels.[45] Like the U.S. navy, the Russian battlefleet did not pose a threat to Britain during the 1870s.[46] Hence, France was the only naval rival that seemed to possess the means to mount offensive operations against Great Britain during the mid-Victorian era.

And even the threat from France during the late 1860s was often overrated by observers on the other side of the Channel. The height of the French naval challenge occurred in the late 1850s and early 1860s. By 1863 a variety of factors had caused the naval scare in Britain to vanish. Most significantly, at least from the British standpoint, it was obvious by 1863–64 that the French shipbuilding program, although ambitious, was badly in arrears. The superiority of Britain's economic and industrial resources enabled it to pull ahead decisively in the ironclad race.[47] Hence, large British shipbuilding programs of 1867 and 1868 undertaken by the Conservative government were conceived to counter an essentially nonexistent French threat.[48] First Lord Sir John Pakington, fueled by alarmist pronouncements from his Naval Lords, claimed that the British navy's position was one of "great relative inferiority" in early 1867, but this assessment is ill-reconciled with subsequent appraisals.[49] The Conservative board's decision to lay down thirteen ironclads in 1867–68, coupled with France's preoccupation with continental matters after 1870, enabled Britain to maintain its naval supremacy in armored vessels for the next dozen years, despite the fact that at the time the reason for their authorization was largely fallacious. In addition, many of these ships could boast a qualitative, as well as a quantitative superiority over French ironclads. Of the latter's twenty-three "first-class" armored ships laid down between 1858 and 1870, all but three had hulls of wood, rather than iron. This fact had bearing on matters beyond the simple question of durability. Most significantly, wooden hulls lacked the structural rigidity imparted by iron and could not, therefore, have effective internal compartmentalization. As a consequence, the majority of British ironclads boasted watertight compartments below decks: their French counterparts lacked this important safety feature. The consequences of this difference, in terms of battleworthiness, are too obvious to require elaboration. Likewise, no fewer than sixteen of the "first-class" French ironclads had armor no thicker than 6 inches, a standard surpassed by Britain in 1867.[50]

The British lead became even more pronounced in the early 1870s as the ships laid down by Pakington and his successor, Henry Corry, came into service. In the first four years of the decade the number of British ironclads afloat increased by fourteen, ten of which were first-class, seagoing vessels. Well could Goschen state in 1873 that Britain possessed "twelve ships which were so strong" that they had no peers in rival navies."[51] Nor was British production the sole factor in the equation, for French shipbuilding, already hamstrung by financial and industrial shortcomings, was virtually paralyzed by military defeat in 1870–71. An Admiralty intelligence report of January 1872 observed that the French minster of marine had issued a circular "calling attention to the absolute necessity for rigid economy in the present state of financial difficulty," and the author of the report added that "[t]he diminution of ships and men forms only a portion of the saving to be effected in the Navy."[52] The saving was to be substantial.

French naval budgets of the early 1860s amounted to between £8.1 million and £8.8 million a year: consistently more than 60 percent of British spending, and as high as 77 percent in 1862. During the latter half of the 1860s the level of French naval spending dropped off.[53] Although 1867 witnessed the outlay of £7.9 million, during no other year from 1865 through 1870 did the figure climb as high as £7 million; further, the ratio of French to British spending did not edge above 74 percent, and the peak was in 1870, when France was at war. With the further exception of 1867, French spending from 1865 to 1870 remained slightly less than two-thirds that of Britain. Following the Franco-German War, however, the French naval budget plummeted to less than £5.9 million in 1871, and under £4.9 million the following year. Not until 1876 did it climb above £5.2 million, and only during the final three years of the decade did it transcend £6 million. In 1871 the French navy received 58.7 percent of the amount granted its cross-Channel rival. That figure, as matters turned out, was generous. For the subsequent two years it dropped to barely half, and in 1874 and 1875 fell below 50 percent, reaching 46.9 percent the latter year. Not until 1878 did the figure rebound significantly above the 50 percent level; only in 1880 did it reach two-thirds. For the majority of the decade, therefore, the French navy was deprived of the funding to maintain its existing navy, much less renew the challenge to Britain. The immediate need to rebuild and remodel the French military establishment, coupled with the futility of naval operations during the war and the necessity of paying a huge war indemnity, made naval reconstruction a low-priority item during the years immediately following the humiliation.[54]

The diminution of the threat from across the Channel was too marked to be missed by British politicians and administrators. In the course of his struggle over the level of defense spending with Edward Cardwell and Goschen in 1873–74, William Gladstone remarked to Foreign Secretary Lord Granville that the French naval budget was then a million pounds below the level of 1869.[55] Goschen, in turn, despite his differences with the prime minister, bluntly told Alexander Milne in 1873 that the latter's proposal for a large unarmored shipbuilding program was out of the question "with our chief naval rival France disabled and doing very little."[56] Moreover, Admiralty intelligence reports, almost uniformly alarmist through August 1870, took on a decidedly different tone in subsequent years. Augustus Spalding, a departmental clerk, prepared a report on French naval strength in September 1871 that stressed that virtually all the French ironclads were wooden-hulled, with armor no more than five and a half inches thick, which made them "almost obsolete" in comparison with recent British vessels.[57] At this point Britain was constructing ironclads boasting ten to twelve inches of armor at the waterline. The growing optimism in Britain regarding the relative position of the navy was by no means restricted to civilians. In late July 1871 Rear-Admiral Robert Hall, Spencer Robinson's successor as controller, stated that Britain's preponderance of seagoing ironclads at that point was such that "we are fairly strong for a maritime war with any

TABLE 12
British and French Ironclads Laid Down,
Ordered, Converted, or Purchased, 1858–90

Year	British	French
1858		*1st class:* Gloire, Invincible, Normandie
1859	*1st class:* Warrior, Black Prince, Defence, Resistance	*1st class:* Couronne, Magenta, Solferino
1860		
1861	*1st class:* Hector, Valiant, Achilles, Minotaur, Agincourt, Northumberland, Prince Consort, Caledonia, Ocean, Royal Oak, Royal Alfred, Zealous, Repulse *2nd class:* Research	*1st class:* Flandre, Gauloise, Guyenne, Magnanime, Provence, Revanche, Savoie, Surveillante, Valeureuse, Heroine
1862	*2nd class:* Enterprise *Coastal defense:* Royal Sovereign, Prince Albert	
1863	*1st class:* Lord Clyde, Lord Warden, Bellerophon *2nd class:* Favourite, Pallas	*2nd class:* Belliquese *Coastal defense:* Taureau
1864	*2nd class:* Scorpion, Wivern	
1865	*2nd class:* Penelope	*1st class:* Ocean, Marengo, Friedland *2nd class:* Alma, Armide, Atalante, Jeanne d'Arc, Montcalm, Reine Blanche, Thetis *Coastal defense:* Belier, Bouledogue, Cerbere, Tigre
1866	*1st class:* Hercules, Monarch	*1st class:* Suffern
1867	*1st class:* Captain *2nd class:* Audacious, Invincible, Vanguard *Coastal defence:* Cerberus	*Coastal defense:* Rochambeau
1868	*1st class:* Sultan *2nd class:* Iron Duke, Swiftsure, Triumph *Coastal defense:* Magdala, Abyssinia, Glatton, Hotspur	*2nd class:* La Galissoniere
1869	*1st class:* Devastation, Thunderer *Coastal defense:* Rupert	*1st class:* Richelieu *2nd class:* Triomphante, Victorieuse
1870	*1st class:* Dreadnought *Coastal defense:* Cyclops, Gorgon, Hecate, Hydra	*1st class:* Colbert, Trident
1871		
1872		
1873	*1st class:* Alexandra, Temeraire *2nd class:* Shannon	*1st class:* Redoubtable *Coastal defense:* Tonnerre, Fulminant, Tempete

TABLE 12 (CONTINUED)
British and French Ironclads Laid Down,
Ordered, Converted, or Purchased, 1858–90

Year	British	French
1874	*1st class:* Inflexible *2nd class:* Nelson, Northampton	
1875		*1st class:* Courbet *Coastal defense:* Vengeur, Tonnant
1876	*1st class:* Agamemnon, Ajax	*1st class:* Devastation *2nd class:* Bayard, Turenne
1877		*1st class:* Amiral Duperre, Terrible
1878	*1st class:* Superb, Neptune *2nd class:* Bellisle, Orion	*1st class:* Caiman, Indomptable, Requin *2nd class:* Duguesclin *Coastal defense:* Furieux
1879	*1st class:* Colossus, Edinburgh *Coastal defense:* Conqueror	*1st class:* Amiral Baudin, Formidable *2nd class:* Vauban
1880	*1st class:* Collingwood	
1881	*2nd class:* Imperieuse, Warspite	*1st class:* Hoche, Marceau
1882	*1st class:* Camperdown, Howe, Rodney, Benbow	*1st class:* Neptune
1883	*1st class:* Anson	*1st class:* Magenta
1884	*Coastal defense:* Hero	
1885	*1st class:* Victoria, Sans Pareil *2nd class:* Australia, Galatea, Narcissus, Orlando, Undaunted	
1886	*1st class:* Nile, Trafalgar *2nd class:* Aurora, Immortalite	
1887		
1888	*2nd class:* Blake, Blenheim	*2nd class:* Dupuy de Lome, Amiral Charner
1889	*1st class:* Empress of India, Royal Sovereign, Hood *2nd class:* Edgar, Endymion, Gibraltar	*1st class:* Brennus

SOURCE: Roger Chesnau and Eugene Kolesnik, eds., *Conway's All the World's Fighting Ships, 1860–1905.*

Foreign power, or even in the event of a combination of one of the larger with one of the lesser powers" and that, consequently, "we may pause in building ironclads until we have fully tried the vessels of new type now ready or nearly so."[58]

In the initial burst of enthusiasm that accompanied the transition to ironclads, the French by 1861 had laid down no less than sixteen first-class armored ships and started a further four in 1865, one in 1869, and two in 1870.[59] Of the latter seven, however, only one was complete by the outbreak of war in 1870, and the fortunes of the remaining six are indicative of the navy's standing following the conflict. Three ships laid down in 1865 were completed in 1872, 1875, and 1876, respectively; the *Richelieu*, begun in 1869, was completed in seven years; the two vessels commenced in 1870 were ready for sea in 1877 and 1878. Moreover, the Third Republic did not attempt to build an ironclad until 1873, when a single vessel was laid down. A further nine first-class armored ships were begun over the latter half of the decade, but none were completed prior to 1882 and seven were finished between 1886 and 1889. Seven ships were added to the French battlefleet during the 1870s, therefore, three of them designed in 1865 or earlier. During the same period the British enlarged their already larger front-line force by thirteen units, along with eight coastal-defense ironclads.[60] Not surprisingly, Goschen made much of the slow pace of French ship construction, addressing the Commons in 1873: "Since 1866 . . . we had commenced and finished fifteen ironclads, while France in the same time only commenced two new ships [three, actually], which were not yet finished."[61]

In 1870 the *Statesman's Yearbook*'s account of the French navy, taken from official statements, put the size of the armored fleet at sixty-two. By 1876 the number had, owing to decay, shrunk to fifty-four, only twenty-one rated as first-class seagoing vessels. Even this figure was optimistic: it included eleven first-generation French ironclads, with wooden hulls and inadequate 4.5-inch armor protection. As the Admiralty's parliamentary secretary, George John Shaw-Lefevre, noted a few years later, "[F]or three or four years succeeding the Franco German war, very little was done towards adding to the *matériel* of the French Fleet. It was described by the Minister of Marine in 1874 as perishing from want of means; and as the building of ironclads was maintained in England during this period the superiority of the British fleet was assured."[62] As late as 1879 the Admiralty's director of naval construction, Nathaniel Barnaby, employing both qualitative and quantitative criteria, calculated Britain's ironclad fleet to be superior to France's by a margin of nine to five.[63] Barnaby's superior, Controller Admiral William Houston Stewart, did, it should be added, take a gloomier view of the balance between the two fleets, concluding that the British battlefleet comprised twenty-nine modern armored vessels, the French, twenty. It is worth noting, however, that there was not another naval power in the world, with the possible exception of Germany, that might have supplied the nine seagoing ironclads that would have evened the scales.

Indeed, given the clear disparity of available naval force it is difficult to believe that any continental power or the United States would have considered challenging the British navy, no matter how strained their relations became, and between 1860 and 1885 Britain was on tolerable terms with every naval rival save Russia. No other navy maintained a force of ironclads in commission anywhere near the size of Britain's.[64] Moreover, any attempt by a rival power to fit out and commission a larger force would have drawn the attention of British naval attachés in Europe and the United States, of British naval officers traveling on the Continent, and of the now-ubiquitous British press. Even an attempt to enforce an increased degree of secrecy in Continental dockyards would have aroused the suspicions of the Admiralty and prompted countermeasures. In other words, Britain boasted a "two-power standard" throughout the navy's "dark ages," contrary assessments by Parkes and others notwithstanding.

CHAPTER 11

Strategic Planning and Imperial Defense

The charge that strategic naval planning received short shrift from the Admiralty during the mid-Victorian era has become virtually a truism. "A relentless flow of administrative questions," notes one recent authority, "came before the Board and claimed its attention.... The larger questions of policy and strategy which the First Lord and his principal naval adviser [the First Naval Lord] were especially charged with were at first neglected, and then forgotten."[1] Indeed, it is alleged that the administration established by Sir James Graham and modified by Hugh Childers and George J. Goschen managed to forget the primary reason for the service's, and hence the board's, existence. Possibly the Admiralty's structure, especially the underrepresentation of naval professionals within it, militated against the evolution and enunciation of a coherent, overarching general naval strategy. But far more important factors influenced the formulation of policy and strategy, not least among them the lack of strategic or tactical certainty that confronted Admiralty planners as a consequence of the ongoing technological revolution. The development of a coherent naval strategy in the industrial era was complicated immensely by "the development and application of the new technologies to the practicalities of war at sea[,] ... by the lack of experience of a major war at sea between 1815 and 1914 and by the increased vulnerability of Britain to attacks on her seaborne trade as she became increasingly dependent on imported food and raw materials."[2]

Furthermore, the indictment that the Admiralty's "central direction of naval policy had almost evaporated" during the second half of the nineteenth century is both erroneous and anachronistic. There was a generally shared—if not always consciously or coherently articulated—conception of policy and strategy that informed the course of British naval administration and decision making between 1850 and 1890. As a corollary, many of the limitations hampering the implementation of a general strategy suitable for a mechanized navy were beyond the Admiralty's, and often the government's, control. Furthermore, most modern critics have generally failed to assess mid-Victorian British naval administration in a contemporary comparative context, judging it instead by the standard of subsequent developments.[3] Finally, the reluctance of successive ministries to act forcefully on matters of naval policy and strategy was in large part justified, or at least quite understandable, given the contemporary foreign political and naval situations.

British strategic aims were ordinarily no more clearly articulated during any period of peace than they were during the 1860s and 1870s. Nor, for the most part, was any greater attention paid by the government or the Admiralty to contingency planning in the event of war, as the unprepared state of the navy at the commencement of Britain's eighteenth-century wars, the Crimean War, and even at the end of the evanescent Peace of Amiens attests. In short, it is misleading to single out the mid-Victorian Admiralty for shortcomings that were endemic to British naval administration—indeed to the structure of British politics—prior to the twentieth century and, arguably, since then as well. Without the concurrent technological revolution, the absence of an enunciated strategic doctrine in the second half of the nineteenth century would have garnered little comment. The strategy of the British navy in the event of a general European war was no more clearly articulated in 1820, 1830, or even 1850, than it was in 1870 or 1880. But it did not have to be, since it was fundamentally unchanged from the days of William Pitt the Elder. This inherited policy consisted of using the battlefleet to maintain a close blockade on the enemy's ports and coasts, while employing smaller units to sweep the seas of enemy commerce and hunt down privateers and commerce-destroyers. The twofold consequences of the policy were economic and commercial deprivation for the blockaded country, and, generally, opportunities for colonial aggrandizement for Britain. In this strategic framework, based on the all-but-universal (if also often unarticulated) assumption that the principal enemy would be France, several geographic areas were particularly crucial to Britain: the Channel, for obvious reasons; the Mediterranean, because of Toulon and the need to protect the shortest route to India; the Caribbean, arising from the ancient Franco-British rivalry over the lucrative sugar islands, and, until the late eighteenth century, the North Atlantic and the routes to and around India.

It is worth considering what havoc the "march of technology" wrought on this set of inherited strategic assumptions. Although the navy continued to advocate the strategy of close blockade for another half-century, by the 1850s perceptive observers in Britain had concluded that it would no longer work.[4] Ships no longer dependent on the wind would be able to evade a blockade virtually at will: "[S]team has bridged the Channel" was Palmerston's famous observation. Of course, there was another side to the story, since a blockading steam fleet would be freed from reliance on the wind, too, and could descend on the enemy's coast at will, but the successive invasion scares in Britain from 1847 through 1861, all of them centered on perceived French designs, testify not only to the widespread distrust and fear felt for the ancient foe, but also to the confounding role steam played in the application of traditional British naval strategy.[5] Equally important, steamships could not keep the sea for weeks, much less months, at a time, at least not after sails had been wholly abandoned, in the manner that blockading fleets under sail could and repeatedly had. Aside from suggesting one of the reasons for the seemingly prolonged retention of sails on some British ironclads, this fact also points to the corollary that, owing to the frequent need to coal, the mere maintenance of a close blockade in the days of steam was attended with far greater difficulties than hitherto. While freeing vessels from the vagaries of the wind, the steam engine, ironically, tied them to the depot and the collier.[6]

But if the advent of steam cast doubts on the continued efficacy of the close blockade, the widespread adoption of the locomotive torpedo in the early 1870s was a direct threat to its feasibility. No longer could those "far distant, storm-beaten ships" vessels so celebrated in British maritime literature cruise with virtual impunity off the enemy's ports and coasts.[7] That the Whitehead torpedo was, for at least a decade after its commercial introduction (1870), a primitive and limited weapon, both in terms of range and of speed, was irrelevant; its mere existence created a huge risk that had not previously existed.

The close blockade would, it was soon perceived—at least in France—be dangerously vulnerable to a massed attack by small torpedo boats, sallying forth from a protected harbor. This vision was seized upon and transformed into the basis of an alternative maritime strategy by the French strategists of the *Jeune Ecole*, who envisioned in an inexpensive fleet of torpedo boats, the key to negating Britain's industrial superiority and preponderance in capital ships.[8] Given strategic imperatives, however, a *Jeune Ecole*-type fleet was utterly impracticable for Britain; torpedo boats lacked the endurance and seaworthiness necessary either to maintain a blockade or to operate worldwide on the high seas.

On the high seas themselves, the technological revolution had a similarly unhappy impact on traditional British naval strategy. The exploits of the Confederate commerce-raider *Alabama*—built in a British shipyard—focused the attention of naval strategists throughout Europe on the enhanced possibilities for commercial warfare that accrued from steam power. Commerce-raiding or privateering had flourished in the days of sail, to be sure. Indeed, it was the favored strategy of inferior naval powers and the strategy of last resort for navies unable to stand up to Britain in the traditional *guerre d'escadre*. But if steam appeared to confound offensive blockading strategy of the *guerre d'escadre*, it appeared simultaneously to open new vistas for the offensive strategy of the *guerre de course*.

Freedom from reliance on the wind seemed to impart a huge advantage to the steam commerce-raider, for it must be borne in mind that even into the 1880s, the majority of merchant vessels, transoceanic as well as coasting, were still sail-powered.[9] A becalmed merchantman in the days of sail was relatively safe; any pursuing commerce-raider would, of course, be becalmed as well. Such was not the case after the advent of steam, as the career of the *Alabama* amply attested. In twenty months one steam ship—not an especially well-armed or seaworthy one, by British standards—captured seventy-one Union ships, and was instrumental in hastening the "flight from the flag," the transfer of much of the formidable United States merchant fleet to neutral registry. Even were the quarry a steamer, a slow-moving merchantman was still at the mercy of a swift commerce raider. When these factors, to say nothing of significant problems of technological transformation, such as the limitations of boilers and engines and the relative ineffectiveness of naval gunnery in the late nineteenth century, are taken into account, it should scarcely be cause for surprise that the Admiralty, which in the space of two decades witnessed the complete overthrow of the foundations on which traditional British wartime strategy rested, responded hesitantly and often incoherently.

Yet it is erroneous to conclude that, inundated by paperwork and routine, British naval administration lost sight of "all considerations of general policy."[10] The mere fact that the Admiralty responded to and incorporated the revolutionary technology testifies to contemporary consideration of what the navy was supposed to do, regardless of how incoherent, inconsistent, short-sighted, or even contradictory the overall response might appear. There was no solution to the close-blockade quandary, admittedly. The imposition of a distant blockade on imperial Germany during World War I was an expedient only possible under unique geographic circumstances: Britain controlled the crucial routes of egress—the "choke-points"—from the North Sea: the Channel and the expanse of sea between Scotland and the west coast of Norway. From Scapa Flow, Harwich, Rosyth, and other east-coast naval bases these choke-points could be covered, and there was no alternative route of escape for the German high seas fleet. A distant blockade of France would have been much more problematic—if not wholly unfeasible—given the length of coastline to be masked both in the Atlantic and the Mediterranean, the lack of convenient choke-points (especially in the Atlantic), the concurrent lack of strategically situated British bases for covering every French port, and the multiplicity of escape routes for French warships, to say nothing of the proximity of French colonies—especially in North Africa—that could serve as sanctuaries for vessels that managed to evade the blockade.

Yet critics have managed to miss the crucial point that the British navy *did*, during the 1860s and 1870s, evolve an alternative strategy to the close blockade. The solution was suggested by noted gunnery and fortifications expert General Sir Howard Douglas in 1859. "[A] steam fleet superior in strength to the fleet blockaded," Douglas conjectured, "if well supplied with Armstrong's incomparable guns . . . and with abundance of mortars for firing at high elevations—will be able to destroy from afar the fleet, or the arsenal in which the ships are crowded, and probably both at the same time. Thus it will not be necessary to keep a steam fleet before an enemy's port during long intervals of time, as was the case formerly with our blockading fleets of sailing ships."[11] Rather than rely on blockading enemy vessels in port, the Admiralty designed and built low-freeboard, heavily armored coastal-assault ships with which to steam into naval arsenals and destroy enemy shipping before it could escape. These ships were passed off as "coastal-defence" vessels, presumably to placate Liberal and Radical politicians who decried the use of the navy as an offensive weapon, but there is no want of evidence that their designers envisioned just such a role for them. In advocating the construction of several such vessels in 1866, Controller Robert Spencer Robinson explicitly acknowledged that they were for defense or attacking "shipping in an enemy harbour."[12] In an equally unequivocal admission of the offensive role of the so-called "coastal-defence" ships, Sir Sydney Dacres complained of the deficient stability of one such vessel: "The ship only half meets the purposes for which she was ordered for she could hardly be trusted across the Channel to attack an Enemy's port—much less venture to the Baltic."[13] Moreover, many of the "seagoing" ironclads of the 1870s and 1880s, in particular the "breastwork monitors" of the *Devastation* type, were more suited to coastal operations than fleet encounters on the high seas.[14]

In other words, the nature of the early ironclad British battlefleet was itself paramount evidence that the Admiralty took strategic concerns into account, although they may not have been as prominent or as well-articulated as were the corresponding tactical considerations. The continued masting of certain ironclads well into the 1870s testified not to a hidebound, blinkered, and backward-looking mentality at the Admiralty, but to a very real appreciation both of the limits of contemporary steam technology and of the relative paucity of coaling stations overseas. Equally important, it further demonstrated the strategic vision of those responsible for ship design. Ironclads with both sails and steam may well have been ungainly and unhappy compromises, combining the worst features of both systems, but they were also the logical consequence of strategic necessity. The British navy of the mid-Victorian era, like its wooden and wholly sail-powered forebear, was a worldwide force, expected to cover not merely the Channel, North Sea, and Mediterranean, but every expanse of ocean from the Baltic to the Sea of Japan, from the Arctic to the Antarctic. Ships destined to serve on the high seas or abroad had to carry sails until the late 1880s, when water-tube boilers and triple-expansion engines were demonstrably reliable and a worldwide network of coaling stations was in place. What has traditionally been derided as an instance of Admiralty foot-dragging is simply an indication that strategic and general policy considerations, along with more obvious manifestations of tactical reflections, exercised their sway on Admiralty officials.[15]

The assertion is equally applicable to those ships that were designed to operate wholly or primarily in the Channel and Mediterranean. In those theaters, where coaling stations and repair facilities were both numerous and close at hand, the battlefleet could and did begin to dispense with sails by 1870. The ships thus designed (the *Devastation* and its successors) have been seen by many in retrospect as the precursors of modern battleships, which indeed they were. But to dismiss subsequent ironclad designs with sails as retrogressive is to miss the point both technologically and strategically; what was feasible, even desirable, for ships designed to operate close to home—and in relatively sheltered waters, it might be added—was impractical, regardless of how desirable, for those designed for less circumscribed duties. Failure to appreciate this salient point is simultaneously a failure to appreciate contemporary technological limitations and a failure to comprehend the nature and breadth of the mid- and late-Victorian navy's myriad strategic responsibilities.

Indeed, for the three decades of transition following 1860, the technological and tactical waters became so muddied that the formulation of a coherent, overarching strategic policy was beyond the realm of probability, even had the Lords of the Admiralty been freed from their routine administrative work and assisted by a naval planning staff. Only when design and tactical theory began to regain measures of stability, in the mid- to late 1880s, could planners begin "to consider strategic problems realistically," for only then did they know "within limits, the nature of the counters on the board upon which the games of the next war were to be placed."[16] One need only sample the range of opinions in papers on technological, tactical, and strategic questions given at the Royal United Services Institution during the 1860s, 1870s, and 1880s to appreciate the want of consensus among naval officers themselves and, more importantly as relates to strategic planning, the wide range of views as to what the future of naval warfare would entail.

It must be continually recalled that these men, professionals and civilians alike, were confronted with an ongoing technological revolution and, as a consequence, the assumptions and certainties that had guided the navy's strategy in wartime, save for the overriding necessity of upholding British maritime supremacy, were superseded

Strategic Planning and Imperial Defense 217

by new, and by no means fully appreciated or understood realities. To be sure, the professional element was weakly represented at the Admiralty, and the Naval Lords were inundated with trivial details to the detriment of considering policy questions, but it did not perforce follow that the elimination of these two impediments would have led to an earlier and more comprehensive reformulation of the navy's wartime policy or, for that matter, a more coherent policy of readying the fleet for the war of the future. The circumstances of the time—in which designs representing the state of the art upon commencement were, owing to the rapidity of technological change, obsolete when commissioned; when the appearance of torpedoes and the revival of the ancient tactic of ramming led to the complete (albeit temporary) abandonment of traditional naval tactics based on broadside gunnery; and when the strategy that had governed the conduct of British forces in wartime for a century and more demanded replacement—all but guaranteed that policy was ad hoc, a succession of short-term responses to immediate problems. Certainly there was little, if any, long-term coherence, but it is unrealistic to expect that there should have been.

Moreover, the lack of long-term coherence must not conceal the fact that Admiralty planners gave a good deal of thought to the novel circumstances that confronted them, strategy included. Take the case of the *guerre de course*. By 1865, Admiralty planners were alive to the threat posed by steam-powered commerce raiders. Indeed, by early 1866 Spencer Robinson had urged the board to build a vessel "to meet the large and swift ships that may be built by other powers, on equal terms as to speed and armament," and had received its sanction to proceed on those lines, resulting in the construction of the *Inconstant*.[17] Yet having recognized the new threat, and having responded to it in an intelligent fashion, the Admiralty was left with a quandary as to how such a ship was to be effectively employed. The *Inconstant* carried both sails and engines, and as a consequence of its large size, fine lines, and powerful machinery, was a swift vessel under either mode. But its size, in turn, made it impractical to duplicate in large numbers, given the financial constraints on the navy, and only one further example of the type was built. In addition, its steaming radius at full speed was but 1,170 miles—and at 6.4 knots, 3,020 miles—meaning that, given the paucity of overseas coal depots, for extended operations outside Europe the *Inconstant* would be forced to rely almost wholly on its sails, a serious detriment in a cruiser intended to interdict commerce raiders. Finally, the *Inconstant*'s lack of armor rendered it vulnerable to ironclads, even the small, second-class vessels that France was beginning to deploy on overseas stations by the late 1860s, and would likely be encountered by British cruisers in wartime. Spencer Robinson's response to this development was to urge that foreign squadrons should contain "both a powerful second-class ironclad and a fast steam frigate," but this expedient, not surprisingly, was too expensive to win favor at the Admiralty—much less in Parliament—and after 1870 the navy turned its attention to the task of trying to combine the qualities of cruiser and ironclad in a single vessel. The early attempts were not successful; faced with the need to effect a design compromise, the Admiralty's initial armored cruisers sacrificed speed and coal endurance to armament, protection, and sail power. The results, as embodied in H.M.S. *Shannon* (launched 1875), *Nelson* (1876), and *Northampton* (1876), were vessels that could easily outgun any commerce-raider they might encounter, but which were unlikely to encounter such ships owing to deficiencies of speed and steaming radius.[18]

The matter of sails versus coal endurance cannot be attributed to conservatism or mistaken strategic notions on the part of the board, however. Sir Alexander Milne, it is true, constantly stressed the need for cruising vessels to carry sails. In late 1874 he informed George Ward Hunt: "This coal question will, in any future war, be one of great difficulties which the Admiralty will have to meet; it therefore becomes necessary that our ships should retain their sailing power and be handy under canvas; for there will be some intervals of time when coal may be entirely wanting."[19] Reactionary they may appear in retrospect, but at the time the words were committed to paper, they were irrefutable. Milne obviously erred in the assumption that sails would be required "in any future war," but as of 1874, and for at least another decade thereafter, they were a necessity for any cruising vessel, given the limits of contemporary steam technology and the lack of a comprehensive system of coaling stations worldwide, a shortage to which the third report of the Carnarvon commission on the defense of British possessions and commerce abroad specifically alluded: "In a man-of-war, the limited capacity for carrying coal, taken in connection with the high rate of consumption, necessarily limits the range of effective action. Without secure and well-placed coaling stations Your Majesty's ships, however numerous and powerful, will be unable to protect trade, or perhaps even reach distant parts of the Empire."[20] Even had these facilities existed—and to implement the commission's recommendations would have required government, rather than Admiralty, action—as of the mid-1870s and even the mid-1880s—the state of marine engineering, coupled with the want of repair and docking facilities worldwide, made the attainment of high speed, to say nothing of great range, under steam in regular service overseas a practical impossibility.[21] That the British cruisers of the 1870s were inadequate for their intended role in wartime is unquestionable, but their shortcomings were the consequence of technological and strategic limitations, rather than being attributable to mistaken strategic notions or want of vision at the Admiralty.

Nor should it be overlooked that during the 1860s, 1870s, and early 1880s there existed a potent counterdiscourse to the threat of the *guerre de course*. Aside from tying up the loose ends of the Crimean War, the diplomats who gathered in Paris in 1856 drafted guidelines for the future conduct of naval warfare to which every European power save Spain subscribed.[22] Two of the clauses of the Declaration of Paris outlawed privateering and prohibited attacks on neutral shipping, save that carrying "contraband of war," an elastic and ill-defined term. In retrospect these clauses are facilely dismissed as the products of untempered idealism, not to say naiveté, but many contemporaries, not just "Manchester school" Radicals and Gladstonian Liberals, took their efficacy for granted. "In the eighties the protection of commerce seemed so insoluble a problem that even Arthur Forwood, the great Liverpool shipowner [Sir Charles] Dilke and [Thomas] Brassey . . . saw the transfer of British commerce to the flag of neutrals at the start of a war the only solution."[23] In short, "most people" assumed that neutral shipping would remain inviolable in wartime, and even a figure as pragmatic and worldly as Lord Salisbury observed in 1871 that the Treaty of Paris "had made the fleet 'almost valueless' for anything other than preventing invasion."[24] The *Jeune Ecole* would torpedo this blithe assumption in the mid-1880s, and unrestricted submarine warfare on merchant shipping in the twentieth century makes it difficult to believe that it could ever have been seriously entertained, but it carried considerable currency for a brief era, during which time it strongly militated against systematic planning for commercial defense.

Furthermore, it is clear that by the early 1870s Milne, then serving a second stint as First Naval Lord, was giving thought to cruiser deployment and strategy. In June 1873, little more than six months after he rejoined the board, Milne requested the construction of more cruising ships from First Lord Goschen, and although rebuffed in this instance, he continued his vigorous efforts to enhance the navy's commerce-protection capability throughout the remainder of his tenure at Whitehall.[25] Milne's concern with commerce protection was, in fact, longstanding. He had addressed the topic as early as 1858, when Junior Naval Lord, and some months prior to his exchange with Goschen he had induced the director of naval ordnance, Sir Arthur Hood, to prepare a memorandum on the steps that would have to be taken to put the navy on war footing.[26] Prominent among Hood's conclusions was the observation, "Our policy would probably be to strain every effort for the protection of our trade (this I look on as the point of first importance).... A considerable number of fast unarmoured cruisers for the protection of our enormous trade afloat is indispensable."[27] In December 1874 Milne himself produced a paper for George Ward Hunt in which he put forward his minimum requirement for the size of the cruising fleet, namely, thirty frigates, twenty-five to thirty first-class corvettes, thirty second-class corvettes, and forty-five sloops, as well as 120 gunvessels and gunboats.[28] Even this force, he added ominously, would require augmentation in wartime. The same month he drafted a further paper for the First Lord that dealt explicitly with his favored theme, "Position of Cruising Ships for Protection of Trade."[29]

It is true that none of Milne's immediate successors at the Admiralty could match the breadth of his strategic vision, and that the boards of the late 1870s and 1880s were notably weak on the score of war planning. Sir Astley Cooper Key, who served a lengthy stretch as First Naval Lord from 1879 to 1885 was "no strategic thinker or careful planner." Asked for an estimate of the number of warships required to protect essential convoys, he gave the revealing reply, "I could not answer that question without a great deal of thought and inquiry." Nor was Sir Arthur Hood, who replaced Key in 1885, much more alive to the latent menace to Britain's seaborne trade, his earlier research for Milne notwithstanding. He "obviously never worked out in detail the number and type of ships needed by the navy to fulfil its various tasks."[30]

Likewise, when the navy's attention was focused on the question of commerce protection, the strategy evolved was erroneous. Rather than adopting a policy centered on the convoy system, the strategy of the sailing ship era that would of necessity ultimately be employed in the two world wars, the planners of the 1880s and subsequent decades called for cruisers to "be stationed at points where the stream of trade passes on narrow and well-known bands, to which spots an intelligent naval officer, well acquainted with the lines in which commerce flows, would be most likely to direct his first attention if bent on the destruction of commerce." Such a strategy was, of course, fallacious, since it assumed "that an enemy will attack in the place where you can best deal with him."[31] Yet the obstinance with which the British clung to this mistaken belief in the face of mounting losses to U-boats during the first two and a half years of the Great War should not conceal the fact that it was a sensible approach during the early days of steam, when enemy commerce raiders would have had to stick close to well-established routes or else work almost wholly under sail.

While it is undeniable that contemporary strategic visions regarding commerce and trade-route protection were imperfect, as would become readily apparent in the 1880s, the weakness sprang from a general *mentalité* within the officers corps as a body, and should not therefore be attributed primarily to defects in Admiralty administrative structure or planning. The root cause of this mistake emanated from the prejudices of naval officers themselves: "so called 'defensive methods' [i.e., the convoy system] were rejected as being alien to the British naval genius, irrespective of their efficacy." As one consequence, as a result of the development of practical submarines, "despite the central place of the need to protect merchant shipping in the growth of the British Navy [after 1889], when war came in 1914 this was the one task in which it proved almost fatally incompetent."[32] By plumping for the offensive strategy of interdiction rather than the defensive one of convoys, the Admiralty—or more accurately, the officer corps—put its eggs in the wrong basket. This failure did not, however, result from the failure to evolve a general strategy: it was simply the wrong strategy. Britain, it has been said, did not tend to err by preparing for the last war, but, rather, by incorrectly assessing the shape and nature of future conflict.

It is also worth stressing, when assessing the performance of the Admiralty in planning for the *guerre de course* that, the frequent alarms of Milne notwithstanding, the contemporary threat was more theoretical than real. During the latter half of the 1860s, the French built ten second-class ironclads designed for overseas duties, but they were even less suitable for commerce raiding than the *Shannon* was for defense against it. The seven *Alma*-class ironclads were small (3,500–3,800 tons)—which adversely affected performance on the high seas—lightly armed, and, most significantly, slow. The *Shannon's* top speed of 12.5 knots was inadequate for hunting down swift commerce raiders, but none of the *Alma* class was capable of more than 11.9 knots. In addition, the coal capacity of the French vessels was no greater than their British counterparts, and the *Shannon*, designed, as Goschen put it, to be "more than a match for the second class ironclad[s] of foreign powers," amply fulfilled the board's intentions.[33]

Much attention, both contemporary and subsequent, was focused on Russia, generally held to be the originator of the modern cruiser designed principally for commerce raiding. Early Russian experiments with the type culminated in the 1870s with the *General Admiral*, "generally regarded as the first true armoured cruiser."[34] Russian cruisers differed significantly from the British second-class ironclads of the *Shannon* type, being more lightly armed and armored, while simultaneously faster and longer-ranged, at least as designed.[35] But whatever theoretical threat these ships might have posed to British commerce in the event of war—and war between Britain and Russia was closer to realization in 1878 and 1885 than between Britain and any other power during the era—the Russian cruisers never attained their designed speed, owing to shortcomings in their domestically manufactured machinery. Indeed, they were little faster than the *Shannon*.[36] Moreover, these were the only two vessels of the type with which the British would have had to contend until 1885, when the next Russian cruiser was completed.

During the Eastern crisis of 1876–78, the latter stages of which raised the specter of war between Russia and Great Britain, the czar's navy made frantic attempts to purchase swift merchant steamers abroad—largely in the United States—with which to improvise a "volunteer fleet" for commerce destruction. Whether the forces thus acquired would have been of any value in wartime is debatable, but the Russian action does, if nothing else, indicate its fatal deficiency in the sort of vessel sought.[37] Finally, geographic circumstances operated to Russia's disadvantage, since only Vladivostok and Archangel were situated on the open sea. "Both were remote anchorages, unable to refit, repair, or even coal a major warship, [both were far from highly traveled sea lanes] and both were ice-bound for much of the year. Any raiding cruiser would have to leave either port at or before the outbreak of war, and thenceforth rely on her own resources."[38] Given the lack of coaling stations abroad, it is unlikely that Russian cruisers, forced to rely primarily on sails, would have evaded capture for long in the event of war. While signaling future danger to British commerce, the threat from Russian armored cruisers during the 1870s and 1880s was largely imagined, and the fact that the British vessels designed to interdict them were unsuited for the task would have been of little import, even had war occurred.

No other power offered a significant threat to British commerce during the 1870s either. The United States had laid down five wooden frigates in 1863 "designed as commerce raiders," but these vessels were failures. One of the five was never even launched, and the remaining four were deficient in several ways, with weak hulls and defective machinery among their more glaring shortcomings. With the exception of the wooden frigate *Trenton*, the United States built no new warships until the mid-1880s.[39] The German navy constructed eleven traditional cruisers during the 1870s, but only five were fast enough to have had any value as commerce raiders; the Austrian navy had no such vessels, and the Italian navy one.[40]

Most basically, it is doubtful that a fleet of surface commerce raiders, no matter how numerous, could have seriously endangered Britain's food supply, given the vast resources of the British shipbuilding industry which, even as late as 1914, produced 59 percent of the world's merchant tonnage.[41] Only with the invisibility afforded by submersion could commerce destruction become more than a piecemeal operation. Prior to the appearance of practical submarines it would have been all but impossible to threaten Britain with starvation, regardless of how severe depredations on trade might have been overall. Loss of a war through the effects of the *guerre de course* was not a prospect that troubled Admiralty planners before the turn of the century, even given the pronouncements of the *Jeune Ecole*.

Given this state of affairs, it is unsurprising that even Milne's frequent calls for more cruisers during the 1870s were largely couched in theoretical terms. The first report of the Carnarvon Commission, which included Milne among its members, made reference not to immediate threats but, rather, to latent dangers.[42] And, for that matter, when Milne did cite an immediate danger from a shortage of cruising vessels—which he did repeatedly in his memoranda to Goschen and Ward Hunt—it invariably took the form of a warning that the navy possessed too few ships to provide the necessary reliefs for vessels on peacetime duty overseas.[43] In addition, neither contemporaries like Milne nor subsequent writers seem to have spared much thought for the fact that all the elements that would circumscribe British cruiser operations in the event of war—especially the paucity of coal depots—would similarly limit the operations of those bent on the destruction of British commerce, and probably to a greater extent. Indeed, given the limited coal endurance of warships prior to the introduction of water-tube boilers and triple-expansion engines in the 1880s, coupled with the difficulty of coaling at sea, any attempt at commerce raiding in the early ironclad era would have been carried out by ships operating within fixed radii—tied to their coal depots—or by ships that relied heavily on their sails. In either case they would increase the risk of interception by British cruisers. Perceptive contemporaries appreciated the fact: in 1889 no less an authority than Thomas Brassey noted, "[W]e find the resources of our neighbours for the conduct of naval operations in distant waters slender indeed in comparison with those which we command."[44]

Finally, there was an ideological dimension to the *guerre de course* issue. Commerce raiding was a traditional tool of the French in naval warfare, from the privateers of the seventeenth century onwards (the French were scarcely alone, of course), but typically the *guerre de course* was viewed as an adjunct to the *guerre d'escadre* until the latter was perceived to have failed, as during the latter stages of the Nine Years' War, Seven Years' War, and the Napoleonic wars after 1805. Only with the rise of the *Jeune Ecole* in the 1880s was commerce raiding embraced by some theoreticians as the principal form of naval warfare versus Britain, to which French energies and resources should be wholly devoted. Hence, "commerce protection only became a grave problem to the English with the extension of (theoretical) belligerent practice on the continent, especially in France, in the '80s and '90s."[45]

Assessments of British naval administration, the course of British naval policy, and the coherence and sophistication of the Admiralty's strategic vision, planning, and implementation in the mid-Victorian period have ordinarily been rendered on the basis of comparison with later developments at Whitehall in each of these spheres.[46] Just as the term "dark ages" was applied *ex post facto* to the medieval era, so has it been applied retroactively to the British navy of the 1870s and 1880s. This approach is not surprising, to be sure, but it does betray the lingering influence of the Whig interpretive framework, and is all but guaranteed to cast an unflattering light on the pre-Edwardian Admiralty. Most modern writers have subscribed, often unconsciously, to a nineteenth-century conception of "progress." One, indeed, couches the development of British naval planning in the metaphor of growing up: "The pains and problems of the Admiralty ... were in a sense those of growing from a maritime police force to a warlike service," and the reforms that eventually followed were made possible in part by "the progressive education of public opinion." Hence, "Many of the administrative deficiencies of the 1860s and 1870s persisted long afterwards, but their pernicious effect was enormously alleviated by the changed attitudes of a new generation."[47]

In such an interpretive framework, however, the mid-Victorian navy, its strategic planning and administration included, is doomed to harsh appraisal, given the nearly universal tendency of naval historians to regard the Naval Defence Act, the appearance of Alfred Thayer Mahan's and others' works on the allegedly pivotal role of sea power, and subsequent developments as steps in the "right" direction. Steps in the right direction they may well have been in the context of the late 1880s and 1890s, but they were not by necessity equally "right" or equally crucial at another juncture. Certainly the Admiralty's administrative arrangements in the 1860s and 1870s were primitive by the standards of the Fisher era, and its notions of naval strategy were flawed and sometimes contradictory. But, with the inappropriate and largely ineffectual commerce-protection strategy that was developed in the 1880s and 1890s and clung to zealously until 1917 (even in the face of skyrocketing shipping losses and the looming threat of starvation), not all of what followed was perforce better, or even less flawed or less contradictory. More to the point, the appropriate questions are not whether the mid-Victorian Admiralty's strategic vision was adequate by early-twentieth-century standards, but whether it was adequate in its contemporary context. A less anachronistic standard of comparison might be provided by a brief survey of the strategic policies of Britain's naval rivals.

Insofar as the United States had a naval strategy, it was similar to that which guided British strategy for its "nonfighting" forces: police of the seas and protection of U.S. commercial interests. From being the largest—at least in terms of numbers—navy in the world as of 1865, the U.S. navy had, within a few years, decayed to insignificance.

"In 1880 the journal *The Nation* condemned the service as a 'satirical semblance of a navy.' ... The standing naval war strategy essentially called for nothing more aggressive than coastal defense in combination with commerce raiding."[48] Worse still, it lacked suitable vessels for the latter task. Indeed, after 1880, when the U.S. government began to contemplate naval reconstruction, a rift appeared between those who believed that the navy should be primarily a defensive force, and Mahan's disciples who agitated for an offensive, "blue-water" fleet. The former stance was predicated on several assumptions, principal among them the pragmatic realization that the United States was in no position to compete with European powers and, more important, had no reason to. The course of the initial buildup of the "New" U.S. navy, however, marked a shift in naval strategy: "In the crucial ... years of 1882–86, the navy ... abandoned its traditional mixture of coast defense with commerce raiding capacity, in favor of a near complete reliance upon the ... *guerre de course*." Another, and far more profound, shift was soon to follow. "Between 1886 and 1893 the emphasis of naval construction switched from light cruisers to heavy cruisers and battleships." Along with—one is tempted to say impelled by—this shift came a concomitant change in strategy from *guerre de course* to *guerre d'escadre*.

Yet this wholesale transformation was not based on a similar shift in strategic outlook. Indeed, it was not based on a strategic outlook at all—the United States had no more pressing a need for a blue-water fleet in 1893 than in 1880—but was, rather, the consequence of the spread of navalist ideology, embodied in the works of Mahan and Theodore Roosevelt, "congressional politics, and the popularity of big, steel ships." Hence, the genesis of the blue-water U.S. navy was in large part the consequence of "concerns originating in domestic politics rather than in concerted efforts to form a grand strategy based on geo-strategic realities and international political threats. For the majority, the new naval strategy was an unintended outcome." The British empire, as the oft-repeated aphorism has it, was acquired in a fit of absence of mind. The same assertion can be made for the United States' high-seas battlefleet. In essence, the United States created a navy, and then developed a strategy for its employment, rather than vice-versa. "The rise of American seapower, more than any other innovation of the late nineteenth century, influenced the grand strategy of the emerging nation."[49] Comparatively speaking, contemporary British naval strategy was a paragon, not only of coherence, but of utility.

Strategic dissonance was less of a problem for the navies of Germany and Russia, largely because geostrategic, economic, and political factors narrowly circumscribed the course of each country's naval policy during the 1870s and 1880s. Yet the discrepancy between perceived strategic requirements and the resultant planning and—with regard to ship design and construction—execution was certainly no less pronounced in at least the Russian navy than it was in the British. Germany was certainly more successful in terms of meshing its strategic conception with the means to implement it, though primarily because its maritime goals were very limited. Simultaneously, however, naval strategy per se was wholly subordinated to military considerations. "The German Navy was simply another arm of a rational system of national defense. Strategically, the chief of the General Staff, General Helmuth von Moltke, organized the navy as he organized a defensive sector on land: the navy was merely the part of the army that happened to watch the sea frontier."[50]

With this limited and coherent strategic agenda, the German navy of the 1870s and 1880s faced minimal problems in designing, constructing, and deploying the forces with which to implement it. The core of the battlefleet consisted of small but potent coastal-defense battleships, supplemented by gun vessels. Neither peacetime policing nor wartime commerce raiding played an integral role in German naval strategy. Despite the contemporary enthusiasm for the *guerre de course*, German naval strategy remained resolutely committed to coastal defense throughout the 1880s.[51] What problems remained for German naval planners were manifested more obviously at tactical and operational levels. The subordination of naval forces to military conceptions of strategy to a large degree extended to more prosaic, if no less essential, matters such as training; "the Germans completely neglected squadron tactics."[52]

Germany, the one European power with a coherent conception of naval strategy during the mid-Victorian era, was, in British eyes, among the least threatening of its rivals, in part as a consequence of that strategy. Indeed, it was precisely the limited, wholly defensive nature of the second reich's initial approach to sea power that made it so coherent. Unlike other navies, the German fleet did not have to contend with the insuperable problems of reconciling technologically deficient means to strategic ends. With no pretensions to blue-water power, German naval planners were spared many, if not most, of the architectural and design nightmares that dogged their counterparts in Britain, France, Italy, and Russia throughout the period. A fleet intended to operate entirely within the narrow confines of the Baltic and North seas posed no insoluble problems for either the need for auxiliary sail power or extended steaming capacity. Likewise, the renunciation of the *guerre de course* minimized the need for speed and coal endurance in the few unarmored corvettes the German navy did possess.[53] In time, the German empire amply demonstrated that its strategic vision could be as myopic and wrongheaded as that of any of its rivals, but that revelation awaited the ascendancy of Tirpitz.[54]

Russia's difficulties in reconciling strategic aims with limited means have been considered in some detail in conjunction with the *guerre de course*, but a few further words should be spared for the strategic picture that confronted the czar's naval planners. Russia's chief geographic advantage in defensive terms—its relative inaccessibility by sea—was its gravest strategic drawback in an offensive context. The narrow, twisting, shoal-infested waters of the Gulf of Finland, ice-bound for much of the year to begin with and studded with elaborate fortifications, were an ideal theater for a coastal-defense force of monitors. Likewise, the confined waters of the Black Sea—wholly demilitarized from 1856 to 1871—were also well protected. Indeed, the Franco–British choice of Sevastopol, a relatively unimportant fortress plagued by diabolical supply problems, as its primary objective in 1854 starkly illustrates the obstacles placed in the way of would-be belligerents by geography. For that matter, the Russian Black Sea coast is not ice-free either, as the British unhappily learned during the Crimean War. Only Vladivostok on the Pacific and Archangel in the White Sea offer geographically unhindered access to the open sea. The latter, however, aside from its geographic and strategic remoteness, is ordinarily ice-free from only May to October. Vladivostok, too, is frozen in for part of the year. During the late nineteenth century, moreover, it was a singularly uninviting target for any potential Russian foe, save perhaps for bombardment. A continent away from Europe, equally isolated from the centers of military power, beset with logistical and supply problems that made those of Sevastopol seem paltry, and strategically insignificant, there was little point in capturing Vladivostok, and huge logistical difficulties would have accompanied any western European attempt to do so. Hence, Russia required only modest measures at sea to supplement the geographic and climatic advantages the country enjoyed.

Yet even with these immense geographic advantages, Russian naval defenses were undistinguished, a testament to equally immense problems posed by the empire's underdeveloped economy and industrial infrastructure. By the mid-1870s the Russian navy had acquired or built a numerically respectable coastal-defense force, most of it stationed in the Baltic.[55] But by 1870 most of these ships lacked adequate armor protection and suffered from other ills as well, in particular unreliable machinery. Most of the Russian coastal-defense ships were small, slow, and unseaworthy, limited wholly to defensive employment in enclosed waters. The Russian navy "was inferior even to the Turkish when the two fought in 1878."[56] With but one significant exception, Russia did not attempt to build seagoing capital ships until the 1880s, and only in the following decade was the offensive capacity of the Russian battlefleet capable of posing even a theoretical threat to Britain.

Therefore, Russia's offensive naval strategy in the 1870s and 1880s was perforce limited to the *guerre de course*, although here too the limitations of technology, industrial base, and, again, geography rendered the menace from Russian commerce raiding more imagined than real. Lacking the industrial capacity and technological sophistication to build a significant—much less a successful—armored cruiser force, Russia of necessity turned to merchant auxiliaries purchased overseas. But even had this improvised force possessed the technological and logistical capability of menacing British shipping, the strategic obstacles posed by lack of year-round access to the open sea, the virtually landlocked waters of the Baltic and Black seas and the strategic, geographic, and commercial isolation of Archangel and Vladivostok made the successful Russian application of the *guerre de course* a very dubious proposition indeed. "The Pacific was to be the main field of action, and Russian ships were equipped with charts of the routes followed by English commerce. . . . But the attack was still at the periphery of the British Empire," and if implemented would have probably met only very limited success.[57]

Italy's strategic problems were even more daunting than those of Russia. The lengthy, exposed Italian coastline was a strategic Achilles heel that plagued neither Germany nor far-larger Russia. And, again unlike Russia, Italy faced a naval rival in the form of neighboring France. Following the naval debacle against Austria in 1866 and spurred by France's ongoing interference in Italian affairs, Italy adopted a defensive naval strategy aimed at protecting "the Italian coasts from the French Mediterranean fleet." Further headaches, both geographic and logistical, accompanied the long and vulnerable coastline, dotted with defenseless ports, in the form of an underdeveloped internal transportation system. The consequences for Italian naval strategy were immense. The bulk of Italy's defenses were concentrated in the north, "tied down by the phobia of a French attack through the Alps," while the vital Tyrrhenian Sea—between Sardinia, Corsica, and the Italian mainland—was virtually undefended. As a consequence, Rome was wholly exposed to attack by amphibious forces, and Naples, the second largest port in the country and the site of major shipyards and the navy's gun factory, was "completely at the mercy of an enemy fleet." Moreover, Italian planners, driven by a vague imperial agenda, positioned Italian naval forces in the south at Taranto, rather than Naples, "leaving crucial defense industries even more exposed than they had been.... By pursuing the shadowy advantage of having an offensive base near the Levant," the more crucial concern of defensive security was sacrificed.[58]

Nor were Italy's ship construction and deployment policies coherent reflections of strategic policy, although in the 1870s and early 1880s they were certainly the most radical, creative, and provocative of any of the world's navies. This was an indication that Italian naval planners, in particular Benedetto Brin and Simone de Saint Bon, appreciated the confounding roles in the formulation of a consistent, rational, and realizable naval strategy played by geography, communications, and, certainly not least of all, Italy's industrial and economic backwardness.[59] Unlike the German navy, which, in the narrow confines of the Baltic and North seas, could anchor its naval power on small coastal-defense battleships, Italy, which had over 5,000 miles of coastline to protect in the considerably wider expanses of the Mediterranean could only build a fleet that possessed a large steaming radius: a fleet of "high-seas battleships." But the limitations of finance and industrial capacity prohibited the construction of such a fleet adequate to defend the entire peninsula. "Since she could not attain numerical equality, [Italy] was forced to depend on the superiority of individual ships."[60]

As a consequence, Italy was in the forefront of developments in naval architecture in the 1870s and 1880s, building four battleships unrivaled by any competitors in terms of speed, size, and offensive power. As manifestations of a strategy in which France was the presumed enemy, the Italian battleships were logically conceived.

The mere existence of the Italian vessels, indeed, would have confounded French naval strategy in the event of war, and were thus deterrents. "As long as the Italian battleships were 'in being' and ready for action, they would fulfill their purpose because the French would not dare to launch a major maritime expedition."[61] Four ships do not a fleet make, however, and while the Italian "super ironclads" largely possessed the same operational and tactical advantages over the British battlefleet that they did over the French, the paucity of Italian vessels, coupled with the vast and largely undefended coastline that they would have to cover in wartime led to dissonance between strategic aims and the means by which they were to be realized. In short, the Italian fleet, which should clearly have been designed and built with defense uppermost in mind, was not really capable of defending the country. Moreover, with the exception of a handful of smaller cruising and torpedo vessels, and some old, small ironclads that had survived the Lissa debacle, the Italian navy consisted entirely of its monster ironclads.[62] No effort was made to construct commerce raiders, despite the fact that Italy was ideally situated to interdict both east–west trade—which dramatically increased following the opening of the Suez Canal in 1869—and France's communications with North Africa.

At least Russia and Italy could draw up more or less coherent naval strategies, even if both countries lacked the resources with which to implement their plans. France, whose pretensions to naval power were greater than Italy's, Russia's, or indeed any country's with the sole exception of Britain, faced insoluble problems in the 1870s and 1880s, not only in implementing a naval strategy, but even in arriving at one, and the dissonance between French aims and actions made similar problems within the Admiralty seem comparatively minor. As the world's second maritime power, France had to pursue two strategies simultaneously: one to be employed in a war against an inferior naval power and another applicable to war against Britain, as an inferior power itself.[63] This dilemma was fully recognized by influential French naval strategist Captain Louis-Antoine-Richild Grivel by the late 1860s. Alive to the concept fully articulated by Mahan more than twenty years later as "command of the sea," Grivel concluded that winning control of the high seas was the crucial object of naval warfare: "[B]y gaining command of the great highroad of the sea," Grivel wrote, "one side automatically restricted the other to the defensive and gained the freedom to chose between the enemy's coast or his commerce or to attack both at once." This strategy was applicable to Germany or Italy.

But a strategy suitable for conflicts with inferior rivals was inappropriate when at war with the naval hegemon. Grivel studied France's repeated attempts to challenge British mastery in the late seventeenth and eighteenth centuries, and concluded that such attempts were doomed: "[T]he whole idea of attaining equality with England by achieving in peacetime near equality in numbers and superiority in training and ship design was an illusion." On this score Grivel was unequivocal: "[I]t is not in the power of any human force to displace suddenly . . . a well-established naval preponderance . . . based on the customs, the geographic situation, and the vocation of a people. . . . Our navy cannot permit itself any illusions regarding an inequality so clearly revealed by geography, history, and statistics." Hence, strategy against England would have to depend on coastal defense, supplemented by commerce raiding. The only viable alternative offensive strategy was economic, which seemed a particularly appropriate course of action to Grivel in light of Britain's unparalleled maritime wealth.

In other words, France evolved two naval strategies, one based on the *guerre d'escadre* for employment against inferior powers, and one based on the *guerre de course* to be used against Britain. But two strategies meant, unfortunately, two fleets in order to implement both. Accordingly, the construction program set forth in 1872 called for a fleet of twenty-three first-class and fourteen station (second-class) battleships, the *guerre d'escadre* force. A force of twenty-three commerce raiders, twenty coastal-defense battleships, and thirty-two gunboats was the projected *guerre de course* force. Implementation was another matter. The strategic dilemma gave rise to some comic situations (although the French may not have seen them thus) during the 1870s and 1880s as successive naval administrations struggled to build a fleet based on two incompatible principles. As late as 1890 the French navy had only one fast cruiser suitable for commerce destruction. For the whole of the 1870s "French cruiser policy stood still." To be sure, France built cruisers, but with two exceptions they were virtually identical to their British counterparts: small, unarmored, principally sailing vessels, intended for peacetime duties. Most French cruisers, furthermore, were not merely unarmored, but wholly wooden, whereas almost all British cruisers built after 1870 sported stronger and more durable composite hulls—wooden sheathing over iron frames. In short, the dissonance between strategic aims and the means by which they were to be carried out was as pronounced in the French navy as it was in the British: "Although English commerce was practically unprotected, France possessed almost nothing but merchant cruisers and small scouts for attacking it."

Ironically, the rise of the *Jeune Ecole* in the 1880s only further clouded the strategic picture for France. Neither Grivel nor his successors, most notably Theophile Aube and Gabriele Charmes, understood that the technological revolution had not altered "the old historical truth that it was impossible to attack the English coasts or commerce without first having command of the Channel." Moreover, Aube's and Charmes' single-minded reliance on small torpedo boats which, they argued, could carry out every facet of their strategic vision—coastal defense, commerce raiding, and artillery bombardment of coastal cities—was even more dissonant than the confused situation they sought to supplant. Torpedo boats, small, fragile, poorly armed (aside from the torpedoes), and short-range, were potent coastal defenders (once the torpedo was an effective weapon), but utterly unsuited to extended operations on the high seas. "Aube, a seasoned seaman, should have known better, and except for his total ignorance of the history of the development of these craft, the only possible explanations for his vigorous assertion of their seakeeping ability are psychological and social."

Worse yet, for the sake of strategic coherence, after 1885 neither *Jeune Ecole* nor traditional French naval strategy was entrenched as the navy's policy of preference. "*Jeune Ecole* theories were from time to time in the ascendant at the ministry of marine."[64] Moreover, the legacy of Aube's brief tenure at the head of the navy (January 1886 to May 1887), during which he "threw out nearly all the officers on the navy's Paris staff and most of the ministry's bureau chiefs," was a high command rent into feuding factions. As a consequence, the "*Jeune Ecole* split the French Navy wide open, and the next fifteen years (1885–1900) was a period of incredible confusion. . . . [W]ith an increasingly complicated ministry, an increasing confusion in strategic ideas, and an increasing number of civilian ministers, it is a wonder that France had any naval policy at all. At times it is certainly difficult to find it."[65]

Critiques of British naval administration in the mid-Victorian period for its alleged lack of strategic vision have generally failed to consider its performance in a contemporary, comparative context, preferring to judge it by standards of another era, during which demands on the navy were far greater; an era in which the reemergence of design stability (after roughly 1890) simultaneously made the formulation of a coherent (if not necessarily appropriate) strategy far simpler, and an era in which the navy was the recipient of a measure of parliamentary and popular support that provided funding at a level unknown in the 1870s and 1880s. Muddled as British strategic thinking was, it was a model of coherence and singleness of purpose compared to that of its cross-Channel rival. Furthermore, that some of the lesser European naval powers managed to formulate coherently conceived—if not always coherently executed—strategies was largely a function of the restricted scope of their maritime pretensions. Nor should it be forgotten that significant among the restricting factors was the British navy itself. Russia, after all, turned to the combined approach of coastal defense and commerce raiding owing to its inability to compete with Britain's naval, economic, and industrial superiority in any other way; and the *Jeune Ecole* was a tacit, but nonetheless unmistakable admission that France could not challenge Britain by the *guerre d'escadre*.

In addition, one should not underestimate the influence that the global scope of the navy's operations had upon design and deployment policies. The British navy was expected to (and did) perform a multitude of roles worldwide. This salient fact largely explains why the formulation of a coherent strategy, and, much more, the construction of a fleet with which to implement it, were so problematic during the mid-Victorian era. The masts and sails that so encumbered (and reduced the bunkerage space of) ships charged with protection of commerce in the event of war were necessary—indeed crucial—appendages on vessels that might spend months beyond reach of coal supplies while upholding British interests in some out-of-the-way corner of the globe during peacetime. "The Royal Navy, with its worldwide commitments and its need to counter all kinds of naval threat, could not normally afford to build highly specialized vessels in large quantities. Most Royal navy ships had therefore to possess not only those features necessary for their specific purpose, but also qualities of armament, protection, seaworthiness, reliability, speed and habitability that would enable them to cope with some chance of success in any type of situation."[66] Ironically, only with the strategic constriction that characterized the post-Mahan era, as British focus became increasingly Eurocentric, that coherent strategic policy developed quickly. One should not read too much into this conjunction: there were other factors at work as well. But there can be little doubt that the heterogeneous nature of the navy's duties during the mid-Victorian era, coupled with the radical upheaval in naval architecture, were the bane of those charged with designing the policies that would uphold maritime hegemony and those who designed the ships with which those policies were implemented. That those designs often reflected the predominance of peacetime roles in the minds of their authors was perhaps unfortunate, but certainly not surprising, given the circumstances of the time.

Finally, compromises in designs that limited the wartime utility of the overseas fleet were to a considerable extent the result of circumstances beyond the Admiralty's control, especially with regard to the extension of docking and repair facilities overseas, the establishment of a comprehensive worldwide network of coal depots, and the construction of a fleet of colliers with which to supply them. The report of the 1871 Admiralty committee on designs of ships of war concluded, among other things, "[W]e believe that our transmarine possessions, and other important interests in distant parts of the world, will be more efficiently protected, where requisite, by centres of naval power, from which ships . . . may operate, than by relying upon cruising ships . . . of limited fighting power."[67] There could be no argument with this conclusion, at least on strategic grounds. But to implement the committee's recommendation would have involved vast expenditure that statesmen of the 1870s and 1880s, doubtless aware of the defenselessness of most colonies and trade routes, but also mindful of the fact that there was virtually no threat to them, were unwilling to sanction. Indeed, the suggestions of the committee on designs for imperial defense "proved far too radical and expensive to be implemented, particularly at a time when colonial relations with the mother country were unsettled[;] . . . the committee's majority recommendations found favor in almost no public quarter."[68]

Contemporary politicians, and the public to which they answered, may be judged in retrospect to have been short-sighted for their failure to take steps to redress this defenselessness, but to have taken the opposite course, in the absence of perceptible foreign threats, would have been willfully extravagant if not outright senseless. In short, the Admiralty's scope of action was circumscribed not only by the limitations and confusion of its strategic vision, but also by the realities of domestic political considerations. This situation was, of course, by no means unique, nor even particularly novel, but it was arguably of unusual gravity because of the revolutionary shift in maritime technology, a problem with which their equally short-sighted and cash-starved predecessors had not had to contend.

CHAPTER 12

Conclusion

If England wants a fleet, she can have it, quickly, effectually, completely; but she must be quite decided, prompt, and unhesitating. ... The creation of an effective fleet implies the immediate outlay of fifty million sterling.
— Anonymous pamphlet, *The Coming War: England Without a Navy*, 1875.

There are two cries against the Admiralty which go on side by side: one says, "We have not ships enough, no 'relief' ships, no *navy*, to tell the truth"; the other cry says, "We have all the wrong ships, all the wrong guns, and nothing but the wrong; in their foolish constructive mania the Admiralty have been building when they ought to have been waiting; they have heaped a curious museum of exploded inventions, but they have given us nothing serviceable." The two cries for opposite policies go on together, and blacken our executive together, though each is a defense of the executive against the other.
— Walter Bagehot, *The English Constitution*, 1867.

Naval affairs, even defense policy in general, were not issues of central importance to the mid-Victorians. National security received relatively little attention alongside the major topics of the day. Ireland, the Eastern question, parliamentary and political reform, the abolition of purchase in the army, and many lesser issues garnered greater attention outside of and occasioned more debate within Parliament than the yearly presentation of the navy estimates. Even the Royal Titles Bill of 1876—proclaiming Victoria empress of India—resulted in a far greater, and more acrimonious, legislative battle than any one year's naval debate. Naval affairs were worthy of one, maybe two, editorials a year, save when the estimates showed a large increase, or when accompanied by a more noteworthy occurrence, such as the *Captain* tragedy. But these instances, few and far between, were the exceptions that proved the rule. Public and press opinion could be mobilized on naval matters, as was amply demonstrated by events·in Britain after 1889.[1] Moreover, before the passage of the Naval Defence Act (1889), even prior to W. T. Stead's 1884 "Truth

About the Navy" articles, which painted a thoroughly alarming picture of the state of the service, there had been the periodic convulsions contemporaries dubbed "naval" or "invasion" scares. These were invariably driven by the perceived inadequacy of the navy. But the scares, though lacking little in terms of intensity, were ephemeral. Even the longest of them, corresponding to the introduction of the ironclad, lasted only from late 1858 to 1862. The sustained interest in naval affairs after 1889 was, furthermore, the consequence of a number of concurrent developments: growing international tensions, resurgent (new?) imperialism, perceived challenges to British maritime hegemony, and, certainly not least, the growing volume and stridency of navalist voices led, ironically, by U.S. navy officer Alfred Mahan.

In 1875, however, the last invasion scare was fifteen years in the past and the first of Mahan's major publications fifteen years in the future. Even the Stead alarm was nine years away. The 1870s were a decade of public and press quiescence regarding the state of the navy. The brief panic of 1870 was confined entirely to the Admiralty, and evidence relating to the "war scare purchases" in 1878 does not suggest that they resulted from outside pressure or public apprehension. Perhaps the most notable instance of public alarm over the state of the country's defenses during the decade occurred, curiously, in response to an article written by a British army officer. In early 1871 *Blackwood's Magazine* published an essay by Colonel Sir George Chesney titled "The Battle of Dorking," an imaginative scenario of a successful invasion of Britain, leading to "the collapse of our power and commerce in consequence."[2] Coming hard on the heels of the rapid German victory over France, the timing of Chesney's piece was serendipitous. "The nation was a ready victim for a tale of terror that would realize its fears and the ominous predictions then being made." The *Annual Register*, in summing up the year, remarked that Britain "was in one of her fits of periodical alarm about herself, and to believe those who should know best, she was never in so fatally an unprepared condition as now." But although spectacular, the alarm was brief. Moreover, it had little, if any, influence on public perception of the navy, despite Chesney's scenario having presupposed that the first line of defense had been evaded.[3] Perhaps because the author had, in the words of a contemporary "conveniently disposed of 'a force without rival in the world'" in "an affair of five lines," he failed to arouse apprehensions about the state of the navy. His article, and the alarm that greeted its publication, made no impression on the formulation of the navy estimates for 1871–72.

In one respect, the general lack of interest in naval affairs inside Parliament is understandable. To others than the handful of ardent navalists such as Sir John Hay, Sir James Elphinstone, Sir Edward Reed, and Thomas Brassey, and an equally small contingent of Manchester School Radicals—most notably Peter Rylands and Charles Seely—debates over the estimates were almost without exception deadly dreary affairs. The *Times* noted the "thin attendance" that typically greeted the presentation of the navy budget, politely attributing it to the "technical" nature of the subject.[4] "Technical" it was indeed, and most members of the House of Commons had neither the expertise nor the interest to participate. Even when they did there was little point in challenging the figures brought forward by the government.[5] During the late 1860s and throughout the 1870s, unlike the post-1889 era, naval policy and finance were not issues settled in public, nor even within the walls of Westminster. They were subjects resolved between the First Lord of the Admiralty, the prime minister, and the chancellor of the exchequer—at most the whole cabinet. As Lord Salisbury testified to the Hartington Commission several years later, "Questions of Estimate which are not settled by personal conference between the Chancellor of the Exchequer and the War Office or Admiralty, as the case may be, are usually arranged in concert with the Prime Minister."[6] Hence, as long as the government possessed a secure majority and the obedience of its back-benchers, defense spending was not ordinarily subject to intense parliamentary or public scrutiny.

It is equally apparent, though, that naval finance was at times an issue of pivotal importance at the cabinet level, that it was often an issue of great divisiveness within the cabinet and, implicitly, within the broader scope of Liberalism. Disputes over naval spending influenced the fortunes of the major parties at two points: 1868 and 1874. The Derby-Disraeli ministry's inability to check its spending was a significant factor in the Conservatives' failure to improve their position in the 1868 general election, and Disraeli's failure to impose his will on the Admiralty completely—though hardly for want of trying—figured into the government's poor reputation for finance. Conversely, whatever shortcomings the Gladstone ministry might have possessed, a want of financial prowess was not among them, yet it is plain that in 1874 the prime minister's campaign on behalf of still greater economy in the service departments ran up against the intransigence of George J. Goschen and Edward Cardwell. The upshot was an impulsive decision to dissolve Parliament and appeal to the electorate in search of a fresh mandate. Gladstone based his electoral message largely on financial issues, the linchpin being his pledge to abolish the income tax, a smaller boon than would appear to contemporary Americans, since it then only brought in some £4–5 million of the government's annual revenue of roughly £70–80 million.[7] Small boon Gladstone's promise might have been, but it was nonetheless a boon of sorts, and he remained mystified by the electorate's rejection of the offer he held out in 1874. Recollecting it during the course of the first Midlothian campaign, five years later, he confessed he had yet to discover why "they then preferred having the Income-tax to no Income-tax."[8] Whatever the reason, and it would seem to have had little to do with the income tax, the majority of voters preferred to back the Tories in 1874. Failure to reach an accord on the size of the service estimates accounted largely for the timing, and may have contributed in a smaller way to the outcome of the general election.

More significantly, the battle between Gladstone on the one hand and Goschen and Cardwell on the other served to illuminate one of the many rifts in that rather amorphous group labeled the Liberal party. Gladstone, Hugh Childers, certainly John Bright, Lord Granville, and—until his death in 1870—Lord Clarendon were all "little Englanders" to a greater or lesser degree, and their approach to foreign and imperial policies—conciliation, cooperation, and nonintervention—along with their unquestioned devotion to retrenchment and the exorcism of "bloated armaments" largely informed their strategy towards defense policy and spending. Years later Lord Salisbury observed that in matters of defense finance the cabinet's role was "to arbitrate between rival departments. . . . The Chancellor of the Exchequer, little familiar with the defensive services, is rightly the spokesman of economy. The heads of the War Office and Admiralty, unacquainted with the precise position of the Exchequer, are the natural and proper advocates of efficiency."[9] For most of the five-plus years of the Liberal administration the balance of power rested with the chancellor of the exchequer and the other advocates of economy, foremost among them the prime minister himself. Yet this context did not result in the outright triumph of the "economical wing" of the party. Though it won the bulk of the battles between 1868 and

Conclusion 241

1874, it lost the final struggle, during the waning days of the administration.

For Goschen, Cardwell, later Joseph Chamberlain, and doubtless many other Liberals, economy was desired, to be sure, but it could not become an end in itself. As Goschen's biographer observed, he "could not be induced on grounds of economy to diminish the efficiency of the Navy for performing the work allotted to it."[10] This fundamental divergence of purpose, ultimately of philosophy, led directly to the demise of the Liberal government in 1874, and was to have a legacy extending well beyond this incident. It reappeared in the early 1880s, more dramatically in 1894 with Gladstone's quixotic battle against the Spencer shipbuilding program, and could be detected again during the early years of the Campbell-Bannerman/Asquith ministry of 1905–16. Moreover, in a larger framework, defense policy was so closely tied to imperial and foreign policies as to be inseparable from them, and therefore the split between the "little Englanders" and Liberal imperialists that played a not insubstantial role in the temporary eclipse of the party after 1886, was at root inseparably tied to matters of military and naval policy and spending. In this respect, the controversy between Gladstone and Goschen and Cardwell was a harbinger of the future.

The Conservatives suffered from no such fundamental division, or at least nothing on the scale of the rift among Liberals. Yet it is equally clear that the level of naval expenditure during the 1866–68 ministry was a subject of both divisiveness and acrimony. Disraeli did not share Gladstone's ideological attachment to the principle of nonintervention, but the great rivals were at one on the matter of retrenchment, at least as long as Disraeli was at the exchequer. Pitted against him were navalists Corry and Pakington and, from 1874 through 1877, Ward Hunt, along with the hawks in the Conservative leadership: Lords Malmesbury and Carnarvon. The situation was altered considerably during the second Disraeli ministry. If the prime minister's views on reducing "bloated armaments" did not undergo a transformation between 1868 and 1874 there was an implicit contradiction in his policy from the latter date onward. The government's colonial and foreign adventures, to which he generally lent his approval, were virtually guaranteed to be reflected in higher army and navy expenditures.[11]

Of the six First Lords who served between 1866 and 1880, three were navalists—strong advocates of efficiency. Two were equally zealous proponents of economy, and the one remaining fell somewhere between the two camps. Pakington's and Corry's policies presaged the era after 1889, although at any time prior to the passage of the Naval Defence Act there could always be found a handful of ardent navalist voices in Parliament and elsewhere (not least among them the queen's), decrying Britain's defenselessness. Largely as a consequence of the relatively enormous building programs begun in 1867–68 and 1868–69 the navy managed to add an average of 20,285 tons yearly to the strength of the fleet between 1866 and 1880, despite the chronic failure to measure up to Childers' construction "standard." Put another way, thanks in large part to the programs initiated by Pakington and Corry, the Admiralty was able to "coast" in the matter of ironclad building for much of the 1870s.

Ward Hunt was an equally zealous navalist, although his posthumous reputation as First Lord has not been high. Even in its obituary the *Times* implied that he might have been better suited for another office, and one subsequent commentator dismissed him as perhaps "our most ineffective naval administrator."[12] Yet the course of his administration undermines the charge that Ward Hunt, "although anxious to do his best for the Service, proved quite unable to make any stand against Disraeli's policy of drastic naval economy."[13] Over the course of three years he managed to increase the level of naval spending an aggregate of £2.27 million above 1873–74's sum (the highest of the Liberal government), hardly an insignificant amount when yearly estimates typically ranged between £10 million and £11 million. Indeed, from the standpoint of naval funding Ward Hunt's administration was as "successful," from a purely navalist standpoint, as either Pakington's or Corry's.

It is true, as the *Times* observed, that his tenure at Whitehall was marred "by a melancholy series of mischances."[14] Most notorious were the accidental ramming and sinking of H.M.S. *Vanguard* by another British ironclad on 1 September 1875, and the near-simultaneous promulgation of an unfortunate circular to captains overseas, instructing them to return fugitive slaves who sought sanctuary on board her majesty's ships to their owners. Neither of these acts was perpetrated by the First Lord, but he bore responsibility for them nonetheless, and it was doubtless to his credit that he made no attempt to shirk it. Indeed, he assured Disraeli in October 1875: "You say the Queen thinks the 'affairs of the Admiralty dangerous to the Government'[;] if you think *my* administration of them is not advan-

Conclusion 243

tageous to the Government & the country the slightest hint will be enough for me."[15] The slightest hint was not forthcoming, but Ward Hunt's administration acquired a reputation for weakness and bumbling that, if not altogether unjustified, was considerably exaggerated, and, moreover, has persisted.

It is instructive, therefore, to consider another contemporary assessment of his accomplishments, from no less an observer than Admiral Sir William Houston Stewart, the controller of the navy from 1872 to 1881. Houston Stewart also served under Goschen, W. H. Smith, and Lord Northbrook, but left no doubt as to whom he thought the most effective. "The first steps towards adding to the strength of the Fleet," he wrote Sir Alexander Milne in 1882, "were taken by Mr. Ward Hunt." "He increased the number of men in the Dockyards to 16,000[;] ... the repairs of the armoured ships were taken in hand and systematically carried out to completion. It was always my opinion that he took the first and most effective steps during the whole of his administration for adding to the efficiency of the Navy, which *first steps* having been taken made matters much easier for his successor."[16]

Conversely, as implied by Houston Stewart's final sentence, the success of Smith as First Lord, at least from a navalist point of view, has been exaggerated. His entry in the *Dictionary of National Biography* notes the criticism that greeted his appointment in 1877, since the "office had generally been held by persons of high rank," but adds that his "appointment belied all misgivings and proved a complete success."[17] This perception of success was based on the acquisition of four ironclads during the Eastern Crisis and little else. In summing up the fortunes of the navy in 1878, the *Times* emphatically stated that "[f]ew years since the date of the Crimean War have seen such manifest progress in the Navy as the year which has passed." The reason was not far to seek. "The most important feature in the year is the stimulus given to shipbuilding and the substantial addition made to the material strength of the Navy. The Vote of Credit was not only timely to the naval authorities in enabling them to make up for lost ground, but it was applied at a time when it could be used to the best advantage and in the most judicious and serviceable manner." Nor did the journal leave any doubt as to who deserved the accolades for such a coup: "Since the time when the late Mr. Corry was head of the Admiralty no such energy has been displayed with so practical a result; and Mr. Smith in his first year in office has proved himself a worthy successor to one of the most enthusiastic and capable heads the Admiralty has had for many years [i.e., Corry]."[18]

The navy would have been augmented in 1878, regardless of who was First Lord. Smith was in the right place at the right time. For the remainder of his tenure at the Admiralty he appeared more nearly a worthy successor to Hugh Childers than to Corry. In fact, the *Times* heaped praise upon Smith when he revealed that "naval expenditure" for 1879 was "lower than it had been since the present Administration took office."[19] Certainly Smith did not lack competence. He had a high reputation as an administrator and, by carrying out a comprehensive reform of the Admiralty secretariat, he showed that he shared other qualities with Childers. But as a man of business, he fell squarely into the "economical" camp along with Childers, and both men, unlike Corry, Pakington, and Ward Hunt, seem to have rated political considerations higher than the often alarmist pronouncements of their naval advisors.[20]

Childers himself was far and away the most reform-minded, the most controversial, and, within the service, the most unpopular First Lord during the period, and the hostility of the naval element, to a large extent, continues to inform assessments of both the man and his accomplishments. His administrative restructuring was nowhere near the fiasco that many commentators concluded. His overriding goal was to rationalize a system and a service in serious need of it, and to a remarkable degree he succeeded.[21] Although his attempt to put ship construction policy on a stable, long-term footing suffered from errors of calculation, it should not be condemned out of hand. The periodic "naval scares" that so characterized the years from 1847 through 1862 repeatedly led to hasty, injudicious, and extravagant expenditure and provided ample justification for Childers' attempt. It was obvious that a reduced level of construction—if not outright neglect of shipbuilding—ordinarily preceded the alarms.

Childers' attempt to remedy these shortcomings was understandable, especially to those of Liberal principles, even if the execution left something to be desired. On the basis of the building programs of rival navies during the 1870s, the standard of 12,000 ironclad tons annually, if achieved, would have been more than adequate to uphold the British navy's preeminent position. As matters turned out, the navy did not fare all that poorly during the decade with considerably less. But it was a bad time to embark upon a consistent, long-term naval construction policy, no matter how well conceived and executed it might have been. Childers' successor touched on the reason why in the process of enunciating the building program for 1872–73: "It cannot be said that we ought to have a certain absolute number of ironclads, but that if our neighbours have much fewer, we also require much fewer. It is a question of proportion."[22] A steady program, based on the production of a certain number of ships, or a certain amount of tonnage, was bound to be inappropriate for practical needs at any given time, either because adhering to it would place the navy at a disadvantage vis-à-vis rival forces whose construction had been augmented, or else because it would bind the government to a larger expenditure on ships than was necessary under the circumstances. Any building policy that was not explicitly tied to rivals' strengths—or British perceptions thereof— would have been found wanting, either because it produced too little or because it cost too much.

The only way to calculate the lowest level of requisite naval strength, either in the eyes of the British public, press, or political world or in those of rivals, was by seeming to allow the navy to sink to or below that level; the reflexive response to this state of affairs, when perceived, was not unnaturally a panic or at least a short frenzy of activity. This tendency also adumbrates an implicit inconsistency in the general political attitude toward naval spending, especially pronounced among the Liberals. On the one hand, panic spending was deprecated, the cue being furnished by Cobden, whose *Three Panics* (1862) was an eloquent condemnation not only of the political dimension of scare-mongering, but also of the ill-planned and wasteful expenditure that almost invariably followed.[23] But on the other, to maintain a steady level of expenditure, through which periodic panics might be largely avoided, opened any administration to charges of extravagance. Radical M.P. Peter Rylands demonstrated the other horn of the dilemma in his condemnation of the estimates in 1872. Goschen, he declaimed, "asserted that England was now relatively stronger than ever before. . . . [Hence,] it appeared almost incredible that the Government should be pushing forward the building of new vessels, and incurring an unnecessary and extravagant expenditure, from which no advantage could be derived."[24] Whether or not Goschen was influenced by the arguments advanced by economy-minded Radicals like Rylands, or for that matter those advanced by Gladstone, the following year he announced an ironclad shipbuilding program only half the size of the 12,000-ton "Childers standard." One pretext offered for this deviation was the state of technological uncertainty, which made every new design a risky investment, but underlying the First Lord's rationale was also the assumption that the naval challenge from abroad was relatively trivial. Owing to the increasing favorable situation after 1871, Goschen sounded a note both confident and cautious: "[W]ith respect to ironclads we were so strong that, though we could not altogether suspend shipbuilding, we could afford to proceed with judgment and calmness, and, above all, to avoid the fatal mistake of coming to a decision too soon."[25] Largely as a consequence of the insignificance of rivals' naval pretensions during the 1870s, planned ironclad tonnage was more than two thousand tons per year below the "Childers standard" between 1870–71 and 1879–80, and tonnage built averaged not 12,000 a year, but barely 8,600.

But reciting yearly averages obscures the sporadic nature of British capital ship construction during the Disraeli/Gladstone era. During the two years that the Conservatives were in office during the 1860s the Admiralty laid down no fewer than thirteen ironclads. In five years the first Gladstone administration commenced eleven. The Conservatives laid down only nine during the slightly less than six years of the second Disraeli ministry. The total of the last administration was swollen to thirteen by the four ships purchased under the vote of credit in 1878, but this tactic further illustrates how thoroughly Childers' "standard" had been ignored. No new ironclads were laid down in 1871, 1872, 1875, 1877, or 1878. At the other extreme, three were begun in 1873, 1874, and 1879, five in 1867, six in 1870, and no fewer than eight in 1868. While these fourteen years did not witness any panics on a par with those of 1858–60 and 1884–85, it is difficult to perceive the supplementary building program of 1870, under which five of the six vessels begun that year were authorized, and the purchases of 1878 in any light other than frenzied responses to short-term crises. Not for nothing, after all, were the latter known as the "Russian war-scare purchases." One can appreciate why Lord Salisbury later testified to the Hartington commission "that the annals of our defensive estimates consist of a series of rushes at one time in the direction of saving, at another in the direction of increased efficiency."[26] In both cases, however, what panic or frenzy there was seems to have been entirely confined to the government and the Admiralty. Neither in 1870 nor in 1878 was any alarm manifested in public, press, or parliamentary spheres.

TABLE 13
British Ironclads Laid Down and Completed, 1866–80
(1 = First Class, 2 = Second Class/Armored Cruiser, 3 = Coastal Defense)

Year	Laid Down	Completed
1866	Hercules (1), Monarch (1), Repulse (1)	—
1867	Captain (1), Audacious (2), Invincible (2), Vanguard (2), Cerberus (3)	Lord Warden (1), Royal Alfred (1)
1868	Sultan (1), Iron Duke (2,) Swiftsure (2), Triumph (2), Glatton (3), Hotspur (3), Magdala (3)[a], Abyssinia (3)[a]	Hercules (1), Penelope (2)
1869	Devastation (1), Thunderer (1)	Monarch (1)
1870	Dreadnought (1)[b], Rupert (3), Cyclops (3), Gorgon (3), Hecate (3), Hydra (3)	Captain (1), Repulse (1), Audacious (2), Vanguard (2), Invincible (2), Cerberus (3), Magdala (3), Abyssinia (3)
1871	—	Sultan (1), Iron Duke (2), Hotspur (3)
1872	—	Swiftsure (2), Glatton (3)
1873	Alexandra (1)[c], Temeraire (1), Shannon (2)	Devastation (1), Triumph (2)
1874	Inflexible (1), Northampton (2)	Rupert (3), Gorgon (3)
1875	—	—
1876	Ajax (1)[d], Agamemnon (1)[d]	Hydra (3)
1877	—	Thunderer (1), Alexandra (1), Temeraire (1), Shannon (2), Cyclops (3), Hecate (3)
1878	Neptune (1)[e], Superb (1)[e], Bellisle (3)[e], Orion (3)[e]	Northampton (2), Belleisle (3)
1879	Colossus (1), Edinburgh (1)[f], Conqueror (3)	Dreadnought (1)
1880	Collingwood (1)	Superb (1)

SOURCE: Oscar Parkes, *British Battleships, 1860–1960* (London: Seeley Service Co., 1957), 130–34.
[a]Built for the Indian government, and not ordinarily counted as part of the British battlefleet.
[b]Begun as *Fury* in 1870, construction on this vessel was halted in the wake of the *Captain* disaster. The ship was then redesigned and renamed, and construction began anew in 1872.
[c]Originally named *Superb*.
[d]*Ajax* and *Agamemnon* were conceived as coast-defense ships. In fact, their size and design were more along the lines of second-class vessels, and contemporaries usually referred to them as first-class ironclads.
[e]Purchased through the Vote of Credit in 1878. All of these ships were in an advanced state of construction, although only one was completed in 1878.
[f]Renamed *Majestic* during construction.

Although the building authorized in 1870 and the purchases of 1878 were the products of localized apprehensions, they were nonetheless manifestations of strictly short-term alarm. Confirmation is found in the behavior of the Admiralty once the crises had passed. The four coastal-defense vessels hurriedly begun in 1870 as a part of Spencer Robinson's "crash program" at the outbreak of the Franco-German War, and extolled by that officer in part because they could be completed in eighteen months, were not finished anywhere near that quickly. One of the four was commissioned in 1874, but the remaining three were completed only in 1876 and 1877, when war clouds again loomed on the horizon. Likewise, of the four "war scare" acquisitions of 1878, only one was commissioned that year, although three of the four were virtually complete when purchased by the Admiralty.[27]

Childers had envisioned the yearly addition of three ironclads to the fleet, which would have netted the navy thirty ships over the course of the decade. Practice did not fall short of theory, in terms of numbers. During the years 1870 through 1879 the navy commissioned twenty-seven ironclads and purchased a further four, thereby exceeding Childers' guidelines. A couple of qualifications should be borne in mind, however. Twelve were small vessels, unsuited for service anywhere other than in coastal waters. And while thirty-one vessels were built or purchased during the decade, only twenty-one were laid down, including the "war scare" ships. Again, the figure for the decade reveals a subtext on closer examination. Of these thirty-one vessels, eight were completed in 1870—the first fruits of the building programs initiated by Pakington and Corry—and a further six in 1877, when affairs in the East were beginning to make the employment of the fleet appear possible. Add to the latter the four vessels purchased the following spring and another two completed in the dockyards during the course of 1878, and it becomes apparent that twenty of the thirty-one were added to the navy's strength afloat during two short, frenzied bursts, whose correlations to the crises of 1870 and 1877–78 were hardly coincidental. Of course, it should not be forgotten that by far the most ambitious building programs—those of Pakington in 1867 and Corry in 1868—were begun during years when foreign challenges were muted, during years when the subject of naval strength was not prominent in either political or journalistic discourse, and, when mentioned, was far from panic proportions. The *Times* complained in April 1867, "It has been agreed on all sides that there is no present probability of a naval war, and it has also been conceded that our naval force is certainly not in arrears, as far as strength goes, to that of other countries. This being our position, and there being no special obligation pressing upon us or suggesting unusual exertion, we are asked for eleven millions of money for the service of the navy."[28] Ultimately, the most evanescent of Childers' achievements was that for which he garnered the greatest contemporary accolades: his economizing. The reduction of the estimates to less than £10 million was an impressive accomplishment, but the rise of matériel costs occasioned by increasing technological sophistication would have forced them up before long, even had Childers remained at the Admiralty after 1871.

Goschen is less easy to classify than the other First Lords of the era, at least on the basis of his tenure in the 1870s.[29] His estimates were exceeded only by Childers' in their rigorous economy, and Goschen was confronted with a substantial rise in prices that his predecessor had been spared. By the same token, however, his ongoing contest of wills with Gladstone underscored Goschen's determination to place naval efficiency above political or economic considerations. In one respect he was cut from the same economical bolt of cloth as Childers, but in another he resembled Ward Hunt and Pakington, both of whom refused to budge when they felt they had cut all that could be safely cut.

Finally, fundamental disagreements within the cabinet regarding the size of the navy estimates were endemic between 1866 and 1874, aside from Childers' tenure as First Lord. The evidence regarding Admiralty–cabinet relations during the second Disraeli ministry is scantier. Certainly Disraeli, Northcote, or the whole cabinet quashed any grandiose schemes Ward Hunt may have entertained for naval reconstruction in 1874, but the First Lord did win a supplementary estimate, albeit one of modest proportions. Moreover, a prolonged battle over the size of the estimates took place the following year, a battle that Ward Hunt won, and in 1876 he managed to gain sanction for a substantial unarmored shipbuilding program. For two years thereafter the Eastern Crisis provided the impetus for increased spending. Only during the ministry's final year did "economy" regain predominance over "efficiency" as the prime criterion of naval policy. Aside from 1875, unfortunately, there is little evidence as to how divisive an issue it was.

With very few exceptions, historians of the late-nineteenth-century

British navy have uncritically accepted the theories of naval power and the need for naval preparedness touted by proponents of the "blue-water school." Mahan was, of course, the most famous, and among the most eloquent and persistent, but he was by no means alone. Britain boasted numerous "blue-water" advocates, among them naval officers such as Philip Colomb, John Hay, John Fisher, Lord Charles Beresford, and the ubiquitous Alexander Milne. All sounded the same alarm as Mahan. Milne, for example, noting that no other country could match Britain in terms of colonies or seaborne trade, deprecated the idea of basing guidelines for British naval strength on the size of other navies.[30] Such comparisons, he said, were "no criterion for us in regard to what should be our standard of force." The implication was that even the "two-power standard" was inadequate to safeguard Britain's "immense interests." Milne wrote these words in 1875, fifteen years prior to the publication of the first of Mahan's major works.

Six years after Milne's observations, the Carnarvon commission was appointed "to make inquiry into the condition and sufficiency of the means of the naval and military forces provided for the defence of the more important sea ports within our colonial possessions and dependencies."[31] Its first report concluded ominously, "[T]he strength of our Navy in ironclad ships and in cruisers should be decidedly in excess of any other nation, and even with a considerable increase great difficulty would be found in affording protection to so extended an Empire and so vast a commerce." Eight years after the Carnarvon commission issued its reports the Hartington commission on naval and military administration's report was published—concurrent with Mahan's *Influence of Seapower on History, 1660–1783*. So alarming were some of the allegations it contained regarding the state of the country's defenses that only twenty copies of the full report and minutes of evidence were printed and these marked "strictly confidential."[32] "[I]t does not follow," testified Admiral Geoffrey Phipps Hornby, "that because we have a superiority over, we will say, the French Navy, or we will take any second navy, that we have a superiority absolutely over two navies, therefore we have sufficient ships to protect our commerce at the outbreak of a war; we must have a very considerable superiority of force."[33] Such contemporary pronouncements can be multiplied almost ad infinitum, and, perhaps due to their sheer volume, their slant has generally informed the views of subsequent commentators.[34]

But assessing mid-Victorian British naval policy on the basis of the navalist critique means implicitly accepting Britain's naval policy after 1889, when navalists' dreams were largely realized, as the normative standard, and judging those who pursued alternative policies during the 1860s, 1870s, and 1880s by it. The judgment, not surprisingly, has been largely critical. The most charitable appraisal of the era's political leaders has been that they were attempting (not without short-term success) to stave off the inevitable.[35] This view, however, rests on the assumption that the Naval Defence Act was sooner or later inevitable. Britain *had*, at some point, to "wake up" to reality and take stock of its own defenselessness, as well as that of the empire. This assumption is ripe for reappraisal.

Was the Naval Defence Act of 1889 "inevitable"? Certainly the probability that the act, or something similar to it, would have been implemented in the late 1880s or 1890s was very high indeed, given the circumstances surrounding its passage. "The final two decades of the century were increasingly a period of imperialism, of irredentism, of the growth of fleets and armies."[36] But one must consider whether the same circumstances existed in the two decades prior to 1880 before passing judgment on the statesmen of the era. To a considerable extent they did not. The imperialism that so typified the final two decades of the nineteenth century and first fourteen years of the twentieth was largely muted between 1866 and 1880. There were colonial wars, to be sure, most notably the Ashantee and Abyssinian expeditions and, at the end of the period, the second Afghan, Zulu, and first Boer wars. There were, moreover, colonial annexations, including Fiji in 1874. And to these should be added Disraeli's purchase of the khedive's Suez Canal shares in 1875. But the heightened emphasis on colonies, on trade with colonies, on the necessity of maintaining uninterrupted lines of communication and trade, on securing dependent markets in the face of increasing competition from abroad, and on defending overseas markets and trade routes were considerations largely absent from the world in which politicians of the late 1860s and 1870s operated.

Concurrent with the revival of imperialism and, indeed, spurring it on, was growing tension in intra-European relations. France's defeat in 1870–71 led to an era of relative quiescence. Prior to its recovery, Germany, the new dominant power on the continent, had little to fear from its neighbor to the west, and Bismarck's efforts to maintain amicable relations with Austria and Russia to the east, if rarely wholly or indefinitely successful, nonetheless helped avert any clash between the two, into which Germany would likely have been drawn. The European situation during the 1870s was therefore largely one of calm, the Eastern crisis of 1876–78 notwithstanding. Only in the mid-1880s was Germany—and Britain, for that matter—confronted with a resurgent France. By the early 1890s the Bismarckian system was obviously crumbling, to be replaced in 1894 with a standoff that aligned France with Russia against the two central European empires, but the alignment of continental Europe into two rival alliance blocs, and the tension consequently generated, did not trouble the calculations of British statesmen prior to the era of the Naval Defence Act.

Third, and of probably greater immediate significance to Britain than the situation on the Continent, was the gradual erosion of its industrial lead. In the 1870s the challenge posed to British economic and industrial supremacy was still largely incipient. Thomas Brassey could confidently observe in 1876 that "our unrivalled resources for the construction of the most powerful ships would give us the means of adding to our existing fleet with a rapidity which could not be equalled abroad."[37] Twenty years later Britain's heavy industrial hegemony had vanished; both the United States and Germany were by then challenging it in iron and steel production. France and Russia had also made substantial gains.[38] In 1870 Britain could rest secure in the knowledge that it could mobilize greater shipbuilding, gun founding, and ironworking resources than any enemy or even any likely combination of enemies. By 1895 the comfort and reassurance this knowledge had provided was vanishing, along with Britain's industrial lead.

Under these circumstances the Naval Defence Act, not to mention the increasing popularity of the navy and the "blue-water school" in the press, within political circles, and even with the public at large, are fairly easily understood. What is less easy to comprehend is why politicians and naval administrators of the late 1860s and 1870s have been largely judged by standards relevant to the final decade of the century but anachronistic to the two decades prior to 1880. By the standards of the British battlefleet of the late 1890s, there can be no doubt that that of the 1870s was indeed a small and sorry agglomeration. But it was not the British fleet of the 1890s that it would have faced in the event of war. It was the contemporary French, Russian, or Italian fleets with which the Admiralty of the 1860s and 1870s was concerned, and dispassionate consideration of the evidence suggests that the British navy compared very favorably when stacked up against one, two, or even three of these potential rivals.

Gladstone, Disraeli, and the bulk of their political contemporaries have often been judged short-sighted, or at best penny-wise and pound-foolish, but the criteria employed in reaching this verdict are irrelevant to the situation they faced. France was not yet resurgent; Germany posed no naval threat; the Russian navy was suited almost solely for coastal defense; and the imposing United States navy assembled to defeat the Confederacy had been either laid up or dismantled outright with dramatic haste following the cessation of the Civil War, and by 1870 could no longer be perceived as a significant threat to Britain.[39] Moreover, British shipbuilding resources were so vastly superior to those of any would-be rival that any attempt to engage in a building race would have been futile to the point of foolishness.

There were, to be sure, contemporary observers ready, able, and willing repeatedly to decry the navy's weakness and lack of preparation for war. Milne, distinguished naval officer and twice First Sea Lord, was, of course, one of them, and he regularly produced alarming memoranda on the navy's inadequacy and the defenselessness of sea routes and colonies, themes that culminated in the Carnarvon commission's first report in 1881. Such fellow officers as Hay, Spencer Robinson, and Charles Cooper Penrose Fitzgerald repeatedly urged the wholesale expansion of the navy, and their entreaties were echoed by those of politicians such as Edward Reed, even such cabinet ministers as Lord Carnarvon, the Earl of Malmesbury, and no less a figure than Conservative prime minister Lord Derby, who admitted privately to Disraeli in early 1868, "[W]ithout yielding to panic ... it must be admitted that we do not possess the preponderance of Power which used to be considered as essential for our safety."[40]

Certainly Derby's position and great experience in politics and government informed his view on the subject. Indeed, there can be little doubt that Britain's naval position relative to other powers was not as commanding in the late 1860s as had been the case fifteen, twenty-five, or fifty years earlier. Yet given the rapid technological change that characterized naval architecture during the second half of the nineteenth century there was scant likelihood that it would be. The advent of steam and armor had nullified the value of the reserve of wooden sailing ships on which Britain's margin of superiority was buttressed. Prior to their blanket obsolescence at the beginning of the

1850s, these ships served to reassure public and press and intimidate would-be challengers, although in the event of a crisis their worth was apt to be minimal, due to the deteriorated state of large numbers of the reserve, coupled with the delays and difficulties that would be met when recruiting crews with which to man them.[41] Whether or not it had any fighting value, however, the reserve fulfilled its deterrent and reassurance functions. But after 1860, as Lord Derby pointed out, Britain could no longer pretend that the reserve of wooden battleships was a source of potential naval strength. Nor, by that point, or even by 1868, had the old wooden vessels been replaced by an ironclad reserve, although it was hardly reasonable to expect that they would have been, Derby's strictures notwithstanding. The ironclad age was, as of 1868, less than a decade old: not long enough, without the urgency of a conflict to spur production, to have led to the construction of both an armored battlefleet and an armored reserve. Moreover, given the rapidity with which new ironclads were themselves outmoded—often in one or two years—it would have been extravagant, not to say wasteful, to sink massive outlays into building a reserve force that would in all probability be obsolescent before a situation calling for its employment arose. It had been a simple and inexpensive matter to maintain a reserve of ships captured or built over the course of a conflict during the days of sail, but the coming of the industrial age altered circumstances dramatically. Derby perceived the change without fully comprehending the forces impelling it.

By the time he wrote to Disraeli, moreover, the naval balance was shifting decisively in Britain's favor. The real challenge from France had occurred at the dawn of the ironclad era, and by the mid-1860s it was clear that Britain's financial and industrial superiority had carried the day, almost before the naval race was well under way. Moreover, the situation grew more favorable over the subsequent decade, especially after the Franco-German debacle of 1870–71. Despite the alarmist warnings of several well-placed contemporaries, the British navy during the late 1860s and all of the 1870s was in a very strong, if not wholly commanding, position vis-à-vis its own fleet and that which might be mustered by any likely combination of rivals.

Finally, as to the protection of Britain's vast and far-flung oceanic commerce, Milne and his fellow critics were fond of pointing out the pressing need for cruising vessels to interdict the *guerre de course*. But if British colonies and the trade routes that connected them to

Conclusion

one another and to the home islands were largely undefended—and they certainly were—it must be added that there was not much from which they needed defending during the 1860s and 1870s. The French navy laid down its first fast protected cruiser in 1882.[42] The Russian navy is widely regarded as having built the prototype armored cruisers but these failed to achieve the high speed requisite for successful commerce raiding—and even had they, there were only two.[43] For all the attention given the exploits of a handful of Confederate commerce raiders during the Civil War, the destruction of Union shipping and the accompanying "flight from the flag" did not achieve even the limited aim of raising the coastal blockade, much less endanger the northern war effort. Similarly, the *guerre de course*, although doubtless capable of wreaking isolated havoc—assuming one of Britain's rivals had possessed a force capable of waging such a campaign—was not a threat to British security, much less national survival, prior to the era of the submarine. The fate of imperial Germany's cruisers in the opening months of World War I suggests the limitations of such operations: the surface *guerre de course* was over by December 1914.

If put to the test during the 1860s and 1870s, Britain would have found its navy inadequate for the demands of defending the empire and the intervening sea lanes. But there was not at that time another navy in the world, nor even a likely combination of two navies, that could have supplied the test. As for home defense, the enlargement of the ironclad fleet over the course of the 1860s and 1870s, coupled with the decline of America's navy after 1865 and France's after 1871, meant that Britain maintained the traditional "two-power standard"—or something very close to it—through the years of the great rivalry between Disraeli and Gladstone.[44] Britain's "strategic overstretch" was certainly latent during the mid-Victorian period, but in the absence of sustained and serious shipbuilding challenges it was to remain thus until, ironically, the era of Mahan.

Navalists argued that the votes of credit of 1870 and 1878, used in part to supplement hurriedly the strength of the navy, furnished undeniable proof that politicians realized the inadequacy of the service when war threatened. No doubt they were correct. The navy would not have been adequate for the tasks required of it had Britain become a belligerent in 1870, in 1878, or at any other point during the period. But Britain's rivals were even less prepared for a naval war. Moreover, the condition of the navy in the mid-Victorian era was hardly a novelty. It was ill-prepared for war between 1866 and 1880, but it was equally unprepared in 1739, in 1775, in 1793, in 1854, in 1899, and in 1939. As far as preparation went, in none of the intervals of peace between the frequent wars of the eighteenth century—with the possible exception of 1748–56—or the much rarer conflicts of the nineteenth century was the navy maintained in a state of readiness, much less upon an actual war footing. Even the tenuous and unsatisfactory Peace of Amiens, the brief respite in the struggle against Napoleon, witnessed a reduction in the number of ships of the line at sea from 104 at the beginning of 1802 to thirty-two a year later.[45] To point to the "unreadiness" of the Royal Navy in 1870 or 1878 is merely to illustrate the priority ordinarily assigned to national security by constitutional governments in time of peace.

Milne, Hay, Reed, Beresford, and others could and did repeatedly call for a navy capable of withstanding any possible combination of enemies it might encounter. Hay, for example, wrote in his memoirs (1898) that his "contention was, and is, that for every battleship existing in the world we should possess one equal or superior."[46] But quite aside from the problems that would have been involved in implementing such a program in 1870s or 1880s, given the lack of consensus regarding design policy, to have heeded their cries would have involved maintaining a navy far in excess of that required for its ordinary peacetime duties, to say nothing of the massive expenditure such a fleet would have required. Moreover, Hay did not take into consideration the rapidity of technological and design change in warship construction that rendered it necessary to update—contemporaries used the term "reconstruct," which better conveys the scope of the undertaking—the ironclad fleet every few years. Finally, his policy was based on the assumption that Britain might go to war without an ally, and with the entire naval force of the rest of the world arrayed against it. "Splendid isolation" was, to be sure, a nice catch phrase, but the reality of international relations was very different. In the course of the previous two hundred years Britain had been involved in only one European conflict without an ally. Likewise, the possibility that Britain might have found itself at war against an alliance of France, Germany, Italy, and Russia was, to put it charitably, laughable. To have heeded navalist cries by maintaining a fleet based on an "all-power standard" or by maintaining the fleet on continual wartime footing would have been lunacy. As Goschen stated when confronted with Milne's demand in 1873 for a large increase in the building program, the proposition was "utterly out of the question. No Government could do it."[47] And it is scarcely necessary to add that any government foolish enough to have tried would—apart from running the risk of provoking maritime rivals to retaliate with increased construction of their own—have committed political suicide.[48] The navalists of the 1870s were devoid of any understanding—it is tempting to say awareness—of the domestic and foreign political realities of the time.[49]

There exists neither conclusive proof nor even ambiguous indications that Britain's maritime supremacy was seriously threatened at any point during the period. Thanks in large part to the ambitious building programs initiated by Pakington and Corry, plus the short-term panic of 1870 and the collapse of French naval power for several years after 1871, the British navy enjoyed a decade for which complacency was not only a justifiable but even an appropriate policy to follow regarding ironclad construction. That the pace of building slowed perceptibly as the decade progressed was not a sign of neglect but, instead, the product of Conservative emphasis on unarmored shipbuilding and maintenance of the existing fleet in the event it was needed, coupled with bewilderment at the march of technology that ultimately raised doubts as to the continued efficacy of ironclads themselves.

Navalists could and did argue that it was crucial for Britain to maintain an ambitious ironclad building program, but politicians, well aware of the economic side of the equation, saw matters in a very different light. They had, after all, seen the first generation of ironclads rendered obsolete in less than a decade, and while navalists demanded large-scale replacement building, those who had to vote the estimates viewed increased construction as money thrown into the sea—for today's vessels would, in all probability, be obsolete themselves tomorrow. As the *Times* observed in 1877, "Naval Architecture was never so much at the mercy of experiments as it is today. Ships which were in the first rank a dozen years ago are now out of date."[50] That politicians were grudging with funding for shipbuilding should, under the circumstances, hardly be cause for surprise.

The effects on British naval strength of the succession of flawed designs emanating from the dockyards during the 1870s and early 1880s were minimal. The lack of sustained challenges from abroad allowed the Admiralty the luxury of design experimentation and reduced the cost of failure to insignificance, at least in terms of national security. Moreover, while the various ships built during the decade are perceived in retrospect to have been failures, contemporaries at home and abroad, denied the advantage of hindsight, tended to view most of them in a less critical light, and perception was as important as reality both for deterrence and in shaping the policy of rivals. The course pursued by the Admiralty with regard to ship design during the 1870s was to construct a series of prototypes—one or two vessels of one design—rather than concentrating on multiple production of a specific type. One modern authority characterizes the result of this policy as "the fleet of samples; the miscellaneous collection of bizarre and ill-assorted designs." This assessment is unarguable, at least as far as the miscellany was concerned, yet it is difficult to see what alternative policy might logically have been pursued. To have settled on one design, especially in the absence of any consensus regarding the future of naval warfare, risked at the same time getting left behind technologically and being saddled with a fleet of obsolete vessels. The latter eventuality would, of course, have resulted in a much larger waste of public money than was the case with the policy followed. And that, after all, still allowed the navy to incorporate and grow accustomed to the novelties of the decade: compound engines, torpedoes, compound armor, electric light, the armored deck, *barbettes*, and others. The immediate results were ships that were unquestionably less than ideal, but the failures of the 1870s provided guidance when the designs of subsequent ironclads were mooted.

No coherent, practical strategy was possible given the crucial disharmony between the aims of policy makers and the technologically circumscribed means with which they had to carry them out. The problem was not that the navy failed to build modern, wholly steam-powered, high-seas battleships or fast, extended-range belted cruisers to fulfill an intended role of interdicting commerce-raiders in the 1870s and early 1880s: it could not build such vessels at that time. The technological means, not only in terms of boilers and engines, but also with regard to coaling stations and repair facilities, did not exist, especially for the British navy and its worldwide commitments. Any ship intended for a global role had to carry sails until at least 1885.[51]

Finally, it is worth noting that neither Britain itself nor any part of the empire was threatened with invasion or attack during the period—the 1867 Fenian raid on Canada notwithstanding—under circumstances where naval power could have played a determining role.

Conclusion

As a consequence, one must conclude that the navy accomplished what was required of it between 1866 and 1880. That it may have done so in part because the facade it presented was more imposing than the reality was, if not entirely irrelevant, then certainly not unique. The politicians, administrators, and designers who oversaw the construction of the battlefleet during the 1870s were neither blind nor stupid. Nor, for the most part, were they so conservative as to endanger maritime preeminence through opposition to change. What has been seen in retrospect as backwardness was simply the pragmatic response of men who had an intimate understanding of the limits of contemporary technology, even if they lacked any clear conception of the future of naval warfare. And it is that last fact, rather than lack of competence, foot dragging, or reactionary behavior, that explains the existence of the "fleet of samples."

CHAPTER 13

Epilogue:
The End of an Era

Benjamin Disraeli's death in April 1881 ended the great rivalry. Yet as far as Victorian defense policy is concerned 1881 makes an inappropriate finishing-point. The assumptions that had guided that policy since the late 1860s continued to hold sway amongst the public, the press, and within the dominant political circles at Westminster, and the policy itself remained largely unaltered for another half decade. The 1880s ultimately witnessed a sea change in British naval policy, a significant departure not only from the nonalarmist, generally unprovocative stance of the 1815–47 and 1866–80 eras, but even from the complacency punctuated by successive panics that had characterized the period from 1847 to 1863. This change, however, manifested itself fully only with the passage of the Naval Defence Act in 1889—and arguably not until the panic of 1893–94—although harbingers of the shift in perception were evident by 1884. The bulk of the decade witnessed no fundamental reassessment of the bases on which British naval policy was founded, at least not among the political elite. Certainly there was no inkling of such a reassessment within the upper circles of the governing Liberal party prior to 1884.[1]

Continuity of fiscal policy was guaranteed with Gladstone's return to power following the Liberals' victory in the general election of 1880; his passion for economy was immediately evident with regard to the size of the defense estimates. Barely a month after taking office he wrote the new First Lord of the Admiralty, Thomas George Baring, Earl of Northbrook, "to ask whether there is a likelihood in your

[Department] of making any & [if so] what favorable impression upon the Estimates [which] were handed over to us by our predecessors in office."[2] The estimates that W. H. Smith had extolled for their attention to economy less than two months earlier—stressing that they were the lowest since 1873-74—were not sufficiently economical by Gladstonian standards.[3] Nor, for that matter, were the army estimates, and Hugh Childers, now at the war office, received a query virtually identical to that sent to Northbrook.[4]

Again Gladstone came up against a wall of intransigence at the Admiralty, for the new board, in particular Parliamentary Secretary George John Shaw-Lefevre, maintained that the Conservatives had failed to uphold the requisite yearly construction program of 19,000–20,000 tons as set forth by Childers, and that the fleet—the battlefleet especially—required substantial and immediate augmentation. As Northbrook reported to his chief, "When the Board was constituted, in May 1880, we found that reports had been made in September, 1879, to our predecessors, by Mr. Barnaby, the Director of Naval Construction, and Sir Houston Stewart, Comptroller [sic] of the Navy.... These reports showed that while England possessed a superiority over France in respect to such ships for the time, yet that the French Admiralty had during the last preceding years laid down more ships of that class than we had, and there were 18 French ships building as compared with 9 English; so that unless measures were taken to redress this inequality, the time must arrive when we should be run very close."[5]

The diverging aims of Liberals and Conservatives over the course of naval policy were again adumbrated. The war-scare purchases of 1877-78 notwithstanding, the bulk of Ward Hunt's and Smith's efforts had been directed toward maintaining the existing battlefleet or augmenting the maritime police force. In either case, the impetus sprang from a policy geared toward meeting immediate exigencies. With the return of the Liberals in 1880, however, the focus of policy, especially of construction policy, returned to the party's norm of a long-range program with its implied emphasis on deterrence rather than intervention. Northbrook wrote in 1885, "[W]e saw that it would be necessary to make a considerable addition to the rate of shipbuilding upon armour-plated ships, and that has been the policy which we have steadily pursued." Sir Henry Campbell-Bannerman, who replaced George Otto Trevelyan as parliamentary secretary in May 1882, enunciated the Liberal view during his presentation of the estimates in 1883: "[T]he main principle that underlies these estimates is ... to concentrate as much money as possible upon the Shipbuilding Votes. . . . [W]e have endeavoured to render available for the strengthening of Her Majesty's Fleet a larger proportion of the money which we ask for from Parliament than has, for many years at least, been devoted to that purpose."[6]

Campbell-Bannerman's opposite number, Smith, countered with the Conservative view on the appropriate utilization of funds for matériel. "I entertain the view that the Navy exists for a possibly sudden state of war. . . . [I]t should always be maintained in a state of complete efficiency and readiness for the protection of the country in case of war. . . . [I]t appears to me, therefore, that every ship in Her Majesty's Service should be as rapidly as possible brought into a state of complete efficiency."[7] The dichotomy—not to say want of continuity—was plainly evident to contemporaries outside Parliament. Remarking on the course being steered by the Liberals, the *Times* "hoped . . . that the present Board of Admiralty in its zeal for construction will not neglect the equally important business of repair. Successive Boards of Admiralty are a little too apt to oscillate between the two policies, and each to accuse the other of the neglect of one of them."[8]

Never one to be deterred by a single rebuff when it came to matters of economy, Gladstone renewed his pressure on Northbrook in the latter months of 1880 when the following year's estimates were first mooted by the cabinet. The draft budget that Northbrook initially forwarded to Gladstone was no better received than those tendered by Goschen in the latter years of the previous Liberal ministry, and although the prime minister—concurrently the chancellor of the exchequer, it might be noted—thanked the First Lord "very much for giving me an early intimation as to the character of [your] Estimates," he added "the announcement [i.e., the amount], however, is serious, & and it will be requisite, now that we are in a condition to draw the nation's threads together into something like a common result, that the Cabinet [should] a little consider its position."[9] Gladstone was the recipient of bad news from virtually all sides, it seemed, for he informed Northbrook, "Childers has not yet been able to guarantee me a reduction in the army, . . . [and] [t]he civil charges grow, partly by self acting, partly by exceptional causes, & I fear the growth may be half a million." Moreover, "There will be the subvention for India, [which] I take roughly for the year at half a million more—[and] it may exceed this." As a consequence, he was reduced to pleading with Northbrook to uphold the cherished Liberal principle of retrenchment. "Goschen was not a rigid economist," he noted by way of comparison, "but the Estimates of this year are I think more than half a million in excess of his. I see that they are three quarters. Can it be necessary that we are to go further?"[10]

His plea fell on deaf ears. The figures as published revealed little change from the sums voted over the past several years. Indeed, there was a modest increase. Nor would there be substantial deviation over the next three years: the estimates totaled £10,483,901 for 1882–83, £10,757,000 for 1883–84, and £10,811,770 for 1884–85.[11] These sums were, to be sure, higher than any estimate brought in during the first Gladstone ministry, but while the navy was the recipient of an absolute increase in funding, it suffered a relative decrease. Between 1880–81 and 1883–84 total government outlays rose from £81.5 million to £87.1 million, before dropping off to £85.4 million in 1884–85.[12] Thus sums spent on the navy formed a smaller part of the overall budget than they had between 1868 and 1874: in 1880–81 the navy received 12.5 percent of government outlays; in 1881–82, 13.1 percent; in 1882–83, 12.7 percent; in 1883–84, only 11.8 percent, and in 1884–85, 12.5 percent.

Similarly, the political discourse regarding the overall direction of naval policy during the first three and a half years of the second Gladstone administration was no different from that which had dominated the 1870s. Every year, usually prior to the introduction of the estimates, a handful of parliamentary critics—most prominently perennial alarmists Sir John Hay, Captain George Price, and George Bentinck, joined in 1882 by former Parliamentary Secretary to the Admiralty Lord Henry Lennox—bemoaned Britain's want of naval strength and efficiency. In 1882, to cite a single example, Lennox calculated the British battlefleet to be inferior to a combination of the French navy with that of any tertiary naval power, and, owing, he said, to "the enormous increase in the Iron-clad navies of the world," Britain's and the empire's maritime commerce was "endangered." Acting on this avowed conviction, Lennox brought forward a motion stating, "[I]t is desirable that steps should be at once taken to make an adequate addition to the strength of the navy." With this sentiment Hay cordially agreed, going so far as to claim that should, "under any conditions, the Navies of France and Germany or Italy . . . [combine,] they would outnumber us nearly two to one."[13]

In 1882, however, Lennox's attack on the Liberals' naval policy shared the fate of similar thrusts—directed at both parties—over the previous decade. Parliamentary Secretary Trevelyan refuted the charges leveled by Lennox and his fellow critics, disputing their figures, deprecating their assessments of the French and other foreign navies, and defending the British fleet from imputations of want of strength or efficiency.[14] Parliament, press, and, presumably, the public at large, preferred to accept the gospel according to Trevelyan rather than that proffered by Lennox. "In calling attention to the defective strength and conditions of the British Navy," the *Times* began, Lennox "complains of the difficulty he has found in inducing the public to take any interest in the subject." This state of affairs elicited scant sympathy from the editors: "[A]s well might the shepherd boy in the fable complain of the difficulty he found in inducing his companions to take any interest in his reiterated cries of 'Wolf'! ... Assertions of the most alarming kind cease to produce their effect when it is discovered that they are not true." Noting that Hay and Bentinck had contributed similar, if not more alarmist, pronouncements—the former stating that Britain had become "a second-class naval power" and the latter calling for "[n]inety-two first-rate ironclads in commission and ready for use" (a standard never remotely approached even during World War I)—the recipient of these gloomy assessments might well conclude, "England is in danger ... so far from the English navy being a match for all the navies of the whole world, it is not even strong enough to meet a probable combination of foreign powers. ... At the present day every state has a Navy and every state, it would appear, manages better with it than England does."

There was but one problem with the scenario painted by Lennox and his fellow travelers: few people paid any attention to it and fewer still lent any credence to their pronouncements. "The art of the alarmist," the *Times* sourly remarked, "consists of putting forward fancy figures and arguing as if they were correct. The counter-move is thus not difficult. All that Mr. Trevelyan had to do was bring his audience from the region of fiction into the dry world of fact. One statement after another was disposed of under this treatment until the whole case was changed. ... Lord Henry Lennox has his own way of counting French ships. The case is one in which two and two do not make four, but some considerably larger number." Concluded the paper, "It is right, of course, that we should know the worst that can be said about our navy; but the charges, if they are to be of any use, must bear some proximate relation to facts.... Lord Henry Lennox must not be surprised if the feelings to which he appeals cease to come at his command. He was heard on Thursday with indifference, and we can promise him no other fate when he next addresses the House on the same subject and in the same style."[15]

Such blithe dismissals were the norm in the early 1880s. In 1881 a similarly alarmist speech by Hay was pooh-poohed: "The complaint that the English Navy is not large enough has something of a conventional character. It seems to be repeated only to furnish occasion for a reply which shows it to be baseless."[16] Likewise, when, in 1883 Lennox renewed his entreaties, it was pointedly noted that "[h]e was not very warmly supported even by Mr. W. H. Smith who ... was careful to dissociate himself from a good many of the arguments used by his impetuous colleague."[17] Although the *Times* admitted that "there is no great difficulty in making disquieting comparisons between the navy of England and that of other Powers," it added that "to judge from innumerable debates in Parliament, there is quite as little difficulty in showing ... that the comparison so far as it is disquieting is misleading." In short, Lennox, as was well known, was "in some sort a naval alarmist.... [H]e takes the opportunity of a lull in political activity to appeal to public opinion, and adroitly spreads his sails to take advantage of any popular breeze that may have been stirred up by the recent policy of France."[18]

In 1884, however, the discourse was abruptly jarred from its moorings, never to return entirely to the complacent confidence that had marked the previous decade and a half. The first half of the year passed quietly enough; the annual presentation of the estimates failed to rate a leading article in the *Times*. Only in September, with the parliamentary session winding down, did the navalists finally seize the public's attention. The catalyst was a notorious series of articles by muckraking journalist W. T. Stead in the *Pall Mall Gazette* as "The Truth About the Navy." Stead's exposé ripped the confident and complacent reassurances of such Admiralty officials as Trevelyan and Campbell-Bannerman to shreds; so far from being capable of taking on any probable combination of rivals, the British fleet was, as described by Stead, the "paper" or "phantom" fleet of which Ward Hunt had spoken nine years earlier. Stead's information came for the most part from fellow journalist H. O. Arnold-Forster, and, secretly, from renegade naval officer John Fisher, then captain of the navy's gunnery training school, H.M.S. *Excellent*.[19]

Stead succeeded where Lennox, Hay, Bentinck, Arnold-Forster, and others had failed. The "Truth About the Navy" created an immediate sensation when the first installment appeared on 8 September 1884. In fact, however, its message was little different from that painted by other navalists. "Our risks from war have enormously increased since 1868–9," wrote Stead under the pseudonym "One Who Knows the Facts."

> [T]he naval expenditure of other powers has increased 40 per cent.... So far from being able to demonstrate our "irresistible superiority" in armour, guns and speed to any probable combination of fleets, we are just a little ahead of France in ships, behind her in guns and the age of our ships.... Instead of making up lost ground we are losing it.... A hostile cruiser could, with almost entire impunity, destroy to-morrow the coaling stations of Hong-Kong, Singapore, Bombay, the Cape, Ascension, St. Helena, Mauritius, St. George's Sound, Fiji and Vancouver's Island, which are virtually unprotected.... We have not sufficient trained men to man our fleet when war is declared.... In the cheapest and deadliest mode of defence [torpedo boats] our naval supremacy, instead of being absolutely irresistible, is absolutely non-existent. To bring us into line with our rivals one hundred torpedo boats should be laid down at once.[20]

These "revelations" broke on the country like a storm, and with the bandwagon rolling, other critics lost little time in jumping aboard. By 23 September the *Times*, editorializing upon a letter from W. H. Smith, asserted that, contrary to its previous soothing stance, "The late First Lord of the Admiralty affirms, what cannot be denied, that, notwithstanding the repeated assurances of the Admiralty, there has been for some time a sense of alarm and insecurity in the public mind as to the condition of our naval defenses, and that this feeling has deepened and widened of late."[21] It deepened and widened further still during the waning months of the year. By 20 October the leading journal printed one of Sir Edward Reed's lengthy alarmist letters, adding in its own editorial, "[T]here are the gravest reasons for the apprehension which has been put into definite form by several critics of experience and sagacity, that our naval predominance is no longer either undisputed or indisputable."[22] Two days later, noting that the year's naval budget was barely higher than it had been in 1866, the editors added, "France in the same period has increased her naval expenditure by about one-fifth, Italy by more than one-third, Germany by nearly one-third, and Russia by nearly one-half. It would be difficult to show that any one of those countries has had as powerful reasons as England for strengthening the force which is indispensable to the security of a growing Empire and a spreading commerce."[23] By early November the journal concluded, "[T]he Admiralty cannot possibly, with its present resources, keep the Navy in the same relative position . . . which it occupied beyond dispute at the time, for example, of the outbreak of the Franco-German war."[24]

While the storm was breaking, Northbrook was absent from England, overseeing the establishment of British fiscal control in newly occupied Egypt. Thus he returned in early November to find the naval policy of the government and his administration under assault from all sides. As early as 2 October Campbell-Bannerman had written to Hugh Childers, then chancellor of the exchequer, admitting, "I am growing anxious to know what view the Cabinet is likely to take of the question which has been raised so loudly regarding the Navy. . . . It seems to us [the board] to be nearly certain that the subject will be brought up when Parliament meets, probably by an Amendment to the Address; and although I do not believe that the hysterical excitement of the *P.M. Gazette* extends far beyond London, there is sufficient interest and anxiety felt in the country to prevent the question from being shelved."[25] Under the circumstances a change of policy was unavoidable. On 2 December Brassey, who had replaced Campbell-Bannerman as parliamentary secretary when the latter, like Trevelyan before him, had been transferred to the chief secretaryship for Ireland, addressed the Commons (and Northbrook the Lords) on the government's response to, as Brassey put it, "the present anxiety out-of-doors."[26] A supplementary vote of £5,525,000 was presented, £3,100,000 of it to be devoted to building one ironclad, five protected cruisers, ten protected scout vessels, and thirty torpedo boats.[27]

The Stead agitation provoked the first full-blown navy panic in over two decades. Northbrook's retrospective memorandum, composed in July 1885 for the guidance of his successor, indicated how little credibility he, at least, attached to the public agitation. "In the autumn of 1884 public attention was very much directed to the condition of our Navy, especially in comparison with that of France, and the facts, of which the board was well aware before, were prominently brought to public notice. The Government took advantage of this state of feeling in order to push on still further the construction of the class of ships which we most required, viz., fast cruisers for the protection of our commerce."[28] But the Stead agitation also marked a milestone in British policy; naval affairs, and especially the role of public opinion thereon, never completely returned to the placid state of the late 1860s and 1870s. The presentation of the 1885–86 estimates the following March was occasion for an unprecedented request on the part of Thomas Brassey, who "adopted a tone rather of apology than of confidence.... He asked himself and the House the question 'Are the estimates we are now proposing to Parliament sufficient?' and his answer was sufficiently important to be given *verbatim*: 'It is impossible for those who are responsible for the administration of the Navy to say that any estimates fully provide for the wants of a great sea service. There must be many things less perfect than we could wish.... We are making a great step in response to a strong popular demand. It will be for the Parliaments of the future to provide for these continuous efforts by which alone a great Navy can be maintained.'" In other words, "The Admiralty has been awakened out of its lethargy by a loud voice coming from an alarmed community, and its official representative in the House of Commons practically invites the country to keep it up to the mark for the future."[29] The navy's budget climbed from £10.7 million in 1884–85 to £11.4 million the following year. It was merely the beginning of an upward spiral: in 1886–87 naval spending edged up to £12.7 million; in 1887–88 it broached the £13 million level, before dropping back to £12.3 million the following year. This reduction marked the last gasp of retrenchment, however.

In 1888 another navalist campaign erupted, spearheaded this time by Lord Charles Beresford, naval officer and M.P., who had resigned his seat on the board in 1887 to protest what he believed to be the niggardly treatment of the service.[30] Agitation for naval expansion was boosted by a published report by Admirals Sir William Dowell, Sir Richard Vesey Hamilton, and Sir Frederick Richards on 1888's naval maneuvers, a report that was highly critical of the state of the navy. In December 1888 Beresford unveiled a measure calling for wholesale augmentation of the fleet. At that point the First Lord of the Admiralty, Lord George Hamilton, described him as a "seaman given to exaggeration," but Beresford had done his public relations work well; thanks to his efforts, the report of the three admirals, and the unceasing agitation of navalists like Brassey and Reed, within three months the Admiralty itself was forced to bring forward a measure very similar to Beresford's.[31] As a consequence of the Naval Defence Act—the resulting piece of legislation—the navy was enlarged by eight first-class and two second-class battleships, nine armored cruisers, thirty-three smaller cruisers, and eighteen torpedo gunboats, at a cost of £21,500,000, to be spread over seven years and financed in part out of the consolidated fund, rather than through the navy estimates.[32] Thus, in 1890–91 naval expenditure shot up to £15.3 million, over £2 million above the previous year's figure. Never was it to drop below £15 million, and by 1895 it had topped £17 million.[33]

A year after the passage of the Naval Defence Act, the first of Alfred Thayer Mahan's volumes on the influence of sea power was published, giving further impetus and effect to the navalist agitation. "The change in the press was remarkable. Every newspaper of any prominence now recorded naval intelligence, often dealt with naval affairs in leaders and articles, and sent special correspondents to the annual fleet maneuvers." In December 1894 the Navy League was formed, its aims "[t]o spread information, showing the vital importance to the British Empire of the naval supremacy on which depended its trade, empire and national existence ... [and] to call attention to the enormous demands which war would make upon the Navy, and to the fact that the Navy is not at present ready to meet them."[34] In 1893 yet another "navy panic" broke out, and when Gladstone, serving as prime minister for the fourth time, failed to convince his colleagues to drop plans for a further increase in the strength of the navy, he retired from the government. The arms spiral that was to culminate in the outbreak of World War I was well under way, although it would be several years before imperial Germany joined the contest.

How real was the naval threat from abroad during the 1880s? Most commentators have taken their cue from the repeated alarmist pronouncements of Hay, Price, Lennox, and their ilk, but a balanced appraisal of the relative strengths of British and rival forces makes it very difficult to assign much credence to the figures presented by the navalists.[35] In 1884, for instance, Hay claimed in the House of Commons that the French possessed "20 [ironclad] ships of the first class," but of these twenty, no fewer than seven were first-generation, wooden-hulled ships, all of them upwards of two decades old, none of them of more than 6,500 tons displacement, and none of them with armor more than six inches thick.[36] It was, of course, perfectly legitimate to list these ships as part of the active French fleet; only with considerable hyperbole could they be labeled "first-class" ships.[37] They were, in fact, decidedly inferior to the British ironclads of the *Triumph* and *Audacious* classes, which were as large, more heavily armored, and iron-hulled, but which were nonetheless calculated by the British as "second-class" vessels.

An additional five French ships on Hay's list were of pre-1870 vintage, four of them wooden-hulled; two further—*Colbert* and *Trident*—had been laid down in 1870 and they, too, had wooden hulls. Finally, two of the vessels enumerated by Hay were by 1884 no longer part of the French battlefleet: the *Coronne*, which was being converted to a gunnery training ship, and the *Gauloise*, which had been stricken outright from the French navy list in 1883.[38] In short, the twenty "first-class" ironclads Hay alleged the French to possess were in actual number eighteen, and of these only four—one of them not completed until 1886, it might be added—warranted the description "first class"; the remainder of his list consisted of ships demonstrably not of the first class, in two cases ships not even part of the battlefleet.[39] Had Hay applied similar standards in assessing the British battlefleet he would have come up with a list of at least thirty-eight ships.[40] And, as Campbell-Bannerman reported to Childers at the height of the Stead furor, "It is the ironclad fleet that is generally most discussed in the House of Commons, but I do not think it is on this that my colleagues [the Naval Lords] would spend the money if they had it."[41] Hay's misrepresentation, however, did not stop with the size of the French battlefleet; he added that they had a further six first-class ships available for "coast defence," but of them, three were decidedly less than first-class vessels and, more crucially, as of March 1884, when he spoke, only two were complete.[42] Of the remaining four, three were not finished until 1887 and the fourth only in 1888, having been fully ten years under construction.

Similar misrepresentations, if not outright falsehoods, were sprinkled liberally throughout the remainder of his enumeration. Of the fourteen second-class ironclads he claimed France possessed, one had been removed from the active list the preceding year and a further two were incomplete. Of the remaining eleven, all but two were of pre-1870 vintage, wooden-hulled, and eight were far too small to stand in the line of battle. They were, as the French termed them, "station ironclads," designed for operations in distant waters, and more nearly glorified gunboats than line-of-battle ships. All of this information, it should be stressed, was available to contemporaries. Both the French and the British were remarkably open with what today would be classified information. Any contemporary desiring detailed and generally accurate information about the state of the French battlefleet and the age and efficiency of its units could obtain it without a great deal of difficulty.[43]

Epilogue: End of an Era

In one respect, however, Hay's recitation was on the mark. He stressed that the French were in the midst of an ambitious naval construction program. They certainly were. As of 1884 there were no less than ten first-class, two coastal-defense, and two station ironclads under construction in French dockyards. The navalists invariably pointed to this activity as proof of the menace from France. Calmer heads, however, perceived the French program for what it actually was. Trevelyan provided a succinct refutation of the navalist argument in responding to one of Lennox's forays in April 1882. In the first place, stressed the secretary to the Admiralty, the British had, at that moment, twenty-six ironclads "armed and manned, which were actually ready to fight the day after tomorrow, at the latest . . . only two of which had wooden frames [hulls], while the French had 11 . . . four of which had wooden frames."[44] British superiority in the most modern armored ships, in unarmored cruisers, and in swift vessels for combating the *guerre de course* was similarly pronounced. Campbell-Bannerman was equally explicit in outlining the disparities of strength and modernity: "I find that in 1883 France had in available [ironclad] ships 71,500 tons of iron or steel vessels, and 170,560 tons of wooden vessels, while we have 331,910 tons of iron and steel vessels, and only 14,000 tons of wooden vessels."[45] First Naval Lord Astley Cooper Key provided a similar appraisal in a letter of December 1884: "We now have twenty-seven ironclads in commission. The French have eleven. We could commission thirteen more within a month. I cannot find that the French have more than two ready and one of these has her boilers condemned (*Richelieu*). Many of our ships are of obsolete types—so are many of theirs. Moreover, being of wood theirs cannot last long. I should have no fear whatever of war with France and Russia now, so far as our Navy is concerned."[46]

Insofar as a deficiency did exist within the British fleet, it was among the smaller vessels, in particular torpedo boats, where the weakness was glaring. France steadily increased the size of its torpedo boat forces through the late 1870s and early 1880s: "As a result of this steady construction, France in 1884 with about fifty good-sized boats of various types was second only to Russia, most of whose one hundred-fifteen boats had been bought in 1877."[47] As for England, her nineteen torpedo boats placed her "behind even Holland." But of all things, torpedo boats were the type of ship that the navy could obtain most rapidly and, equally important, most cheaply. The private shipbuilding industry included two firms—Thornycroft and Yarrow—that specialized in the construction of torpedo boats.

As for the ambitious French ironclad building program, Trevelyan noted simply that it was "a temporary measure for the purpose of replacing an obsolete Fleet."[48] This assessment could be gainsaid only with difficulty and by wholesale disregard of the available evidence. Campbell-Bannerman provided the specifics in response to Lennox's perennial posturing the following year. "I believe the object of France is most reasonable and patriotic, and one which we can regard without any alarm. She finds that the great bulk of her Fleet is composed of wooden ships of short lives, some of which are already, probably in a material sense defunct, although they may not be absolutely condemned; and she wishes to substitute for them the more modern style of steel ships." The need for an accelerated construction program was, as Campbell-Bannerman put it, the consequence of prior neglect:

> It is somewhat more than ten years ago since the people of France awoke to the fact that their naval force had not been kept up to the proper level. . . . To make up for this neglect, the people of France resolved, for some years to come, to devote large sums of money to restoring their Fleet to what they believed to be its proper position. . . . [Thus,] the reason why the French have been making great strides in adding to their Navy . . . is that they are engaged in the process of exchanging their wooden ships for iron ships; they, in fact, speak of it themselves as the "transformation" of their Navy.[49]

In addition, as Trevelyan stressed in 1882, "The whole of the extraordinary French Estimates for rebuilding their Fleet had hitherto been provided, not out of revenue, but as an increase to the National Debt." Moreover, "it had been intended" in the French naval budget of 1882 "that the shipbuilding should as usual be paid for out of a loan, but the [Ways and Means] Committee had recommended that for this year and for all the future the shipbuilding should be met out of Revenue," a sign that the parliamentary secretary took to be "a strong confirmation that" with the completion of the rebuilding program the "object at which the French Admiralty had been aiming would have been accomplished, and . . . that they would carry it no further." Hence, he concluded, "it was not necessary for the safety of the country" to augment their own building program "unless the French Admiralty, having completed its programme of 1872 and replaced its obsolete ships, should go on building as fast as ever."[50]

Epilogue: End of an Era

In retrospect it is clear that Trevelyan and Campbell-Bannerman were correct. In 1885 Northbrook noted that his board had laid down no less than ten ironclads, but "this number would have been insufficient if the French had continued the rate of building which they had been following during the previous five years ... but a change took place in the financial arrangements of the French Admiralty. They had supplemented their shipbuilding votes by borrowed money, but that system ceased in 1881, and their rate of expenditure, and what is still more important, their rate of progress, which we carefully watched, fell off considerably."[51] More than the rate of progress dropped off. In 1882 France had commenced two ironclads, another in 1883, and one in 1884. No further battleships were begun until the *Brennus* was laid down in 1889, and no other armored ships were started save for two armored cruisers—these, too, at the end of the decade.[52] In short, the French ceased laying down armored ships between 1883 and 1888, during which time the British began five battleships, one coastal-defense ironclad, and seven armored cruisers, in addition to the four battleships laid down in 1882.[53] It was ironic that the Stead panic broke out just as Britain's position took a noticeable—one is tempted to say dramatic—turn for the better.

Furthermore, the French construction program, although superficially impressive as to the number of ships under construction, was subject to even worse delays and bottlenecks than those that perpetually plagued the British. In 1884 Hay stated, misleadingly and rather disengenuously, "I am not prepared to believe that these [French] ships are not advancing with considerable rapidity."[54] In point of fact, French shipbuilding generally lagged behind British by a considerable margin, no matter how much Britain's allegedly sluggish pace was decried at home. What was more, the British had previous examples of French construction policy to inform their views. The French had laid down a very large number of ironclads between 1858 and 1861—a major factor in the panic that gripped much of Britain during those years—but their practice was subsequently revealed to be the slow, simultaneous construction of those ships. Four of the ten *Provence*-class ironclads laid down in 1861 were not completed until 1867: the British *Lord Clyde* and *Lord Warden*, laid down two years after the *Provence*, were completed before the last of the French ships; the *Bellerophon*, begun in December 1863, was completed by April 1866.[55] The French program of the late 1870s and early 1880s adhered to traditional practice. What was more, this practice was readily evident to the British and appreciated by perceptive observers, Hay's insinuations notwithstanding. As Campbell-Bannerman informed the House of Commons in 1883, "So far from advancing or exceeding their programme, they are falling behind every year in spite of all their efforts. In fact, on a recent occasion, so disheartening in this respect were the comments made in the French Chamber by the Minister representing the Marine Department, that one of the Deputies exclaimed—'*on a fait machine en arrière*'—he complained that progress had actually been made backwards."[56] The exaggeration was minimal: only one of the four battleships of the *Terrible* class was completed in less than ten years; the two battleships of the subsequent *Amiral Baudin* class took nine and ten years, respectively, the *Hoche* took nine years, and all three of the *Marceau* class battleships, laid down in the early 1880s, were not completed for a decade.[57]

Finally, Trevelyan pointed to the views the French themselves held with regard to their naval rivals, pointedly stressing "the freedom with which the French Government had published the facts relating to their shipbuilding," not to mention "the generous admission which they themselves had made. . . . The Commission of 1879, presided over by M. Gambetta, indicated that the naval rivalry between the two countries had passed away. 'No one,' it was stated in a most interesting passage of that Report, 'disputes the first rank with England.'"[58] Even in the latter months of 1884, with the Stead panic bubbling away, the *Times* felt compelled to acknowledge the French themselves freely admitted "that in speaking of foreign Powers we must set aside the English navy, with which our fleet cannot enter into comparison for the number of first-class iron-clads, cruisers, or torpedo boats."[59]

As for other naval forces, navalists painted a similarly alarming picture: Lennox described Germany as having added "twelve iron-clads to her Fleet" since 1876; Italy "has placed herself in the front rank of European Powers by her marvelously rapid creation of a most powerful Iron-clad navy;" even Spain, according to him, displayed naval ambitions. In short, "every country of the world, except England, is taking steps to defend herself in case of war."[60] Again, however, there is little evidence to support the navalist contention. In the course of the 1880s Germany began one seagoing and one coastal-defense ironclad, and Austria-Hungary began two ships of the former type.[61] Slightly more impressive was the Italian navy, which laid down six seagoing ironclads during the decade, but the British laid down ten such vessels prior even to the passage of the Naval Defence Act, to say nothing of eleven armored cruisers. In fact, aside from Britain, the only maritime nation that can reasonably be said to have carried out an extensive shipbuilding program during the 1880s was the one least often mentioned by the navalists: Russia. Between 1880 and 1888 Russia laid down six first-class battleships and four armored cruisers, more capital ships, by a considerable margin, than were begun by France during the decade. Yet even with the completion of these ships the Russian navy was in little position to mount a serious maritime challenge to Britain. At the beginning of the decade it possessed but a single seagoing ironclad of the first rank.

As for the naval expenditures of rival powers, it was true that Italian spending had jumped from about £1.4 million in 1868 to £2.3 million in 1884, but, the first figure was artificially low, coming as it did in the wake of the debacle at Lissa, and the second was barely 20 percent of what Britain spent on its navy in 1884.[62] Likewise, the German navy's budget in 1884 was considerably higher than it had been in the late 1860s for the simple reason that there had been no German navy until 1871. In 1884 it received £2.45 million, but this was only 21.4 percent of the amount the British navy received. The United States navy was allotted 32.2 percent of the British total, and the impoverished Austro-Hungarian navy 8.2 percent. Russian naval expenditures were more substantial, but still less than half of those of Britain in 1884. France was the only power whose naval expenditures exceeded half of Britain's. In 1884, the French navy received £7.8 million, 68.2 percent of the British navy's £11.4 million. Again, the timing of the navalists was off; by the point the Stead agitation seized the public imagination, French naval spending had already peaked. In the early 1880s it had crept above 70 percent of the British level, reaching 83.6 percent in 1883. After 1883, however, the financial situation in France took a turn for the worse, and for the remainder of the decade the figure remained at 70 percent or less. Indeed, for the final three years of the 1880s French spending dropped to less than 60 percent that of its rival. In short, for the whole of the 1880s Britain could claim a "two-power standard," or something very close to it, as regards naval expenditures, save for the combined outlays of France and Russia during the first half of the decade. At their highest point, in 1883, the two powers' naval spending climbed to 127.8 percent of the British figure, but by 1884 it had dropped to 110.9 percent, and by 1888, on the eve of the agitation leading to the Naval Defence Act, it was down to 105.7 percent.

Such facts are difficult to reconcile with pronouncements such as Captain Price's in 1882: "France and Italy combined had 25 first-class ironclads, as against our ten, . . . [and] [t]here was no doubt of this—that both France and Italy were at present contending for that naval supremacy which for so many years we had maintained."[63] In the Lords, Viscount Sidmouth frequently made similar statements, warning in 1883 that "[i]n addition to the French navy, the Italian had also attained a considerable degree of efficiency. Moreover, of late years Germany was making great strides in the direction of becoming a naval power [!], while China, Japan and the United States [!] possessed vessels of great power; and there could be no doubt that foreign nations would have an immense superiority over England in the event of their forming a combination against her which was not impossible."[64]

Navalist hyperbole was incessant. Lennox, for instance, baldly informed the Commons in May 1882 that foreign navies (he did not bother to specify which ones, but given the tone of his screed it would appear he was being inclusive) "go on year after year spending enormous sums of money for the purpose of building up gigantic navies, when they have neither commerce nor Colonies, to speak of, to defend."[65] Up to late 1884 this sort of pronouncement was routinely dismissed. But in the aftermath of Stead's agitation the foundations of British naval policy shifted profoundly, from being based on the professional assessments of Admiralty officials, to being largely a response to popular demands. The *Times* blandly acknowledged the shift in 1885 when it remarked, "It has hitherto been the habit of the country to trust for the efficiency of its naval resources to those who were responsible to Parliament. That habit must now be abandoned. The country must henceforth take the matter into its own hands; it must judge for itself whether the Navy is efficient and sufficient, and if it finds that it is not, it must insist on the Board of Admiralty making it so forthwith, and, what is more, it must not rest until it finds a Board of Admiralty that is ready to do its bidding."[66] And in 1889 it found such a board, despite the fact that Britain already had a battlefleet very close to the two-power standard that was to be embodied in law by the Naval Defence Act.[67]

So far from being responses to legitimate threats to British maritime supremacy, the naval scares of 1884–85 and 1888–89 were internally generated and based on illusions that could have been refuted at the time. This interpretation, if correct, suggests that so far from being driven by external provocation, British naval policy after 1884, and especially after 1889, was itself the chief agent of provocation among the naval powers of the world, and that the British themselves initiated the naval arms spiral among itself, France, and Russia. Such an interpretation is based not on the premise that there were no external factors pushing British policy onwards, but rather that the factors were not specifically naval. Certainly there was growing rivalry and competition, not to say tension and crises, but the sphere in which this tension and rivalry grew was imperial, rather than naval.[68] One can easily note the increasing concern with imperial security in speeches made by the navalists. Lennox's motion in 1882 specifically said that "the Trade and Commerce of the Empire is endangered . . . [by] the enormous increase in the Iron-clad Navies of the World."[69]

Certainly the theoretical scope of the navy's responsibilities in the event of war had increased substantially, but in the absence of a sustained threat or threats from abroad, the expansion remained solely theoretical; true, there was much more of the empire to defend, but there was not much more from which it needed defending during the 1880s, the cries of the navalists notwithstanding, and it is hard to see why public and press bought into the navalist argument when they did, save that the growth of empire, and of imperial competition, made them increasingly uneasy about the future. Likewise, the growth of economic and industrial competition, especially from Germany and the United States but also from France and Russia, may well have pushed public sentiment in favor of naval increases, despite the fact that a substantive naval challenge was not immediately forthcoming. And by so doing, the British themselves contributed to the rise of that challenge.

In 1883 Campbell-Bannerman deprecated the suggestion that the British undertake a large increase in its naval shipbuilding, and his words bear repeating in light of subsequent events. "In the first place," he informed the House, "we believe that we are quietly and steadily making and preparing such additions to the Navy as to fully maintain our position. . . . In the second place, I would ask the Committee what would be the effect in Europe if England were suddenly to embark on a new career of Naval Expenditure, and possibly set the example of a fresh international rivalry on the sea, which could in the end but add to the miseries which the system of portentous military establishments on land already inflict upon the world?"[70] Thirty years later the editor of the *Economist*, F. W. Hirst, reflected on the consequences of Stead's agitation. "Of popular panic there was no trace; but Mr. Stead and his fellow conspirators managed to produce a feeling of nervous disquietude in high society, and although the results were small in comparison with later performances, the year 1884 deserves attention as the beginning of a most disastrous expansion in naval armaments in which the provocative impulse has too often been furnished by Great Britain."[71]

Reference Matter

Notes

Chapter 1

1. Andrew Lambert, *Battleships in Transition*, 28–29.
2. C. J. Bartlett, *Great Britain and Sea Power, 1815–1853*, 190.
3. Ibid., 222; Lambert, *Battleships in Transition*, 21–24.
4. Quoted in Bartlett, 228; see also Lambert, *Battleships in Transition*, 29.
5. Lambert, *Battleships in Transition*, 36.
6. Oscar Parkes, *British Battleships, 1860–1950*, 230.
7. In addition to the works of Bartlett and Lambert already cited, see Andrew Lambert, *The Last Sailing Battlefleet: Maintaining Naval Mastery 1815–1850* and Michael Lewis, *The Navy in Transition*. For a brief account of the early steam ships of the line, see David K. Brown, "The First Steam Battleships." For the Fisher era, see especially Nicholas Lambert, "The Influence of the Submarine Upon Naval Strategy, 1898–1914"; Arthur Marder, *The Anatomy of British Sea Power: A History of British Naval Policy in the Pre-Dreadnought Era, 1880–1905*; idem ed., *Fear God and Dread Nought: The Correspondence of Admiral of the Fleet Lord Fisher of Kilverstone*; idem, *From Dreadnought to Scapa Flow: The Royal Navy in the Fisher Era, 1904–1919*; Ruddock MacKay, *Fisher of Kilverstone*; and Jon T. Sumida, *In Defence of Naval Supremacy: Finance, Technology and British Naval Policy, 1889–1914*.
8. See Parkes, *British Battleships*; William Laird Clowes et al., *The Royal Navy*, vol. 7; Peter Padfield, *Rule Britannia: The Victorian and Edwardian Navy*; Robert Gardiner ed., *Steam, Steel and Shellfire: The Steam Warship 1815–1914*; David K. Brown, *A Century of Naval Construction: The History of the Royal Corps of Naval Constructors*; and J. R. Hill, ed., *The Oxford Illustrated History of the Royal Navy*.
9. Stanley Sandler, *The Emergence of the Modern Capital Ship*; James P. Baxter, *The Introduction of the Ironclad Warship*; C. J. Bartlett, "The Mid-Victorian Reappraisal of Naval Policy"; Kenneth Bourne and D.C. Watts, eds., *Studies in International History*; and C. I. Hamilton, *Anglo-French Naval Rivalry, 1840–1870*.

282 Notes to Pages 3-12

10. This disposition is particularly pronounced in Baxter's *Introduction of the Ironclad Warship*, Sandler's *Modern Capital Ship*, and, of course, Parkes' *British Battleships*, as well as furnishing the raison d'être for Hamilton's *Anglo-French Naval Rivalry*.

11. See Bartlett, "Mid-Victorian Reappraisal"; Marder, *Anatomy*; Parkes, *British Battleships*; Padfield, *Rule Britannia*; George Ballard, *The Black Battlefleet*; N. A. M. Rodger, "The Dark Ages of the Admiralty, 1869-1885"; and Richard Millman, *British Foreign Policy and the Coming of the Franco-Prussian War*.

Chapter 2

1. N. A. M. Rodger, "The Dark Ages of the Admiralty," Part II, 41.
2. Bernard Semmel, *Liberalism and Naval Strategy*, 40.
3. *Hansard's Parliamentary Debates*, 3rd ser., 81 (1845), cols. 1158, 1171-72, cited in ibid., 41.
4. *Hansard*, 3rd ser., 211 (1872), col. 730.
5. Ibid., 3rd ser., 169 (1863), col. 1072.
6. Paul Kennedy, *The Rise and Fall of British Naval Mastery*, 167.
7. The following synopsis of British foreign policy aims during the nineteenth century is largely drawn from Kenneth Bourne, *The Foreign Policy of Victorian England, 1830-1902*; Paul Schroeder, "Old Wine in New Bottles: Recent Contributions to British Foreign Policy and European International Politics, 1789-1848"; idem, "The 19th-Century International System, Changes in the Structure"; idem, *The Transformation of European Politics, 1763-1848*; Kennedy, *Naval Mastery*; idem, *The Rise and Fall of the Great Powers*; idem, "The Tradition of Appeasement in British Foreign Policy, 1865-1939", idem, *Strategy and Diplomacy, 1870-1945*; idem, *The Realities behind Diplomacy: Background Influences on British External Policy, 1865-1980*; and Gerald Graham, *The Politics of Naval Supremacy*.
8. Kennedy, *Rise and Fall of the Great Powers*, 149-51.
9. C. J. Bartlett, "The Mid-Victorian Reappraisal of Naval Policy," 189. See also Kennedy, "The Tradition of Appeasement," 20.
10. Bartlett, "Mid-Victorian Reappraisal," 189; Kennedy, *Naval Mastery*, 181.
11. Bourne, *Foreign Policy of Victorian England*, 369, 374-75.
12. Paul Knaplund, *Gladstone's Foreign Policy*, 4; Bartlett, 189.
13. Kennedy, *Naval Mastery*, 158.
14. Bourne, *Foreign Policy of Victorian England*, 124. See also Kennedy, "The Tradition of Appeasement," 6; Knaplund, *Gladstone's Foreign Policy*, 6; and Martin Swartz, *The Politics of British Foreign Policy in the Era of Disraeli and Gladstone*, 27.
15. Bourne, *Foreign Policy of Victorian England*, 125.
16. Knaplund, *Gladstone's Foreign Policy*, 40.
17. Bourne, *Foreign Policy of Victorian England*, 387, 396.
18. Quoted in ibid., 96.

19. Knaplund, *Gladstone's Foreign Policy*, 42.
20. Kennedy, *Realities Behind Diplomacy*, 79–80.
21. Disraeli to Victoria, Most Confidential, 16 May 1876, printed in Bourne, *Foreign Policy of Victorian England*, 406.
22. Ibid. "With the Cabinet hopelessly divided until March 1878—Disraeli observed that there were twelve members and seven policies—any consistency was impossible."
23. Ibid., 130.
24. Swartz, *Politics of British Foreign Policy*, 112–17.
25. Kennedy, "Tradition of Appeasement," 21–22.
26. C. J. Lowe, *The Reluctant Imperialists: British Foreign Policy, 1878–1902*, 1: 21; Bourne, *Foreign Policy of Victorian England*, 137; Kennedy, *Realities Behind Diplomacy*, 87.
27. Bourne, *Foreign Policy of Victorian England*, 144. See also Barbara Jelavich, "British means of Offense against Russia in the Nineteenth Century," *passim*.
28. Lowe, *Reluctant Imperialists*, 1: 22.
29. Graham, *Politics of Naval Supremacy*, 66–68. See also Arthur Marder, *The Anatomy of British Sea Power: A History of British Naval Policy in the Pre-Dreadnought Era, 1880–1905*, 145, and Theodore Ropp (Stephen Roberts, ed.), *The Development of a Modern Navy: French Naval Policy, 1871–1914*, 250.
30. Ropp, *Development of a Modern Navy*, 90.
31. The most recent and detailed coverage of the invasion scares is C. I. Hamilton, *Anglo-French Naval Rivalry, 1840–1870*.
32. Cited in Marder, *Anatomy of British Sea Power*, 67.
33. *Hansard*, 3rd ser., vol. 211, col. 60.
34. Oscar Parkes, *British Battleships, 1860–1950*, 24–292. Ordinarily another three to five ironclads were stationed overseas.
35. "Augmentation of the Naval Force, in Ships and Stores," Robert Spencer Robinson to Board of Admiralty, 9 August 1870, PRO: ADM1/6159. Spencer Robinson was quoting one of his own memoranda from 1866.
36. For pro-coast-defense rhetoric in Parliament, see *Hansard*, 3rd ser., vol. 166 (1862), cols. 265, 592, 597.
37. Ibid., 3rd ser., vol. 205 (1871), col. 670.
38. Marder, *Anatomy of British Sea Power*, 67; Anthony Preston and John Major, *Send a Gunboat!*, 36.
39. "Report of the Commissioners appointed to inquire into the state and sufficiency of the fortifications existing and projected for the Defence of the United Kingdom; with the Minutes of Evidence and Appendix; also correspondence relative to a site for an internal arsenal," *Parl. Papers*, 1860, vol. 23, x.
40. D. C. Gordon, *The Dominion Partnership in Imperial Defense, 1870–1914*, 48.
41. *Hansard*, 3rd ser., vol. 166 (1862), col. 276.
42. William Laird Clowes et al., *The Royal Navy. A History from the Earliest Times to the Death of Queen Victoria*, 7: 243–47.

43. Ibid., 385.
44. Spencer Robinson to Board of Admiralty, 9 August 1870, PRO: ADM1/6159.
45. I. F. Clarke, *Voices Prophesying War, 1763–1984*, 27. See G. J. Marcus, *Quiberon Bay*, 23–28, for similar fears during the Seven Years' War.
46. Parkes, *British Battleships*, 168–70.
47. For the American Civil War period see Regis Courtmanche, *No Need of Glory: The British Navy in American Waters, 1860–1864*, passim; for the Second Opium War, see Preston and Major, *Send a Gunboat!*, chapter 3.
48. Schroeder, "The Nineteenth-Century International System," 16. See also Kennedy, *Naval Mastery*, 158.
49. I have refrained from counting the Great Lakes, which contained a number of navy vessels. None were in commission after 1820, however.
50. In 1821 there were only two ships of the line in commission outside home waters, one in the Mediterranean and one off South America. At the same time, there were thirty frigates, thirty-two sloops, three brigs, and a schooner in commission abroad.
51. Gordon, *The Dominion Partnership*, 47.
52. The disparity between the total given here and the figure 145 is owing to the inclusion of steam dispatch vessels in the latter calculation.
53. Preston and Major, *Send a Gunboat!*, 32. See also pp. 9–31 for the Crimean origins of the gunboat.
54. *Parl. Papers*, 1862, 34: 881–85.
55. Two other requests were rejected owing to the want of suitable vessels, and of the remaining two, the consul at Biafra's request for a vessel to be permanently stationed at the port was denied on the grounds "that British interests [were] sufficiently protected by cruizers [sic] on [the] station," and the Cotton Supply Association, which asked for a vessel to be sent up the Niger from time to time was "[i]nformed that this service can only be undertaken under special circumstances, and for some specific object."
56. Clowes, *The Royal Navy*, 7: 218–385.
57. Preston and Major, *Send a Gunboat!*, 127: "As late as 1871 it was estimated that 2,000 negroes were being shipped to the French settlements in Nossi-Bé (off the north-west coast of Madagascar), Reunion and Mayotta (in the Comoro Islands), on the pretext that they had volunteered to work for five years."
58. *Hansard*, 3rd ser., vol. 210 (1872), col. 460.
59. Gladstone to Somerset (Copy), 13 December 1864, Gladstone Papers, BL, 44304, fols. 203–6.
60. Bartlett, "Mid-Victorian Reappraisal," 198.
61. The *Times* (London), 4 April 1867, 9; see also ibid., 19 April 1867, 8.
62. *Hansard*, 3rd ser., vol. 185 (1867), col. 1838.
63. Ibid., cols. 1853–54.
64. Ibid., 3rd ser., 192 (1868), col. 46.
65. Gladstone to Goschen (Copy), 23 September 1871, Gladstone Papers, BL, 44540, fols. 238–39.

66. Goschen to Gladstone, 19 September 1871, ibid., 44161, fols. 178, 182.
67. Bartlett, "Mid-Victorian Reappraisal," 189.

Chapter 3

1. John Henry Briggs, *Naval Administrations, 1827 to 1892: The Experience of 65 Years*, 97–104.
2. Cited in J. T. Ward, *Sir James Graham*, 128, and N. A. M. Rodger, *The Admiralty*, 98 (unattributed). See also Christopher Lloyd, *Mr. Barrow of the Admiralty: A Life of John Barrow, 1764–1848*, 98–99, and Charles Stuart Parker, *Life and Letters of Sir James Graham, Second Baronet of Netherby, P.C., G.C.B.*, 1: 147.
3. Byam Martin was eased out of office a few months prior to the abolition of the navy board. For his account of the proceedings leading to his departure, see Richard Vesey Hamilton, ed., *Letters and Papers of Admiral of the Fleet Sir Thomas Byam Martin, G.C.B.*, 2: 239–65.
4. John Barrow, *An Auto-biographical Memoir of Sir John Barrow, Bart., Late of the Admiralty: Including Reflections, Observations, and Reminiscences at home and abroad from early life to advanced age*, 408–9; Lloyd, *Mr. Barrow*, 99.
5. Barrow, *Auto-biographical Memoir*, 414–18.
6. Rodger, *Admiralty*, 100.
7. See for instance "Report from the Select Committee of the House of Lords on the Board of Admiralty; Together with the Proceedings of the Committee, Minutes, Appendix, and Evidence (generally known as the Somerset Committee), *Parl. Papers*, 1871, 7:34, and Lord Ellenborough to Hamilton, 6 July 1846, PRO: ADM1/5564, cited in C. J. Bartlett, *Great Britain and Sea Power, 1815–1853*, 10n.
8. Barrow, *Auto-biographical Memoir*, 418.
9. "Report of the Select Committee appointed to inquire into the Constitution of the Board of Admiralty, and the various Duties devolving thereon; also, as to the general effect of such a system on the Navy, and who were instructed to consider the present system of Promotion and Retirement in the Royal Navy, and to report their Opinion thereon," *Parl. Papers*, 1861, 5: 640.
10. Cited in Oswyn Murray, "The Admiralty," Part VII, 464.
11. "Report of the Commissioners appointed to Inquire in the Control and Management of Her Majesty's Naval Yards; together with the Minutes of Evidence and Appendix," *Parl. Papers* 1861, 26: 413.
12. *Hansard's Parliamentary Debates*, 3rd ser., 161 (1861), cols. 1240–69.
13. "Report of the Select Committee on Admiralty Administration," *Parl. Papers*, 1861, 5: 39–343.
14. Ibid., 182.
15. Ibid., iii.
16. *Hansard*, 3rd ser., 165 (1862), col. 1263.
17. Ibid., 3rd ser., 168 (1862), cols. 986, 995, 1144–46.

18. Arthur D. Elliot, *The Life of George Joachim Goschen, First Viscount Goschen 1831–1907*, 1: 65.

19. See *Hansard*, 3rd ser., 169 (1863), cols. 697, 755, 823, 1089; 170 (1863), col. 905; 171 (1863), cols. 657–69, 1398–1415; 173 (1864), cols. 905–6, 1299; 177 (1865), cols. 1016, 1385; 178 (1865), cols. 678–97.

20. [Seymour, Edward, 12th Duke of Somerset], *The Naval Expenditure from 1860 to 1866, and its Results*, 3.

21. The *Times* (London), 11 February 1867, 9.

22. Ibid. For further criticism of naval administration, see the *Times*, 20 February 1867, 9; 21 February 1867, 9; 16 March 1867, 9; 26 November 1867, 6; 26 December 1867, 6; 17 January 1868, 5; 7 April 1868, 8; 15 July 1868, 9; 27 July 1868, 9; 15 December 1868, 9; 23 December 1868, 9.

23. *Naval and Military Gazette* (London), 8 February 1868, 88. For further adverse commentary on naval administration, see *Naval and Military Gazette*, 25 January 1868, 51; 22 February 1868, 120; 29 February 1868, 136; 14 March 1868, 169; 4 April 1868, 216; 12 September 1868, 584; 19 December 1868, 808; *United Service Gazette* (London), 18 April 1868, 4–5; 9 May 1868, 4; the *Standard* (London), 9 March 1869, 4.

24. The *Times* (London), 26 December 1867, 6; 7 April 1868, 8.

25. Ibid., 4 April 1868, 9.

26. *Naval and Military Gazette* (London), 29 February 1868, 136.

27. *United Service Gazette* (London), 4 January 1868, 4.

28. The *Times* (London), 3 February 1868, 9.

29. *Hansard*, 3rd ser., 161 (1861), col. 1129.

30. Ibid., 3rd ser., 161 (1861), cols. 1129, 1139; "Report of the Select Committee on Admiralty Administration," *Parl. Papers*, 1861, 5: 736.

31. Theodore Ropp (Stephen Roberts, ed.), *The Development of a Modern Navy*, 52–55.

32. *Hansard*, 3rd ser., 149 (1858), col. 126.

33. Ibid., 227 (1876), cols. 1873–91; 268 (1882), col. 1046; the *Times* (London), 14 March 1876, 9. Bentinck spoke to the subject in 1858, 1859, 1860, 1863, 1864, and 1865. He was in poor health from 1866 through 1868, and retired from Parliament in the latter year. He returned, however, in 1871, and renewed his campaign in 1872, 1873, and 1876. See *Hansard*, 3rd ser., 149 (1858), col. 126; 154 (1859), cols. 939–40; 159 (1860), cols. 352–54; 169 (1863), cols. 702–3, 822; 173 (1864), col. 900; 178 (1865), cols. 685–86; 210 (1872), cols. 418–22; 215 (1873), col. 83; 227 (1876), cols. 1873–79.

34. The *Times*, 15 December 1868, 9.

35. Ibid., 21 April 1871, 9.

36. Ibid. The *Times*' reference is to gross expenditure. In introducing the navy estimates the spokesman for the government ordinarily stressed the *net* sum, thus accounting for apparent discrepancies in the figures.

37. Ibid., 26 April, 9. See also A. Patchett Martin, *Life and Letters of Robert Lowe, Viscount Sherbrook G.C.B., D.C.L.*, 2: 366–71.

38. The *Times* put expenditure for 1870–71 at £69,548,000, up from the original estimate of £67,303,000 owing to the Franco-German War. It placed

the estimated expenditure for 1871–72 at £72,308,000. The *Times*, 21 April 1871, 9. B. R. Mitchell, on the other hand, puts the figures at £67.8 million for 1870–71 and £69.9 million for 1871–72. See Mitchell and Phyllis Deane, *Abstract of British Historical Statistics*, 397. The *Parliamentary Papers* agree with the *Times*' figure for 1870–71 and put the actual expenditure for 1871–72 at £71,490,020 6/5. See "Finance Accounts," *Parl. Papers*, 1871, 37: 11; 1872, 26: 11.

39. Robert Blake, *Disraeli*, 307–9. See also Andrew Lambert, *Battleships in Transition*, 38–39.

40. Blake, *Disraeli*, 324–25. See also Robert Stewart, *The Politics of Protection*, 208.

41. Disraeli to Derby, 9 October 1858: Derby Papers, Liverpool Record Office, 920 DER (14), 145/5. For an assessment of Walker's capabilities as Surveyor, see Lambert, *Battleships in Transition*, passim.

42. Blake, *Disraeli*, 378–79.

43. The *Times* (London), 21 April 1871, 9.

44. On the invasion scare in general, see C. J. Bartlett, "The Mid-Victorian Re-appraisal of Naval Policy," 190. See also D. Southgate, "*The Most English Minister*" *The Politics and Policies of Palmerston*, 474–75.

45. Oscar Parkes, *British Battleships, 1860–1950*, 16–117.

46. Bartlett, "Mid-Victorian Reappraisal," 190. See also Palmerston's letters to Gladstone of 19 July and 21 July 1861, printed in Philip Guedalla ed., *The Palmerston Papers: Gladstone and Palmerston; Being the Correspondence of Lord Palmerston with Mr. Gladstone, 1851–1865*, 171–74, 181–87. On Somerset's tenure at the Admiralty, see Colin Baxter, "The Duke of Somerset and the Creation of the British Ironclad Navy, 1859–1866," 279–84.

47. Palmerston to Gladstone, 19 October 1864, printed in Guedalla, ed., *Gladstone and Palmerston*, 302.

48. "Finance Accounts," *Parl. Papers*, 1861, 34: 143; 1862, 29: 115; 1864, 32: 117; 1866, 39: 111.

49. Philip Magnus, *Gladstone*, 141. See also Southgate, *Most English Minister*, 470–71, 474–75.

50. Parkes, *British Battleships*, 108. See also Stanley Sandler, *The Emergence of the Modern Capital Ship*, 255.

51. Sandler, *Modern Capital Ship*, 254.

52. Bartlett, "Mid-Victorian Reappraisal," 197. See also Magnus, *Gladstone*, 168.

53. Mitchell and Deane, *Abstract of British Historical Statistics*, 397.

54. Ibid., 396–97. In addition, the idea of setting aside surplus revenue in order to reduce the principal of the debt was popular among both mid-Victorian financiers and journalists.

55. Army strength typically hovered around 130,000 regulars, exclusive of militia, "volunteers," and, after the Cardwell reforms, reservists.

56. Out of the consolidated fund came allocations for annuities and pensions, salaries and allowances, courts of justice, and miscellaneous serv-

ices. Independent of the consolidated fund were the headings public works and buildings, public departments, law and justice, education, science and art, foreign, consular, and colonial services, superannuations, and miscellaneous and special services.

57. Herbert C. F. Bell, *Lord Palmerston*, 2: 237.

58. Gladstone to Goschen (Copy), 16 September 1871, Gladstone Papers, BL, 44540, fol. 111; Gladstone to Goschen (Copy), 23 September 1871, ibid., 44540, fol. 238.

59. Bartlett, "Mid-Victorian Reappraisal," 189.

60. These figures were swollen by a substantial inflationary trend from the mid-1890s on. Prices climbed some 30 percent during the two decades prior to World War I. Naval spending still rose dramatically; the "adjusted figure" for the period 1910–14 would be in the range of £28 million a year at 1895 prices. The appearance is hence a bit more dramatic than reality.

61. Lambert, *Battleships in Transition*, 13.

62. To get a sense of contemporary perception, see *Hansard*, 3rd ser., 208 (1871), col. 1528, and the *Times* (London), 3 April 1874, 5.

63. The *Times* (London), 2 March 1876, 9.

64. Ibid., and 21 April 1874, 9.

65. The figure was £10,382,908.

66. *Hansard*, 3rd ser., 210 (1872), col. 429; 215 (1873), col. 38.

67. Ibid., 3rd ser., 156 (1860), col. 984.

68. Ibid., 3rd ser., 181 (1866), col. 1322.

69. Ibid., 3rd ser., 199 (1870), col. 896.

70. Ibid., 3rd ser., 215 (1873), col. 36.

71. Ibid., 3rd ser., 244 (1879), col. 561.

72. Ibid., 3rd ser., 205 (1871), col. 699.

73. Ibid., 3rd ser., 222 (1875), cols. 1637–38.

74. Goschen to Gladstone, 19 September 1871, Gladstone Papers, BL, 44161, fol. 181.

Chapter 4

1. Pakington to Derby, 18 July and 21 July, 1866, Derby Papers, Liverpool Record Office, 920 DER (14), 141/11. Emphasis in original.

2. Disraeli to Derby, 20 August 1866, ibid., 920 DER (14), 146/2. Robert Stewart, *The Foundation of the Conservative Party, 1830–1867*, 360.

3. "Report of the Committee on Dockyard Economy appointed by the Admiralty," *Parl. Papers*, 1859, 18: 1, "Report of the Commissioners Appointed to Inquire into the Control and Management of Her Majesty's Naval Yards," *Parl. Papers*, 1861, 26: 1. Seely was responsible for introducing yearly balance sheets showing cost of manufacture and repair in the dockyards.

4. Disraeli to Derby, 20 August 1866, Derby Papers, Liverpool Record Office, 920 DER (14), 146/2.

5. Pakington to Derby, 7 February 1867, ibid., 920 DER (14), 141/12. Emphasis in original.

Notes to Pages 71–76 289

6. Stanley Sandler, *The Emergence of the Modern Capital Ship*, 255.
7. Derby to Pakington (Copy), Confidential, 15 September 1866, Derby Papers, Liverpool Record Office, 920 DER (14), 191/2, fol. 111.
8. Derby to Pakington (Copy), Confidential, 16 January 1867, ibid., 920 DER (14), 192/1, fol.
9. Pakington to Disraeli (Copy), 25 January 1867, ibid., 920 DER (14), 141/12.
10. The naval stores vote increased from £855,511 to £1,003,501 while contract shipbuilding rose from £338,000 to £860,559. "Navy Estimates," *Parl. Papers*, 1867, 44: 5; 1867–68, 40: 5. The *Parliamentary Papers* put the total estimates at £11,477,290 for 1867–68, but in introducing them, Lord Henry Lennox stated the figure as £10,926,253 (See *Hansard's Parliamentary Debates*, 3rd ser., 185 [1867], col. 1825.) Final expenditure for the year 1867–68 was £11,342,798 5/6, exclusive of the navy's share of a vote of credit for the Abyssinian expedition. See "Finance Accounts," *Parl. Papers*, 1868–69, 38: 5.
11. Disraeli to Derby, 2 February 1867, Derby Papers, Liverpool Record Office, 920 DER (14), 146/3.
12. John C. D. Hay, *Lines from My Logbooks*, 261–63.
13. Disraeli to Derby (Fragment), n.d. Derby Papers, Liverpool Record Office, 920 DER (14), 141/12.
14. *Dictionary of National Biography*, 4:1179–80. See also Disraeli's recommendation of Corry to Victoria in George Earle Buckle, ed., *The Letters of Queen Victoria*, 2nd ser., 1: 397–98.
15. Corry to Cabinet (Copy), 2 December 1867, Milne Papers, NMM, MLN/143/3/10.
16. Corry to Disraeli, 11 January [1868], Hughenden (Disraeli) Papers, Bodleian Library, B/XXI/C, Box 123/3, fol. 73.
17. Ibid., fols. 73–74.
18. Lennox to Disraeli, Most Private, 5 January 1868, ibid., B/XX/Lx/270.
19. Corry to Disraeli, 11 January [1868], ibid., B/XXI/C, Box 123/3, fol. 75.
20. Lennox to Disraeli, Most Private, 23 January 1868, ibid., B/XX/Lx/271. Emphasis in original.
21. Disraeli to Derby, Confidential, 28 January 1868, Derby Papers, Liverpool Record Office, 920 DER (14),146/4, and Lennox to Disraeli, Most Private, 23 January 1868, Hughenden (Disraeli) Papers, Bodleian Library, B/XX/Lx/271.
22. Disraeli to Derby, Confidential, 28 January, 1868, Derby Papers, Liverpool Record Office, 920 DER (14), 146/4. See also Treasury to Admiralty, 6 January 1868, PRO: ADM12/818/91.1.
23. Ibid. See also Sandler, *Modern Capital Ship*, 59–63, esp. 62.
24. "Finance Accounts," *Parl. Papers*, 1878–79, 42: 733. There were three votes of credit: £2 million in 1867–68, £5 million in 1868–69, and £1.3 million in 1869–70.
25. Disraeli to Derby, Confidential, 28 January 1868, Derby Papers, Liverpool Record Office, 920 DER (14), 146/4.

26. Derby to Disraeli (Copy), Confidential, 30 January [1868], ibid., 920 DER (14), 193/1, fols. 199–202.

27. Lennox to Disraeli, Confidential, 28 January 1868, Hughenden (Disraeli) Papers, Bodleian Library, B/XX/Lx/272.

28. For support for this hypothesis, see Milne's memorandum of 7 November 1867 in the Milne Papers, NNM, MLN/143/3/8; the comments of Sir John Hay and George Seymour, MLN/143/3/9, and Corry's own paper of 2 December 1867, MLN/143/3/10.

29. Memorandum of the Naval Members of the Board, for the Consideration of the First Lord of the Admiralty (Copy), 16 December 1867, Milne Papers, NMM: MLN/143/3/11.

30. Derby to Disraeli (Copy), Confidential, 30 January [1868], Derby Papers, Liverpool Record Office, 920 DER (14), 193/1, fols. 199–202.

31. Corry to Disraeli, 11 January [1868], Hughenden (Disraeli) Papers, Bodleian Library, B/XXII/C/442.

32. Lennox to Disraeli, Confidential, 1 February 1868, ibid., B/XX/Lx/273.

33. Lennox to Corry (Copy), n.d., ibid., B/XX/Lx/277a.

34. Lennox to Disraeli, Most Private, 15 February 1868, ibid., B/XX/Lx/277.

35. Ibid. See also Disraeli to Queen Victoria, 15 February 1868, University of Illinois Library (microfilm copy), Royal Archives, E52/26. Lennox meant not that £124,000 would pay in full for three ironclads but that it was the sum to be spent on three ironclads over one year out of the several needed to complete the vessels. Each would cost some £250,000–400,000 to complete.

36. *Hansard*, 3rd ser., 192 (1868), cols. 34–35, 51, 59.

37. On 15 September 1866 Malmesbury wrote Derby: "I have been a long time anxious about the state of our *Navy* [which] from unavoidable circumstances does not bear nearly the same relative position as regards other navies [which] it formerly did, & [which] it should do." Quoted in Richard Millman, *British Foreign Policy and the Coming of the Franco-Prussian War*, 149. See also Malmesbury's own *Memoirs of an Ex-Minister*, 624.

38. Robert Blake, *Disraeli*, 379; Sandler, *Modern Capital Ship*, 38.

39. Sandler, *Modern Capital Ship*, 62–63.

40. *Evidence, Written and oral, taken by the Royal Commission appointed to Enquire into the Civil and Professional Administration of the Naval and Military Departments and the Relationship of those Departments to each other and to the Treasury* (generally known as the Hartington Commission), PRO: HO73/35/3, 7.

41. Gladstone to Goschen (Copy), 7 November 1872, Gladstone Papers, BL, 44542, fol. 41. Gladstone, in a struggle with George J. Goschen over naval spending in 1872, intimated that the Liberals had "promised" the electorate substantial savings in the cost of government during the campaign of 1868: "I must own we do not at present stand four-square with the (very reasonable) Election pledges of 1868." See also the *Times* (London), 2 January 1880, 9, in which the editors claim that naval expenditure was a large factor in the election of 1868. More recently, C. J. Bartlett stated that the issue of

government expenditure was second only to that of Ireland in 1868. Bartlett, "The Mid-Victorian Reappraisal of Naval Policy," 198.

42. The *Times* (London), 23 October 1868, 8.

43. Ibid., 27 August 1868, 6. In comparing government expenditure, the *Times* noted that by 1864 Gladstone's expenditure, exclusive of servicing the debt, was £39,680,000, and that between 1862 and 1866 he reduced revenue from taxation by £13,693,000. In contrast, after two years with the Conservatives in office, expenditure was up to £43,730,000, again exclusive of debt service. For another leading article of similar tenor, see the *Times*, 21 September 1868, 8. See also Arthur D. Elliot, *Life of George Joachim, Viscount Goschen*, 1: 98.

44. Financial Reform Union, *Papers on Taxation and Expenditure Issued by the Financial Reform Union*.

45. Ibid., No. 1. *Naval Mal-Administration*, 8.

46. Ibid., No. 3. *A Budget for 1869*, 2.

47. The *Times* (London), 31 January 1868, 7.

48. *Pall Mall Gazette* (London), quoted in the *Times* (London), 17 January 1868, 5.

49. *Naval and Military Gazette* (London), 8 February 1868, 88.

50. Blake, *Disraeli*, 492–93.

51. Philip Magnus, *Gladstone*, 193.

52. The *Times* (London), 23 December 1868, 9.

Chapter 5

1. For Childers' life, see Spencer Childers, *The Life and Correspondence of the Rt. Hon. Hugh Culling Eardley Childers*.

2. Childers to Gladstone, 3 August 1865, Gladstone Papers, BL, 44128, fol. 1.

3. *Dictionary of National Biography*, 22: 424.

4. The *Times* (London), 9 March, 1869, 9.

5. *Hansard's Parliamentary Debates*, 3rd ser., 199 (1870), cols. 914–17.

6. Ibid.

7. In 1867 Lord Henry Lennox termed the four earliest British ironclads "not perfect specimens." Childers himself was more specific in 1869, noting that the first-generation British ironclads—not one of which at that moment was as much as a decade old—were "very badly protected." In 1872 George J. Goschen alluded to the need "to replace, as we have begun to do, our older ironclads by other ships." This criticism should not suggest that these ships were wholly useless. Most still had sound hulls, and were more than a match for foreign ships of a similar vintage.

8. *Hansard*, 3rd ser., 199 (1870), col. 918.

9. Spencer Robinson to Admiralty [1870], PRO; ADM12/853/69.1, S. 2254.

10. The figure was £3,208,071.

11. As a result of significant additions made to the fleet through the vote

of credit of the previous year, the program for 1879–80 called for building slightly more than 15,000 tons. In 1870–71 the program was also inflated by a vote of credit, and in 1876–77 George Ward Hunt introduced an ambitious unarmored shipbuilding program.

12. "Return of the Amount of Shipping—Tons Weight of Hull—Estimated for and Calculated to have been Built in each Year from 1865–66 to 1884–85," *Parl. Papers*, 1884–85, 48: 539–42.

13. *Hansard*, 3rd ser., 227 (1876), col. 1926. See also the *Times* (London), 14 October 1876, 9. "It has long been customary for the work of the Dockyards to fall short of the amount predicted in the Navy Estimates, and for which votes have been taken."

14. *Hansard*, 3rd ser., 222 (1875), cols 1653–54.

15. The shortfall was 13,925 tons over ten years.

16. Robinson to Dacres (Copy), 9 August 1870, PRO; ADM1/6159; *Hansard*, 3rd ser., 208 (1871), col. 1445.

17. "Navy Estimates," *Parl. Papers*, 1873, 42: 165; 1875, 45: 171.

18. *Hansard*, 3rd ser., 199 (1870), col. 917.

19. Ibid., 3rd ser., 162 (1862), col. 666.

20. Derby to Pakington (Copy), 15 September 1866, Derby Papers, Liverpool Record Office, DER 920, 191/2, fols. 111–12; Disraeli to Derby, 20 August 1866, Confidential, ibid., 146/2.

21. Derby to Pakington (Copy), 15 September 1866, ibid., DER 920 (14), 191/2, fol. 114.

22. The *Times* (London), 7 April 1868, 8. See also for 26 December 1867, 6 and 31 January 1868, 7.

23. "Navy Estimates," *Parl. Papers*, 1871, 40: 183.

24. *Hansard*, 3rd ser., 210 (1872), col. 469.

25. Ibid., 3rd ser., 215 (1873), cols. 58–61.

26. Ibid., 3rd ser., 218 (1874), col. 870.

27. Ibid., 3rd ser., 227 (1876), col. 1927.

28. K. T. Rowland, *Steam at Sea: A History of Steam Navigation*, 106.

29. *Hansard*, 3rd ser., 238 (1878), col. 1453.

30. Ibid., 3rd ser., 215 (1873), col. 61.

31. Ibid., 3rd ser., 218 (1874), col. 854.

32. Ibid., 3rd ser., 238 (1878), col. 1429. See also Rowland, *Steam at Sea*, 136. The Committee issued a preliminary report in 1877 and a final report in 1880. See "Third Report of the Committee appointed by the Admiralty to inquire into the causes of the deterioration of boilers &c, and to propose measures which would tend to increase their durability, with Appendices containing the précis and analysis of the evidence, the results of the experiments, the photographs of specimens, the preliminary and other reports of the Committee &c," *Parl. Papers*, 1877, 19: 1, and "Final Report of the Committee appointed by the Admiralty to inquire into the causes of the deterioration of Boilers, &c, and to propose measure which would tend to increase their durability; with Appendices containing results of Experiments," *Parl. Papers* 1880, 13: 417.

Notes to Pages 91–97

33. Given Ward Hunt's bulk, physical force might have done the trick.

34. Rowland, *Steam at Sea*, 106, 136. The committee recommended placing "sacrificial anodes" in boilers, "used to protect steel and other metals from electrochemical corrosion. The anodes gradually corrode away in preference to the steelwork [or iron] and are periodically replaced": 136.

35. *Hansard*, 3rd ser., 218 (1874), col. 856.

36. The *Daily News* (London), 9 March 1869, 4. For the political affiliations of journals, see Lucy Brown, *Victorian News and Newspapers*, 61–65.

37. *Hansard*, 3rd ser., 194 (1869), col. 864.

38. The *Daily News* (London), 9 March 1869, 4.

39. The *Standard* (London), 9 March 1869, 4.

40. *Hansard*, 3rd ser., 194 (1869), cols. 903–4.

41. The *Standard* (London), 9 March 1869, 4.

42. Woolwich Dockyard to Admiralty, 22 September 1869, PRO: ADM12/828/5.1. See also Spencer Childers, *Hugh Childers*, 1: 169; *Naval and Military Gazette* (London), 30 January 1869, 72; 13 February 1869, 105–6; 27 February 1869, 136–37; and 20 March 1869, 200–201.

43. The *Times* (London), 1 March 1870, 9.

44. The *Daily News* (London), 1 March 1870, 4.

45. *Naval and Military Gazette* (London), 13 February 1869, 105–6; 5 March 1870, 223.

46. *Hansard*, 3rd ser., 199 (1870), cols. 896–97.

47. Ibid., col. 940.

48. The *Standard* (London), 1 March 1870, 4.

49. *Hansard*, 3rd ser., 199 (1870), col. 897.

50. Childers to Granville, 11 July 1870, Granville Papers, PRO: PRO30/29/54.

51. William E. Gladstone (H.G.C. Matthew, ed.), *The Gladstone Diaries, with Cabinet Minutes and Prime-Ministerial Correspondence*, 7: 330.

52. Gladstone to Queen Victoria (Copy), 16 July 1870, PRO: CAB41/2/34.

53. Robinson to Dacres (Copy), 4 August 1870, PRO: ADM1/6159.

54. Dacres to Childers, ibid.

55. Comments of Spencer Robinson, ibid.

56. Gladstone to Queen Victoria (Copy), 30 July 1870, PRO: CAB41/2/38.

57. *Hansard*, 3rd ser., 205 (1871), col. 695.

58. The Navy Estimates display a figure of £9,875,981, the finance accounts show £9,900,486.

59. Memorandum of 22 December 1868, printed in "Report from the Select Committee of the House of Lords on the Board of Admiralty; Together with the Proceedings of the Committee, Minutes of Evidence, and Appendix" (generally known as the Somerset Committee), *Parl. Papers*, 1871, 7: 129.

60. *Hansard*, 3rd ser., 194 (1869), col. 871.

61. Memorandum of 22 December 1868, printed in "Somerset Committee Report," *Parl. Papers*, 1871, 7: 129.

62. *Hansard* 3rd ser., 194 (1869), cols. 870–71.

63. Memorandum of 22 December 1868, printed in "Somerset Committee Report," *Parl. Papers*, 1871, 7: 129–30.

64. *Hansard*, 3rd ser., 194 (1869), col. 872.

65. Ibid., cols. 872–74.

66. Leslie Gardiner, *The British Admiralty*, 17; John Henry Briggs, *Naval Administrations 1827–1892*, 188; C. I. Hamilton, *Anglo-French Naval Rivalry, 1840–1870*, 234. The primary reason the offices were maintained separately was shortage of office space in Admiralty House. The surveyor's (controller's) department was moved to the Admiralty in 1855, but other departments remained at Somerset House until Childers' consolidation.

67. *Hansard*, 3rd ser., 194 (1869), cols. 873–75.

68. Childers provided additional assistance for the controller by the creation of the post of director of naval ordnance, and appointed a naval chief of staff to help the First Naval Lord.

69. Order in Council of 14 January 1869, printed in "Somerset Committee Report," *Parl. Papers*, 1871, 7: 131.

70. Ibid., 12.

71. "Report of the Commissioners appointed to inquire into the case of H.M.S. '*Megaera*,' together with Minutes of Evidence and Appendix (generally known as the *Megaera* Commission)," *Parl. Papers*, 1872, 15: 502, 508.

72. "Report of the Commissioners appointed to inquire into the Control and Management of Her Majesty's Naval Yards, Together with the Minutes of Evidence and Appendix," *Parl. Papers*, 1861, 26: vi–vii.

73. Printed in the "Somerset Committee Report," *Parl. Papers*, 1871, 7: 45–49.

74. "*Megaera* Commission Report," *Parl. Papers*, 1872, 15: 501.

Chapter 6

1. N. A. M. Rodger, "The Design of the *Inconstant*," 13. Rodger furnishes a vivid description of Spencer Robinson's personality.

2. John Beeler, "'Fit for Service Abroad': Promotion, Retirement, and Royal Navy Officers, 1830–1890," 300–312.

3. John Henry Briggs, *Naval Administrations, 1827–1892: The Experience of 65 Years*, 170. See also "Correspondence between Flag Officers and the Admiralty relating to the late scheme of retirement," *Parl. Papers*, 1871, 40: 723.

4. *Hansard's Parliamentary Debates*, 3rd ser., 199 (1870), cols. 931, 935.

5. Spencer Robinson to Childers (Copy), 6 June 1870, Gladstone Papers, BL, 44614, fol. 100; "Copy of Scheme for Increasing the flow of Promotion amongst the Executive Classes," *Parl. Papers*, 1866, 46: 627–28.

6. "Report from the Select Committee of the House of Lords on the Board of Admiralty; Together with the proceedings of the Committee, Minutes of Evidence, and Appendix" (generally known as the Somerset Committee), *Parl. Papers*, 1871, 7: 37, 112–13; *Hansard*, 3rd ser., 204 (1870), cols. 322–23.

7. Dacres to Milne, 26 March [1870], Milne Papers, NMM, MLN/165/3.

Notes to Pages 103–8

8. Spencer Robinson to Childers (Copy), 6 June 1870, Gladstone Papers, BL, 44614, fol. 100; also, Spencer Robinson to Childers (Copy), Confidential, 1 June 1870, ibid., fol. 95, in which Spencer Robinson requested that he be exempted from the workings of the retirement scheme.

9. Spencer Robinson to Childers (Copy), 6 June 1870, ibid., fol. 102. He added Childers had said "provided you [Childers] could do so consistently with your public duty."

10. Gladstone to Spencer Robinson (Copy), 23 June 1870, ibid., 44538, fol. 173.

11. Childers to Gladstone, 19 March 1870, ibid., 44128, fol. 161.

12. Childers to Spencer Robinson (Copy), 4 June 1870, ibid., 44614, fol. 96.

13. Ibid., fols. 98–99.

14. Ibid., fol. 98.

15. Spencer Robinson to Childers (Copy), 1 June 1870, ibid., 44614, fol. 95.

16. Spencer Robinson to Childers (Copy), 6 June 1870, ibid., 44614, fols. 104–5.

17. Spencer Robinson to Childers (Copy), 10 June 1870, ibid., 44614, fols. 113–14.

18. Spencer Robinson to West, 5 April, 6 April, 13 June 1870, ibid., 44426, fols. 93, 102; 44427, fols. 42–49; Spencer Robinson to Gladstone, 20 June, 25 June 1870, ibid., 44427, fols. 87, 103.

19. Dacres to Milne, Private, nd [spring or early summer 1870], Milne Papers, NMM, MLN/165/3.

20. Rodger, "Design of the *Inconstant*," 13–14; Stanley Sandler, *The Emergence of the Modern Capital Ship*, 29–31.

21. Seymour to Milne, Private, 5 May 1870, Milne Papers, NMM, MLN/165/11.

22. Seymour to Milne, Private, 5 July 1870, ibid., MLN/165/11.

23. Childers to Gladstone, 27 June 1870, Gladstone Papers, BL, 44128, fol. 174.

24. Childers to Milne, 7 May 1870, Milne Papers, NMM, MLN/165/1; Seymour to Milne, Private, 5 May 1870, ibid., MLN/165/11.

25. Gladstone to Fortesque (Copy), 21 June 1870, Gladstone Papers, BL, 44538, fol. 170.

26. Childers to Milne, 3 July 1870, Milne Papers, NMM, MLN/165/1.

27. Seymour to West, Strictly Private, 21 June 1870, Gladstone Papers, BL, 44341, fols. 39–40.

28. Seymour to West, Quite Confidential, [22 June 1870], ibid., fols. 41–42.

29. West to Fortesque (Copy), 22 June 1870, ibid., fol. 37. West wrote: "Beauchamp Seymour and Camperdown are both in a great state of mind about the present insubordination & confusion in the Admiralty."

30. *The Times* (London), 27 June 1870, 11.

31. Gladstone to Spencer Robinson (Copy), 23 June 1870, Gladstone Papers, BL, 44538, fol. 173.

32. *Hansard*, 3rd ser., 202 (1870), cols. 1003–05.

33. Spencer Robinson to Gladstone, 25 June 1870, Gladstone Papers, BL, 44427, fol. 103.

34. Childers to Gladstone, 4 July 1870, ibid., 44128, fol. 183.

35. *Hansard*, 3rd ser. 203 (1870), cols. 413–14. Childers read the letter in the House of Commons on 18 July 1870. At this point Reed explicitly downplayed any appearance of discord with the Childers administration.

36. Seymour to Milne, Private, 5 July 1870, Milne Papers, NMM, MLN/165/11.

37. Milne to the Admiralty, 7 September 1870, PRO: ADM1/6159. There were actually eighteen survivors.

38. Prince Albert to Somerset, 10 December 1860, printed in Theodore Martin, *The Life of His Royal Highness the Prince Consort*, 5: 257–58.

39. Spencer Robinson to Admiralty, 14 March 1868, PRO: ADM12/818/91.1.

40. The *Times* (London), 11 May 1868, 9.

41. Ibid., 13 May 1868, 9.

42. *Naval and Military Gazette* (London), 22 February 1868, 120. For further press attacks on the Admiralty's construction policy, see the *Times* (London), 11 February 1867, 9; 3 February 1868, 9; 11 May 1868, 9; 18 May 1868, 9; 4 June 1868, 8; 4 July 1868, 9; 15 July 1868, 9; 27 July 1868, 9; 5 August 1868, 6; 24 September 1868, 6; 1 March 1869, 8, 9; 12 April 1869, 9; 28 September 1869, 6; 9 June 1870, 9; 27 June 1870, 11; 8 August 1870, 8. In the *Naval and Military Gazette* (London), see 25 January 1868, 51; 8 February 1868, 89; 14 March 1868, 169; 23 March 1868, 329; 30 May 1868, 346; 6 June 1868, 363; 13 June 1868, 377–78; 11 July 1868, 440; 18 July 1868, 456; 12 September 1868, 586; 14 November 1868, 728–29. In the *United Service Gazette* (London), see 4 January 1868, 4; 14 March 1868, 4; 6 March 1869, 4; 10 April 1869, 4; 12 November 1870, 4; 19 November 1870, 4.

43. Halifax to Gladstone, 12 October 1870, Gladstone Papers, BL, 44185, fol. 62.

44. *Hansard*, 3rd ser., 185 (1867), col. 1843.

45. *United Service Gazette* (London), 4 January 1868, 4.

46. See also the *Times* (London), 15 July 1868, 9.

47. Dacres was one of few senior navy officers to argue unequivocally against the use of turrets in masted, seagoing ironclads, informing Sir Alexander Milne in August 1870, "I don't believe in a *Cruising* [i.e., masted] Turret [ship]." At the end of the same month, barely a week before the disaster, he warned Milne, "I can never believe in a Cruising Turret ship of any class and [you] be careful in any report of the *Captain* to look to her weights." Dacres to Milne, 5 August 1870 and 27 August [1870], NMM, MLN/165/3.

48. Childers to Milne, 16 September 1870, Milne Papers, NMM, MLN/165/1.

49. There is extensive correspondence in the Gladstone Papers from both Halifax and Northbrook on naval matters—especially the loss of the *Captain*—during the fall and winter of 1870–71. See Halifax to Gladstone, BL,

44185, fols. 58–61, 62–69, 70, 74–75, 125–32, 133–37; and Northbrook to Gladstone, ibid., 44266, fols. 8–12, 13–14, 15, 17–19, 21–22, 23. See also Seymour to Milne, Private, 5 July 1870, Milne Papers, NMM, MLN/165/3. Seymour wrote, "[Y]ou will see that Lord Halifax has joined the Cabinet which looks as if Mr. Gladstone wanted to have a First Lord available if by any chance Mr. [Childers'] health should fail."

50. The *Times* (London), 26 September 1870, 9.

51. The navy's legal system mandated a court martial whenever a ship was lost, regardless of the circumstances. In this case, the surviving sailors were ostensibly on trial. In actuality, it was a court of inquiry, and the acquittal of the eighteen men in the dock a foregone conclusion.

52. "Minute of the First Lord of the Admiralty, with reference to H.M.S. 'Captain,' with the Minutes of the Proceedings of the Court Martial, and the Board Minute thereon," *Parl. Papers*, 1871, 42: 177–79.

53. Dacres to Milne, 5 August 1870, Milne Papers, NMM, MLN/165/3.

54. Dacres to Northbrook (Copy), received 8 October 1870, Gladstone Papers, BL, 44266, fol. 15. As for the possibility that Reed did warn Childers in private, the chief constructor never made a specific claim to that effect, and it is unlikely that the First Lord would have disregarded an explicit warning from a naval architect of Reed's stature.

55. Reed to the *Times* (London), 8 August 1870, printed in [Edmund R. Fremantle], "The Loss of H.M.S. *Captain*," *Fraser's Magazine* 183, January 1871: 77.

56. "Captain Minute," *Parl. Papers*, 1871, 42: 179.

57. Ibid., 161.

58. Ibid., 158. Spencer Robinson managed to evade testifying at the court martial himself. Instead he provided the court with a written statement, a course contrary to established precedent, and one criticized by several observers. The other principal who did not testify—Hugh Childers—was still abroad, attempting to regain his health.

For details on the physical characteristics and seaworthiness of the *Captain*, see Stanley Sandler's exhaustive treatment of the construction of the ship and the publicity surrounding it in *Modern Capital Ship*, 177–233.

59. "Captain Minute," *Parl. Papers*, 1871, 42: 183.

60. The *Times* (London), 22 December 1870, 9.

61. Ibid., 23 January 1871, 9.

62. *Hansard*, 3rd ser., 205 (1871), col. 880.

63. Northbrook to Dacres (Copy), 8 October 1870, Gladstone Papers, BL, 44266, fols. 17–18.

64. Northbrook was aware of how close he was cutting it. His final words to Dacres were "there is very little time to lose before the Court closes."

65. "Captain Minute," *Parl. Papers*, 1871, 42: 183.

66. Northbrook to West, 8 October 1870, Gladstone Papers, BL, 55266, fols. 7–11.

67. Childers to Gladstone, 18 October 1870, ibid., 44128, fols. 193–95.

68. "Captain Minute," *Parl. Papers*, 1871, 42: 280–81.

69. Ibid., 6–38. Only Childers' signature was affixed to the minute. No contemporary doubt existed as to whose opinions it contained. For confirmation, see the *Times* (London), 16 December 1870, 9; and especially the *Daily News* (London), 23 February 1871, 5.

70. Sandler, *Modern Capital Ship*, 232.

71. "Captain Minute," *Parl. Papers*, 1871, 42: 18–40.

72. Reed to Admiralty, 14 March 1870, printed in ibid., 18.

73. The center of gravity was determined experimentally (it had already been figured quite accurately by calculation) by a process called "inclining," which involved weighting one side of the ship to produce a list. Accurate results could be obtained only in calm water, hence Reed's reference to the weather.

74. The *Times* (London), 16 December 1870, 9.

75. Robert Hastings Harris, *From Naval Cadet to Admiral*, 109.

76. "Captain Minute," *Parl. Papers*, 1871, 42: 161.

77. Reed to the *Times* (London), 21 December 1870, 12.

78. "Captain Minute," *Parl. Papers*, 1871, 42: 41.

79. Reed to the *Times* (London), 21 December 1870, 12.

80. Osborn to ibid., 15 November 1870, 6.

81. The *Daily News* (London), 23 February 1871, 5.

82. *Pall Mall Gazette* (London), 19 December 1870, 2.

83. *United Service Gazette* (London), 24 December 1870, 5.

84. The *Times* (London), 16 December 1870, 9.

85. Ibid., 22 December 1870, 9.

86. See *Naval and Military Gazette* (London), 22 April 1871, 190.

87. See, for instance, the *Times* (London), 15 November 1870, 9.

88. Halifax to Gladstone, 2 October 1870, Gladstone Papers, BL, 44185, fol. 58.

89. Gladstone to Halifax (Copy), 13 October 1870, ibid., 44539, fol. 53.

90. Childers to Gladstone, 18 October 1870, ibid., 44128, fols. 194–95.

91. That the Committee was impartial seems beyond dispute, if on no other evidence than the frequent lack of consensus amongst the members themselves. Indeed, it issued both majority and minority reports, although on the crucial question of the safety of the navy's existing ironclads there was across-the-board agreement.

92. William E. Gladstone (H. C. G. Matthew, ed.), *The Gladstone Diaries, with Cabinet Minutes and Prime-Ministerial Correspondence*, 7: 390–92.

93. *Hansard*, 3rd ser., 210 (1872), cols. 451–52.

Chapter 7

1. Spencer Robinson to Gladstone, 26 October 1870, Gladstone Papers, BL, 44428, fols. 152–57.

2. Spencer Robinson to Gladstone, 5 November 1870, ibid., 44428, fol. 180; Gladstone to Spencer Robinson (Copy), 7 November 1870, ibid., 44539, fol. 68. There is no reply to Gladstone's request among his papers, and no evidence that the interview took place.

3. Spencer Robinson to Gladstone, addendum by Childers, 5 November 1870, ibid., 44428, fol. 181.

4. Halifax to Gladstone, Confidential, 30 January 1871, ibid., 44185, fols. 126–27; Gladstone to Spencer Robinson (Copy), 31 January 1871, ibid., 44539, fol. 147. Spencer Robinson was first appointed to the controllership for five years in February 1861, and reappointed for another term in 1866.

5. Spencer Robinson to Childers, 17 December 1870, printed in "Copy of the Reply made by Sir Spencer Robinson to the Minute by the First Lord of the Admiralty (Published by order of the Lords Commissioners of the Admiralty)," *Parl. Papers*, 1871, 40: 687–89. A similar claim can be found in Spencer Robinson to Gladstone, 6 March 1871, printed in the *Times*, 7 March 1871, 10.

6. Spencer Robinson to Admiralty, 25 November 1871, PRO: ADM1/6221. This denunciation prefaced Spencer Robinson's comments on the committee's report.

7. Halifax to Gladstone, Confidential, 30 January 1871, Gladstone Papers, 44185, fol. 127.

8. Spencer Robinson to Gladstone, 31 January 1871, printed in the *Times*, 15 February 1871, 10.

9. The *Times* (London), 30 December 1870, 7.

10. Childers to Gladstone, 6 January 1871, Gladstone Papers, 44128, fols. 198–99.

11. Gladstone to Childers (Copy), 8 January 1871, ibid., 44539, fol. 127.

12. Gladstone to Ellis (Copy), 10 January 1871, ibid., 44539, fol. 136.

13. Childers to Gladstone, 15 January 1871, 21 January 1871, ibid., 44128 fols. 200–201, 202–3.

14. The *Lancet*, reprinted in the *Times* (London), 20 January 1871, 9.

15. Memorandum by Halifax, Confidential, 30 January 1871, Gladstone Papers, 44185, fol. 131.

16. Gladstone to Spencer Robinson (Copy), 30 January 1871, ibid., 44539, fol. 147.

17. Gladstone to Spencer Robinson (Copy), 31 January 1871, ibid., 44539, fol. 149.

18. The *Times* (London), 7 February 1871, 7. The *Times* reported rumors of Spencer Robinson's departure on the 7th.

19. *United Service Gazette* (London), 18 February, 5.

20. The *Times* (London), 18 February, 9.

21. The *Daily News* (London), 23 February 1871, 9.

22. The *Times* (London), 18 February 1871, 9. See also *Army and Navy Gazette* for 11 February 1871, for perhaps the most balanced contemporary appraisal.

23. Cited by Childers and printed in "Report of the Commissioners appointed to inquire into the case of H.M.S. '*Megaera*'; together with Minutes of Evidence and Appendix" (generally known as the *Megaera* Commission), *Parl. Papers*, 1872, 15: 521–22.

24. The *Times* (London), 9 March 1869, 9.

25. *United Service Gazette* (London), 6 March 1869, 4.
26. The *Standard* (London), 9 March 1869, 4.
27. The *Times* (London), 1 March 1870, 9.
28. Ibid., 23 January 1871, 9.
29. *United Service Gazette* (London), 14 January 1871, 4. See also the same journal for 18 February 1871, 5.
30. There were nine debates on naval administration and related subjects—the forced resignation of Spencer Robinson and responsibility for the loss of the *Captain*—during the 1871 Session: 16 February (Lords), *Hansard's Parliamentary Debates*, 3rd ser., 204 (1871), cols. 295–315; 17 February (Commons), 204 (1871), cols. 455–76; 18 April (Commons), 204 (1871), cols. 1280–1332; 27 April (Commons), 205 (1871), cols. 1810–22; 3 July (Lords), 207 (1871), cols. 963–76; 11 July (Commons), 207 (1871), cols. 1445–8; 7 August (Commons), 208 (1871), cols. 1019–61; 8 August (Commons), 208 (1871), cols. 1147–75; and 9 August (Commons), 208 (1871) cols. 1195–1254.
31. *United Service Gazette* (London), 25 March 1871, 4.
32. Ibid., 3 December 1870, 4.
33. "Report from the Select Committee of the House of Lords on the Board of Admiralty; Together with the Proceedings of the Committee, Minutes of Evidence, and Appendix," (generally known as the Somerset Committee), *Parl. Papers*, 1871, 7: ix–x. For further contemporary criticism, see John Henry Briggs, *Naval Administrations, 1827–1892: The Experience of 65 Years*, 186–87.
34. The *Times* (London), 18 February 1871, 9.
35. *Hansard*, 3rd ser., 204 (1871), col. 299.
36. The *Times* (London), 18 February 1871, 9.
37. "Somerset Committee Report," *Parl. Papers*, 1871, 7: xi.
38. The *Times* (London), 7 March 1871, 9.
39. Ibid., 18 February 1871, 9; 28 March 1871, 9.
40. *United Service Gazette* (London), 18 February, 1971, 5.
41. *Hansard*, 3rd ser., 204, (1871) cols. 304, 315. The entire debate occupies cols. 295–315.
42. Ibid., col. 462. The entire debate occupies cols. 455–75. Gladstone was the principal spokesman for the government.
43. Ibid., 3rd ser., 205, col. 1295. The entire debate occupies cols. 1280–1332.
44. Norman McCord, "A Naval Scandal of 1871: The Loss of H.M.S. *Megaera*," 123.
45. Ibid., 116–17.
46. The *Times* (London), 8 August 1871, 9. There were other editorials on the subject as well: see 4 August 1871, 9; 25 September 1871, 9; and 24 October 1871, 9.
47. McCord, *Megaera*, 122–30.
48. "*Megaera* Commission Report," *Parl. Papers*, 1872, 15: 355.
49. See the *Times* (London), 20 January 1872, 9, and 24 January 1872, 9.
50. Cited in McCord, *Megaera*, 131.

51. Gladstone to Halifax (Copy), 27 February 1871, Gladstone Papers, BL, 44539, fol. 168.
52. Gladstone to Halifax (Copy), 1 March 1871, ibid., 44539, fol. 169.
53. The *Times* (London), 4 March 1871, 9.
54. Ibid., 7 March 1871, 9.
55. Ibid.
56. *Naval and Military Gazette* (London), 11 March 1871, 113.
57. *Hansard*, 3rd ser., 204 (1871), col. 1505.
58. Arthur D. Elliot, *Life of George Joachim Goschen, First Viscount Goschen, 1831–1907*, 1: 3–4, 46, 90–91.
59. Goschen to Gladstone, 18 November 1871, Gladstone Papers, BL, 44161, fol. 192.
60. The *Times* (London), 3 February 1872, 9. For ongoing journalistic calls for Admiralty reform during the first year of Goschen's administration, see the *Times*, 5 May 1871, 9; 26 June 1871, 9; 5 July 1871, 9; 13 July 1871, 9; 8 January 1872, 8; 20 January 1872, 9; 24 January 1872, 9; 29 January 1872, 9; 3 February 1872, 9; 21 March 1872, 9; and the *United Service Gazette* (London), 20 May 1871, 4; 1 July 1871, 4; 8 July 1871, 4; 9 September 1871, 4; 6 January 1872, 4; 27 January 1872, 4.
61. Memorandum to the Cabinet by Goschen (Copy), Confidential, 6 March 1872, Gladstone Papers, BL, 44161, fols. 197–201.
62. See the *Times* (London), 20 April 1870, 9. The same criticism was voiced in Briggs, *Naval Administrations*, 186–89. Most subsequent commentators have taken their cue from Briggs.
63. "Somerset Committee Report," *Parl. Papers*, 1871, 7: ix.
64. Memorandum to the Cabinet by Goschen (Copy), Confidential, 6 March 1872, Gladstone Papers, BL, 44161, fols. 198–200.
65. *Hansard*, 3rd ser., 210 (1872), cols. 204–5.
66. Memorandum to the Cabinet by Goschen (Copy), Confidential, 6 March 1872, Gladstone Papers, BL, 44161, fol. 199.
67. Ibid., fols. 199–201; "Copies of the Orders in Council relating to the Construction of the Board of Admiralty and the Professional Staff of the Controllers' Department," *Parl. Papers*, 1872, 39: 339–40. From the subsequent order in council (19 March 1872) it appears that Goschen did not carry the cabinet with him on this point. The text states only that "[t]he Civil Lord, the Permanent Secretary, and the Naval Secretary, to have such duties as shall be assigned to them by the First Lord."
68. Gladstone to Goschen (Copy), 16 September 1871, Gladstone Papers, BL, 44540, fol. 111.
69. Gladstone to Queen Victoria (Copy), 18 December 1871, PRO: CAB41/3/48.
70. Goschen to Gladstone, 19 September 1871, Gladstone Papers, BL, 44161, fols. 177–82.
71. Gladstone to Goschen (Copy), 23 September 1871, ibid., 44540, fol. 119.
72. Goschen to Gladstone, 29 September 1871, ibid., 44161, fol. 184.

73. "Navy Estimates," *Parl. Papers*, 1870, 44: 5; 1871, 40: 5; 1872, 39: 5. Aside from the increase resulting from the vote of credit, the estimates for 1870–71 also bore a surplus of £120,000 caused by the cost of pensions in implementing Childers' retirement scheme for the officer corps.

74. *Hansard*, 3rd ser., 210 (1872), col. 460.

75. Ibid., 3rd ser., 211 (1872), cols. 723–30.

76. Goschen to Gladstone, 8 July 1872, Gladstone Papers, BL, 44161, fol. 206.

77. Gladstone to Goschen (Copy), 9 July 1872, ibid., 44541, fol. 151.

78. Shaw-Lefevre to Gladstone, 7 December 1872, ibid., 44153, fols. 18–26.

79. For details on the wrangle over dockyard salaries, see William E. Gladstone (H. G. C. Matthew, ed.), *The Gladstone Diaries, with Cabinet Minutes and Prime-Ministerial Correspondence*, 8: 283. In the Cabinet meeting of 8 February 1873, Goschen carried his views in the face of considerable opposition.

80. Shaw-Lefevre to Gladstone, 7 December 1872, Gladstone Papers, BL, 44153, fols. 18–26.

81. Gladstone to Goschen (Copy), 7 November 1872, ibid., 44542, fol. 41.

82. Goschen to Gladstone, 29 January 1873, ibid., 44161, fols. 233–34. Emphasis in original.

83. *Hansard*, 3rd ser., 215 (1873), cols. 32–38.

84. Ibid., col. 38.

85. The *Times* (London), 25 March 1873, 9.

86. "Finance Accounts," *Parl. Papers*, 1859, 14: 15; 1860, 39: 155; 1861, 34: 143; 1862, 29: 115; 1863, 29: 137; 1864, 32: 117; 1865, 30: 113; 1866, 39: 111; 1867, 39: 99; 1867–68, 40: 107; 1868–69, 34: 107.

87. Gladstone to Goschen (Copy), 24 November 1873, Gladstone Papers, BL, 44542, fol. 17.

88. Gladstone to Goschen (Copies), 1 December 1873, 22 December 1873, ibid., 44542, fols. 20, 34.

89. Gladstone to Granville, 3 January 1874, ibid., 44542, fol. 44.

90. Gladstone to Granville, 8 January 1874, printed in John Morley, *Life of Gladstone*, 2: 482.

91. Ibid. See also Philip Magnus *Gladstone*, 226. Emphasis in original.

92. Goschen to Gladstone, [11?] January 1874, Gladstone Papers, BL, 44161, fol. 253.

93. Gladstone to Goschen (Copy), 17 January 1874, ibid., 44543, fol. 53.

94. Gladstone to Cardwell (Copy), 15 October 1873, ibid., 44542, fol. 198. See also Morley, *Gladstone*, 2: 483.

95. Paul Knaplund, *Gladstone's Foreign Policy*, 4.

96. Memorandum, marked "Secret," 19 January 1874, Gladstone Papers, BL, 44762, fol. 4.

97. Gladstone to Cardwell and Goschen (Copy), 22 January 1874, ibid., 44762, fol. 8.

98. Goschen to Gladstone, 22 January 1874, ibid., 44161, fol. 256.

99. Gladstone to Cardwell and Goschen (Copy), 22 January 1874, ibid., 44762, fol. 8. See also Gladstone to Queen Victoria (Copy), 21 January 1874, PRO: CAB41/6/1; George Earle Buckle, ed., *The Letters of Queen Victoria*, 2d ser., 2: 303–4; and Philip Guedalla, ed., *The Queen and Mr. Gladstone*, 1: 435–73.

100. *Gladstone Diaries*, 8: 447.

101. Ibid. See also Gladstone to Queen Victoria, 23 January 1874, PRO: CAB41/6/2, printed in Morley, 2: 485–87, and Guedalla, ed., *The Queen and Mr. Gladstone*, 441–42.

102. Magnus, *Gladstone*, 226. Magnus attributes the decision to impulsiveness and depression on Gladstone's part.

103. Morley, *Gladstone*, 2: 374.

104. C. J. Bartlett, "The Mid-Victorian Reappraisal of Naval Policy," 206.

105. Goschen to Gladstone, 19 September 1871, Gladstone Papers, BL, 44161, fol. 177. See also *Hansard*, 3rd ser., 205 (1871), cols. 694–95.

106. Bartlett, "Mid-Victorian Reappraisal," 200, 207.

107. Goschen to Gladstone, 19 September 1871, Gladstone Papers, BL, 44161, fol. 178.

108. Spencer Walpole, *The History of Twenty-Five Years*, 2: 290.

Chapter 8

1. Derby to Northcote, 5 April 1874, Iddesleigh (Northcote) Papers, BL, 50022, fol. 99.

2. Robert Blake, *Disraeli*, 517. See also George Earle Buckle, ed., *The Letters of Queen Victoria*, 2nd ser., 2: 321.

3. Lennox to Disraeli, 9 February, 6 August, and 23 August 1868: Hughenden (Disraeli) Papers, Bodleian Library, B/XX/Lx/274, 308, 309.

4. *Dictionary of National Biography*, 10: 263–64; the *Times* (London), 30 July 1877, 9.

5. Hunt to Disraeli, 9 October 1868, Hughenden (Disraeli) Papers, Bodleian Library, B/XX/Hu/41.

6. Ibid., and Hunt to Disraeli, 3 October 1867, ibid., B/XX/Hu/25.

7. Memorandum to Cabinet on the State of the Navy (Copy), April 1874, ibid., B/XX/Hu/59.

8. Remarks of Sir Alexander Milne, 3 April 1874, ibid.

9. Remarks of John Walter Tarleton, 15 April 1874, ibid. See also the comments of Lord Gilford, 18 April 1874, ibid.

10. Goschen to Milne, 8 May 1873, Milne Papers, NMM, MLN/165/5.

11. *Hansard's Parliamentary Debates*, 3rd ser., 218 (1874), cols. 867–71.

12. See also A. G. Gardiner, *Life of Sir William Harcourt*, 1: 233.

13. *Hansard*, 3rd ser., 194 (1869), col. 887; 199 (1870), cols. 916–17.

14. Ibid., 3rd ser., 218 (1874), cols. 866, 871.

15. Ibid., 3rd ser., 222 (1875), col. 1653.

16. Ibid., 3rd ser., 238 (1878), col. 1410.

17. Ibid., 3rd ser., 244 (1879), col. 557.

18. Disraeli to Queen Victoria (Copy), 24 May 1876, PRO: CAB41/7/11. See also Disraeli to Queen Victoria (Copy), 30 June 1877, ibid., CAB41/8/24; Disraeli to Queen Victoria (Copy), 14 December 1877, ibid., CAB41/9/18; letter to Queen Victoria of 10 August 1877, and "Note on Cabinet Meeting of 15 August 1877" printed in William Monypenny and George Earle Buckle, *The Life of Benjamin Disraeli, Earl of Beaconsfield*, 6: 170–72.

19. The Liberals provided an average of £90,000 a year more than the Conservatives, or about 13 percent. But their estimates for Vote 6 were also considerably below those of the Conservatives; dropping to less than £1 million three times and less than £900,000 once, while never climbing above £1.15 million. The Conservatives, on the other hand, never allotted less than £1.25 million to dockyard wages and in five of the six years they were in power, the outlay was more than £1.3 million.

20. *The Times* (London), 21 April 1874, 9.
21. Ibid., 3 April 1874, 5; 4 April 1874, 9; 22 April, 9.
22. Ibid., 21 April, 1874, 9.
23. Ibid., 25 April 1874, 9.
24. *The Standard* (London), 22 April, 1874, 4.
25. *The Times* (London), 1 May 1874, 9.
26. *Hansard*, 3rd ser., 218 (1874), cols. 1445, 1468, 1475.
27. Ibid., col. 1852.
28. *The Times* (London), 7 May 1874, 5.
29. John Henry Briggs, *Naval Administrations 1827–1892: The Experience of 65 Years*, 200.
30. *The Times* (London), 1 May 1874, 9.
31. Ibid., 7 May 1874, 5.
32. Disraeli to Queen Victoria, 10 November 1874, printed in *The Letters of Queen Victoria*, 2nd ser., 2: 356–57.
33. Gathorne Hardy (Nancy Johnson, ed.), *The Diary of Gathorne Hardy, Later Lord Cranbrook, 1866–1892: Political Selections*, 224.
34. Hunt to Disraeli, Confidential, 4 January 1875, Hughenden (Disraeli) Papers, Bodleian Library, B/XX/Hu/67.
35. Ibid. See also Northcote to Disraeli (Copy), Confidential, 28 January 1875, Iddesleigh (Northcote) Papers, BL, 55017, fol. 5.
36. *Diary of Gathorne Hardy*, 224.
37. Northcote to Disraeli (Copy), Confidential, 28 January 1875, Iddesleigh (Northcote) Papers, BL, 50017, fol. 5. Emphasis in original.
38. *Diary of Gathorne Hardy*, 226.
39. Disraeli to Queen Victoria (Copy), 14 January 1875, PRO: CAB41/6/20.
40. Ibid. See also Disraeli to Queen Victoria (Copy), 7 February 1875, ibid., PRO: CAB41/6/22.
41. Spencer Walpole, *The History of Twenty-Five Years*, 4: 364–66. See also the *Times* (London), 16 April 1875, 9.
42. *The Times* (London), 27 February 1875, 9.

Notes to Pages 161–65

43. *Hansard*, 3rd ser., 222 (1875), cols. 1644–48.
44. Memorandum on H.M. Fleet (Copy), Confidential, November 1875, Carnarvon Papers, PRO: PRO30/30/6/115, fol. 61.
45. Remarks of Sir Alexander Milne, 29 October 1875, ibid.
46. Remarks of Geoffrey Phipps Hornby, 30 October 1875, ibid.
47. Ibid., comments of Ward Hunt. Emphasis in original.
48. Hunt to Disraeli, Private, 15 December 1875, Hughenden (Disraeli) Papers, Bodleian Library, B/XX/Hu/75.
49. Northcote to Hunt (Copy), 11 October 1875, Iddesleigh (Northcote) Papers, BL, 50052, fol. 136.
50. The *Times* (London), 2 March 1876, 9.
51. *Hansard*, 3rd ser. 227 (1876), cols. 1928–30. Hunt's program was eighteen gunboats, two sloops, and six corvettes to be built by contract, plus another three sloops to be built in the dockyards and three torpedo vessels to be purchased. Geoffrey Phipps Hornby, testifying before the Hartington Commission eleven years later, claimed that part of Hunt's "minimum requirements" had been deleted without the knowledge of the Naval Lords. See *Evidence, Written and Oral, taken by the Royal Commission appointed to Enquire into the Civil and Professional Administration of the Naval and Military Departments and the Relationship of those Departments to each other and to the Treasury* (generally known as the Hartington Commission), PRO: HO73/35/3, 104.
52. The *Daily News* (London), 2 March 1876, 4.
53. The *Times* (London), 4 April 1876, 10.
54. Speech of Sir Stafford Northcote at Liverpool, 25 January 1877, printed in Andrew Lang, *Life, Letters, and Diaries of Sir Stafford Northcote, First Earl of Iddesleigh*, 2: 67.
55. The *Times* (London), 13 April 1877, 9, and 5 March 1879, 10.
56. Walpole, *History of Twenty-Five Years*, 4: 366.
57. *Hansard*, 3rd ser., 232 (1877), cols. 1810–11.
58. The *Daily News* (London), 13 March, 1877, 4.
59. For Hunt's health, see Hunt to Disraeli, 21 June 1877, Hughenden (Disraeli) Papers, Bodleian Library, B/XX/Hu/93. For the offer to Lord Sandon, see Viscount Chilston, *W. H. Smith*, 94.
60. Hunt and Disraeli were already exchanging letters regarding the state of the British Mediterranean Squadron—should its presence be needed in the East, by May 1876. See Hunt to Disraeli (with enclosures), 20 May 1876, Hughenden (Disraeli) Papers, Bodleian Library, B/XX/Hu/77, 78a, and 78c. On the Eastern Crisis of 1875–78, see Richard Millman, *The Eastern Question, 1875–1878*; R. W. Seton-Watson, *Disraeli, Gladstone, and the Eastern Question*; and B. H. Sumner, *Russia and the Balkans, 1870–1880*.
61. The *Times* (London), 13 March 1877, 9.
62. Walpole, *History of Twenty-Five Years*, 4: 369.
63. *Hansard*, 3rd ser., 238 (1878), col. 1404.
64. *Hansard*, 3rd ser., 236 (1877), index; 242 (1878), index; the *Times* (London), 4 March 1878, 10.

65. *Hansard*, 3rd ser., 237 (1878), col. 1375. For the debate, see cols. 535–85, 729–870, 926–57, 1211–30, 1326–1417.

66. Northcote to Hunt (Copy), 11 October 1875, Iddesleigh (Northcote) Papers, BL, 50052, fol. 136; *Diary of Gathorne Hardy*, 251.

67. Disraeli to Queen Victoria (Copy), 10 June 1876, PRO: CAB41/7/13.

68. Northcote to Smith (Copy), 4 November 1876, Iddesleigh (Northcote) Papers, BL, 50053, fol. 37.

69. *Hansard*, 3rd ser., 242 (1878), cols. 1567–68, index; 244 (1879), col. 557.

70. Northcote to Salisbury (Copy), 25 September 1878, Iddesleigh (Northcote) Papers, BL, 50053, fol. 124.

71. Northcote to Smith, Confidential, 1 October 1878, Hambleden (W. H. Smith) Papers, W. H. Smith Archives, Milton Hill House, Abingdon, PS6/212.

72. Northcote to Salisbury (Copy), 25 September 1878, Iddesleigh (Northcote) Papers, BL, 50053, fol. 124.

73. *Hansard*, 3rd ser., 234 (1877), col. 557.

74. The *Times* (London), 13 May, 1878, 9. See also *Hansard*, 3rd ser., 239 (1878), cols. 1757–58.

75. Included in the Treaty of Berlin's terms were reduction in size of the autonomous province of Bulgaria and the reaffirmation of the principle of closure of the Straits of Constantinople to ships of war in time of peace. In addition, by the terms of the Cyprus Convention between Britain and the Ottoman Empire the former was permitted to occupy that island and this agreement, too, was ratified at Berlin.

76. Northcote to Salisbury (Copy), 25 September 1878, Iddesleigh (Northcote) Papers, BL, 50053, fol. 124.

77. Salisbury to Northcote, 27 September 1878, ibid., 50019, fol. 120.

78. *Hansard*, 3rd ser., 244 (1879), cols. 557, 569; 242 (1878), index; 249 (1879), index.

79. Walpole, *History of Twenty-Five Years*, 4: 376. The final figure was £3.2 million. The breakdown of expenditure was: South Africa: £2,722,720; Griqualand: £222,000; Sikukuni expedition: £250,000. See "Finance Accounts," *Parl. Papers*, 1878–79, 40: 11.

80. For 1877–78, a deficit of £3,640,197; for 1878–79, a deficit of £2,241,817; for 1879–80, a deficit of £3,090,698. See "Finance Accounts," *Parl. Papers.*, 1876, 42: 9–10; 1877, 49: 10, 13; 1878, 46: 10, 13; 1878–79, 46: 10, 13; 1879–80, 40: 10, 13.

81. Walpole, *History of Twenty-Five Years*, 4: 382.

82. *Hansard*, 3rd ser., 251 (1880), col. 607.

83. The *Times* (London), 1 March 1880, 8.

84. Blake, *Disraeli*, 667–69.

85. Trevor Lloyd, *The Election of 1880*, 674.

86. The *Times* (London), 12 March 1880, 9.

87. William Gladstone, *Midlothian Speeches, 1879*, 130–57. The statement was made in the Corn Exchange Speech, delivered on 29 November 1879.

88. Disraeli to Queen Victoria (Copy), 14 January, 1875, PRO: CAB41/6/20.

Chapter 9

1. Oswyn Murray, "The Admiralty," Part VII, 476; N. A. M. Rodger quotes Murray's opinion in *The Admiralty*, 112.
2. Milne to Goschen (Copy), 13 September 1873, Milne Papers, NMM, MLN/165/5. Emphasis in the original.
3. Ibid. Milne also addressed a series of letters to his fellow Naval Lord, Admiral John Walter Tarleton, in the fall of 1873, that dealt with the burden of work and suggested redistributing duties between the First and Second Naval Lords. See Milne to Tarleton, 28 [August?] 1873, Tarleton Papers, Liverpool Record Office, 5/10, fol. 164 (microfilm copy), reel 5/7, item 122; Milne to Tarleton, n.d., ibid.
4. Goschen to Milne, 17 September [1873], Milne Papers, NMM, MLN/165/5.
5. Milne to Goschen (Draft), n.d., ibid., MLN/165/5.
6. Rodger, *The Admiralty*, 105.
7. *Hansard's Parliamentary Debates*, 3rd ser., 210 (1872), col. 183.
8. Hornby to Cooper Key (Copy), 12 October 1876, Hornby Papers, NMM, PHI/121 A(1). See also Hornby's diary entry for 13 January 1877, printed in Mary Augusta Egerton (née Hornby), *Admiral of the Fleet Sir Geoffrey Phipps Hornby, G.C.B. A Biography*, 192–95.
9. Egerton, *Phipps Hornby*, 183, 195.
10. N. A. M. Rodger, "The Dark Ages of the Admiralty," Part II, 38–39; Egerton, *Phipps Hornby*, 195–96. A similar account is found in Philip H. Colomb, *Memoir of Admiral the Right Honble Sir Astley Cooper Key, G.C.B., D.C.L., F.R.S., etc.*, 412–13.
11. Rodger, "Dark Ages," Pt. III, 125–26.
12. "First Report of the Royal Commissioners appointed to inquire into the Civil Establishments of the different offices of State at Home and Abroad; with Evidence and Appendix," *Parl. Papers*, 1887, 19: xvi.
13. "Preliminary and Further Reports (With Appendices) of the Royal Commissioners appointed to enquire into the Civil and Professional Administration of the Naval and Military Departments and the Relation of those Departments to each other and to the Treasury" (generally known as the Hartington Commission), *Parl. Papers*, 1890, 19: viii–xii.
14. Murray, "The Admiralty," Part VII, 465–66, 477.
15. See Stanley Sandler, "'In Deference to Public Opinion': The Loss of H.M.S. *Captain*," 61–62; Norman McCord, "A Naval Scandal of 1871: The Loss of H.M.S. *Megaera*," 118; and Rodger, "Dark Ages," Part I, 343–44.
16. Seymour to Milne, Private, 5 July 1870, Milne Papers, NMM, MLN/165/11.
17. Dacres to Milne, January 1870, ibid., MLN/165/3. In a letter of late 1869 he also stated that he had "a multiplicity of work on my shoulders[:] I have been unable to do anything but the 'drudgery' work of the office." (Dacres to Milne, n.d. [late 1869], ibid.)
18. "Report from the Select Committee of the House of Lords on the Board

of Admiralty; Together with the Proceedings of the Committee, Minutes of Evidence, and Appendix" (generally known as the Somerset Committee), *Parl. Papers*, 1871, 7: 8, 27, 39, 104.

19. John Henry Briggs, *Naval Administrations 1827–1892: The Experience of 65 Years*, 187.

20. Dacres to Milne, n.d. [late 1869], Milne Papers, NMM, MLN/165/3.

21. "Somerset Committee Report," *Parl. Papers*, 1871, 7: 30.

22. Memorandum to the Cabinet by Goschen (Copy), Confidential, 6 March 1872, Gladstone Papers, BL, 44161, fols. 197, 201.

23. "Somerset Committee Report," *Parl. Papers*, 1871, 7: 11. Lushington had no first-hand acquaintance with the old system, having been appointed in mid-1869, a fact which he admitted to the Committee. He was, however, in close contact with many who had been employed prior to Childers' reforms.

24. Rodger, "Dark Ages," Part I, 337.

25. "Somerset Committee Report," *Parl. Papers*, 1871, 7: 34, 50, 51, 92–93; "Report of the Commissioners appointed to inquire into the case of H.M.S. '*Megaera*,' together with Minutes of Evidence and Appendix (generally known as the *Megaera* Commission), *Parl. Papers*, 1872, 15: 508.

26. "Somerset Committee Report," *Parl. Papers*, 1871, 7: 8, 13, 111.

27. Briggs, *Naval Administrations*, 189.

28. "Somerset Committee Report," *Parl. Papers*, 1871, 7: ix.

29. The *Times* (London), 18 February 1871, 9.

30. Ibid., 5 July 1871, 9. The debate in the Lords took place on 3 July and is found in *Hansard*, 3rd ser., 207 (1871), cols. 963–76.

31. Childers, it appears, was solely responsible for insisting that the First Lord's supremacy be explicitly acknowledged by the order in council of January 1869, and it was certainly he who devised the office of financial secretary. Likewise, the tripartite division of business was his innovation, although it would logically have followed once the controller had charge of all matters relating to matériel and Edward Baxter had been assigned the task of overseeing finance.

32. "Somerset Committee Report," *Parl. Papers*, 1871, 7: 41–42.

33. Memorandum by Spencer Robinson, 1867, printed in ibid., 45–49.

34. "*Megaera* Commission Report," *Parl. Papers*, 1872, 15: 501.

35. Although Childers made these remarks on 27 January 1872, by which point his system had been pilloried inside and outside Parliament, he and Spencer Robinson had been at loggerheads for more than a year, and his promotion of the controller to board membership was about to be reversed by Goschen, he nonetheless maintained that the controller's memorandum of 1867 was "a most admirable statement of the faults which then existed in the system."(501) It hardly seems likely, therefore, that Childers was attempting to shift the blame for the system's apparent failure to Spencer Robinson.

36. The *Times* (London), 20 April 1871, 9.

37. See Sandler, "In Deference to Public Opinion," 61; McCord,

"*Megaera*," 118–19; Rodger, "Dark Ages,: Part I, 338; idem, *The Admiralty*, 109–10.

38. The *Times*, 23 January 1871, 9.
39. Briggs, *Naval Administrations*, 191.
40. *United Service Gazette* (London), 25 March 1871, 4. Spencer Robinson testified before Somerset's Committee on 13 March.
41. The worst that Dacres appears to have written about his superior was that he was stubborn. See Dacres to Milne, January 1870, Milne Papers, NMM, MLN/165/3. Likewise, there is no indication in any of Beauchamp Seymour's letters to Milne that he had any problems in his dealings with Childers. See Seymour to Milne, ibid., MLN/165/11, *passim*.
42. Briggs, *Naval Administrations*, 190–93.
43. The *Times* (London), 20 April 1871, 9.
44. Briggs, *Naval Administrations*, 188–89.
45. "Somerset Committee Report," *Parl. Papers*, 1871, 7: 64–66.
46. The *Times* (London), 20 April 1871, 9; see also 3 February 1872, 9.
47. Draft minute by Milne on "Proposals by Spencer Robinson," [1867], Milne Papers, NMM, MLN/165/11. With Milne's views presumably conveyed to Pakington and Corry, it is hardly surprising that neither saw fit to act on Spencer Robinson's proposal. Childers, on the other hand, evidently never perceived the outcome Milne sketched.
48. *Hansard*, 3rd ser., 267 (1882), col. 446.
49. Leslie Gardiner, *The British Admiralty*, 283.
50. Northbrook to Algernon West, 12 October 1870, Gladstone Papers, 44266, fol. 21.
51. "*Megaera* Commission Report," *Parl. Papers*, 1872, 15: 502.
52. Murray, "The Admiralty," Part VII, 476.
53. Rodger, "Dark Ages," Part II, 46; Part III, 128.
54. Alexander Milne (1872–76); Hastings Yelverton (1876–77); George Wellesley (1877–79), and Astley Cooper Key (1879–85).
55. Colomb, *Cooper Key*, 413; see also Rodger, *The Admiralty*, 113.
56. Bryan Ranft, "The Protection of British Seaborne Trade and the Development of Systematic Planning for War, 1860–1906," idem ed., *Technical Change and British Naval Policy, 1860–1939*, 7; *Dictionary of National Biography: 1901–1911 Supplement*, 293.
57. Bernard Mallet, *Thomas George, Earl of Northbrook, G.C.S.I. A Memoir*, 151.
58. The *Times* (London), 13 July 1871, 9.
59. Ibid., 5 July 1871, 9.
60. "Somerset Committee Report," *Parl. Papers*, 1871, 7: xi.
61. Sandler, "In Deference to Public Opinion," 61–62; Rodger, "Dark Ages," Part I, 341–43; idem, *The Admiralty*, 111–12.
62. Memorandum for the Cabinet by Goschen (Copy), Confidential, 6 March 1872, Gladstone Papers, BL, 44161, fol. 197.
63. For a recent enunciation of this interpretation, see C. I. Hamilton, *Anglo-French Naval Rivalry, 1840–1870*, 264–66. Hamilton writes, "[I]n

certain regards," Childers' reforms "were salutary, above all in the way they divided administration on functional lines, distinguishing between personnel, *matériel* and finances. Moreover, Childers was responsible for physically concentrating the London offices, certainly long overdue. Departmental heads were given slightly more authority than previously, satisfying some complaints." Yet he adds that otherwise, Childers' reform "had been misconceived from the very beginning.... He moved in quite the wrong direction. Instead of developing the Admiralty brain, he lobotomized it."

64. *Hansard*, 3rd ser., 171 (1863), col. 1402. The thirteen branches to which Hay alluded were 1. manning the navy, 2. discipline, 3. construction, marine engines and dockyards, 4. public works, docks, 5. paymaster or accountant-general, 6. storekeeper general, 7. victualling, 8. ordnance, 9. medical, 10. hydrographical, 11. marines, 12. coast guard, 13. transport board.

65. The *Times* (London), 20 April 1871, 9.
66. Ibid., 21 March 1872, 9.
67. Ibid., 18 February, 1871, 9.
68. "First Report of Civil Establishments Commission," *Parl. Papers*, 1887, 19: xv.
69. Briggs, *Naval Administrations*, 189; Rodger, "Dark Ages," Part I, 342.
70. Memorandum to the Cabinet by Goschen (Copy), Confidential, 6 March 1872, Gladstone Papers, BL, 44161, fol. 198. It should be added that the controller could not vote at the board when present, although Spencer Robinson's experience of being outvoted by the First Lord and First Naval Lord over the designs of frigates in 1870 suggests this rule was of little practical significance. See also *Hansard*, 3rd ser., 210 (1872), cols. 206–8 for Goschen's explanation of his changes.
71. Murray, "The Admiralty, Part VII," 478. For his assessment of Childers, see 470–75.
72. The *Times* (London), 19 March 1872, 9.
73. Briggs, *Naval Administrations*, 193–94.

Chapter 10

1. Paul Kennedy, *The Rise and Fall of British Naval Mastery*, 156–57.
2. For a recent articulation, see Robert K. Massie, *Dreadnought*, xiii. For similar statements, see R. R. Palmer and Joel Colton, *A History of the Modern World*, 6th ed., 395, and Michael Lewis, "Armed Forces and the Art of War: Navies," *The New Cambridge Modern History, Vol. 10: The Zenith of European Power*, 274.
3. Oscar Parkes, *British Battleships, 1860–1950*, 232.
4. N. A. M. Rodger, "The Dark Ages of the Admiralty," Part I, 331; Roger Chesneau and Eugene M. Kolesnik, eds., *Conway's All the World's Fighting Ships, 1860–1905*, 282.
5. C. J. Bartlett, "The Mid-Victorian Reappraisal of Naval Policy," 189; Paul Kennedy, *The Rise and Fall of the Great Powers*, 153.
6. The *Times* (London), 21 April 1874, 9.

7. In 1866–67 the army and navy combined consumed 61.6 percent of nondebt outlays; in 1870–71, 53.3 percent; 1874–75, 52.6 percent; 1876–77, 51.6 percent; and in 1879–80, 46.4 percent.

8. The *Times* (London), 21 April 1874, 9.

9. The statistical data that follows are drawn from *Conway's*, 7–29, 360–74, 380–81, 387, 401, 405–6, 410–11, 418–19.

10. Lawrence Sondhaus, *The Habsburg Empire and the Sea: Austrian Naval Policy, 1779–1866*, 266–67; idem, *The Naval Policy of Austria-Hungary, 1867–1918: Navalism, Industrial Development, and the Politics of Dualism*, 20–28, 35–69; Anthony E. Sokol, *The Imperial and Royal Austro-Hungarian Navy*, 57.

11. *Conway's*, 389.

12. *Hansard's Parliamentary Debates*, 3rd ser., 227 (1876), col. 1897.

13. *Conway's*, 242. See also Holger Herwig, *"Luxury" Fleet: The Imperial German Navy 1880–1918*, 12.

14. *Conway's*, 243–45.

15. Frederick Martin, ed., *The Statesman's Yearbook: A Statistical and Historical Account of the States of the Civilized World*, 1881: 104.

16. The *Times* (London), 22 September 1874, 7.

17. On Anglo-German relations during the 1860s and 1870s see Paul Kennedy, *Rise of Anglo-German Antagonism, 1860–1914*.

18. Herwig, *"Luxury' Fleet*, 13.

19. *Statesman's Yearbook*, 1881: 313–14.

20. *Conway's*, 339–40.

21. Parkes, *British Battleships*, 244. Parkes terms the *Duilio* and the *Dandolo*, along with Dupuy de Lome's *Gloire* and Fisher's *Dreadnought*, "the most provocative capital ships ever built."

22. J. W. King, *European Ships of War and Their Armament, Naval Administration, etc.*, 156.

23. Parkes, *British Battleships*, 283. By the time they had been completed the lack of horizontal protection had become a serious drawback, owing to the appearance of the high explosive shell. Mostly for this reason, the ships had been superseded by the time they were commissioned.

24. John Ericsson to the *Times* (London), 31 March 1862, cited in *Hansard*, 3rd ser., 166 (1862), col. 270.

25. These were two ironclads built at Birkenhead for the Confederacy. The *Alabama*, similarly, had been constructed in a British shipyard, but following the latter's depredations the U.S. minister to Great Britain, Charles Francis Adams, threatened that should the British government allow the Confederates to take possession of the Laird ships it would mean war between the United States and Britain. The vessels were eventually bought by the Royal Navy, which found them manifestly unsatisfactory.

26. *Conway's*, 119. The *Monitor's* freeboard was "only 14 in when fully laden," although "waves washing over the low hull served to limit rolling." As for conditions below, "Even with the blowers running and hatches open,

178°F in the engine room and 120°F in the berth deck were recorded in the summer of 1862."

27. *Hansard*, 3rd ser, 166 (1862), col. 441.
28. Ian Hogg and John Batchelor, *Naval Gun*, 52, 65.
29. Ward to Admiralty, 4 July 1870, PRO: ADM1/6169. By mid-1870 the naval attaché in Washington, Captain Ward, could report that although the U.S. ironclad fleet numbered 51, no more than a handful of those vessels were fit for service.
30. Kennedy, *Great Powers*, 251.
31. Spencer Robinson to Admiralty, 22 January 1870, PRO: ADM1/6177.
32. Remarks of Edward J. Reed, printed in ibid.
33. See N. A. M. Rodger, "The Design of the *Inconstant*," 9–22.
34. Inglefield to Admiralty, 20 April 1872, PRO: ADM1/6255.
35. Gore Jones to Admiralty, 4 January 1875, PRO: ADM1/6351. This report is confirmed in the following year's *Statesman's Yearbook*, which lists the U.S. ironclad fleet at twenty-seven. See *The Statesman's Yearbook*, 1876: 580.
36. Cited in *The Statesman's Yearbook*, 1874: 575–76.
37. *The Statesman's Yearbook*, 1870: 378; 1878: 382; *Conway's*, 173–77, 186.
38. Goodenough to Admiralty, 6 January 1871, PRO: ADM1/6198.
39. Remarks of Barnaby in ibid. Goodenough and Barnaby counted twenty-nine Russian ironclads, rather than the twenty-four listed in *The Statesman's Yearbook*.
40. Many naval historians see the *Devastation* as "the genesis of the modern capital ship," to use Stanley Sandler's description.
41. *Hansard*, 3rd ser., 215 (1873), col. 44.
42. King, *European Ships of War*, 167.
43. Goodenough to Admiralty, 6 January 1871, PRO: ADM1/6198.
44. *Hansard*, 3rd ser., 244 (1879), col. 609; see also Hood to Admiralty, [18]78, NMM: ADM138/47.
45. Foreign Office to Admiralty, PRO: ADM1/6456 and 6457, *passim*.
46. Donald Mitchell, *A History of Russian and Soviet Sea Power*, 178–97.
47. Theodore Ropp (Stephen Roberts, ed.), *The Development of a Modern Navy*, 10.
48. France laid down several ironclads in 1865–66, but most were small, thinly armored vessels designed for service on foreign stations rather than as units of the battlefleet.
49. Pakington to Derby, Confidential, 7 February 1867, Derby Papers, Liverpool Record Office, 920 DER, 141/12; for a judicious modern assessment, see Stanley Sandler, *The Emergence of the Modern Capital Ship*, 59.
50. Twenty-five seagoing British ironclads labored under the same disadvantage, be it noted. Only one, however, was routinely included in assessments of front-line British battlefleet strength during the 1870s. The early French ironclads, by contrast, continued to be counted as part of the battlefleet even into the 1880s.

51. *Hansard*, 3rd ser., 215 (1873), cols. 44–45.
52. Goodenough to Admiralty, 3 January 1872, PRO: ADM1/6238.
53. France, Ministère de la Marine et des Colonies, *Revue Maritime et Coloniale*, 28 (1869): 456–57. At the same time French naval expenditure was tailing off the number of overseas services demanded of the navy was on the rise. In 1862, for instance, the original credits voted for the navy amounted to 126,015,419 francs, whereas the sum expended reached 206,989,919 francs. Part of the excess was attributable to naval reconstruction ("transformation de la flotte"), but also imperial operations in China, Indochina, and Mexico also drove up sending. From 1862 through 1867 each of these theaters witnessed French naval activity.
54. Ropp. *Development of a Modern Navy*, 31; see also Arthur J. Marder, *The Anatomy of British Sea Power: British Naval Policy in the Pre-Dreadnought Era*, 20.
55. Gladstone to Granville (Copy), 3 January 1874, Gladstone Papers, BL, 44542, fol. 44.
56. Goschen to Milne, 8 May 1873, Milne Papers, NMM, MLN/165/5.
57. Spalding to Admiralty, 25 September 1872, PRO: ADM1/6214.
58. Hall's remarks on the *Report of the Committee on Designs of Ships of War*, 26 July 1871, PRO: ADM1/6212.
59. *Conway's*, 286–91.
60. Ibid., 15–25.
61. *Hansard*, 3rd ser., 215 (1873), col. 46.
62. Shaw-Lefevre to Admiralty, 1 August 1881, PRO: ADM1/6608.
63. Remarks of Nathaniel Barnaby in ibid.
64. Thomas Brassey, ed., *Naval Annual*, 1888: 583–86, 684–87.

French and British Forces in Commission, 1887

	Britain	France
Ironclads	26	7
Cruisers	50	21
Gunvessels	12	—
Gunboats	24	33
Dispatch Vessels	2	34
Schooners	—	4
Others	7	2
Total	121	101

Chapter 11

1. See N. A. M. Rodger, *The Admiralty*, 99–105; Bryan Ranft, "The Protection of British Seaborne Trade and the Development of Systematic Planning for War," idem ed., *Technical Change and British Naval Policy, 1860–1939*, 4; D. C. Gordon, *The Dominion Partnership in Imperial Defence, 1870–1914*, xi, 46–50.

2. Ranft, "Protection of British Seaborne Trade," 1.

3. Theodore Ropp's *Development of a Modern Navy* is a noteworthy exception to this tendency.

4. See especially Howard Douglas, *Observations on Modern Systems of Fortification*, 191.

5. I. F. Clarke, *Voices Prophesying War*, 22–29.

6. Arthur Marder, *The Anatomy of British Sea Power: A History of British Naval Policy in the Pre-Dreadnought Era*, 107; John Beeler, "Steam, Strategy, and Schurman: Imperial Defence in the Post-Crimean Era, 1856–1905," Greg Kennedy and Keith Neilson, eds., *Far Flung Lines*, 31.

7. Marder, *Anatomy of British Sea Power*, 108–9.

8. Ibid., 107–12. See also Theodore Ropp (Stephen Roberts, ed.), *The Development of a Modern Navy*, 155–80, esp. 161, and Paul Kennedy, *The Rise and Fall of British Naval Mastery*, 199.

9. Great Britain, *Statistical Abstract for the United Kingdom*, 23 (1876): 96; 37 (1890): 157. In 1861 total British sailing merchant tonnage was 3,918,511 tons, while steamers accounted for only 441,184 tons. A decade later the figures were 4,343,588 tons sailing ships and 1,290,003 steamers. As late as 1878 there were more than twice as many tons of sailing vessels as steamers (4,138,149 to 1,977,489), but thereafter the gap narrowed very rapidly, and by 1883 steamers had achieved parity (3,369,959 sailing tons to 3,656,103 steaming). By the end of the decade steamers had moved decisively ahead (2,976,346 tons sailing ships, 4,664,808 tons steamers).

10. Rodger, *The Admiralty*, 105.

11. Douglas, *Modern Systems of Fortification*, 191.

12. "Augmentation of the Naval Force, in Ships and Stores" (Copy), 9 August 1870, PRO: ADM1/6159.

13. Remarks of Dacres on the design of H.M.S. *Glatton*, 12 December 1871, NMM, ADM138/64.

14. Andrew Lambert, "The Royal Navy, 1856–1914: Deterrence and the Strategy of World Power," 13. I am indebted to Dr. Lambert for permission to cite his unpublished paper.

15. Stanley Sandler, *The Emergence of the Modern Capital Ship*, 87–88.

16. Donald M. Schurman, *The Education of a Navy: The Development of British Naval Strategic Thought, 1867–1914*, 3–5.

17. N. A. M. Rodger, "The Design of the *Inconstant*," 12–22.

18. N. A. M. Rodger, "British Belted Cruisers," *passim*.

19. "Paper Relative to Unarmored Ships, and Proposal for an Establishment" (Copy), Confidential, December, 1874, Milne Papers, NMM, MLN/144/3/1.

20. "Third and Final Report of the Royal Commissioners Appointed to Inquire into the Defence of British Possessions and Commerce Abroad" (Generally known as the Carnarvon Commission), Confidential, 1882, Milne Papers, NMM, MLN/163/12; "Paper Relative to Unarmored Ships, and Proposal for an Establishment" (Copy), Confidential, December, 1874, ibid., MLN/144/3/1.

Notes to Pages 219–23

21. See K. T. Rowland, *Steam at Sea: A History of Steam Navigation*, 105–30; A. E. Seaton, *A Manual of Marine Engineering: Comprising the Designing, Construction, and Working of Marine Machinery*, 228–29.

22. Bernard Semmel, *Liberalism and Naval Strategy: Ideology, Interest and Sea Power during the Pax Britannica*, 56–59.

23. Marder, *Anatomy of British Sea Power*, 89.

24. Kennedy, *Naval Mastery*, 199.

25. Goschen to Milne, 8 June 1873, Milne Papers, NMM, MLN/165/5.

26. Ranft, "Protection of British Seaborne Trade," 2.

27. Hood to Milne, Confidential, 5 February 1873, Milne Papers, NMM, MLN/144/1/3.

28. "Paper Relative to Unarmoured Ships, and Proposal for an Establishment" (Copy), December 1874, ibid., MLN/144/3/1.

29. "Position of Cruising Ships for Protection of Trade" (Copy), December 1874, ibid., MLN/144/3/1. A year later he produced yet another memorandum on the subject: "Unarmoured Ships" (Copy), Confidential, 11 November 1875, ibid., MLN/144/4/2.

30. Ranft, "Protection of British Seaborne Trade," 3.

31. "The Protection of Commerce by Patrolling the Ocean Highways and by Convoy," Foreign Intelligence Committee Papers, Ministry of Defence Library, cited in ibid., 6.

32. Ranft, 3.

33. Goschen Minute on Design of H.M.S. *Shannon*, 7 April 1873, ADM138/43, fol. 22; Rodger, "Design of *Inconstant*," 19; Roger Chesneau and Eugene M. Kolesnik, eds., *Conway's All the World's Fighting Ships, 1860–1905*, 46–57, 308, 315–19.

34. Rodger, "Belted Cruisers," 24–26.

35. Ibid., 26; *Conway's*, 63. The *General Admiral* and *Gertzog Edinburghski* had six 8" guns, 6" armor, and were designed to steam at 13 1/2 knots with a cruising range of 6,000 miles at 10 knots. The *Shannon* had two 10" and six 8" guns, 6–9" armor, steamed at 12.25 knots, and had a far smaller cruising radius under steam.

36. The *General Admiral* attained only 12.3 knots, the *Gertzog Edinburghski* 13.2 knots.

37. Ropp, *Development of a Modern Navy*, 88; Rodger, "The Dark Ages of the Admiralty," Part II, 43.

38. Rodger, "Belted Cruisers," 24. Any Russian cruiser attempting to operate in the Baltic, where British trade was extensive, would have been hunted down with relative ease, being circumscribed by the surrounding landmass. For that matter, Russian egress on the Baltic was frozen for much of the year too.

39. Rodger, "Design of *Inconstant*," 10–12; *Conway's*, 124, 150.

40. *Conway's*, 251, 275, 345.

41. Sidney Pollard and Paul Robertson, *The British Shipbuilding Industry, 1870–1914*, 6–7.

42. *First Report of the Royal Commission appointed to make Enquiry*

into the Condition and Sufficiency of the Means of the Naval and Military Forces provided for the Defence of the more important Sea-ports within our Colonial Possessions and Dependencies (generally known as the Carnarvon Commission), 9 July 1881, Carnarvon Papers, PRO: PRO30/6/131.

43. See, for instance "Unarmoured Ships" (Copy), Confidential, 11 November 1875, Milne Papers, NMM, MLN/144/4/2; "Paper Relative to Unarmoured Ships, and Proposal for an Establishment" (Copy), Confidential, December 1874, ibid., MLN/144/3/1; Milne to Ward Hunt, 29 October 1874, ibid., MLN/144/2/5.

44. Thomas Brassey, ed., *Naval Annual*, 1889: 231.

45. Marder, *Anatomy of British Sea Power*, 86.

46. Schurman's *The Education of a Navy* is a noteworthy exception. See esp. 2–6.

47. Rodger, "Dark Ages, Part III," 127–28.

48. Mark Shulman, *Navalism and the Emergence of American Sea Power, 1882–1893*, 96.

49. Ibid., 117–19, 158.

50. Ropp, *Development of a Modern Navy*, 28.

51. Ivo Lambi, *The Navy and German Power Politics, 1862–1914*, 7.

52. Ropp, *Development of a Modern Navy*, 30.

53. *Conway's*, 251. Germany built nine unarmored iron corvettes during the 1870s and the navy possessed another nine wooden vessels built prior to unification.

54. Lambi, *The Navy and German Power Politics*, 91–112.

55. *Conway's*, 173–77.

56. Ropp's *Development of a Modern Navy* remains the best English-language treatment of the Italian and Russian navies in the 1870s and 1880s. The following paragraphs are based largely on his work, 77–87.

57. Ibid., 88.

58. Ibid., 80.

59. On the policies of Brin and Saint Bon, see Ropp, *Development of a Modern Navy*, 79; and *Conway's*, 336.

60. Ropp, *Development of a Modern Navy*, 81.

61. Ibid., 84.

62. *Conway's*, 345–47.

63. Again, this section is drawn largely from Ropp's analysis, 20–21, 107–9, 155–80, 212, 362, and *Conway's*, 316–19.

64. Marder, *Anatomy of British Sea Power*, 87.

65. Ropp, *Development of a Modern Navy*, 178, 180.

66. Hugh Lyon, "The Relations Between the Admiralty and Private Industry in the Development of Warships," Bryan Ranft, ed., *Technical Change and British Naval Policy, 1860–1939*, 58.

67. "Report of the Committee appointed by the Lords Commissioners of the Admiralty to examine the Designs on which Ships of War have Recently been Constructed, with Analysis of Evidence" (generally known as Dufferin's Committee), *Parl. Papers*, 1872, 14: xiv.

68. Sandler, *Modern Capital Ship*, 165–66.

Chapter 12

1. Arthur Marder, *The Anatomy of British Sea Power: A History of British Naval Policy in the Pre-Dreadnought Era, 1880–1905*, 44–61.
2. Quoted in I. F. Clarke, *Voices Prophesying War*, 31–36.
3. Ibid., 34–36. The bulk of the fleet was sent "on a fool's errand to the Dardanelles" and the remainder was sunk by "secret weapons," evidently torpedoes.
4. The *Times* (London), 13 March 1877, 9.
5. *Hansard's Parliamentary Debates*, 3rd ser., 169 (1863), col. 698.
6. *Evidence, Written and Oral, taken by the Royal Commission appointed to Enquire into the Civil and Professional Administration of the Naval and Military Departments and the Relationship of those Departments to each other and to the Treasury* (generally known as the Hartington Commission), Strictly Confidential, PRO: HO73/35/3, p. 7.
7. B. R. Mitchell and Phyllis Deáne, *Abstract of British Historical Statistics*, 393–94. Even when Northcote raised the income tax to 5 pence in the pound it, along with property tax, produced only £8.7 million out of a total of £81.2 million.
8. William E. Gladstone, *Midlothian Speeches, 1879*, 137.
9. "Hartington Commission Report," PRO: HO73/35/3, p. 7.
10. Arthur D. Elliot, *The Life of George Joachim, First Viscount Goschen 1831–1907*, I: 141.
11. Freda Harcourt, "Disraeli's Imperialism, 1866–1868: A Question of Timing," 87–109.
12. The *Times* (London), 30 July 1877, 9; Oscar Parkes, *British Battleships, 1860–1950*, 230. For a further assessment in the same vein, see N. A. M. Rodger, "The Dark Ages of the Admiralty," Part II, 34.
13. Parkes, *British Battleships*, 230.
14. The *Times* (London), 30 July 1877, 9.
15. Hunt to Disraeli, 15 October 1875, Hughenden (Disraeli) Papers, Bodleian Library, B/XX/Hu/72.
16. Houston Stewart to Milne, 29 January 1882, Milne Papers, NMM, MLN/165/12.
17. *Dictionary of National Biography*, 18: 567.
18. The *Times* (London), 31 December 1878, 3.
19. Ibid., 1 March 1880, 8.
20. Foreign Office to Admiralty, 15 November 1877, PRO: ADM1/6424. To a report by naval attaché Captain Nicholson on the French Navy in late 1877, Controller Houston Stewart added a minute that stated that the French "are rapidly going ahead of us, and unless it is decided to lay down *12 Armoured Battle Ships* to be completed by the end of 1881, that year will find the Navy of France decidedly superior to that of Great Britain in ships & guns, as it undoubtedly is at present in the number and quality of *Trained* Seamen."

Similar pronouncements were recorded by Second Sea Lord Sir Arthur Hood and First Sea Lord Sir George Wellesley, but Smith's sole comment was "a very interesting paper." The votes for matériel were not increased in the following year's navy estimates, no new ironclads were laid down in 1877–78, and only one in 1878–79.

21. For a differing assessment, see Rodger, "Dark Ages," Part I, 331–44.
22. *Hansard*, 3rd ser., 210 (1872), col. 450.
23. Richard Cobden, *The Three Panics, An Historical Episode*, 135–38.
24. *Hansard*, 3rd ser., 211 (1872), col. 729.
25. Ibid., 3rd ser., 215 (1873), col. 45.
26. "Hartington Commission Report," PRO: HO73/35/3, p. 7.
27. Parkes, *British Battleships*, 212–13, 267–80.
28. The *Times* (London), 4 April 1867, 9; also ibid., 1 June 1870, 9, and 12 May 1868, 9.
29. He again served in the office during the third Salisbury administration, this time much more in sympathy with the navalist viewpoint, not surprising given the change in public and political sentiments regarding the service after 1889.
30. Memorandum on Her Majesty's Navy, Remarks of Alexander Milne (Copy), 3 April 1874, Hughenden (Disraeli) Papers, Bodleian Library, B/XX/Hu/59.
31. *First Report of the Royal Commission appointed to make Enquiry into the Condition and Sufficiency of the Means of the Naval and Military Forces provided for the Defence of the more important Sea-ports within our Colonial Possessions and Dependencies* (generally known as the Carnarvon Commission), 9 July 1881, Carnarvon Papers, PRO: PRO30/6/131.
32. "Hartington Commission Report," PRO: HO73/35/3.
33. Ibid., 107.
34. Rodger, "Dark Ages," Part I, 331; Richard Millman, *British Policy and the Coming of the Franco-Prussian War*, 151; C. J. Bartlett, "The Mid-Victorian Reappraisal of Naval Policy," 207.
35. Rodger, "Dark Ages," Part III, 127; Bartlett, "Mid-Victorian Reappraisal," 207.
36. Rodger, "Dark Ages," Part III, 127.
37. Thomas Brassey, "On Unarmoured Vessels," *Transactions of the Institute of Naval Architects* 17 (1876): 14.
38. B. R. Mitchell, *Abstract of European Historical Statistics*, 2nd rev. ed., 420. German steel production surpassed British output by 1893. Sidney Pollard and Paul Robertson, *The British Shipbuilding Industry, 1870–1914*, 45.
39. Foreign Office to Admiralty, 4 July 1870, PRO: ADM1/6169. An intelligence report revealed that of the fifty-one monitors on the U.S. navy list, no fewer than thirty-four were under 1,000 tons and only seven of more than 3,000 tons. Moreover, it was stated that of the latter vessels, three were "on the stocks with machinery on board but unarmoured. Said to be built of Green timber; . . . a fourth did not even have the machinery on board, and a

fifth was simply labelled 'incomplete.'" And a whole class of twelve of 773 tons were dismissed out of hand: "This class of monitors are acknowledged failures. They have never carried their intended armament." Even Spencer Robinson, never one to understate a threat from abroad, acknowledged the "amount of failure, very considerable in many cases, that has attended the efforts of the U.S. to produce a fast and powerfully armed navy."

40. Derby to Disraeli (Copy), Confidential, 30 January [1868], Derby Papers, Liverpool Record Office, 920 DER (14), 193/1, fols. 199–202.

41. Britain lacked any organization akin to a naval reserve until the French invasion scare of 1859 prompted the formation of such a body. Prior to that date political leaders hoped that the fleet could be manned by volunteers in the event of a crisis, but continued to regard impressment as a possibility under extreme circumstances.

42. Theodore Ropp (Stephen Roberts, ed.), *The Development of a Modern Navy*, 40.

43. Roger Chesneau and Eugene M. Kolesnik, eds., *Conway's All the World's Fighting Ships, 1860–1905*, 186, 284, 308; Ropp, *Development of a Modern Navy*, 87.

44. George Modelski and William R. Thompson, *Seapower in Global Politics, 1494–1993*, 78.

45. William James, *The Naval History of Great Britain from the Declaration of War by France in 1793, to the Accession of George IV*, 3: 504–5.

46. John C. D. Hay, *Lines From My Logbooks*, 248.

47. Goschen to Milne, 8 April 1873, Milne Papers, NMM, MLN/165/5.

48. Paul Kennedy, "The Tradition of Appeasement in British Foreign Policy, 1865–1939," idem ed., *Strategy and Diplomacy, 1870–1945. Eight Studies*, 18.

49. Milne once claimed he "by no means advocate[d] any large expenditure of public money" when pushing a characteristic demand for more ships, but there is no indication that any of his numerous recommendations were based primarily upon considerations of economy. See Memorandum on Her Majesty's Navy (Copy), Remarks of Milne, 3 April 1874, Hughenden (Disraeli) Papers, Bodleian Library, B/XX/Hu/59.

50. The *Times* (London), 13 March 1877, 9; see also ibid., 16 March 1878, 9.

51. See Bartlett, "Mid-Victorian Reappraisal," 207–8, and Rodger, "Dark Ages," Part II, 38.

Chapter 13

1. Arthur Marder, *The Anatomy of British Sea Power: A History of British Naval Policy in the Pre-Dreadnought Era, 1880–1905*, 59.

2. Gladstone to Northbrook, *Private*, 31 May 1880 (Copy), Gladstone Papers, BL, 44543, fol. 14.

3. *Hansard's Parliamentary Debates*, 3rd ser., 251 (1880), col. 607.

4. Gladstone to Childers, *Private*, 31 May 1880 (Copy), Gladstone Papers, BL, 44543, fol. 14.

5. Minute by Lord Northbrook (Printed), July 1885, PRO: ADM1/7465c. See also *Hansard*, 3rd ser., 252 (1880), cols. 1383-95 for Shaw-Lefevre's speech.

6. *Hansard*, 3rd ser., 277 (1883), col. 602.

7. Ibid., col. 613. See also Smith's remarks in ibid., 3rd ser., 273, (1882), cols. 416, 418, and those of Northbrook, ibid., 3rd ser., 272 (1882), col. 846.

8. The *Times* (London), 19 March 1881, 11. See also 13 September 1884, 9.

9. Gladstone to Northbrook, 15 December 1880 (copy), Gladstone Papers, BL, 44544, fol. 112.

10. Ibid. Gladstone added, "I doubt any member of the Cabinet [would] wish it reduced."

11. *Hansard*, 3rd ser., 277 (1883), col. 599; 286 (1884), col. 363.

12. B. R. Mitchell, *British Historical Statistics*, 588. The remaining yearly figures were: 1881-82, £80.6 million; 1882-83, £83.3 million. These figures depict spending, rather than the estimates given in the yearly budgets. The analogous figures for the navy are: 1880-81, £10.2 million; 1881-82, £10.5 million; 1882-83, £10.6 million; 1883-84, £10.3 million; 1884-85, £10.7 million.

13. *Hansard*, 3rd ser., 268 (1882), cols. 1037-38, 1051.

14. Ibid., cols. 1053-64. For similar debates, see ibid., 3rd ser., 273 (1882), cols. 362-68, cols. 409-52; 278 (1883), cols. 40-52; 279 (1883), cols. 75-143; 286 (1884), cols. 336-62; 294 (1884), cols. 395-431, 448-555.

15. The *Times*, 26 April 1882, 11.

16. Ibid., 15 August 1881, 9.

17. Ibid., 3 October 1883, 9.

18. For further editorials in a similar vein, see ibid., 17 August 1881, 9; 9 December 1881, 7; 12 January 1882, 9; 8 May 1883, 9.

19. Frederic Whyte, *The Life of W. T. Stead*, 1: 146-48. Arnold-Forster first brought the topic to Stead's attention.

20. "The Truth About the Navy," *Pall Mall Gazette*, 8 September 1884, cited in John Henry Briggs, *Naval Administrations, 1827-1892: The Experience of 65 Years*, 216-17.

21. The *Times* (London), 23 September 1884.

22. Ibid., 20 October 1884, 9.

23. Ibid., 22 October 1884, 9.

24. Ibid., 12 November 1884, 9. For further editorials on the subject, see the *Times*, 27 November 1884, 9; 2 December 1884, 9; 17 December 1884, 9; 26 December 1884, 7; 19 February 1885, 9; 12 March 1885, 9.

25. Campbell-Bannerman to Childers, 2 October 1884, cited in J. A. Spender, *The Life of the Right Hon. Sir Henry Campbell-Bannerman*, 1: 53-54.

26. *Hansard*, 3rd ser., 294 (1884), col. 448. Brassey's statement in the Commons and the ensuing debate occupy columns 448-555.

27. Ibid., col. 412. Northbrook's statement in the Lords and the ensuing debate occupy columns 395-432. This was the program as originally envi-

Notes to Pages 268–71

sioned. As carried out it was modified to two battleships (*Victoria* and *Sans Pareil*), seven belted cruisers of the *Australia* class, six torpedo cruisers of the *Archer* class, and fourteen torpedo boats. See Oscar Parkes, *British Battleships, 1860–1950*, 328.

28. Minute by Lord Northbrook (Printed), July 1885, PRO: ADM1/7465c.
29. The *Times* (London), 17 March 1885, 9–10.
30. For Beresford's actions, see Marder, *Anatomy of British Sea Power*, 133–34.
31. Briggs, *Naval Administrations*, 244.
32. Parkes, *British Battleships*, 352. For financing the provisions of the Naval Defence Act, see Jon T. Sumida, *In Defence of Naval Supremacy: Finance, Technology and British Naval Policy, 1889–1914*, 13–17.
33. All figures are drawn from Mitchell, *British Historical Statistics*, 588. The figures were: 1891–92, £15.6 million; 1892–93, £15.6 million; 1893–94, £15.7 million; 1894–95, £15.5 million; 1895–96, £17.5 million.
34. Marder, *Anatomy of British Sea Power*, 48–49.
35. Marder, *Anatomy of British Sea Power*, 16; Norman McCord, "A Naval Scandal of 1871: The Loss of H.M.S. *Megaera*," 133; A. P. Thornton, *The Imperial Idea and its Enemies: A Study in British Power*, 29–30; N. A. M. Rodger, "The Dark Ages of the Admiralty," Part I, 331; Richard Millman, *British Foreign Policy and the coming of the Franco-Prussian War*, 151; C. J. Bartlett, "The Mid-Victorian Reappraisal of Naval Policy," 207.
36. Roger Chesneau and Eugene Kolesnik, eds., *Conway's All the World's Fighting Ships, 1860–1905*, 287.
37. Hansard, 3rd ser., 286 (1884), cols. 340–41.
38. *Conway's*, 288–91.
39. The four were the *Redoutable* (completed 1878), *Amiral Duperre* (1883), *Devastation* (1882), and *Courbet*, which Hay called the *Foudroyant*, its original name, and which was two years short of completion at the time.
40. I.e., *Warrior, Black Prince, Defence, Resistance, Hector, Valiant, Achilles, Minotaur, Agincourt, Northumberland, Caledonia, Royal Oak, Royal Alfred, Zealous, Repulse, Lord Warden, Bellerophon, Sultan, Hercules, Alexandra, Temeraire, Superb, Monarch, Devastation, Thunderer, Dreadnought, Neptune, Inflexible, Ajax, Agamemnon, Swiftsure, Triumph, Audacious, Invincible, Iron Duke, Shannon, Nelson,* and *Northampton*.
41. Campbell-Bannerman to Childers, 2 October 1884, cited in Spender, *Campbell Bannerman*, 1: 54–55.
42. Hansard, 3rd ser., 286 (1884), col. 340. His list consisted of the *Caiman, Indomptable,* and *Terrible*, all of them first-class ships, and all of them at least three years from completion (Conway, 291). The remaining three were the *Tonnerre* and *Fulminant*, both complete but both strictly coastal-defense monitors, and the *Furieux*, another coastal-defense vessel which was not completed until 1887 (*Conway's*, 299–300).
43. See, for instance, Frederick Martin, *The Statesman's Yearbook: A Statistical and Historical Account of the States of the Civilized World*, 1881: 72–75. Martin provides a table of the ships of the French navy, accurately

giving displacement, armament, and thickness of armor. Those ships not yet complete are marked with asterisks. In the following explanatory text, Martin lists the most recent fifteen ships as making up the first line of the French navy, adds that six of those fifteen are incomplete, and concludes, "Most of the remaining ironclads of the 'batiments de combat' class are of antiquated construction, and, as will be seen from the list, with armour of not more than from 5 to 7 1/2 inches in thickness. By a recent decision of the Minister of Marine, the majority of them are to be struck off from the 'efectif normal' in 1885."

44. *Hansard*, 3rd ser., 268 (1882), col. 1062.
45. Ibid., 3rd ser., 279 (1883), cols. 134–35.
46. Cooper Key to Geoffrey Phipps Hornby, 2 December 1884, printed in Parkes, *British Battleships*, 328.
47. Theodore Ropp (Stephen Roberts, ed.), *The Development of a Modern Navy*, 132.
48. *Hansard*, 3rd ser., 268 (1882), col. 1063.
49. Ibid., 3rd ser., 279 (1883), cols. 133–35.
50. Ibid., 3rd ser., 268 (1882), col. 1063.
51. Minute by Lord Northbrook (Printed), July 1885, PRO: ADM1/7465c.
52. *Conway's*, 303–4. The *Dupuy de Lome* was begun in 1888 and the *Amiral Charner* in 1889; see also Ropp, *Development of a Modern Navy*, 140, for a concise appraisal of the French program of the 1880s.
53. *Conway's*, 29–31, 64–66.
54. *Hansard*, 3rd ser., 286 (1884), col. 341.
55. *Conway's*, 13, 287.
56. *Hansard*, 3rd ser., 279 (1883), col. 139.
57. *Conway's*, 292–93. Years under construction: *Caiman*, 1878–88; *Indomptable*, 1878–87; *Requin*, 1878–88; *Terrible*, 1877–87; *Amiral Baudin*, 1879–88; *Formidable*, 1879–89; *Hoche*, 1881–90; *Magenta*, 1883–93; *Marceau*, 1881–91; and *Neptune*, 1882–92.
58. *Hansard.*, 3rd ser., 268 (1882), col. 1064.
59. The *Times* (London), 23 September 1884, 7. It may be noted that not all French naval officials took the same view. Auguste Gougeard, minister of marine during the brief Gambetta ministry of 1881–82, formulated strategic plans that called for "a ruthless attack on English trade," especially in the Mediterranean, coupled with "the threat of a cross-Channel invasion" (Ropp, *Development of a Modern Navy*, 127–28). Later in the decade, Theophile Aube, one of the leaders of the *Jeune Ecole*, advocated unrestricted warfare against merchant shipping in the event of a war with Britain. Also, the French statement was not true with regard to torpedo vessels.
60. *Hansard*, 3rd ser., 279 (1883), cols. 80–81.
61. *Conway's*, 246, 271.
62. John Beeler, "'A One Power Standard?' Great Britain and the Balance of Naval Power, 1860–1880," 551–54.
63. *Hansard*, 3rd ser., 268 (1882), cols. 1072, 1078.
64. Ibid., 3rd ser., 278 (1883), col. 42.

65. Ibid., 3rd ser., 279 (1883), col. 79.
66. The *Times* (London), 17 March 1885, 9–10.
67. Parkes, *British Battleships*, 352–53. Parkes lists the British fleet at twenty-two first-class battleships, fifteen second-class battleships, and eleven coastal-defense ironclads, whereas the French and the Russians between them had twenty-one of the first category (fourteen French and seven Russian), fifteen of the second (seven French and eight Russian) and thirteen of the third (six French and seven Russian). In other words, Britain possessed a two-power force with the sole exception of the third class, where the deficiency was two vessels.
68. Ropp, *Development of a Modern Navy*, 210–12. Ropp argues otherwise. "Did England and Italy, or Russia and France, start the great naval competition of the 1890s?" he asks. "England and Italy began the augmentation of naval expenses, but fears of the Jeune Ecole clearly motivated both the English and the Italian programs.... If England set the pace for extravagant naval construction ... she did so because technological advances and the new system of warfare preached in France had overthrown the very bases of the naval strategic system on which the British Empire had been founded."
69. *Hansard*, 3rd ser., 268 (1882), 1037–39.
70. Ibid., 3rd ser., 277 (1883), col. 603.
71. F. W. Hirst, *The Six Panics and Other Essays*, 42.

Bibliography

Archival and Other Primary Sources

A Clear Anchor [pseud.]. *The Board of Admiralty. Can it not be Reformed, or must it be Wholly Reconstructed?* London: Harrison, 1871.

A Flag Officer [pseud. for William Fanshawe Martin]. *The Admiralty.* Portsmouth: Griffin and Co., 1870.

A Gunnery Officer [pseud.]. *A Few Words About Our Navy.* London: Edward Stanford, 1867.

A Lieutenant, R. N. [pseud. for ? Beresford]. *Another View of the British Navy in the Present Year of Grace.* London: Simpkin, Marshall, and Co., 1886.

A Retired Naval Officer [pseud.]. *British Maritime Supremacy: A Brief Analysis of Its Past, Present, and Possible Future Condition; shewing the Necessity for a Division of the Duties of the Fleet, and the Establishment of a Coast Defence Militia.* London: Hamilton Adams and Co., 1876.

An Undistinguished Naval Officer [pseud. for Henry James Boyle Montgomery]. *The British Navy in the Present Year of Grace.* London: Hamilton Adams and Co., [1886]. 3 vols.

[Anonymous]. *A Soft Answer Turneth Away Wrath.* London: Harrison, 1875.

[Anonymous]. *An Important Question for the Constituencies by A Taxpayer.* London: Edward Stanford, 1884.

[Anonymous]. *Admiralty Administration: Its Faults and Defaults.* London: Longman, Green, Longman, and Roberts, 1861.

[Anonymous]. *British and French Ships.* London: Harrison and Sons, 1883.

[Anonymous]. *Naval Efficiency: A Statement of Facts Bearing on this Important Subject with some Suggestions for Increasing it, together with Economy.* [London: n.p., 1877].

[Anonymous]. *Naval Mal-Administration.* London: n.p., 1868.

[Anonymous]. *On the Economy of the Navy Estimates in Certain Departments.* London: Lockwood and Co., 1868.

[Anonymous]. *Our Nautical School, Wh*****ll, London: Giving a Description of its proceeding from the First Reformed Parliament, in 1832, up to* the present time; concluding with a brief allusion to the loss of the 'Captain,' and the resignation of Mr. Chil***s. London: Simpkin, Marshall, and Co., 1871.

[Anonymous]. *The Battle of the Ironclads; or, England and her foes in 1879.* London: G. J. Palmer, 1871.

[Anonymous]. *The Coming War: England Without a Navy.* London: Longmans, Green, and Co., 1875.

Bacon, Reginald H. *A Naval Scrapbook.* London: Hutchinson and Co., 1925. 2 vols.

Bagehot, Walter. *The English Constitution.* reprint, Ithaca, NY: Cornell University Press, 1986.

Barfleur [pseud. for Reginald Custance]. *Naval Policy: A Plea for the Study of War.* Edinburgh: William Blackwood and Sons, 1897.

Barnaby, Nathaniel. "Armour for Ships," *Transactions of the Institute of Naval Architects,* 20 (1879): 27–32.

———. "Battleships, A Forecast," *Journal of the Royal United Services Institution,* 27 (1883): 127–44.

———. *Comparison of the Navies of England and France, January, 1870.* London, n.p., For Admiralty Circulation, 1870.

[———]. *Comparison between Armoured Ships of England and France as to New Types.* [London]: n.p., For Admiralty Circulation, [1880].

———. *Comparative Progress of European Ironclad Navies.* [London]: n.p, For Admiralty Circulation, 1884.

———. *H.M.S. 'Inflexible.'* London: Eyre and Spottiswoode, 1878.

———. *Memorandum on the Relative Strengths of British and French Ships.* London: n.p., For Admiralty Circulation, 1883.

———. *Naval Development in the Century.* London: Linscott Publishing Co., 1902.

———. "On Iron and Steel for Shipbuilding," *Transactions of the Institute of Naval Architects* 16 (1875): 131–46.

———. "On Ships of War," *Transactions of the Institute of Naval Architects* 17 (1876): 1–12.

———. "On Some Recent Designs of Ships of War for the British Navy, Armoured and Unarmoured," *Transactions of the Institute of Naval Architects* 15 (1874): 1–21.

———. "On the Fighting Power of the Merchant Ship in Naval Warfare," *Transactions of the Institute of Naval Architects* 18 (1877): 1–23.

———. "On the Nelson Class," *Transactions of the Institute of Naval Architects* 21 (1880): 59–68.

———. "On the Unmasted Sea-going Ships *Devastation, Thunderer, Fury,* and *Peter the Great,*" *Transactions of the Institute of Naval Architects* 14 (1873): 1–20.

———. *The Naval Review of British, French, Italian, German, and Russian Large Ships of War, Being an Inspection of Two Hundred and Fifty-Three Sea-Going Fighting Ships.* London: E. Marlborough and Co., [1885?].

Bibliography

———. *The Proper Form and Construction of the Rams or Spurs of Ironclads.* London: n.p., For Admiralty Circulation, 1875.

———. *To the Members of the Royal Corps of Naval Constructors. January 1, 1885.* [London]: n.p., For Admiralty Circulation, 1885.

Barrow, John. *An Auto-biographical Memoir of Sir John Barrow, Bart., Late of the Admiralty: Including Reflections, Observations, and Reminiscences at home and abroad from early life to advanced age.* London: John Murray, 1847.

Beresford, Charles de la Poer. *The Memoirs of Admiral Lord Charles Beresford.* London: Methuen and Co., 1914. 2 vols.

Biddlecomb, George. *Changes in the Royal Navy During the Last Half Century.* Glasgow: Anderson Eadie, 1872.

Block, Maurice. *Le Budget, Revenus et Dépenses de la France.* Paris: J. Hetzel et Cie, [1881].

Brassey, Thomas. *Comparison of the French and English Ironclads.* London: n.p., For Admiralty Circulation, 1881.

[———]. *English and Foreign Opinions on the Types of Ships Best Adapted for Modern Naval Warfare.* London: n.p., For Admiralty Circulation, 1881.

———. "On Unarmoured Vessels," *Transactions of the Institute of Naval Architects* 17 (1876): 13–28.

———. "Our Naval Strength and Policy," *Contemporary Review* 27 (1876): 791–802.

———. *Papers and Addresses.* London: Longmans, Green, and Co., 1894. 2 vols.

———. "Recent Designs for Ships of War," *Macmillan's* 36 (1877): 257–66.

———. *Recent Naval Administrations.* London: Longmans, Green, and Co., 1872.

———. "The Administration of the Navy, 1880–1885," *Nineteenth Century* 19 (1886): 106–26.

———. *The British Navy: Its Strength, Resources, and Administration.* London: Longmans, Green, and Co., 1882. 6 vols.

——— (ed). *Naval Annual.* Portsmouth: J. Griffin and Co., 1886–.

Bridge, Cyprian A. G. *Some Recollections.* London: John Murray, 1919.

Briggs, John Henry. *Naval Administrations 1827 to 1892. The Experience of 65 Years.* London: Sampson, Low, Marston, and Co., 1897.

Bright, John. *Selected Speeches of the Right Hon. John Bright on Public Questions.* London: J. M. Dent and Co., n.d.

Brooke, John, and Mary Sorenson, (eds.). *The Prime Ministers' Papers: W. E. Gladstone.* London: Historical Manuscripts Commission, 1971.

Buckle, George Earl (ed.). *The Letters of Queen Victoria. Second Series. A Selection from Her Majesty's Correspondence and Journal between the Years 1862 and 1878.* London: John Murray, 1926. 2 vols.

Cardwell Papers. The Papers of Edward, First Viscount Cardwell. Public Record Office, Kew, London, PRO 30/48/27, 30/48/36.

Carnarvon Commission. See Great Britain. Parliament.

Carnarvon Papers. The Papers of Henry Howard Molyneux Herbert, 4th Earl of Carnarvon. Public Record Office, Kew, London, PRO 30/6/5, 30/6/115, 30/6/131.

[Chesney, George]. "The Battle of Dorking," *Blackwood's* 109 (1871): 539–72.

Childers Papers. The Political Correspondence of Hugh Culling Eardley Childers. Royal Commonwealth Society Library, London, file 5/1–228.

Childers, Hugh C. E. *Naval Policy. A Speech Delivered in the House of Commons on the 21st March, 1867, During the Debate on the Naval Estimates*. London: Longmans, Green, and Co., 1867.

———. *Results of Admiralty Organization*. London: n.p., 1871.

———. *The Naval Power of England*. London: n.p., 1874.

Clarendon Papers. The Papers of George William Frederick Villiers, Fourth Earl Clarendon. Bodleian Library, Oxford University, MSS. Clare Dep. c.499.

Cobden, Richard. *The Three Panics: An Historical Episode*. London: Cassell and Co., 1862.

Cohn, S. *Die Finanzen des Deutschen Reich seit seiner Begründung*. Berlin: J. Guttentag, 1899.

Coles, Cowper Phipps. "Shot-proof Gun-shields as Adapted to Iron-cased Ships," *Journal of the Royal United Services Institution* 4 (1860): 280–90.

———. "The Turret *versus* the Broadside System," *Journal of the Royal United Services Institution* 11 (1867): 436–84.

Colomb, John C. R. *Imperial Defence*. London: Edward Stanford, 1880.

———. *Imperial Strategy*. London: Edward Stanford, 1871.

———. *Naval Intelligence and Protection of Commerce in War*. London: W. Mitchell and Co., 1881.

———. *The Defence of Great and Greater Britain*. London: Edward Stanford, 1880.

Colomb, Philip Howard. *Great Britain's Maritime Power: How Best Developed as Regards: Fighting Ships, Protection of Commerce, Naval, Volunteer, or Supplemental Force, Colonial and Home Defence*. London: Harrison and Sons, 1878.

———. "Great Britain's Maritime Power, How Best Developed as Regards Fighting Ships, etc.," *Journal of the Royal United Services Institution* 22 (1878): 1–55.

———. *Naval Warfare: Its Ruling Principles and Practice Historically Treated*. London: W. H. Allen and Co., 1891.

Colson, Percy (ed.). *Lord Goschen and His Friends (The Goschen Letters)*. London: Hutchinson and Co., 1946.

Corry, Henry Thomas Lowry. *The Navy. Speeches of the Right Hon. H. T. L. Corry on Subjects Relating to the Navy, in the House of Commons, on August 7, 8, 11 and 12, 1871*. London: Cornelius Buck, 1872.

Cross Papers. The Papers of Richard Assheton Cross. British Library (BL), London, Additional Manuscript 51268.

Cross, Richard Assheton. *A Political History*. London: Eyre and Spottiswoode, For Private Circulation, 1903.

Daily News. London.
Derby, Earls of. *See* **Stanley Papers.**
Disraeli, Benjamin. *Disraeli's Reminiscences*, Helen and Martin Swartz (eds.). London: Hamish Hamilton, 1975.
Disraeli, Benjamin: *See also* **Hughenden Papers.**
Douglas, Howard. *Observations on Modern Systems of Fortification.* London: John Murray, 1859.
———. *On Naval Warfare With Steam.* London: n.p., 1857.
Dundas, Charles. *An Admiral's Yarns.* London: H. Jenkins, 1922.
Eardley-Wilmot, Sydney M. *An Admiral's Memories.* London: Sampson, Low, Marston, and Co., 1906.
———. *The Development of Navies.* London, 1892.
Elliot, George. "The Ram: The Prominent Feature of Future Naval Victories," *Journal of the Royal United Services Institution* 27 (1883): 357–78.
Fairbairn William. *Treatise on Iron Ship Building: Its History and Progress.* London: Longmans, Green, and Co., 1865.
Financial Reform Union. *Papers on Taxation and Expenditure Issued by the Financial Reform Union. No. 1 Naval Mal-Administration.* London: G. Hill, [1868].
———. *Papers on Taxation and Expenditure Issued by the Financial Reform Union. No. 3 A Budget for 1869. Based on Mr. Cobden's "National Budget" proposed in 1849.* London: G. Hill, [1868].
Fisher, John A. *Memories.* London: Hodder and Stoughton, 1919.
———. *Naval Tactics.* [London]: n.p., For Private Circulation, 1871.
———. *Records.* London: Hodder and Stoughton, 1919.
Fitzgerald, Charles Cooper Penrose. *From Sail to Steam: Naval Recollections, 1878–1905.* London: E. Arnold, 1916.
———. *Memories of the Sea.* London: E. Arnold, 1913.
Flannery, J. Fortesque. "On Water-tube Boilers," *Transactions of the Institute of Naval Architects* 17 (1876): 259–82.
France. Ministère des Finances. *Bulletin de Statistique.* Paris: Imprimerie Nationale, 1878–90.
———. Ministère des Finances. *Compte Général de l'Administration des Finances* Paris: Imprimerie Nationale, 1871–92.
———. Ministère de la Marine et des Colonies. *Revue Maritime et Coloniale.* Paris: Imprimerie Administrative de Paul Dupont, 1869.
[Fremantle, Edmund R. (signed E. R. F.)]. "The Loss of the Captain," *Fraser's Magazine* 83 (1871): 68–83.
———. *The Navy as I have Known it: 1849–1899.* London: Cassell and Co., 1904.
Germany. Kaiserlichen Statistischen Amt. *Statistisches Jahrbuch für das Deutsche Reich.* Berlin: Puttkammer und Mühlbrecht, Buchhandlung für Staats- und Rechtswissenschaft, 1872–90.
Gladstone Papers. The Papers of William Ewart Gladstone. British Library (BL), Additional Manuscripts 44117, 44128, 44131, 44153, 44161, 44185, 44266, 44267, 44300, 44338, 44341, 44417, 44421, 44422, 44426, 44427,

44428, 44429, 44430, 44434, 44439, 44443, 44463, 44473, 44474, 44492, 44536, 44537, 44538, 44539, 44540, 44541, 44542, 44543, 44544, 44545, 44546, 44547, 44548, 44614, 44637, 44639, 44641.

[Gladstone, William E.]. "Germany, France and England," *Edinburgh Review* 132 (1870): 554–93.

———. (H. C. G. Matthew, ed.). *The Gladstone Diaries, with Cabinet Minutes and Prime-Ministerial Correspondence.* Oxford: Clarendon Press, 1978–82. Vols. 6–8.

———. *The Midlothian Speeches, 1879.* reprint, New York: Humanities Press, 1981.

Goodrich, Caspar F. *Report of the British Naval and Military Operations in Egypt, 1882.* Washington: U.S. Government Printing Office, 1885.

Granville Papers. The Papers of Granville George Leveson Gower, Second Earl Granville. Public Record Office, Kew, London, PRO 30/29/54.

Great Britain. Admiralty. *Comparative Progress of the European Ironclad Navies: Comparison of Armoured Ships of England and France.* [London]: n.p., 1884.

———. *Condition of the Ironclad Fleet.* [London]: n.p., 1874.

———. Parliament. *Parliamentary Debates.* 3rd Series. London: Hansard (generally known as *Hansard's Parliamentary Debates*).

———. *British Parliamentary Papers.* London: HMSO (generally known as *Parliamentary Papers*)

———. *Report of the Royal Commission appointed to Enquire into the Civil and Professional Administration of the Naval and Military Departments and the Relationship of those Departments to each other and to the Treasury* (generally known as the Hartington Commission). London: HMSO, 1890. Strictly Confidential.

———. *Report of the Royal Commission appointed to make Enquiry into the Condition and Sufficiency of the Means of the Naval and Military Forces provided for the Defence of the more important Sea-ports within our Colonial Possessions and Dependencies* (generally known as the Carnarvon Commission). London: HMSO, 1881. Confidential.

Grey, Frederick. *Admiralty Administration, 1861–1866.* London: n.p., 1867.

Guedalla, Philip, (ed.). *The Palmerston Papers: Gladstone and Palmerston; Being the Correspondence of Lord Palmerston with Mr. Gladstone, 1851–1865.* New York: Harper and Brothers, 1928.

———. (ed.). *The Queen and Mr. Gladstone.* London: Hodder and Stoughton, 1933. 2 vols.

Halifax Papers. The Papers of Charles Wood, First Viscount Halifax. British Library (BL), London, Additional Manuscript 49561.

Hall, William H. *Our Naval Defences.* London: J. Wakeham, 1871.

Hambleden Papers. The Papers of W. H. Smith. W. H. Smith Ltd. Archives, Didcot Parkway, manuscripts PS5/30–64, PS6/1–646, PS17/1–72, PS18/1–18, PS19/1–82, PS20/1–21.

Hamilton, Richard Vesey, ed. *Letters and Papers of Admiral of the Fleet Sir Thomas Byam Martin, G.C.B.* London: Naval Records Society, 1901. 2 vols.

Bibliography

———. *Naval Administration. The Constitution, Character, and Functions of the Board of Admiralty, and of the Civil Departments it Directs*. London: George Bell and Sons, 1896.

Harcourt Papers. The Papers of William George Granville Venables Vernon Harcourt. Bodleian Library, Oxford University, MS. Harcourt Dep. Adds. 18, 19.

Hardy, Gathorne. *The Diary of Gathorne Hardy, Later Lord Cranbrook, 1866–1892: Political Selections*. Nancy Johnson (ed.). Oxford: Clarendon Press, 1981.

Harris, Robert Hastings. *From Naval Cadet to Admiral*. London: Cassell and Co., 1913.

Hartington Commission. See Great Britain. Parliament.

[Hay, John C. D.]. "Continued Mismanagement of the British Navy," *Quarterly Review* 131 (1871): 440–60.

[———]. "Efficiency of the Navy," *Quarterly Review* 126 (1869): 207–18.

———. *Lines From My Logbooks*. Edinburgh: David Douglas, 1898.

[———]. "Mismanagement of the British Navy," *Quarterly Review* 129 (1870): 392–415.

———. *Speech of Rear-Admiral Sir John Hay, Bart., to the Electors of Stamford, November 13, 1868 with Remarks on the Naval Policy of the Conservative Government*. London: Edward Stanford, 1868.

[Hope, C. W.]. "Ironclads and Torpedoes: The *Inflexible* and Mr. Reed," *Blackwood's* 123 (1878): 153–71.

[———]. "Our Ironclad Ships," *Blackwood's* 107 (1870): 706–24.

[———]. "The Progress of Naval Architecture," *Blackwood's* 125 (1879): 507–24.

Hornby Papers. The Papers of Geoffrey Thomas Phipps Hornby. National Maritime Museum, Greenwich, London, PHI/103/17, PHI/109/1–7, PHI/110/1–4, PHI/118a/I–IV, PHI/120a/I–VIII, PHI/121a2/II–VI, PHI/126, PHI/127, PHI/132/11.

Hughenden Papers. The Papers of Benjamin Disraeli, First Earl Beaconsfield. Bodleian Library, Oxford University, Political Correspondence, files B/XX/Hu, B/XX/Lx, B/XX/N, B/XX/S, B/XXI/C, B/XXI/H.

Hunt, George Ward. *Speech of the Right Hon. George Ward Hunt, M.P. (First Lord of the Admiralty), on Moving the Navy Estimates in the House of Commons, Monday, April 20, 1874*. London: Cornelius Buck, [1874].

Hunt, George Ward: See also Wadenhoe Papers.

James, William. *Naval History of Great Britain, From the Declaration of War by France in 1793, to the Accession of George IV*. London: R. Bentley, 1837. 5 vols.

Kebbel, T. E. "A Conservative view of the Election," *Nineteenth Century* 7 (1880): 905–16, 1057–64.

Kemp, Peter (ed.). *The Fisher Papers*. London: Navy Records Society, 1960.

Keppel, Henry. *A Sailor's Life Under Four Sovereigns*. London: Macmillan and Co., 1889. 3 vols.

Key, Astley Cooper. "Naval Defence of the Colonies," *Nineteenth Century* 20 (1886): 284–93.
King, J. W. *European Ships of War and Their Armament, Naval Administration, etc.* Washington: U.S. Government Printing Office, 1877.
King-Hall, L. (ed.). *Sea Saga: Being the Naval Diaries of Four Generations of the King-Hall Family.* London: Victor Gollancz, 1935.
[Laughton, John Knox]. "Naval Warfare," *Edinburgh Review* 162 (1885): 234–64.
[———]. "Past and Present State of the British Navy," *Edinburgh Review* 161 (1885): 492–513.
———. "The Sovereignty of the Sea," *Fortnightly Review* 5 (1866): 718–33.
[———]. "Thomas Brassey on the British Navy," *Edinburgh Review* 155 (1882): 477–504.
Layard Papers. The Papers of Andrew Layard. British Library (BL), London, Additional Manuscripts 39011, 39032.
Lennox, Henry Gordon. *Forewarned, Forearmed.* London: William Ridgway, 1882.
Main, Robert. *The British Navy in 1871.* London: Smith, Elder, and Co., 1871.
Malmesbury, Earl of. *Memoirs of an Ex-Minister.* London: Longmans, Green, and Co., 1884.
Marder, Arthur J. (ed.). *Fear God and Dread Nought: The Correspondence of Admiral of the Fleet Lord Fisher of Kilverstone. Volume I: The Making of an Admiral 1854–1904.* London: Jonathan Cape, 1952.
Martin, Frederic (ed.). *The Statesman's Yearbook: A Statistical and Historical Account of the States of the Civilized World.* London: Macmillan and Co., 1864–90.
Martin, Thomas Byam (Richard Vesey Hamilton, ed.). *Letters and Papers of Admiral of the Fleet Sir Thomas Byam Martin, G.C.B.* London: Naval Records Society, 1901. 2 vols.
[Martin, William Fanshawe]. "The Admiralty," *Blackwood's* 107 (1870): 763–71.
Milne Papers. The Papers of Alexander Milne. National Maritime Museum, Greenwich, London, Manuscripts MLN/143/1–4, MLN/144/1–5, MLN/145/2–5, MLN/146/2, 4, MLN/147/3–5, MLN/148/1–3, MLN/163/12, MLN/165/1, 3, 5, 7, 10, 11, 12, MLN/166/3, 4, MLN/169/9, 13, 18.
Milton, J. "Strength of Boilers," *Transactions of the Institute of Naval Architects* 21 (17): 318–26.
Mitchell, W. F. *The Royal Navy.* Portsmouth: Griffin and Co., 1872, 1881. 2 vols.
Naval and Military Gazette. London.
NMM: ADM National Maritime Museum, Greenwich, London, Admiralty Papers, File ADM 138 (Ships' Covers).
Northcote Papers. The Papers of Stafford Northcote, First Earl Iddesleigh. British Library (BL), London, Additional Manuscripts 50016, 50017, 50019, 50022, 50040, 50052, 50053.
Osborn, Sherard. *Our Admiralty.* London: n.p., 1867.

Otway, A. (ed.). *Autobiography and Journals of Admiral Lord Clarence E. Paget, G.C.B.*. London: Chapman and Hall, 1896.
Pall Mall Gazette. London.
Palmer's Index to the Times. London: Samuel Palmer, 1867–86.
Parkes, W. "On the Use of Steel for Marine Boilers, and some Recent Improvements in Their Construction," *Transactions of the Institute of Naval Architects* 19 (1878): 172–92.
PRO: ADM Public Record Office (Kew, London), Admiralty Papers, Files ADM 1 (Secretary's In Letters), ADM 12 (Digest), and ADM 116 (Cases).
PRO: CAB Public Record Office, Kew, London, Cabinet Papers, file 41 (Cabinet Correspondence to the Queen).
PRO: HO Public Record Office, Kew, London, Home Office Papers, file HO 73/35/3 (*Evidence, written and Oral, taken by the Royal Commission appointed to Enquire into the Civil and Professional Administration of the Naval and Military Departments and the Relationship of those Departments to each other and to the Treasury, Strictly Confidential*, London: HMSO, 1890).
Ramm, Agatha (ed.). *The Political Correspondence of Mr. Gladstone and Lord Granville, 1868–1876*. London: Royal Historical Society, 1952. 2 vols.
Reed, Edward J. "On Citadel Ships," *Transactions of the Institute of Naval Architects* 18 (1877): 24–36.
———. *Our Ironclad Ships*. London: John Murray, 1869.
———. (ed.). *Naval Science. A Quarterly Magazine for Promoting the Improvement of Naval Architecture, Marine Engineering, Steam Navigation, and Seamanship*. London: Lockwood and Co., 1872–75.
———, and Edward Simpson. *Modern Ships of War*. New York: Harper and Bros., 1888.
Robinson, Robert Spencer. "England as a Naval Power," *Nineteenth Century* 7 (1880): 389–405.
———. "On Armour-plating Ships of War," *Transactions of the Institute of Naval Architects* 20 (1879): 1–26.
———. *On the State of the British Navy; With Remarks on one Branch of Naval Expenditure*. London: Harrison, 1874.
———. *Remarks on H.M.S. 'Devastation.'* London, 1873.
[———]. *Results of Admiralty Organization as Established by Sir James Graham and Mr. Childers; with some Suggestions for Improvements*. London: Harrison, 1871.
———. "The Dangers and Warnings of the *Inflexible*," *Nineteenth Century* 3 (1878): 278–95.
———. "The Navy and Its Rulers," *Contemporary Review* 51 (1887): 252–73.
———. "The Navy and the Admiralty," *Nineteenth Century* 17 (1885): 185–200.
[———]. "The State of the British Navy," *Quarterly Review* 134 (1873): 77–107.
Russia. Ministry of Finance. *Bulletin Russe de Statistique, Financière et de Legislation*. St. Petersburg: Imprimerie du Ministère des Finances.

Scott, Percy. *Fifty Years in the Royal Navy.* New York: George H. Doran and Co., 1919.
Seaton, Albert E. *A Manual of Marine Engineering, Comprising the Designing, Construction, and Working of Marine Machinery.* London: C. Griffin and Co., 1907.
[Seymour, Edward, 12th Duke of Somerset]. *The Naval Expenditure from 1860 to 1866, and its Results.* London: William Ridgway, 1866.
Shaw-Lefevre, George J. "British and Foreign Ships of War," *Macmillan's* 35 (1877): 257–65.
Smith, W. H. "The Navy: its duties and capacity," *National Review* 4 (1884): 259–99.
Smith, W. H.: *See also* Hambleden Papers.
Standard, The. London.
Stanley Papers. (1) The Papers of Edward Geoffrey Stanley, 14th Earl of Derby, Liverpool Record Office, William Brown Library, Liverpool, Manuscripts 920 DER (14), 141/11, 141/12, 146/2, 146/3, 146/4, 164/1, 191/2, 192/1, 193/1.
Stanley Papers. (2) The Papers of Edward Henry Stanley, 15th Earl of Derby, Liverpool Records Office, William Brown Library, Liverpool, Manuscripts 920 DER (15), 13/2/1, 13/2/2, 16/2/4, 17/2/5.
Stead, W. T. "Government by Journalism," *Contemporary Review* 49 (1886): 653–74.
Stewart Papers. The Papers of William Houston Stewart. National Maritime Museum, Greenwich, London, Manuscripts SWT/101, SWT/102.
Tarleton Papers. The Papers of John Walter Tarleton (Microfilm Copy). Liverpool Record Office, William Brown Library. Group 5, Reels 7, 8, 10.
The Annual Register: A Review of Public Events at Home and Abroad. London: Rivingtons, 1866–81.
Times, The. London.
United Service Gazette. London.
United States. (Lerner, William, et al., eds.). *Historical Statistics of the United States.* Washington: U.S. Government Printing Office, 1975.
Very, Edward W. *Navies of the World; Giving Concise Descriptions of the Plans, Armament, and Armour of the Naval Vessels of Twenty of the Principal Nations. Together with the Latest Developments in Ordnance, Torpedoes, and Naval Architecture, and a Concise Summary of the Principal Naval Battles of the Last Twenty Years, 1860–1880.* London: Sampson, Low, Marston, Searle, and Rivington, 1880.
Vincent, John (ed.). *Derby, Disraeli, and the Conservative Party: The Political Journals of Lord Stanley.* Hassocks, Sussex: The Harvester Press, 1979.
Wadenhoe Papers. The Papers of George Ward Hunt. Northamptonshire Record Office, Northampton, Letters WH 205, WH 222, WH 225, WH 282–90.
Watt, Henry F. *The State of the Navy, 1878.* Liverpool: William Potter, 1878.
White, William H. *A Manual of Naval Architecture.* London: John Murray, 1877.

[Willis, William]. *Remarks on Naval Administration*. London: n.p., 1871.
Wilson, Herbert W. *Ironclads in Action: A Short Sketch of Naval Warfare from 1855 to 1895*. London: Sampson, Low, and Co., 1896.

Secondary Sources

Aldcroft, Derek H. (ed.) *The Development of British Industrial and Foreign Competition, 1875–1914*. Toronto: University of Toronto Press, 1968.
Arnold-Forster, Mrs. Hugh. *The Right Honourable Hugh Oakley Arnold-Forster. A Memoir*. London: Edward Arnold, 1910.
Bacon, Reginald. *The Life of Lord Fisher of Kilverstone, Admiral of the Fleet, KCB, KCVO, DSO*. London: Hodder and Stoughton, 1929. 2 vols.
Ballard, George. *The Black Battlefleet*. Annapolis, Maryland: Naval Institute Press, 1980.
Ballock, W. H. *Letters, Remains, and Memoirs of Edward Adolphus Seymour, Twelfth Duke of Somerset*. London: Richard Bentley and Sons, 1893.
Barnaby, Kenneth. *The Institution of Naval Architects 1860–1960: An Historical Survey of the Institution's Transactions and Activities over 100 Years*. London: The Royal Institution of Naval Architects, 1960.
Bartlett, Christopher J. *Great Britain and Sea Power: 1815–1853*. Oxford: Clarendon Press, 1963.
———. "The Mid-Victorian Reappraisal of Naval Policy," in Kenneth Bourne and D. C. Watts (eds.), *Studies in International History*. London: Longmans, 1967, 189–208.
———. (ed.). *Britain Pre-eminent: Studies of British World Influence in the Nineteenth Century*. London: Macmillan and Co., 1969.
Bassett, Arthur Tilney. *Gladstone's Speeches, Descriptive Index and Bibliography*. London: Methuen and Co., 1916.
Baxter, Colin. "Lord Palmerston: Panic Monger or Naval Peacemaker," *Social Science* 47 (1972): 203–11.
———. "The Duke of Somerset and the Creation of the British Ironclad Navy, 1859–1866," *Mariner's Mirror* 63, no. 3 (1977): 279–84.
Baxter, James Phinney. *The Introduction of the Ironclad Warship*. Cambridge, MA: Harvard University Press, 1933.
Beeler, John, "'A One Power Standard?': Great Britain and the Balance of Naval Power, 1860–1880," *Journal of Strategic Studies* 15 (1992): 548–75.
———. "'Fit for Service Abroad': Promotion, Retirement, and Royal Navy Officers, 1830–1890," *Mariner's Mirror*, 81 (1995): 300–312.
———. "Steam, Strategy, and Schurman: Imperial Defence in the Post-Crimean Era, 1856–1905," in Greg Kennedy and Keith Neilson (eds.), *Far-Flung Lines: Essays in Honor of Donald Schurman*. London: Frank Cass and Co., 1996.
Bell, Herbert C. F. *Lord Palmerston*. London: Longmans, Green, and Co., 1933. 2 vols.
Blake, Robert. *Disraeli*. New York: St. Martin's Press, 1967.

———. *The Conservative Party from Peel to Churchill*. London: St. Martin's, 1971.
Bonnett, Stanley. *The Price of Admiralty*. London: Robert Hale Ltd., 1968.
Bourne, H. R. Fox. *English Newspapers: Chapters in the History of Journalism*. New York: Russell and Russell, 1966 (reprint).
Bourne, Kenneth. *The Foreign Policy of Victorian England, 1830–1902*. Oxford: Clarendon Press, 1967.
———, and D. C. Watts (eds.). *Studies in International History*. London: Longmans, 1967.
Bradford, Edward E. *Life of Admiral of the Fleet Sir Arthur Knyvet Wilson*. London: John Murray, 1923.
Brandes, Georg. *Lord Beaconsfield, A Study*. R. Bentley and Son, trans. by Mrs. G. Sturge, 1880.
Brodie, Bernard. *Sea Power in the Machine Age*. Princeton: Princeton University Press, 1947.
Brown, David K. *A Century of Naval Construction: The History of the Royal Corps of Naval Constructors*. London: Conway Maritime Press, 1983.
———. "The First Steam Battleships," *Mariner's Mirror* 63, no. 4 (1976): 327–33.
Brown, Lucy. *Victorian News and Newspapers*. Oxford: Clarendon Press, 1985.
Chamberlain, Muriel. *Pax Britannica? British Foreign Policy 1789–1914*. London: Longman, 1988.
Chesnau, Roger, and Eugene Kolesnik (eds.). *Conway's All the World's Fighting Ships, 1860–1905*. London: Conway Maritime Press, 1979.
Childers, Spencer. *The Life and Correspondence of the Rt. Hon. Hugh Culling Eardley Childers*. London: John Murray, 1901. 2 vols.
Chilston, Viscount. *W. H. Smith*. London: Routledge and Kegan Paul, 1965.
Clapham, J. H. *An Economic History of Modern Britain*. Cambridge: Cambridge University Press, 1926. 3 vols.
Clarke, I. F. "The Battle of Dorking, 1871–1914," *Victorian Studies*, 8 (1965): 309–28.
———. *Voices Prophesying War, 1763–1984*. London: Oxford University Press, 1970.
Clowes, William L., with Clements Markham, Alfred Thayer Mahan, H. W. Wilson, and Theodore Roosevelt. *The Royal Navy. A History from the Earliest Times to the Death of Queen Victoria*. London: Sampson, Low, and Co., 1897–1903. 7 vols.
Colomb, Philip Howard. *Memoir of Admiral the Right Honble Sir Astley Cooper Key, G.C.B., D.C.L., F.R.S., etc*. London: Methuen and Co., 1898.
Conacher, J. B. *The Peelites and the Party System, 1846–1852*. Newton Abbot, Devon: David and Charles, 1972.
———. (ed.). *The Emergence of British Parliamentary Democracy in the Nineteenth Century*. New York: John Wiley and Sons, 1971.
Cook, Edward T. *Delane of the Times*. New York: Henry Holt, 1916.
Courtmanche, Regis. *No Need of Glory: The British Navy in American*

Bibliography

Waters, 1860–1864. Annapolis, Maryland: Naval Institute Press, 1977.
Cowpe, Alan. "The Royal Navy and the Whitehead Torpedo," in Bryan Ranft, (ed.), *Technical Change and British Naval Policy, 1860–1939*. London: Hodder and Stoughton, 1977, 12–36.
Crouzet, François. *The Victorian Economy*. Trans. A. S. Forster. London: Methuen and Co., 1982.
Dasent, Arthur I. *John Thaddeus Delane*. New York: Charles Scribners, 1908. 2 vols.
Dawson, William H. *Richard Cobden and Foreign Policy*. London: George Allen and Unwin, 1926.
Dictionary of National Biography. Reprint edition, Oxford: Oxford University Press, 1967–68. 22 vols.
Egerton, Mary Augusta. *Admiral of the Fleet Sir Geoffrey Phipps Hornby, G.C.B. A Biography*. Edinburgh: William Blackwood and Sons, 1896.
Eldridge, C. C. *England's Mission: The Imperial Idea in the Age of Gladstone and Disraeli*. London: Macmillan, 1973.
———. *Victorian Imperialism*. London: Hodder and Stoughton, 1978.
Elliot, Arthur D. *The Life of George Joachim, First Viscount Goschen, 1831–1907*. London: Longmans, Green, and Co., 1911. 2 vols.
Erickson, Arvell B. *The Public Career of Sir James Graham*. Oxford: Basil Blackwell, 1952.
Fanshawe, Alice E. J. *Admiral Sir Edward Gennys Fanshawe*. London: Spottiswoode and Co. For private circulation, 1904.
Fitzgerald, Charles Cooper Penrose. *Life of Vice-Admiral Sir George Tryon, K.C.B*. Edinburgh: William Blackwood and Sons, 1897.
Fitzmaurice, E. *The Life of Granville George Leveson Gower, Second Earl Granville, K.G., 1815–1891*. London: Longmans, Green, and Co., 1905. 2 vols.
Gardiner, A. G. *The Life Of Sir William Harcourt*. London: Constable and Co., 1923. 2 vols.
Gardiner, Leslie. *The British Admiralty*. Edinburgh: William Blackwood and Sons, 1968.
Gardiner, Robert (ed.), *Steam, Steel, and Shellfire: The Steam Warship 1815–1914*. London: Conway Maritime Press, 1992.
Gathorne-Hardy, Alfred E. *Gathorne Hardy, First Earl of Cranbrook: A Memoir. With Extracts from His Diary and Correspondence*. London: Longmans, Green, and Co., 1910. 2 vols.
Goodman, Jordan, and Katrina Honeyman. *Gainful Pursuits: The Making of Industrial Europe 1600–1914*. New York: Edward Arnold, 1988.
Gordon, D. C. *The Dominion Partnership in Imperial Defence, 1870–1914*. Baltimore: Johns Hopkins University Press, 1965.
Graham, Gerald S. *The Politics of Naval Supremacy*. Cambridge: Cambridge University Press, 1965.
Grenville, John A. S. *Lord Salisbury and Foreign Policy*. London: Athlone Press, 1964.
Gritzen, Edward (ed.). *Introduction to Naval Engineering*. Annapolis, Naval Institute Press, 1980.

Hamilton, C. I. *Anglo-French Naval Rivalry, 1840–1870.* London: Oxford University Press, 1994.
Hamilton, W. Mark. *The Nation and the Navy: Methods and Organization of British Navalist Propaganda, 1889–1914.* New York: Garland Publishing Co., 1986.
Hanham, Harold J. *Elections and Party Management: Politics in the Time of Disraeli and Gladstone.* London: Longmans, 1959.
Harcourt, Freda. "Disraeli's Imperialism 1866–1868: A Question of Timing," *The Historical Journal* 23, no. 1 (1980): 87–109.
Hardie, Frank. *The Foreign Policy Influence of Queen Victoria, 1861–1901.* London: Oxford University Press, 1935.
Hawkey, Arthur. *H.M.S. 'Captain.'* London: George Bell and Sons, 1963.
Hawkins, Angus. "Lord Derby and Victorian Conservatism, A Reappraisal," *Parliamentary History* 5 (1987).
Headrick, Daniel. *The Tentacles of Progress: Technology Transfer in the Age of Imperialism.* New York: Oxford University Press, 1988.
———. *Tools of Empire.* New York: Oxford University Press, 1981.
Herwig, Holger. *"Luxury" Fleet: The Imperial German Navy, 1880–1918.* London: George Allen and Unwin, 1980.
Higham, Robin (ed.). *Guide to the Sources of British Military History.* Berkeley: University of California Press, 1971.
Hill, J. R. (ed.). *The Oxford Illustrated History of the Royal Navy.* New York: Oxford University Press, 1995.
Hirst, F. W. *The Six Panics and Other Essays.* London: Methuen and Co., 1913.
History of the Times. New York: Macmillan, 1935–52. 5 vols.
Hodges, Peter. *The Big Gun: Battleship Main Armament 1860–1914.* Annapolis, Maryland: Naval Institute Press, 1981.
Hogg, Ian, and John Batchelor. *Naval Gun.* Poole, Dorset: Blanford Press, 1978.
Houghton, Walter E. (ed.). *The Wellesley Index to Victorian Periodicals, 1824–1900.* London: University of Toronto Press/Routledge and Kegan Paul, 1966–89. 5 vols.
Hovgaard, William. *Modern History of Warships.* London: E. and F. N. Spon, 1920.
Jane, Frederick T. *Heresies of Seapower.* London: Longmans, Green, and Co., 1907.
———. *Jane's Fighting Ships.* New York: Jane's Publishing Co., 1897.
———. *The British Battle Fleet. Its Inception and Growth Throughout the Centuries.* London: S. W. Partridge and Co., 1912. 2 vols.
———. *The Imperial Russian Navy.* London: W. Thacker and Co., 1904.
Jelavich, Barbara. "British Means of Offense Against Russia in the Nineteenth Century," *Russian History/Histoire Russe* 1, pt. 2 (1974): 119–35.
Jenkins, Ernest H. *A History of the French Navy from its Beginnings to the Present Day.* London: Macdonald and Janes, 1979.

Jones, Howard. *The Union in Peril: The Crisis over British Intervention in the Civil War*. Chapel Hill: University of North Carolina Press, 1992.

Jones, Wilbur D. *Lord Derby and Victorian Conservatism*. Athens, University of Georgia Press, 1956.

Kemp, Tom. *Industrialization in Nineteenth Century Europe*. 2nd edition, London: Longman, 1985.

Kennedy, Paul. "Arms Races and the Causes of War, 1850–1945," in idem (ed.), *Strategy and Diplomacy, 1870–1945. Eight Studies*. London: George Allen and Unwin, 1983, 163–177.

———. *The Realities Behind Diplomacy: Background Influences on British External Policy, 1865–1980*. London: George Allen and Unwin, 1981.

———. *The Rise of Anglo-German Antagonism, 1860–1914*. London: Allen and Unwin, 1980.

———. *The Rise and Fall of British Naval Mastery*. Malabar, FL: Robert Krieger, 1976.

———. *The Rise and Fall of the Great Powers*. New York: Random House, 1987.

———. *Strategy and Diplomacy 1870–1945. Eight Studies*. London: George Allen and Unwin, 1983.

———. "The Tradition of Appeasement in British Foreign Policy, 1865–1939," in idem (ed.), *Strategy and Diplomacy, 1870–1945. Eight Studies*. London: George Allen and Unwin, 1983, 13–39.

Knaplund, Paul. *Gladstone's Foreign Policy*. New York: Harper and Row, 1935.

Lambert, Andrew. *Battleships in Transition: The Creation of the Steam Battlefleet 1815–1860*. London: Conway Maritime Press, 1984.

———. *The Crimean War: British Grand Strategy Against Russia, 1853–1856*. Manchester: Manchester University Press, 1990.

———. *The Last Sailing Battlefleet: Maintaining Naval Mastery 1815–1850*. London: Conway Maritime Press, 1991.

———. "The Royal Navy 1856–1914: Deterrence and the Strategy of World Power." Unpublished paper.

Lambert, Nicholas. "The Influence of the Submarine Upon Naval Strategy, 1898–1914," Unpublished Oxford University dissertation, 1992.

Lambi, Ivo. *The Navy and German Power Politics, 1862–1914*. Boston: Allen and Unwin, 1984.

Landes, David. *The Unbound Prometheus: Technological Change and Industrial Development in Western Europe from 1750 to the Present*. Cambridge: Cambridge University Press, 1969.

Lang, Andrew. *Life, Letters, and Diaries of Sir Stafford Northcote, First Earl of Iddesleigh*. Edinburgh: William Blackwood and Sons, 1890. 2 vols.

Lee, Alan J. *The Origins of the Popular Press in England, 1855–1914*. London: Croom Helm, 1976.

Lewis, Michael. "Armed Forces and the Art of War: Navies," *The New Cambridge Modern History, Vol. 10: The Zenith of European Power*. Cambridge: Cambridge University Press, 1960.

———. *The Navy In Transition, 1814–1865*. London: Hodder and Stoughton, 1965.
Livezey, William. *Mahan on Sea Power*. Rev. ed. Norman, Oklahoma: University of Oklahoma Press, 1981.
Lloyd, Christopher, *Mr. Barrow of the Admiralty: A Life of John Barrow, 1764–1848*. London: Collins, 1970.
Lloyd, Trevor. *The Election of 1880*. London: Oxford University Press, 1968.
Lowe, C. J. *The Reluctant Imperialists: British Foreign Policy, 1878–1902*. New York: Macmillan and Co., 1969. 2 vols.
Lyon, Hugh. "The Relations Between the Admiralty and Private Industry in the Development of Warships," in Bryan Ranft (ed.), *Technical Change and British Naval Policy, 1860–1939*. London: Hodder and Stoughton, 1977, 37–64.
Mackay, Ruddock. *Fisher of Kilverstone*. Oxford: Clarendon Press, 1973.
McCord, Norman, "A Naval Scandal of 1871: The Loss of H.M.S. *Megaera*," *Mariner's Mirror* 57, no. 2 (1972): 115–33.
McNeill, William H. *The Pursuit of Power: Technology, Armed Force, and Society Since A.D. 1000*. Chicago: University of Chicago Press, 1982.
Magnus, Philip. *Gladstone*. New York: E. P. Dutton and Co., 1964.
Mahan, Alfred Thayer. *Naval Administration and Warfare: Some General Principles*. London: Sampson, Low, and Co., 1908.
———. *Naval Strategy Compared and Contrasted with the Principle and Practice of Military Operations on Land*. London: Sampson, Low, and Co., 1911.
———. *The Influence of Sea Power upon History, 1660–1783*. Boston: Little, Brown and Co., 1890.
———. *The Influence of Sea Power upon the French Revolution and Empire, 1793–1812*. Boston: Little, Brown and Co., 1892. 2 vols.
Mallet, Bernard. *Thomas George Earl of Northbrook, G.C.S.I. A Memoir*. London: Longmans, Green, and Co., 1908.
Manning, Frederic. *The Life of Sir William White*. New York: E. P. Dutton and Co., 1923.
Marcus, Geoffrey J. *Quiberon Bay*. Barre, MA: Barre Publishing Co., 1963.
Marder, Arthur J. *The Anatomy of British Sea Power: A History of British Naval Policy in the Pre-Dreadnought Era 1880–1905*. Reprint edition, New York: Pantheon Books, 1976.
———. *From Dreadnought to Scapa Flo: The Royal Navy in the Fisher Era, 1904–1919*. New York: Oxford University Press, 1961–70. 5 Vols.
Markham, Clements. *Life of Admiral Sir Leopold McClintock*. London: John Murray, 1909.
Martin, A. Patchett. *Life and Letters of the Right Honourable Robert Lowe, Viscount Sherbrook, G.C.B., D.C.L.* London: Longmans, Green, and Co., 1893. 2 vols.
Martin, Theodore. *The Life of His Royal Highness the Prince Consort*. London: Smith, Elder and Co., 1875–80. 5 vols.

Massie, Robert K. *Dreadnought*. New York: Random House, 1991.
Maxwell, Herbert. *Life and Times of the Right Honourable William Henry Smith, M.P.* Edinburgh: William Blackwood and Sons, 1893. 2 vols.
———. *Life and Letters of George William Frederick, Fourth Earl of Clarendon*. London: Edward Arnold, 1913. 2 vols.
Millman, Richard. *British Foreign Policy and the Coming of the Franco-Prussian War*. Oxford: Oxford University Press, 1965.
———. *The Eastern Question, 1875–1878*. Oxford: Clarendon Press, 1979.
Mitchell, B. R. *British Historical Statistics*. Cambridge: Cambridge University Press, 1989.
———. *European Historical Statistics*. Second edition, New York: Facts on File, 1980.
———, and Phyllis Deane. *Abstract of British Historical Statistics*. Cambridge: Cambridge University Press, 1962.
Mitchell, Fred, and Conrad Dixon. *Ships of the Victorian Navy*. Southampton: Ashford Press Publishing, 1987.
Mitchell, Donald. *A History of Russian and Soviet Seapower*. New York: Macmillan and Co., 1974.
Modelski, George, and William Thompson. *Sea Power in Global Politics, 1494–1993*. Seattle: University of Washington Press, 1988.
Monypenny, William F., and George Earl Buckle. *The Life of Benjamin Disraeli, Earl of Beaconsfield*. New York: Macmillan and Co., 1910–20. 6 vols.
Morley, John. *The Life of Richard Cobden*. London: Chapman and Hall, 1883.
———. *The Life of William Ewart Gladstone*. New York: Macmillan and Co., 1903. 3 vols.
Mosse, W. E. "Public Opinion and Foreign Policy: The British Public and the War Scare of Nov 1870," *Historical Journal* 6 (1963): 38–58.
Murray, Oswyn. "The Admiralty, Part VII: Naval Administration from 1832 Onwards," *Mariner's Mirror* 24 (1932): 470–78.
Neilson, Keith, "'Greatly Exaggerated': The Myth of the Decline of Britain before 1914," *International History Review* 13 (1991): 695–725.
Owen, Edward. "The Rt. Hon. Hugh Childers," *Army Quarterly and Defence Journal* 117, no. 1 (1987): 67–79.
Padfield, Peter. *Rule Britannia: The Victorian and Edwardian Navy*. London: Routledge and Kegan Paul, 1981.
———. *The Battleship Era*. New York: David MacKay Co., 1972.
Palmer, R. R., and Joel Colton. *A History of the Modern World*. 6th ed. New York: A. A. Knopf, 1984.
Parker, Charles S. *Life and Letters of Sir James Graham, Second Baronet Netherby, P.C., K.C.B., 1792–1861*. London: John Murray, 1907. 2 vols.
Parkes, Oscar. *British Battleships, 1860–1950*. London: Seeley Service Co., 1957.
Parry, Ann (ed.). *The Admirals Fremantle*. London: Chatto and Windus, 1971.
Partridge, Michael. *Military Planning for the Defence of the United Kingdom, 1814–1870*. New York: Greenwood, 1989.

Patterson, Temple. "Captain Cowper Coles and Palmerston's Folly," *Mariner's Mirror* 51, no. 1 (1965): 19–25.

Pearson, Hesketh. *Dizzy. The Life and Nature of Benjamin Disraeli, Earl of Beaconsfield*. London: Methuen and Co., 1951.

Pemsel, Helmut. *A History of War at Sea*. Annapolis, Maryland: Naval Institute Press, 1979.

Pollard, Sidney, and Paul Robertson. *The British Shipbuilding Industry, 1870–1914*. Cambridge, Massachusetts: Harvard University Press, 1979.

Preston, Anthony, and John Major. *Send a Gunboat!* London: Longmans, Green, and Co., 1967.

Ranft, Bryan. "The Protection of British Seaborne Trade and the Development of Systematic Planning for War, 1860–1906," in idem, *Technical Change and British Naval Policy, 1860–1939*. London: Hodder and Stoughton, 1977.

Rasor, Eugene. *British Naval History since 1815: A Guide to the Literature*. London/New York: Garland Publishing Co., 1990.

Reynolds, Clark G. *Command of the Sea*. Malabar, FL: Robert Krieger Co., 1983. 2 vols.

Richmond, Herbert W. *Statesmen and Seapower*. Oxford: Clarendon Press, 1946.

Robinson, Ronald, John Gallager, and Alice Denny. *Africa and the Victorians*. New York: St. Martin's Press, 1961.

Rodger, Nicholas A. M. "British Belted Cruisers," *Mariner's Mirror* 64, no. 1 (1978): 23–35.

———. "British Naval Thought and Naval Policy, 1820–1890: Strategic Thought in an Era of Technological Change," in Craig L. Symonds (ed.), *New Aspects of Naval History*. Annapolis: Naval Institute Press, 1981.

———. *The Admiralty*. Lavenham, Suffolk: Terence Dalton Ltd., 1979.

———. "The Dark Ages of the Admiralty, 1869–1885," *Mariner's Mirror* 61, no. 4 (1975): 331–42; 62, no. 1 (1976): 33–46; no. 2 (1976): 121–28.

———. "The Design of the *Inconstant*," *Mariner's Mirror* 61, no. 1 (1975): 9–22.

Ropp, Theodore. *The Development of a Modern Navy: French Naval Policy, 1871–1914*. Stephen Roberts (ed.). Annapolis, Maryland: Naval Institute Press, 1987.

Rowland. K. T. *Steam at Sea: A History of Steam Navigation*. Newton Abbot: David and Charles, 1970.

Sainty, John C. (ed.). *Office Holders in Modern Britain: Volume IV: Admiralty Officials, 1660–1870*. London: Athlone Press, 1975.

Sandler, Stanley. "'In Deference to Public Opinion': The Loss of H.M.S. *Captain*," *Mariner's Mirror* 59, no. 1 (1973): 57–68.

———. "The Day of the Ram," *Military Affairs* 40 (1976): 175–78.

———. "The Emergence of the Modern Capital Ship," *Technology and Culture* 11, no. 3 (1970): 576–95.

———. *The Emergence of the Modern Capital Ship*. Newark, DE: University of Delaware Press, 1979.

Schroeder, Paul. "Old Wine in New Bottles: Recent Contributions to British Foreign Policy and European International Politics, 1789–1848," *Journal of British Studies*, 26 (1987): 1–25.

———. *Strategy and Diplomacy, 1870–1945*. London: George Allen and Unwin, 1983.

———. "The 19th-Century International System: Changes in the Structure," *World Politics*, 39 (1986): 1–25.

———. *The Transformation of European Politics, 1763–1848*. Oxford: Clarendon Press, 1994.

Schurman, Donald M. "Imperial Defence 1868–1887: A Study in the Decisive Impulses behind the Change from 'Colonial' to 'Imperial' Defence." Unpublished Ph.D. thesis, Cambridge University, 1955.

———. *Julian S. Corbett, 1854–1922*. London: Royal Historical Society, 1981.

———. *The Education of a Navy: The Evolution of British Naval Strategic Thought, 1867–1914*. London: Cassell and Co., 1965.

Semmel, Bernard. *Liberalism and Naval Strategy: Ideology, Interest and Sea Power during the Pax Britannica*. Boston: Unwin Hyman, 1986.

Seton-Watson, R. W. *Disraeli, Gladstone, and the Eastern Question*. London: Macmillan and Co., 1935.

Shannon, Richard. *Gladstone*. London: Hamish Hamilton, 1982.

———. *The Crisis of Imperialism*. London: Hart-Davis Macgibbon, 1974.

Shaw, Stanford J. *History of the Ottoman Empire and Modern Turkey*. Cambridge: Cambridge University Press, 1977. 2 vols.

Shulman, Mark R. *Navalism and the Emergence of American Sea Power, 1882–1893*. Annapolis: Naval Institute Press, 1995.

Sokol, Anthony E. *The Imperial and Royal Austro-Hungarian Navy*. Annapolis: Naval Institute Press, 1968.

Sondhaus, Lawrence. *The Habsburg Empire and the Sea: Austrian Naval Policy, 1779–1866*. West Lafayette, Indiana: Purdue University Press, 1989.

———. *The Naval Policy of Austria-Hungary, 1867–1918: Navalism, Industrial Development, and the Politics of Dualism*. West Lafayette, Indiana: Purdue University Press, 1994.

Southgate, D. *"The Most English Minister": The Politics and Policies of Palmerston*. New York: St. Martin's Press, 1966.

Spender, J. A. *The Life of the Right Hon. Sir Henry Campbell-Bannerman*. Boston: Houghton Mifflin Co., 1923. 2 Vols.

Stenton, Michael (ed.). *Who's Who of British Members of Parliament*. Hassocks, Sussex: The Harvester Press, 1978.

Stewart, Robert. *The Foundation of the Conservative Party, 1830–1867*. London: Longmans, 1978.

———. *The Politics of Protection: Lord Derby and the Protectionist Party, 1841–1852*. Cambridge: Cambridge University Press, 1971.

Strakhovsky, Leonind. "Russia's Privateering Projects of 1878," *Journal of Modern History*, 7 (1935): 22–40.

Sulivan, Henry Norton. *Life and Letters of the Late Admiral Bartholomew James Sulivan.* London: John Murray, 1896.

Sumida, Jon T. *In Defence of Naval Supremacy: Finance, Technology and British Naval Policy, 1889–1914.* Boston: Unwin Hyman, 1989.

Sumner, Benedict Humphrey. *Russia and the Balkans: 1870–1880.* Oxford: Oxford University Press, 1937.

Swartz, Martin. *The Politics of British Foreign Policy in the Era of Disraeli and Gladstone.* London: Macmillan, 1985.

Taylor, Alan John Percivale. *The Struggle for Mastery in Europe, 1848–1918.* Oxford: Clarendon Press, 1954.

Thornton, A. P. *The Imperial Idea and Its Enemies.* London: Macmillan and Co., 1959.

Tunstall, W. C. B. "Imperial Defence, 1815–1870," in *Cambridge History of the British Empire.* Cambridge: Cambridge University Press, 1940, 2: 807–41.

———. "Imperial Defence, 1870–1897," in *Cambridge History of the British Empire.* Cambridge: Cambridge University Press, 1959, 3: 230–54.

Vincent, John R. *The Formation of the British Liberal Party, 1857–1866.* London: Constable and Co., 1966.

Walpole, Spencer. *The History of Twenty-Five Years, 1856–1880.* London: Longmans, Green, and Co., 1904–8. 4 vols.

Ward, John T. *Sir James Graham.* London: Macmillan and Co., 1967.

Ward, Thomas Humphry. *The Reign of Queen Victoria: A Survey of Fifty Years of Progress.* London: Smith, Elder, and Co., 1887. 2 vols.

Webster, Charles K. *The Foreign Policy of Lord Palmerston.* London: George Bell and Sons, 1951. 2 vols.

White, Colin. *Victoria's Navy: Volume II, The Heyday of Steam.* Annapolis, Maryland: Naval Institute Press, 1983.

Whyte, Frederic. *The Life of W. T. Stead.* New York: Houghton Mifflin Co., 1925.

Wiener, Martin. *English Culture and the Decline of the Industrial Spirit, 1850–1980.* Cambridge: Cambridge University Press, 1981.

Woodward, Ernest Llewellyn. *The Age of Reform, 1815–70.* 2nd ed. Oxford: Clarendon Press, 1962.

Index

In this index, an "f" after a number indicates a separate reference on the next page, and an "ff" indicates separate references on the next two pages. A continuous discussion over two or more pages is indicated by a span of numbers, e.g., "57–58." *Passim* is used for a cluster of references in close but not consecutive sequence.

Aberdeen administration (1852–55), 41
Abyssinian War (1867–68), 33, 59, 76, 251
Adams, Charles Francis, 309
Admiralty, 2, 20, 25, 27, 32–35 *passim*, 40, 46, 50–51, 69–80, 82–96 *passim*, 102, 110–12, 123–26 *passim*, 134–35, 136, 143, 150–67 *passim*, 197–225 *passim*, 231, 235–49 *passim*, 257–69 *passim*, 276, 312; administration, 4, 38–48, 81–82, 96–102, 104–8, 126–39, 171–90, 233–34, 293, 298; and H.M.S. *Captain*, 117–23. *See also* Naval Lords
Adriatic Sea, 22, 195
Aegean Sea, 165
Afghanistan, 15–16, 167, 251
Africa, 26f, 33–34, 168, 214, 231
Alabama, C.S.S., 11, 213
Alabama claims, 11–12, 59, 200, 201
Albert, Prince, 110
Alexander II (Russian Czar), 14
Alexandria, 15, 18, 22, 33, 155
Algeria, 17
Alma (French warship), 222
Amethyst, H.M.S., 25
Amiens, Peace of, 211, 256
Amiral Baudin (French warship), 274
Annual Register, 238

Arabi Pasha, 16–17
Archangel, 222, 228f
Archbishop of Canterbury, 27
Argentina, 195
Armstrong, William, 197, 214
Army, 42, 48, 53–54, 55, 287
Arnold-Forster, H. O., 265–66
Ashantee War (1873–74), 33, 59, 251
Asquith, H. H., 241
Aube, Theophile, 233
Audacious, H.M.S., 202, 269
Australia, 20, 24, 33
Australian station, 26
Austria-Hungary, 10, 13, 14, 22, 197, 229, 251–52; navy, 195, 198, 223, 274
Austro-Prussian war, 9f

Bagehot, Walter, 1, 237
Balkans, 13, 16, 165
Baltic Sea, 27, 202, 215, 228ff
Baring, Francis, First Baron Northbrook, 42
Baring, Thomas George, Second Baron and First Earl Northbrook, 112, 184, 185–86, 243, 260–63, 267–68, 273, 294, 318–19; and H.M.S. *Captain*, 113, 115–16, 120, 124
Barnaby, Nathaniel, 114, 121, 202f, 208, 261
Barnes, Frederick, 119

Barrow, Sir John, 40
Bartlett, C. J., 3, 18, 36
"Battle of Dorking" (George Chesney), 238–39, 315
Batum, 16
Baxter, Edward, 99, 127
Baxter, James P., 3
Belgium, 16, 56
Bellerophon, H.M.S., 273
Bentinck, George, 46f, 97, 263–66 *passim*, 286
Beresford, Charles, 250, 256, 268
Berlin, Congress of (1878), 14–15, 167, 304
Berlin Memorandum (1876), 13
Bismarck, Otto von, 10f, 14, 251–52
Black Prince, H.M.S., 91
Black Sea, 10f, 16, 26, 176, 203, 228f
Blackwood's Magazine, 238
Blake, Robert, Lord, 50
"Blue water" strategy, 18–24
Board of Trade, 32
Boer War, first (1880–81), 33, 251
Boilers, naval, 90–91, 215, 258, 292f
Bon, Cape, 17
Brassey, Thomas, 20, 219, 224, 239, 252, 267–68
Brazil, 75, 166, 195
Brennus (French warship), 273
"Brick and mortar" strategy, 18, 20–21, 23–24
Briggs, John Henry, 158, 176–83 *passim*, 190
Bright, John, 11, 20, 49, 146, 240
Brin, Benedetto, 197, 230
British Columbia, 32
British empire, 12–13, 219, 226, 229, 255, 267, 269, 277
British Museum, 27, 32
British Navy; and technological change, 1–2, 3–8 *passim*, 18, 19, 21–23, 65, 204, 211–14, 256, 257–58, 291, 310; debates over strength of, 69–80 *passim*, 95–96, 151–52, 159, 261–62, 263–77 *passim*; maintenance and repair of, 85–92; policy, 3f, 16–27 *passim*, 32–37 *passim*, 61–71 *passim*, 78–79, 141, 147f, 154, 210–25 *passim*, 237–59, 260–78 *passim*; shipbuilding policy, 20, 66–68, 84–88, 244–49, 257–58, 261–62; strength of, vis-à-vis foreign fleets, 71–80 *passim*, 95, 159, 191–209, 261–77 *passim*, 315. *See also* Boilers, naval
Bulgaria, 13, 14, 16, 165, 166, 304
Bulgarian Horrors and the Question of the East (W. Gladstone), 13
Burgoyne, John, 116, 120
Burma, 33

Cabinet, 72–76 *passim*, 95, 147–53 *passim*, 162–66 *passim*, 239, 249, 267
Campbell-Bannerman, Henry, 241, 261–62, 265–77 *passim*
Camperdown, Earl of, *see* Haldane-Duncan, Robert Adam Philips, Third Earl of Camperdown
Canada, 12, 258
Cape Hatteras, 199
Cape of Good Hope (Cape) station, 26
Captain, H.M.S., 5, 39, 102, 109, 112–24, 126–27, 132f, 179, 187, 190, 237, 294ff
Cardwell, Edward, First Viscount, 140, 146–47, 149, 205, 240, 241
Caribbean Sea, 26, 212
Carnarvon, Lord, *see* Herbert, Henry Howard Molyneux, Fourth Earl of Carnarvon
Carnarvon Commission on Colonial Defense, 174, 218–19, 223, 250, 253
Cartagena (Spain), 22
Cavendish, Spencer Compton, styled Marquess of Hartington, later Eighth Duke of Devonshire, 169
Cecil, Robert Arthur Talbot Gascoyne-, Third Marquess of Salisbury, 14, 16, 80, 167–68, 219, 239f, 246
Chamberlain, Joseph, 241
Charleston, 199
Charmes, Gabriele, 233
Chatham, 70, 96
Chesney, George, 238–39, 315
Childers, Hugh Culling Eardley, 4, 23, 34, 67, 82f, 95–96, 102, 141, 153, 157, 240, 244, 261f, 267, 270, 300; and H.M.S. *Captain*, 112, 113, 116–23, 126–27; collapse of health, 106, 109, 127–28, 134–35, 295; difficulties with subordinates, 102–6, 107f, 125–27; reduces naval spending, 59, 64, 66, 92–95, 140, 144–45, 148; reduces

naval forces overseas, 35–36, 37, 52, 78–79, 147, 148, 154, 159; reforms naval administration, 48, 96–101, 129–35, 137–38, 172, 175–90, 210, 292, 306ff; shipbuilding and dockyard policies, 84–89, 92, 154–55, 242, 244–49, 261–62
Childers, Leonard, 112
Chile, 24, 75, 195
China, 162, 276
China station, 24, 26, 27
Civil service expenditures, 55–56, 286–87
Civil War, see United States; Civil War
Clarendon, Lord, see Villiers, George William Frederick, Fourth Earl of Clarendon
Clarke, I. F., 24
Clausewitz, Karl von, 49
Close blockade, 211–13
Clowes, William Laird, 33, 36
Coal, 7, 235
Coastal defense, 18. See also "Palmerston's follies"
Coastal defense ironclads, 19–20, 22–24, 95, 215
Cobden, Richard, 7, 10, 20, 49, 245
Coles, Cowper Phipps, 109–12, 114, 120–21, 124
Colomb, Philip H., 185, 250
Colonial office, 27
Commerce-raiding, 200–201, 203, 213–14, 217–21, 225–34 *passim*, 254–55, 271, 313
Commerell, Edmund, 116
Congo River, 33
Conservative party, 15f, 34, 45, 50f, 58, 71, 73, 80–84 *passim*, 93, 111, 149–53 *passim*, 164–69 *passim*, 183, 185, 239, 241, 246, 257; naval and shipbuilding policy, 154–56, 261–62, 302. See also Tory party
Constantinople, 13–14, 16, 21, 155, 165, 201
Constantinople, Straits of, 14, 17, 165, 201, 304. See also Dardanelles
Controller of the Navy, 97–98, 131, 137, 172, 177, 179–84, 189, 307, 308. See also Surveyor of the Navy; Robinson, Robert Spencer; Stewart, William Houston

Conway's All The World's Warships, 193
Cooper Key, Astley, see Key, Astley Cooper
Coronne (French warship), 270
Corry, Henry Thomas Lowry, 34, 38, 59, 67, 73–81, 84, 93f, 135, 150–55 *passim*, 180, 203f, 241–48 *passim*, 257, 307
Crete, 33
Crimean War, 9f, 26f, 41, 51, 56, 109, 140, 144, 211, 219, 228, 243
Cyprus, 14, 17f, 304
Cyrenia, 32

Dacres, Sydney, 75, 77, 95–96, 127, 192, 215, 294; and loss of H.M.S. *Captain*, 112, 113–16, 120; difficulties of at the Admiralty, 103, 104–5, 107, 109, 176–77, 305
Dahomey, King of, 32
Daily News (London), 92, 94, 122, 129, 150, 163f
Dandolo (Italian warship), 197
Dardanelles, 17, 155. See also Constantinople, Straits of
Debt, national, 53, 160–61, 169, 287
Defence, H.M.S., 91, 202
Delane, John T., 48
Derby, Lord, see Stanley, Edward George Geoffrey, Fourteenth Earl of Derby; Stanley, Edward Henry, Fifteenth Earl of Derby
Derby (Conservative) ministries, 1852: 39, 50; 1858–59: 50–51, 58
Derby-Disraeli (Conservative) ministry (1866–68), 34, 58, 69–83, 93, 148, 159, 203, 239, 246
Detached squadron, 26
Devastation, H.M.S., 20, 202, 215, 216, 310
Devonport, 21
Dictionary of National Biography, 243
Dilke, Charles, 219
Disraeli, Benjamin, First Earl of Beaconsfield, 3, 12–16 *passim*, 34–35, 48, 61, 68, 88, 143, 149, 150f, 164, 186, 242, 251–55 *passim*, 260; and naval spending, 50–51, 69–81, 83, 93, 153, 158–60, 162, 170, 239, 241, 249; and Eastern Crisis (1875–78),

13–14, 155, 164–67, 201, 303
Disraeli administration (1874–80), 53, 150–70, 196, 246
Dockyards, 62, 84–90, 92, 243, 257; administration, 42, 46, 69–70, 88–89, 97, 100, 155–56, 179–80, 184
Douglas, Howard, 214
Dowell, William, 268
Dry docks, 21
Dufferin, Lord, *see* Temple, Frederick, First Marquess of Dufferin and Ava
Duilio (Italian warship), 197
Dulcigno (Balkans), 22
Duncombe, Admiral, 44

East Indies station, 26, 27
Eastern Crisis; 1839–41, 56; 1875–78, 10, 13–14, 19, 60, 62, 155, 164–68, 201, 203, 222–23, 237, 243, 248–52 *passim*
Economist, the, 278
Ecuador, 32
Eden, George, First Earl of Auckland, 2
Education Act (1870), 53
Egypt, 13, 15ff, 22, 33, 56, 267
Elliot, George, 124
Ellis, Robert, 127
Elphinstone, Sir James, 44, 46–47, 142, 239
Engagé trade (indentured servitude), 33–34, 284
English Channel, 203, 205, 212–16 *passim*, 233, 234
Ericsson, John, 109f
Esher Committee, 175, 189
Europe, 6, 9, 11, 15, 21, 24, 143, 157, 164, 191, 202, 208, 211, 219, 227f, 234, 251–52, 278
Excellent, H.M.S., 265
Exchequer, Chancellor of, 50, 80, 239, 240

Far East, 23, 27
Fiji, 251
Financial Reform Union, 81
Finland, Gulf of, 228
Fisher, John A., later Baron Fisher of Kilverstone, 184, 225, 250, 265
Fitzgerald, Charles Cooper Penrose, 253
Florida, C.C.S., 11
Foreign Office, 27, 32

Foreign stations, *see* Overseas stations
Fortesque, Chichester, 106
Forwood, Arthur, 219
France, 1, 4, 8–19 *passim*, 23f, 33–34, 56, 61, 152, 191, 194, 212–18 *passim*, 228–31 *passim*, 238, 250–57 *passim*, 277; navy, 2, 47–48, 50–52, 193, 203–9, 221–22, 231–33, 270–76, 310f; British views of, 71, 77, 145, 261–70 *passim*, 315
Franco-German War, 9f, 16, 20, 59, 87, 89, 95–96, 108, 123, 205–8 *passim*, 247f, 254, 267, 286
Free trade, 11
French Revolution, 9
Froude, William, 124

Gambetta, Leon, 274
Gathorne Hardy, Gathorne, 159, 160, 170
Gauloise (French warship), 270
General Admiral (Russian warship), 222
General Election; of 1868, 80–82, 239, 290–91; of 1874, 147, 149, 150, 153, 240; of 1880, 169, 260
Geneva, 12
Germany, 4, 8–16 *passim*, 21–23, 153, 191–95 *passim*, 208, 214, 229, 232, 238, 251–56 *passim*, 269, 277; navy, 196, 198, 223–28, 230 *passim*, 264, 267, 274–76
Gibraltar, 17, 18
Gladstone, William E., 3, 8–20 *passim*, 34–37 *passim*, 49ff, 61–83 *passim*, 95, 116f, 123f, 134ff, 154, 167–70 *passim*, 186, 219, 245, 253, 255, 269, 290, 295f; and naval spending, 52, 58f, 140–49, 150, 205, 239–41, 249, 260–61, 262–63; and Robert Spencer Robinson, 103–8 *passim*, 125–28 *passim*, 133
Gladstone (Liberal) ministries, 1868–74: 35, 49, 59f, 82, 144, 150–59 *passim*, 182, 239–40, 246; 1880–85: 134, 169; 1886: 134
Gloire (French ironclad), 80
Goodenough, James, 124, 202
Gordon, General Charles, 16
Goschen, George J., First Viscount, 19, 35–37 *passim*, 43, 52, 59, 64, 67,

87–91 *passim*, 96, 124, 148–59 *passim*, 185, 190, 202–23 *passim*, 243–49 *passim*, 256–57, 262–63, 290, 299, 316; and naval spending, 140–50, 205, 240–41, 300; reforms naval administration, 135–39, 171–77 *passim*, 184–89, 210, 308
Graham, Gerald S., 17
Graham, Sir James, 39–42, 46, 133, 172, 175, 210
Granville, Lord, *see* Leveson-Gower, Granville George, Second Earl of Granville
Great Britain; foreign policy, 8–16, 164, 169, 252; government fiscal policy, 53–56, 59, 60, 61, 146, 148, 163, 168–70, 260–61
Greece, 15, 21–22, 32, 195
Grey, Henry George, styled Viscount Howick, later Third Earl Grey, 39
Grivel, Louis-Antoine-Richild, 231–32
Grosser Kurfürst (German warship), 196
Guerre de course, see Commerce-raiding

Haldane-Duncan, Robert Adam Philips, Third Earl of Camperdown, 103, 107, 127, 293
Halifax, 26
Hall, Robert, 205
Hamilton, C. I., 3, 307–8
Hamilton, George, 268
Hamilton, Richard Vesey, 268
Harcourt, William, 158
Harris, James Howard, Third Earl of Malmesbury, 79, 241, 253, 290
Hartington, Lord, *see* Cavendish, Spencer Compton, styled Marquess of Hartington, later Eighth Duke of Devonshire
Hartington Commission, 175, 239, 246, 250, 303
Hay, Lord John, 103, 176, 178
Hay, Sir John C. D., 71–77 *passim*, 142, 187–88, 239, 250–56 *passim*, 263–73 *passim*, 308, 319
Herbert, Henry Howard Molyneux, Fourth Earl of Carnarvon, 14, 79, 241, 253
Herbert, Sidney, 112

Hirst, F. W., 278
Hoche (French warship), 274
Home Islands, 8, 18–21, 255
Hong Kong, 9, 24
Hood, Arthur, 185, 186, 220, 316
Hornby, Geoffrey Phipps, 21, 124, 161–62, 173–74, 250, 303
House of Commons, 19, 42–51 *passim*, 61, 72–84 *passim*, 91, 93, 98, 123f, 133f, 142, 149–57 *passim*, 164–67 *passim*, 185, 190, 239, 265–77 *passim. See also* Parliament
House of Lords, 267. *See also* Parliament
Houston Stewart, William, *see* Stewart, William Houston
Huascar (Peruvian ironclad), 25
Hunt, George Ward, 43, 66f, 89–91 *passim*, 151, 164, 166, 172f, 185, 218–23 *passim*, 241–44 *passim*, 261, 265; and the state of the navy, 151–60 *passim*, 249, 303
Hutt, W. H., 7, 35

Inconstant, H.M.S., 200, 217–18
Independência (Brazilian warship), 166
India, 13–20 *passim*, 201, 212
Indian Ocean, 33
Inflexible, H.M.S., 197
Influence of Sea Power on History, 1660–1783 (Alfred T. Mahan), 250
Inglefield, Edward A., 200
Intransigentes (Spain), 21–22
Invasion scare (1858–62), 18f, 57–58, 136, 238
Ireland, 237
Ironclads; British, 6, 8, 19–25 *passim*, 46, 51f, 145, 165–67, 254–57 *passim*, 291, 310; ratio of to foreign battlefleets, 71–77 *passim*, 95, 162, 191–209, 261–62, 263–76; foreign, 194–98, 309; French, 50, 203–9, 232, 269–74, 310; Russian, 201–3, 310; United States, 198–201, 203, 310, 316–17
Italia (Italian warship), 197
Italy, 17, 22, 228, 232, 252, 256; navy, 195–98 *passim*, 223, 229–31, 264, 267, 274–76 *passim*, 309

Jane's Fighting Ships, 191

Japan, 24, 191, 276
Jellicoe, John R., 184
Jeune Ecole, 213, 219–24 *passim*, 233f
Jones, Gore, 201, 203

Kabul, 15
Key, Astley Cooper, 173–74, 185, 186, 220, 271
King, James W., 197, 202

Lagos (Nigeria), 32
Laird Brothers (shipbuilders), 70, 111, 118, 199, 309
Lamb, William, Second Viscount Melbourne, 61
Lancet, the, 128
Lauderdale, Earl of, *see* Maitland, Thomas, Eleventh Earl of Lauderdale
Lefevre, George John Shaw, *see* Shaw-Lefevre, George John
Lebanon, 32
Leghorn (Livorno, Italy), 17
Lennox, Henry, 52, 74–77, 89, 111, 133–34, 150–51, 263–77 *passim*; and reduction of naval forces overseas, 34–35, 36f, 75, 78–79
Lepanto (Italian warship), 197
Leveson-Gower, Granville George, Second Earl of Granville, 12, 95, 145–46, 205, 240
Liberal party, 6f, 15–19 *passim*, 34, 49, 51, 60, 81–93 *passim*, 111, 140–60 *passim*, 169, 215, 239–41, 242–45 *passim*, 260–64 *passim*; naval and shipbuilding policy, 154–56, 261–62, 302
Lindsay, William, 35
Lissa, battle of (1866), 195, 197, 231, 275
Liverpool, 11
Livingstone, David, 32
London Conference (1871), 11
Lord Clyde, H.M.S., 273
Lord Warden, H.M.S., 273
Lowe, Robert, 49, 52
Lushington, Vernon, 127, 134, 176ff, 306

Madagascar, 33
Mahan, Alfred T., 3, 23f, 225f, 234, 238, 250, 269
Maitland, Thomas, Eleventh Earl of Lauderdale, 115
Malaysia, 32
Malmesbury, Lord, *see* Harris, James Howard, Third Earl of Malmesbury
Malta, 17, 166
"Manchester school" radicals, 11, 49, 219, 239
Marceau (French warship), 274
Marder, Arthur J., 3
Martello (coastal defense) towers, 24
Martin, Sir Thomas Byam, 40, 285
Meade, Richard, styled Lord Gilford, later Fourth Earl of Clanwilliam, 161
Mediterranean Sea, 14–19 *passim*, 23, 26, 132, 165, 195–201 *passim*, 212, 214ff, 230
Mediterranean Squadron, 14f, 21–33 *passim*, 105, 115, 120, 152, 155, 201, 284, 303
Megaera, H.M.S., 133–34, 136, 180, 181, 187
Mehemet Ali, 56
Mexico, 32, 34
Midlothian campaign, 169–70, 240
Miliutin, Dimitri, 14
Milne, Alexander, 71, 77, 151, 174ff, 205, 218, 243, 250–56 *passim*, 294f, 307, 317; and commerce protection, 219–24 *passim*; and H.M.S. *Captain*, 103–12 *passim*, 116, 120; and naval administration, 171–72, 183–84, 305, 307; and the state of the navy, 152–53, 161, 186
Minin (Russian warship), 202
Mobile, 199
Moltke, Helmuth von, 227
Monitor, U.S.S., 110, 199, 309–10
Montenegro, 15, 22
Morley, John, later First Viscount, 147–48
Mozambique, 33
Napoleon (Napoleon Bonaparte), 1, 17, 256
Napoleon, Louis (Napoleon III), 10, 50
Napoleon (French warship), 2
Naval and Military Gazette, the (London), 45–46, 82, 94, 111, 122, 135
Naval budget; expenditure on personnel, 62–66; expenditure on matériel, 66–68, 289, 302; expenditure on

Index

dockyards, 84–88, 92–94, 96, 155–56, 158, 161–63
Naval Defence Act (1889), 3, 191, 225, 237, 242, 251–52, 260, 268–69, 275–76
Naval Lords, 35, 43, 80, 97–98, 137–38, 171, 175–76, 185, 186, 217, 270; advisory duties of, 39, 41, 96, 138–39; and shipbuilding policy, 70–78, 95–96, 151–52, 161–62, 203, 315. *See also* Admiralty
Naval reserve, 19, 317
Naval spending, 48–52, 66–68, 239–41, 249, 278, 288, 317; as a portion of the budget, 54–62; Conservative policy toward, 50–51, 69–80, 150–66 *passim*; Liberal policy toward, 93–94, 96, 140–49 *passim*; compared to foreign navies, 193–95, 197–200, 201–2, 204–5; after 1880, 260–61, 262–63, 267–69
Naval strategy; British, 210–25; foreign, 225–33
Naval staff, 173–75
Navy Board, 39, 40, 172
Navy estimates, *see* Naval spending
Navy League, 269
Nelson, Horatio Lord, 1f, 24, 42, 191
Nelson, H.M.S., 218
Netherlands, 194, 272
Newdegate, Charles, 167
Newfoundland, 26
New Hebrides, 33
New Orleans, 199
Nigeria, 32
Niger River, 33
North America and West Indies station, 24, 26, 27, 167–68
North Sea, 214f, 228, 230
Northbrook, Lord, *see* Baring, Thomas George, First Earl Northbrook
Northcote, Stafford, First Earl of Iddesleigh, 150, 159–70 *passim*, 249, 315
Northampton, H.M.S., 218
Norway, 214

Officers, navy, 44, 300
Opium war, second (1859–62), 25
Osborn, Sherard, 112
Ottoman Empire, 13–14, 15f, 22, 164, 166, 201, 304; navy, 195–96. *See also* Turkey
Overseas (foreign) naval stations, 24–34; reduction of ships serving on, 34–37, 78–79, 147f, 154, 159. *See also* Australian station; Cape of Good Hope station; China station; East Indies station; Mediterranean Squadron; North America and West Indies Station; Pacific station; Southeast Coast of America (South America) station

Pacific station, 24–25
Paget, Clarence, 44–45
Pakington, John, later First Baron Hampton, 42–49 *passim*, 58f, 79, 84, 88, 112, 135, 150–55 *passim*, 179f, 203f, 242, 244, 248, 257, 307; and naval spending, 50–51, 69–73
Pall Mall Gazette (London), 81, 122, 265–68
Palmerston, Lord, *see* Temple, John Henry, Third Viscount Palmerston
Palmerston (Liberal) ministry, (1859–65), 58, 79, 83, 84
"Palmerston's follies" (coastal fortifications), 18, 20, 24, 59, 71
Paris, Declaration of (1856), 219
Paris, Treaty of (1856), 10, 165, 176, 219
Parkes, Oscar, 3, 191, 209
Parliament, 38–49 *passim*, 61, 76, 78, 82, 95, 114, 117, 123, 132, 134, 138, 144, 147, 154, 158, 165–69 *passim*, 218, 237–42 *passim*, 262–68 *passim*, 276, 298. *See also* House of Commons; House of Lords
Parliamentary Reform Act (1867), 4, 45, 73
Peel, Robert, 61, 73
Pembroke, 70
Penjdeh incident (1885), 16, 22, 174
Percy, Algernon, Fourth Duke of Northumberland, 38–39, 50
Persia (Iran), 16
Peru, 24f, 32, 75, 195
Peter the Great (Russian warship), 202–3
Piracy, 27, 32
Pitt, William, the Elder, 211
Plate River, 75
Plevna, 165

Port Hamilton (Korea), 16
Port Mahon (Balearic Islands), 17
Porter, David Dixon, 201
Portsmouth, 19, 21, 70
Press, the, 144, 110–12, 269, 277; criticism of Admiralty administration, 45–46, 80–82, 129–32
Price, George, 263, 269, 276
Provence (French warship), 273
Prussia, 10, 196

Radicals (political), 7, 34f, 88, 142, 148, 215, 219, 239, 245
Rankine, William, 124
Reed, Edward J., 105–8 *passim*, 134, 156–57, 182, 200, 239, 253, 256, 266, 268; and H.M.S. *Captain*, 110–23 *passim*
Reichstadt Accord (1877), 14
Repairs, *see* British navy, maintenance and repair
Resistance, H.M.S., 91
Richards, Frederick, 268
Richelieu (French warship), 208, 271
Robinson, Robert Spencer, 23, 71–78 *passim*, 83, 95–96, 102–9 *passim*, 200, 205, 215–18 *passim*, 247, 293–97 *passim*, 317; and H.M.S. *Captain*, 110, 112–16, 118–23, 295; and the office of Controller of the Navy, 100, 178–84, 306, 307, 308; forced resignation of, 125–29, 132f, 296, 297
Roebuck Commission (Crimean War), 41
Roosevelt, Theodore, 226
Royal Sovereign, H.M.S., 111–12
Royal United Services Institution, 216
Russell, John, later First Earl Russell, 2, 10, 11–12, 45, 51, 61
Russia, 10–17 *passim*, 21–27 *passim*, 56, 174, 176, 191, 194, 209, 227, 234, 251–56 *passim*, 271, 272, 277; navy, 201–3, 222–23, 228–29, 267, 275, 310
Russo-Turkish War (1877–78), 13–14, 155, 164–67, 196, 201, 246
Ryder, A. P., 124
Ryder, Dudley Francis Stewart, styled Viscount Sandon, later Second Earl of Harrowby, 164
Rylands, Peter, 7, 35, 142, 239, 245

Saint Bon, Simone de, 230
St. Paul's Island, 133
Salisbury, Lord, *see* Cecil, Robert Arthur Talbot Gascoyne-, Third Marquess of Salisbury
Samoa, 33
Sandler, Stanley, 3
Sandon, Viscount, *see* Ryder, Dudley Francis Stewart, styled Viscount Sandon, later Second Earl of Harrowby
San Stephano, Treaty of (1878), 14, 165, 167
Schleswig–Holstein crisis, 9, 10
Schroeder, Paul, 25
Scotland, 214
Seely, Charles, 69, 239
Serbia, 13
Sevastopol, 109, 228
Seymour, Edward Adolphus, Twelfth Duke of Somerset, 34, 42–45 *passim*, 51, 58, 103f, 110f, 145, 148, 179f, 184, 199
Seymour, Frederick Beauchamp (later Lord Alcester), 105–8 *passim*, 171–76 *passim*, 182, 293, 295, 307
Seymour, George, 72–77 *passim*
Shah, H.M.S., 25
Shannon, H.M.S., 218, 222
Shaw-Lefevre, George John, 91, 143, 208, 261
Sheerness, 70, 103, 133
Sicily, 17
Slave trade, 7, 26f, 32ff
Singapore, 9, 32
Smith, W. H., 43, 64, 66, 90–91, 154, 164–70, 185, 243–44, 261–66 *passim*, 316
Somerset committee on Admiralty administration (1871), 131–32, 133, 176–86 *passim*
South Africa, 15, 168
South-East Coast of America (South America) station, 26, 27, 284
Spain, 21f, 219, 274
Spalding, Augustus, 205
Spencer Robinson, Robert, *see* Robinson, Robert Spencer
Stafford, Augustus, 50
Standard, the (London), 93, 94, 130, 156–57

Index

Stanley, Edward George Geoffrey, Fourteenth Earl of Derby, 12, 35, 50f, 58, 69–83 *passim*, 88, 124, 253–54
Stanley, Edward Henry, Fifteenth Earl of Derby, 13, 14, 124, 150
Stansfeld, James, 34
Statesman's Yearbook, 196, 208, 319–20
Stead, W. T., 237–38, 265–68, 270–78 *passim*
Steam power, 1–2, 18–21, 23, 61, 65, 212–14
Stewart, William Houston, 90, 208, 243, 261, 315
Sudan, 15f
Suez Canal, 13–18 *passim*, 231 *passim*
Surveyor of the Navy, 40. *See also* Controller of the Navy; Walker, Baldwin Wake
Symonds, Thomas, 116
Syria, 32

Tarleton, John Walter, 152, 171, 305
Temple, Frederick, First Marquess of Dufferin and Ava, 124
Temple, John Henry, Third Viscount Palmerston, 8–12 *passim*, 18, 36, 42–45 *passim*, 51–52, 58, 145, 212
Terrible (French warship), 274
Thomson, William, later Lord Kelvin, 124
Times, the (London), 34, 51, 82, 96, 107, 110–14 *passim*, 127–29 *passim*, 134–35, 156–59, 163, 167, 196, 239, 242ff, 257, 262; and H.M.S. *Captain*, 113f, 120, 121–23 *passim*; on naval administration, 45–46, 48, 89, 129–36 *passim*, 179–90 *passim*; on naval spending, 61–62, 80–81, 93–94, 144, 161–69 *passim*, 193–94, 248–49, 286–87; on the state of the navy, 264–67, 274, 276
Tirpitz, Alfred, 196, 228
Torpedoes, 160, 212–13, 217, 233, 271–72
Tory party, 40, 163, 169f, 240. *See also* Conservative party
Toulon, 17, 212
Trafalgar, 1, 191
Treasury, 72, 73, 81, 153
Trenton, U.S.S., 200, 223

Trevelyan, George Otto, 261–67 *passim*, 271–74 *passim*
Trident (French warship), 270
Triumph, H.M.S., 269
"Truth about the navy" (W. T. Stead), 237–38, 265–68
Turkey, 13–14, 22, 165, 201, 229. *See also* Ottoman Empire

United Service Gazette, the (London), 46, 122, 129–32 *passim*, 181
United States, 8, 12, 24–27 *passim*, 34, 59, 143, 191, 208, 213, 222, 277, 309; Civil War, 25, 26, 198–99, 252–55 *passim*; navy, 198–201, 203, 223, 225–26, 253, 275f, 310, 316–17

Vancouver, 32
Vanguard, H.M.S., 242
Victoria, Queen, 13, 18, 95, 147, 159, 166, 237, 242
Victoria (Australian colony), 33
Victualling Board, 39f, 172
Villeneuve, Pierre, 23
Villiers, George William Frederick, Fourth Earl of Clarendon, 12, 240
Virginius affair (1873–74), 200
Vladivostok, 222, 228f
Volunteers, 19
Votes of Credit, 1870: 96, 255; 1878: 165–67, 243, 246, 255

Walker, Baldwin Wake, 50–51, 179
"War in sight" crisis (1875), 10, 13
Ward Hunt, George, *see* Hunt, George Ward
Warrior, H.M.S., 91, 202
Washington, Treaty of (1871), 12
Waterloo, 56
Welby, Robert, 145
Welles, Gideon, 200
Wellesley, George, 316
Wellington, Duke of, 18
West, Algernon, 104, 116
West Africa station, 7
West Indies, 23. *See also* North America and West Indies station
Whitworth, Joseph, 108
Wilhelm II, German emperor, 196
Wilson, Arthur K., 184
Wizard, H.M.S., 33

Wood, Sir Charles, First Viscount Halifax, 42, 112, 123–34 *passim*
Woolley, Joseph, 124
Woolwich, 54, 93
World War I, 60, 214, 221, 255, 269

Yelverton, Hastings, 174

Zambesi, 32
Zanzibar, 33–34
Zulu War (1878–79), 33, 168, 251

Library of Congress Cataloging-in-Publication Data

Beeler, John F. (John Francis), 1956–
　British naval policy in the Gladstone-Disraeli era, 1866–1880 / John F. Beeler.
　　p.　cm.
　Includes bibliographical references and index.
　ISBN 0-8047-2981-6 (alk. paper)
　1. Great Britain—History, Naval—19th century. 2. Gladstone, W. E. (William Ewart), 1809–1898—Views on military policy. 3. Disreali, Benjamin, Earl of Beaconsfield, 1804–1881—Views on military policy. 4. Great Britain—History—Victoria, 1837–1901. 5. Great Britain—Military policy. I. Title.
　DA88.B44　1998
　359'.00941'09034—DC21　　　97-33038
　　　　　　　　　　　　　CIP

　This book is printed on acid-free paper.